Expecting the End

Expecting the End

Millennialism in
Social and Historical Context

edited by

Kenneth G. C. Newport
Crawford Gribben

BAYLOR UNIVERSITY PRESS

Cover Design: Cynthia Dunne, Blue Farm Graphics
Cover Image: Bobby Bible Holds Up Cross and Prophecy Book Overlooking
    Old City of Jerusalem © Reuters/CORBIS. Used by permission.

Scripture quotations are from the New Revised Standard Version Bible,
copyright 1989, Division of Christian Education of the National Council of
the Churches of Christ in the United States of America. Used by
permission. All rights reserved.

Library of Congress Cataloging-in-Publication Data

Expecting the end : millennialism in social and historical context / Kenneth
G.C. Newport, Crawford Gribben, editors.
    p. cm.
Includes bibliographical references and index.
Millennium (Eschatology)
ISBN-13: 978-1-932792-38-6 (pbk. : alk. paper)
1. Millennialism. I. Newport, Kenneth G. C. II. Gribben, Crawford.

BT892.E97 2006
202'.3--dc22

                    2006024991

Printed in the United States of America on acid-free paper with a 50% pcw
recycled content.

Contents

Preface

In the few years leading up to the year 2000 there was, quite understandably we might at first presume, something of a boom in millennial expectation. An informed observer, however, might wonder why—after all, January 1, 2000 is an entirely human, and indeed Christian, construct: a date that ought to be without much significance at all to most of the people in the world. And even for those for whom the Christian faith is a matter of ultimate concern, there is still a question of why the year 2000 should mean anything in particular, since even if we were to think that God would indeed do something special to mark his Son's two thousandth birthday, it surely would not have come with the turn of the year 2000. This is not simply to argue that Jesus was born in 7 or perhaps 4 B.C.E. (though he probably was), nor yet to note that if December 25 is correct (and there is about a 1 in 365 chance that it is) the big apocalyptic bang should perhaps have been set to occur on that day and not at the New Year. It is not even to note that for much of Christian history each new year began on March 1 and not on January 1 (which is why the month we now call September is called September—it is the seventh and not the ninth month of the year, according to the "old style"). In fact, while all these points are valid, the nonsignificance of the year 2000 is perhaps even more transparent than this: there was no year zero. This being the case, if God were going to do something in the two thousandth year after the birth of his Son, even a very uncritical reading of the timescale ought to have meant that this something should have been due to happen not in 2000 but in 2001.

It is possible, of course, that it is simply wrong to think the reason that the year 2000 was important to some Christians was because of its assumed connection with the birth of Jesus. Perhaps we ought instead to be thinking more in terms of the much older tradition that the earth would last for six thousand years and then be followed by a Sabbath-millennium. After all, to the Lord a day is as a thousand years and a thousand years as one day (2 Pet. 3:8), and the week of creation, including the Sabbath day of rest, might be a foreshadowing of the history of the world. Such a view was embedded in the Christian tradition at least as early as the second-century work the Epistle of Barnabas (and in Jewish sources it is probably older than that). It can be seen also in the writing of William Whiston (1667–1752), who charts the six thousand years of Christian history from creation to the dawn of the millennium in his work (published in 1706) on the interpretation of the book of Revelation.[1] But again there is a problem here. Archbishop Ussher, whose chronology is accepted by many fundamentalists, worked out that creation was in 4004 B.C.E., which means that, again taking a rather uninformed view, the end should have come in 1996 and not in 2000. However, the absence of the year zero is again a factor: accepting Ussher's chronology but allowing for this absence of year zero would mean that the end should have been due in 1997 rather than 1996 or 2000. The interested observer might then indeed wonder why the year 2000 became so important in popular culture. But that it did so is beyond question—many will well remember the buildup to the year 2000.

The discussion above is designed to illustrate a point: millennial apocalypticism operates much more at an emotional than a cerebral level. No one who had given more than a moment's thought to the issue could really have come to the conclusion that the year 2000 would see anything particularly significant happen. Nevertheless "PMT" (premillennial tension) was evident on all sorts of fronts as the year 2000, or Y2K as it became colloquially known, loomed large. Something in the individual and collective consciousness simply would not give in to the dictates of plain reason. The number with those many noughts on the end surely must herald the event of something, even if most were not sure what.

As Y2K drew close, there were warnings that chaos might break out as computer systems crashed, fears that the antichrist might arise, and hopes

---

[1] See K. G. C. Newport, *Apocalypse and Millennium: Studies in Biblical Exegesis* (Cambridge: Cambridge University Press, 2000).

that Jesus would appear. As is so often the case with these things, however, it all went with more of a whimper than a bang. Nothing of any significance happened on a global scale. Indeed, in comparison with 2001 (the year of the attack on the World Trade Center) or 2002 (the launch of the "war on terror"), the year 2000 seems to have been something of a backwater in the flow of apocalyptic time, and the end is yet awaited.

The Center for Millennial Studies at Boston University charted some of these developments. Its work spanned Y2K and observed and documented both the buildup to it and the anticlimax that followed the wake of the nonevents of that year. It is a great shame that the work of the Center has not continued, though Brenda Brasher, one of the contributors to this book, has sought to progress things through a series brought out with Equinox Publishing. There is a need, however, to continue the discussion viva voce, especially so since the Millennial Studies group that once met as part of the American Academy of Religion has also now gone. Millennialism was bound to be a matter of more general interest around the year 2000, but for some, including some academics, it remains a matter of fascination and serious academic inquiry.

It is in recognition of this fact that the project represented in this book was launched at Liverpool Hope University and at, initially, Trinity College, Dublin, but now the University of Manchester. This "Hope-Manchester Colloquium on Millennialism" has met twice, and on both occasions the format has been the same: a small group of scholars interested in, and academically capable of, commenting on millennial thought have come together over the course of a few days to discuss issues relating to belief in the coming of the millennial age. Most of the essays found in this book are those that were presented at the inaugural meeting held at Trinity College, Dublin, and the editors are deeply appreciative of the support offered by the college that enabled the meeting to take place and this subsequent volume to appear. A second colloquium was held in September 2005 at Ripon College Cuddesdon, and the editors are similarly appreciative of the hospitality afforded by the college and in particular by Professor Martyn Percy, the principal.

All the essays presented here relate to the broad theme of millennialism. They are masterfully introduced in chapter 1 by the former director of the Center for Millennial Studies at Boston, Professor Richard Landes. Some of the essays are pictures of popular culture painted with fairly broad brushstrokes, but others treat individual millennial topics and groups in some finer detail. It is the hope of the editors that this collection of essays will keep alive the academic discussion on this extremely important aspect of the thought world in which we all live. As the truly massive popularity of the *Left Behind* series of novels shows clearly enough, millennial expectation is probably as vibrant today as it has ever been, and to ignore it is not a responsible option for the academy.

This volume would not have been possible but for the very kind and unconditional support of the Panacea Society. Not only did the Society provide initial funding to enable scholars to convene in Dublin, but in addition assisted financially with the inevitable costs of editing a volume of essays written by scholars used to a variety of house styles. Much of the smoothing out of those diverse styles has been undertaken by Alf Westwell, whose eye for detail, competence, and sheer hard work have done much to make this volume not only professional, but readable. Carey Newman at Baylor University Press has been extremely helpful both in negotiating the initial publishing contract and also by being an able and competent guide during the production process.

This foreword was written just a few days after it was revealed in a U.K. newspaper, *The Independent*, that President Bush was told by God to go to war in Iraq. It was written at a time, too, when the Internet was positively buzzing with speculation that Cardinal Ratzinger, recently elected Pope Benedict XVI, might in fact turn out to be the antichrist! Y2K has indeed come and gone, but there are always new challenges, new opportunities, new threats, and new hopes to excite the millennially inclined mind. In this book scholars attempt to explore and explain such dimensions in both historical and contemporary contexts. The debate must continue.

Kenneth G. C. Newport

Chapter One

Millenarianism and the Dynamics of Apocalyptic Time

Richard Landes

Francis Danby's painting *The Opening of the Sixth Seal* (1828) is one of the great forgotten icons of Ireland's millennial past. Exhibited today in the National Gallery of Ireland, it is an impressive and massive work that immediately catches the eye of anyone entering the room in which it is displayed. The grand canvas presents a cataclysmic scene in the background and a group of humans in varying postures of abject terror in the foreground. At the centre of the human group stands a seminude woman with her back to the viewer, looking at the oncoming destruction—it looks like a waterfall of blood—with her arms outstretched as if in welcome. On her right lies an old king, prostrate at her feet with his crown fallen to the ground. Danby's contemporaries immediately understood this detail as antislavery, with the woman slave welcoming the apocalyptic devastation and the king paralyzed with fear and remorse. The picture codifies the radical possibilities of millennial and apocalyptic thought.

The picture was enormously successful, so much so that at its opening exhibition in London in 1834 it was given its own room to accommodate the crowds of viewers who came to see it. This response illustrates the kind of enthusiasm and excitement such prophetic assaults on the powers that be can generate. But two years later, at another exhibition, an anonymous figure stole in one night and mutilated the picture. The portion of the canvas he removed was that of the woman and the king. Although there are other explanations for this mutilation, the most likely explanation has the vandal as one who found unbearable so popular and public a depiction of a king prostrate at the feet of a slave. As the high priest Amaziah complained to King Jeroboam of the vitality of prophecy, "the land is not able to bear all his words" (Amos 7:10).

As with artwork, so with millennial movements: the key to millennial progress is neither the agency of the "roosters" (those who announce the imminent dawn of the apocalyptic transformation) nor that of the "owls" (those who insist that the night is still long and wish the roosters to be silenced), but rather the reaction of their audiences. Had Danby's painting not attracted attention, made a sensation, and brought a "hidden transcript" of antimonarchical sentiment into the open, it probably would not have been mutilated. Leaders who draw upon this apocalyptic interest with even a fraction of 1 percent of an audience wield a weapon of enormous potency. Messiahs exercise immense influence over their followers. Charismatic leaders demand total response, and the rewards of apocalyptic belief are commensurate with the intensity of the commitment.[1] No rhetoric is more powerful than apocalyptic rhetoric; no greater motivation exists in the repertoire of human behavior than the belief that one's every action is crucial to the final destiny of the human race.[2] If the leader can convince his followers that God or the historical dialectic calls for ruthless destruction, there is almost no limit to the damage they can do, trying to save the world by destroying it.[3] And every movement, no matter how large it becomes, starts small. But without the tacit or, still better, warm approval of the public, without the ability to enter the public sphere with apocalyptic proposals and get a hearing, such dedicated troops can do little.

Millennialism brings out the most noble and most base elements of human behavior, inspiring anything from the genocidal rage of Crusaders and Nazis to the extravagant love of a Francis of Assisi or a George Fox. It continues to operate in this modern age where we, having dismissed God from the apocalyptic scenario, have replaced his immense destructive powers with our own. If we do not understand the appeal, the varieties and the dynamics of millennialism, we do not understand a critical element of one of our own and other cultures' greatest passions.[4]

Millennial Perception in Apocalyptic Time

Millennialists view a dramatically different world from the grey complexities we denizens of normal time have come to live with. They pay close attention to human suffering and its causes: evil, injustice, and oppression. The religious among them believe that a benevolent and omnipotent God, gods, or ancestors do exist and intervene in the *saeculum*. Monotheistic millennialists, the most common variant, believe in a God of justice and await his day of judgment, arguing that he allows evil to flourish as a test. For them, the unhappy anomalies that most sweep under their mental rugs occupy the center of attention. God's unwillingness to intervene in history stems not from indifference or incapacity, but from a desire to test us. Then at last, on a great Judgment Day—Doomsday—the evil will get their just punishment and the good their just reward.

Indeed, the transformation that will take place on this day will be so great and dramatic that the world will then enter a wondrous period (conventionally one thousand years—*mille anni*, "millennium") of justice, joy, fellowship, and abundance. Here the rapacious social world will be turned upside down. Here the lamb shall lie down with the lion and get a good night's sleep.[5] Here the weapons of elite dominion—sword and spear—become the tools of honest labor—ploughshare and pruning hook. Here people will enjoy and share the fruits of their honest labor undisturbed: "On that day, says the Lord of hosts, you shall invite each other to come under your vine and fig tree" (Zech. 3:10). Here nations will live at peace because they do not study war, but peace, because, fearing the Lord, they will have taken upon themselves the yoke of a heavenly kingdom, to walk in God's paths, to earn their bread by the sweat of their brow, to treat their fellow humans fairly. At its heart, millennialism, certainly the demotic millennialism described above, contains a fundamental and profound act of the will—both a willingness and a wilfulness. Such attitudes of empowerment generally get crushed under the heavy atmospheric pressure of authoritarian societies and their ideologies of submission and passivity. They rarely lead to peremptory actions in public.

Millennialists have a passion for justice. They think they know good and evil well. When they look at humanity, many see not various kinds of peoples, but a few saints and a vast sea of sinners, some redeemable, some, perhaps most, not. They see quite clearly who will suffer punishment (above all the abusively powerful) and who will gain reward (those faithful willing to risk all for the kingdom of heaven) at the final revelation. And they do not believe in compromise. They anticipate the absolute eradication of evil—corruption, violence, oppression—and the wondrous bliss of the just kingdom for the good. Millennialists reject tepidity: "So, because you are lukewarm, and neither cold nor hot, I am about to spit you out of my mouth," says Jesus to the church of Laodicea (Rev. 3:16). For millennialists, the grey world of the *corpus permixtum* will—and must—pass away.

Some of these believers hold that the abuse of power, the use of violence for selfish purposes—in a word, injustice—constitutes the greatest of sins, bringing humanly induced suffering into the world. They look forward to the day when such violence, and all its institutional trappings, will vanish.

Thus millennial thinking, however spiritually put, is political thinking. All millennialists hope that commitment to their beliefs will spread far and wide enough to bring about a transformation of the social, and therefore the political, universe. That is the very essence of millennialism, as opposed to other forms of eschatology: the just live free in this world.[6] It might be by-and-by, but the messianic promise is no pie in the sky. It is a transformation of humanity, an evolutionary leap to a different way of human interaction. To use the language of evolutionary epidemiology, millennialism is a meme programmed to spread as far and wide as possible.[7] To use the language of political science, millennialism is a (the first?) revolutionary ideology.[8]

Revolutionary ideologies only begin to appeal to large numbers of people (that is, the meme only spreads widely) when they feel themselves close to the moment of turning, of transformation. For millennialists, this means apocalyptic time, the process that extends from the moment before the individual enters the vortex of the *eschaton*. For some Christians, apocalyptic time means the temporary victory of the antichrist and the return (*parousia*) of Jesus; for some Jews, the coming of the messiah; for some Muslims, the arrival of the Dajjal (antichrist) and the Mahdi; for the communist, the withering away of the state; for the Nazi, the rule of the master race over the planet; for the Islamist, the rule of Islam over the planet.

The historian gets to see millennialism only when apocalyptic time activates it. But long before his or her highly trained mind is set upon the literate precipitation that such apocalyptic movements set in motion, a town, region, or generation of people have gone into a psychological arena where anything becomes possible, where grown men can cry, lifelong enemies can forgive and embrace, and the magical forces of the universe will come to the aid of those who long for help. To people who believe themselves in the midst of apocalyptic time, many things become possible. Such people have included saintly men wandering through Europe preaching peace, and warriors with crosses "wading in blood up to their horses' bridles,"[9] believing that this was the Day our Lord promised us, the day in which to rejoice (Ps. 118:24). To the people who inhabit this apocalyptic time, we who read about them so many years later should never have been. We are their unthinkable universe. And they were quite wrong in so thinking. But just because they were wrong does not mean they were inconsequential.

For people who have entered apocalyptic time, everything quickens, everything enlivens, everything coheres. In apocalyptic time, believers become semiotically aroused—everything has meaning, patterns. The smallest incident can have immense importance and open the way to an entirely new vision of the world, one in which forces unseen by other mortals operate.[10] The whole world is watching, and millennialists believe that their deeds are known to all—"the shot heard round the world," as the American Revolutionaries put it. And all the signs they now can "read" point in one direction: now is the time! Believers commit themselves to this world of transformation, convinced of the superiority of their perceptions, convinced that the uncomprehending mass (including the old elites) will either soon join them or get shredded in the cosmic transformation. The believer's semiotic arousal leads him or her straight into the apocalyptic vortex.

Such believers have varied careers. Apocalyptic time is always in the offing, although uncertain conditions certainly encourage it. But rarely do such conditions give birth to millennial movements; still more rarely do those movements make a lasting mark on the public consciousness, making it into the record; and still more rarely do millennial movements take power. And of that small minority who do take power, no millennial movement can sustain for more than a short while the hallucination that the new world is indeed messianic. The most sustained period for such episodes of mass delusion generally last less than twenty years, to judge by one of the earliest (led by Akhenaten) and one of the most recent (led by Hitler). Faced with erratic documentation from movements so short-lived and, in their passing, so reviled, historians have a decided disadvantage in trying to understand what the history of millennialism involves. The record is written by people deeply hostile to the millennial actors (in the case of Protestants and Catholics documenting the history of Matthew of Münster), or, if not to the actors, to their incorrect apocalyptic expectations and calculations (in the case of such otherwise respected figures as Martin Luther or Isaac Newton). And, as Wessinger demonstrates later in this volume, the same tendencies towards demonizing can be found in the "cult" hysteria of popular media representations of significant millennial players.

The key to millennial studies lies in our imagining the beginning of these movements (using extensive ancillary material from anthropology), then our following the dynamics of apocalyptic time as the movement enters into that period, takes shape, reaches its height, then handles the terrifying disorientation of acknowledging failure and reentering normal time, into a world they had never imagined would still exist. At this later point they stand, not glorious, as apocalyptic prophets commanding the faithful, but ashamed and impotent before the very people they had dismissed with contempt. The chapters below by Newport and by Allan trace a similar trajectory in the history of two important prophetic movements, the Davidians (as opposed to the Branch Davidians) and the Southcottians. How do these groups and the individuals within them handle the cognitive dissonance of having embraced a prophecy that failed?

Here, among other places, we find the origins of totalitarianism, that uncontrollable urge to hide one's shame by coercing purity, even at the cost of huge numbers of lives. Here the apocalyptic imagination is quite capable of contemplating with enthusiasm the death of most of the six billion people now alive. At their worst, paranoid messianic emperors such as

Hitler, Mao, Stalin, or Hong Xiu Chang have tried to carve the millennium out of the social body over which the forces of the universe have given the true believers power. One cannot do millennial historiography if one cannot talk about the motivating power of shame.

Varieties of Millennial Experience

In order to understand millennial beliefs and their apocalyptic movements, we must become familiar with their fundamental tensions. Eschatology holds that at the end (*eschaton*) of "time," the Lord will judge the quick and the dead, all, together, publicly. This apocalyptic theodicy can give rise to two possible aftermaths: an "eschatological" (final) one, in which the earthly world is consumed in purifying fires, and individuals are assigned to eternal heavenly rewards or hellish punishments; or a "millennial" one, in which the new world of justice appears on earth and marks a messianic age of abundance and the joy of fellowship.

Eschatological thought tends toward totalism: the conclusion is ultimate and decisive, a closed, final solution. The messiness of earthly existence must itself burn up in the process. This vision of an ultimate solution welcomes zero-sum thinking (dualism), imagining a closed form of redemption: the good in heaven, the evil in hell; the earthly body and all its messy delights, gone, permanently. Here Allan's discussion of Southcottian universalism appears to be almost as totalizing as Jones's reading of the much more dichotomous world of the *Left Behind* novels.[11] Tertullian's vision of a heaven where the saved got to watch the torments of the damned in all their locations in hell (an idea that later inspired Dante to visionary poetry) may well represent a high-water mark in millennial *ressentiment*,[12] but it also illustrates the workings of closed (zero-sum) images of redemption. When the body and soul are separated, the very drama of moral existence has been resolved. There is no future, no more tests, no more hopes. The story has ended. Future generations, and the open-ended directions in which they might move, no longer have any say in the redemptive process. For the apocalyptic eschatological thinker, this is the End of the World. The earthly game is over.

Millennialism

Millennialism moves in the opposite direction in its search for justice—it needs to happen in this world. It is an open challenge to the narrative that claims everybody is morally corrupt, no real change is possible, and this is how things have to be. It expects that spiritual strength will transform this world by transforming society. By transforming the way people interact, it will bring a time of justice here on earth. Thus millennialism is a deeply politically subversive form of social mysticism.

The essays that constitute the chapters of this volume use the term "millennial" to designate the belief that at some point in the future our world will be radically transformed into a world of peace, justice, fellowship, and plenty. Millennialism can, but need not, entail a belief in God. The earliest recorded millennial movements all invoked God or gods. But possibly as early as ancient Greece, and with increasing frequency in the course of the last half-millennium (1500–2000 C.E.), the West has produced and exported a number of secular, indeed atheistic, forms of millennialism. Marx's vision of the future, for example, fits all the criteria for demotic millennialism—from the vision of a noncoercive society (the withering away of the state), to the dignity of manual labor (the workers of the world), to the radical egalitarianism (the renunciation of private property), to the semiotic arousal of reading the signs indicating imminent apocalypse (historical dialectic).

Some historians object to so capacious a definition for millennialism. They suspect that this breadth is merely a ploy for claiming a whole range of subject matter, and that the definition comes close to including every radical movement in history within the purview of millennial studies. My suggestion is that we are far too early in our research to decide what relevance millennial studies might have for these topics. Given that most people have never thought about Nazism as a millennial movement—and this includes scholars who know that the Nazis claimed to inaugurate the *tausendjähriger Reich*—it seems too early to decide how useful or bloated the definition might be.[13] Nevertheless, my contention is that by understanding movements that share the simple combination of a millennial vision of the world to be transformed, and an apocalyptic belief in that transformation's imminence, one can make sense of these movements in significant ways. They participate in an unusual and characteristic dynamic that is well worth understanding. These movements form a natural grouping of sociocultural phenomena that cut across all cultures and regions and periods of history. They are still with us. We are in their current.

Millennial beliefs stand out as particularly important among eschatological beliefs in that they anticipate the rewards of the good times coming on earth, in the flesh, within the *saeculum*.[14] As a result, millennialism takes on more active forms than other eschatologies since, in these scenarios, the dramatic changes happen in this world, in time. Thus we find especially strong tendencies toward both social perfectionism and human agency. More cosmic scenarios, on the other hand, are those in which only God can effect any significant change. These discourage precisely these activist tendencies, and produce passive apocalyptic scenarios, whether they are cataclysmic (as in contemporary premillennial dispensationalism, described in this volume by Sweetnam, Gribben, and Jones), or more gradually transformative (as in the charismatic manifestations described by Hunt, or the missionary vision described by Pierce).

Although not all millennial beliefs are activist, all secular millennial movements have active apocalyptic scenarios. There is no one but "us" (however defined) to bring about this transformation. The *secular*[15] dimension of millennialism—its insistence that redemption occurs in the world of time and history, in the *saeculum*—makes it possible for nontheistic versions to emerge, like utopianism and communism. Until the advent of nuclear weapons, cosmic apocalyptic scenarios necessitated a deity.

Although millennialism can by this definition cover a very wide range of beliefs and behavior patterns—from active to passive, violent to pacifist—all of these patterns relate significantly to one another. When we work with these definitions, we keep company with both the church fathers, who despised precisely this "earthly" element of millennialism, and modern anthropologists who want to study it in all its forms, from the tribal cargo cults of Melanesia to the postmodern cargo cults of UFOs, whose theology is described in this volume by Partridge.[16]

Those who want to limit millennialism to its pursuit of radical social change through violence miss a key dynamic.[17] Individual millennial believers or groups can move from one extreme of their options for dealing with others in apocalyptic time to the other: from peace to violence, from reconciliation to extermination. However radically different these individuals or groups may seem to us, as reported in the documents, they can and often do participate in the same trajectories. The wave of new religious movements that we call the Protestant Reformation produced the exceptionally egalitarian and pacifist Anabaptist communities, which gave women a prominent role and renounced all forms of coercion. But under the pressures of a public breach of apocalyptic time in 1533 in the town of Münster, they turned to violent, patriarchal, and hierarchical behavior.[18] There is a similar difference between the passive nonviolence of dispensational responses to World War I, as described below by Sweetnam, and the aggressive and violent response to modernity chronicled by Jones and Gribben. To understand this kind of development, we need to focus on its key components: a belief in the possibility of radical social change; perfection, in this world (millennialism); and an expectation that this revolution is now occurring (apocalyptic).

"Demotic millennialism" represents bottom-up and egalitarian ideals. The inhabitants of the messianic world act justly by choice, and thus there will be no need for government. The Zealots of Jesus' time cried, "No king but God," the demotic political formula of monotheism;[19] Marx spoke of the "withering away of the state." Demotic millennialists view empire and hierarchy as the incarnation of evil.[20] For them, freedom and justice in the messianic age will abolish the dominion of individual over another, promoting a kind of holy anarchy in which the "saved" behave justly from love and not from fear. Although some forms of demotic millennialism look for a "unified" population of believers, as Jones explains, others involve a multicultural world, where "nation shall not lift up sword against nation" (Is. 2:4; Mic. 4:3), and honest, hardworking people enjoy the fruits of their labour regardless of their form of worship.[21]

The danger run by these egalitarians is described by Nietzsche as "slave morality," that is, the whining argument of the weak that the powerful do not have the right to push them around.[22] Once they take power, their demotic principles, which they only invoked to advance their (weak) case, are jettisoned for the dominating imperative. As the Athenians put it: "Those who can do what they will; those who cannot suffer what they must."[23] The large numbers of demotic millennial movements that turn into totalitarian adventures (like the Taiping or Communists[24]) reflect precisely the kind of reversal that so many cynics anticipate from the proponents of equality: they only speak of fairness when they are weak, and with power—in millennial cases, absolute power—such discourse rapidly turns to coercive purity.[25]

Hierarchical or imperial millennialism proposes a top-down model of the perfect society. It thus reverses the monotheistic political formula of anarchic millennialism. Rather than "No king but God," they insist "One God, one king, one religion."[26] This scenario views the cosmic battle for the world pitting chaos (evil) against order (good), and calls for the establishment of justice and peace from the top down, by a hierarchy on earth that mirrors the hierarchy in heaven, with an emperor-messiah, world conqueror who is the image or icon of God on earth.[27] In Christianity this tradition dates back to the time of Constantine and produces the notion of a "last" or messianic emperor who will conquer the world and bring all within the just confines of true Christianity.[28] This tradition of a final "world conqueror" who will inaugurate the golden age appears in many world historical traditions, including both Buddhism and Hinduism.[29]

Apocalypticism

The millennial vision of a transformable man and society is ultimately a discourse about time. It interprets the present in terms of the future and therefore places timing at the center of its rhetoric.[30] If one believes that the great transformation is far off in the future, millennialism tends to have a pacifying effect: it gives meaning to one's sufferings in the long run but discourages any action in the present. The time is not "ripe." If, on the other hand, one believes the transformation is imminent—that is, apocalyptic—then one becomes far more active. Then one joins with others to start revivalist movements, rich in emotion and tears of joy.[31]

The obviously important role of apocalypticism (signifying imminence) in bringing millennialism to light has tended to blind many to the distinction between the two terms. Indeed most definitions of millennialism—including Norman Cohn's—subsume the apocalyptic under the millennial.[32] We only see the phenomenon in action when millennialists believe the end is imminent; but that does not mean that we cannot see it in our documents, that it is not present. On the contrary, when we attend to apocalyptic beliefs and their inevitable disappointment, we find a richly textured narrative about how once-eager public advocates of eschatological faith do their best to disappear after the failure, *ex post defectu*.[33]

Thus, despite key "common" traits, especially in comparison with those approaches that "accept" the world "as is," millennial beliefs take a wide variety of forms. We can profitably divide them into several polar attitudes towards key issues: the apocalyptic question of when and how the millennial transformation would come about; the question of agency, that is, who does what to bring about this transformation; and the millennial question which asks what the millennial kingdom would look like. In answer to the first question, we have cataclysmic versus transformational apocalypticism; in answer to the second, we have a continuum from divine to human agency, human to divine passivity; and in answer to the third, we have authoritarian or hierarchical versus anarchic or demotic millennialism.

Cataclysmic apocalyptic scenarios foresee enormous destruction preceding the advent of God's kingdom. They tend to emphasize the depravity of man—most people are damned and must perish before any truly just society can come about. This apocalyptic scenario thus involves staggering levels of violence and destruction: rivers of blood, plague, earthquakes, floods, and famines—devastation from wars and natural calamities. Religious forms of cataclysmic apocalyptic belief, like modern "premillennial dispensationalism" among evangelical Protestants, tend to emphasize the central role of God and divine agents in bringing about the millennium. In these scenarios evil forces control the world either openly or, as in many Christian and antimodern versions, secretly, as Jones describes. This latter version, the conspiracist, imagines a worldwide conspiracy that will soon—at the apocalyptic moment—spring its trap and enslave the world.

The most widespread and familiar form of this belief in the coming of a world in the grip of a totalitarian cabal fears is the emergence of a New World Order.[34] Modern Protestant "premillennialism" expects Jesus to return before the millennium to destroy the antichrist and his agents in the battle of Armageddon and then to found the kingdom of the saints (the millennium). Here humanity has a passive role, largely limited to penitence and preaching (which was at the very heart of the Davidian movement, as Newport demonstrates). There are exceptions to this, of course: for example, Gribben notes the transformation of passivity in one recent series of rapture novels.[35] Though, as Partridge demonstrates, its theology borrows from dispensational ideas, Heaven's Gate, and many other Gnostic apocalyptic approaches, view this physical world as a prison from which we need to be released, and this planet (*saeculum*) as something that will be "ploughed under" at the great transformation. When we imagine apocalyptic as disastrous and speak of Doomsday as a day of terror, we are referring primarily to various manifestations of the cataclysmic millennial scenario.

Transformational apocalyptic scenarios, on the other hand, emphasize humanity's voluntary and peaceful change. A massive collective change of heart, perhaps divinely inspired, brings on the messianic age. This mood was epitomized, as Hunt demonstrates, in the "Toronto Blessing." Transformational scenarios assume that large numbers of people can transcend their current social paradigms and move into a messianic mode voluntarily—the lion lies down with lamb, aristocrats beat their swords into ploughshares and their spears into pruning hooks and earn their food by the sweat of their brow. Transformational millennialism tends to foster programs of radical and often unrealistic social change (peace movements, universal temperance, emancipation, utopian communes, or the healing water of the Panacea Society described by Allan below); it places great emphasis on educational reforms that create "new" people (citizens, comrades, believers).

Currently, the most prominent form of transformational millennialism comes from the New Age movements set in motion by the millennial wave of the 1960s: environmentally harmonized communes. In Protestant circles, transformational millennialism is known as "postmillennialism" (that is, Jesus comes back after his faithful create the millennium on earth), although there are cataclysmic variants of postmillennialism.[36] Historically, transformational (post)millennialism has contributed to a number of typically American "reformist" developments: the Great Awakenings, the Civil War, utopian farming and industrial communities (from the Shakers and Amish to the Oneida and Fourier communities), the profession of social work, and the civil rights movement, and, arguably, the ecumenical movement described here by Pierce.

Both active and passive apocalyptic scenarios vary internally according to the various roles they assign to God and humans in bringing about the transformation. The most passive scenarios are eschatological (because redemption is not in time, there is nothing to change on earth) and cataclysmic (only superhuman forces can effect the necessary destruction). Such scenarios relegate humans to a passive role: they must wait for God's "appointed" time, and their task calls for repentance, not for social transformation.

Paul apparently embraced such a notion when he called on Christian slaves to accept their status and Christian subjects to accept the rule of the existing powers (1 Cor. 7:20-24; Rom. 13). It is difficult to imagine Paul expecting slavery and the rule of unjust pagans (especially those of the Roman Empire) as a feature of the coming kingdom. But he does not think that one should expend one's final efforts, just before the return of Christ in power and glory, resisting a doomed system: "You know what time it is, how it is now the moment for you to wake from sleep. For salvation is nearer to us now than when we became believers; the night is far gone, the day is near" (Rom. 13:11-12).[37]

Passive nonmillennial scenarios are largely apolitical and tend, therefore, to be more "respectable" to owls in "normal time." But one can certainly find cases of passive transformational and millennial scenarios. Movements that stress individual transformation, meditation, and limited participation in the larger culture—on the basis that the kingdom of heaven is within—discourage any visible millennial activity, while ardently using apocalyptic rhetoric. In certain cases this passive stance can shift to active by holding out millennial goals (for example, being part of the intellectual vanguard of the revolution)—a line of inquiry that might usefully be applied to the Davidians and Branch Davidians, described in this volume by Newport and by Wessinger.

Active scenarios, on the other hand, place agency in human hands: mankind, perhaps inspired by God, brings about the dramatic events. Most active apocalyptic scenarios at least start out as transformative: human beings, transfigured by God's grace (or that of the historical dialectic), inaugurate the millennial world. All secular scenarios are activist (there is no God upon whom to wait), but so are many religious ones. The messianic vision of Isaiah and Micah places the key in the actions of the nations who flow to Jerusalem. But their action consists of accepting the yoke of God's justice, voluntarily submitting to God's kingship. Nations turn to his paths, and they convert the weapons of aristocratic violence (swords and spears) into tools of honest manual labour (ploughshares and pruning hooks).[38]

Active apocalypticism, however, tends to prefer cataclysmic variants since they promise more readily tangible results to an impatient enthusiast. With the advent of serious technological empowerment, they have become the most likely apocalyptic scenario of this next millennium. From the revolutions of France, Russia, Germany, and China, to the feverish apocalyptic visions induced by nuclear weapons, we have a growing array of cataclysmic apocalyptic thinking that is vigorously activist.[39] Such groups, starting out small, tend to view the social world as if it were a set of high-pressured tectonic plates where a small but well-aimed explosion can trigger a massive quake (Aum Shinrikyo and the Tokyo subway system, here described by John Walliss). What they lack in strength, they make up for in enhanced technology and the true understanding of who is good and who evil.

Now while all these apocalyptic and millennial variants appear to have mutually exclusive traits, this is only the deception of a categorical approach that tries to define a movement by a single set of beliefs. On the contrary, as the chapters of this volume suggest, millennialism is a dynamic phenomenon, and in the course of an apocalyptic episode, a movement can literally flip from one extreme to the other. Among the classic cases are the Anabaptists who, in the course of their failed millennium at Münster, 1533–1535, moved from being the most radically pacifist and egalitarian of the new Protestant groups to one of the most radically violent and authoritarian: their transformational demotic millennialism became cataclysmic and hierarchical.[40] Conversely, a violently revolutionary group like the Bahai transformed into a radically demotic, transformative millennial religion in the aftermath of their military failure. Indeed, one might suspect that the inevitable disappointment and failure of any apocalyptic group will act as a trip-switch to flip it back and forth from active to passive, or, vice versa, demotic to hierarchic, cataclysmic to transformational. In this paradoxical volatility we may find some of the keys to the strange relationship between millennial vision and violence, here analyzed by Walliss.[41]

So, the apocalyptic and millennial variants presented above should not be taken as a series of discrete categories, but as a map of terrain over which millennial groups, in the course of an apocalyptic episode, may travel. In order to understand the phenomenon in practice, rather than in theory, we must turn to the great "activator" of millennial hopes—apocalyptic expectations. These convictions of the imminence of the transformation drive millennialists out of the closet and into the public arena.

Apocalyptic Expectations—The Disinhibiting Imminent Transformation

The apocalyptic scenario stands firmly in the realm of "hidden transcripts," and most of us do not even notice the nonapocalyptic millennialists in our very midst. They can live among us invisibly, adapting to our secular world, while nurturing outrageous hopes. China has a long tradition of "secret societies" whose centuries-long, possibly millennia-long, history is punctuated by apocalyptic outbursts, revolts, and revolutions.[42] These believers have accepted the current rules "under protest" even if that protest is, provisionally, silent. They eagerly await the moment when the rules will change, and change dramatically. In the early fifth century, a rooster bishop named Hesychius wrote to Augustine a veiled reproach for his opposition to the widespread apocalyptic expectation of the day: "The coming of the Lord is to be loved and expected, for it is a great bliss for those who love His coming."[43] In the mid-nineteenth century, Aggy, an African American slave woman, put it somewhat more vehemently:

> There's a day a-coming! I hear the rumbling of the chariots, I see . . .
> white folks' blood a running on the ground like a river and the dead
> heaped up that high! O Lord! Hasten the day when the blows and the
> bruises and the aches and the pains shall come to the white folks.
> . . . O Lord! Give me the pleasure of living to that day.[44]

James C. Scott has called these sentiments a "full throated hidden transcript," the most elaborate and all-encompassing of the resentments that people, forced to pretend to like what they hate, tell themselves and their trusted friends in times of unguarded candour.[45] The fact that Aggy had a rich Christian apocalyptic imagination—despite the fact that slaves' access to Christian beliefs was, in principle, severely restricted—underlines the radical split between public and private discourse. Aggy, like so many other commoners who normally do not count, had access to an aural biblical tradition, far more radical than the one taught in the schools she could not attend.[46] And although Scott does not say so explicitly, it seems implicit in his thesis that the more violence goes into enforcing the "public transcript" and its prime divider, the more violence fills the apocalyptic visions of its disappearance. The powerful—the *potentes*—often know that such transcripts exist and have them as targets.

> For then shall end the tyranny of kings and the injustice and rapine
> of reeves and their cunning and unjust judgments and wiles. Then
> shall those who rejoiced and were glad in this life groan and lament.
> Then shall their mead, wine and beer be turned into thirst for them.[47]

These are the future rejoicings of people who truly hate their elites and look forward to their demise.

The elites know about hidden transcripts, but they generally consider such expressions of ill will as acceptable pressure-valve releases—as long as they remain private. The danger comes when such hidden transcripts go public, when the status quo and its rules are openly challenged. These are moments of great emotion, when public discourse can change dramatically, challenging and even overthrowing the prevailing transcripts.[48] And millennialists are, at heart, people who hope and dream of this day. For them, it is a day of pleasure.

Apocalyptic expectations—suggesting the imminence of the day—provide one of the most powerful dynamics for bringing hidden transcripts, many and loud ones, to the surface. The whole point of public transcripts is that they get everyone to pretend that they voluntarily accept the current situation. Violence, almost by definition, should not play a visible role in their maintenance, except in specific, often ritually defined conditions (for example, sacrifice or execution). The public transcript is the very quintessence of self-imposed inhibition, and it is the threat of future punishment for transgressions that keeps people in line. We, denizens of society, learn to inhibit ourselves by understanding this predictable future.[49] But when people believe that the future will be radically different from the past, they become radically uninhibited, at least in terms of the current public transcript. None of the "normal" threats work to intimidate someone who, to those on the outside, appears literally "mad." Nothing frightens the guardians of the public transcript more than such a rogue voice. Of all hidden transcripts, the most dangerous—unless one can ridicule it—is the apocalyptic voice of prophetic vengeance. And most elites generally respond by attempting its extermination.

However frightening to the guardians of order, apocalyptic time is a literal deliverance for millennialists. Convinced that the moment for the great transformation is at hand, they step into a dramatically different universe where the final, cosmic revelation, the final resolution of good and evil, enters the public sphere. Here the "powers" that rule this world receive their just humiliation, if not eternal punishment. Here "saints" who have suffered—at least humiliation, at most real pain and even death—at last have their day of vindication. Here all earlier suffering becomes meaningful, all the turned cheeks, the humiliations, the crushing burdens. Here, at last, the millennial believer gets to say a resounding, cosmic, "I told you so!" Like roosters, apocalyptic believers crow to signal that the long night has passed, and the dawn of the great and terrible day of rejoicing is at hand.

Apocalyptic millennialists live in a world overflowing with meaning and purpose. They live at the climax of human and sacred history and have at least a front-row seat, maybe even a speaking role, in this ultimate cosmic drama. For them there is no "chance," no grey zones of suspended meaning. They become semiotically aroused—everything is a sign, every event is a message about the unfolding drama, every encounter is destined.[50] When the signs indicate that final drama, their readers enter apocalyptic semiosis. From the people they meet and the texts they read to the events that happen around them, everything coheres as part of a huge apocalyptic plan, crystalline in its clarity and glorious in its implications. Sometimes the plan is nefarious—an international conspiracy by the forces of evil to enslave mankind; sometimes, benevolent—the dawn of a new age. In any case, whereas it once existed only in the shadows, scarcely discernible, the signs of its advent are now legible, visible, and clear to anyone with discernment.

Such semiotic arousal fires the imagination, loosening the tongue, the hand, and the body to write, speak, sing, paint, and dance the visions, to communicate the good news to as many as possible, if they have eyes to see and ears to hear. Thus those in apocalyptic semiosis become the vocationally aroused, stepping out of their closets and into the public arena, burning with enough fervor and conviction that they are ready to forsake the safety of convention, the anonymity of consensus, the protection of mimetic desire in public. Believers who have received this calling burn bridges to past lives: they give away their wealth, they leave their homes, forsaking spouse and family, friendships, jobs and professions. "Whoever comes to me and does not hate his father and mother, wife and children, brothers and sisters, yes, and even life itself, cannot be my disciple" (Luke 14:26).[51] They say things that alienate the powerful and influential, they are capable of both sacred joy (Francis of Assisi) and sacred violence (Hitler). Such behavior is always radical, whether it benefits others—as emotional and material charity—or harms them—as violence aimed at eradicating evil. In any case, because the believer has broken with the past, he has made a leap of faith into a future whose advent he or she has seen coming.

Apocalyptic Community and Apocalyptic Disappointment

Apocalyptic zealots leave old, organic communities, ones they inherited by birth, and join voluntary communities. At their outset, all apocalyptic millennial movements are voluntary. That is the meaning of *ana*baptism—to be baptized again—because the first baptism, received as an infant, was a meaningless ceremony. Only the "called," only those capable of a self-conscious voluntary engagement in the process of transformation (repentance and return) can become members of an apocalyptic community. That is why so many movements demand great sacrifice to enter, as with the Xhosa.[52]

These voluntary communities are temporal hothouses. They represent brief moments when a self-selecting group of strangers comes together in circumstances where all "normal existence" ceases and a series of interlocking and energizing paradoxes come to life.

- The loss of one's "organic" community precedes entry into a still more intensely intimate voluntary community. The sense of spiritual connection, mutual purpose, and cosmic commitments that believers feel in these groups is perhaps the single most powerful motivator behind both the formation of millennial groups and of their persistence after prophecy fails.[53]
- The radical act of individualism that leads believers to break with their past can turn into a radical act of submission and ego renunciation to the cause, to the new group, to the leader. The kinds of mental vulnerabilities—especially at the hands of trusted spiritual

leaders—that members of apocalyptic groups necessarily experience leads those on the outside to attribute it to weak-minded and
brainwashed lack of will.[54]

- The shorter the temporal horizon, the more intense the apocalyptic expectations become. Every apocalyptic episode is a game of
chicken with the approaching end as the crack-up. The trade-off is
between caution and passion, and what seems irrational if not
insane from the outside—picking a specific date, for example—
fuels ardor on the inside, hence upping the ante.

- The apocalyptic moment induces extreme behavior of wildly
opposing types, from radical asceticism (extreme self-deprivation)
to extravagant antinomianism (murder, sexual license, taboo
breaking). The same wild swings hold for apocalyptic "social structures." All movements are violently antiauthoritarian (at least
where older authorities are concerned) and often begin in a radical egalitarianism (communal property). But they can, in certain
circumstances, develop into still more intense forms of authoritarianism with equally radical inequalities.[55]

Living in such a world carries obvious advantages. Believers are true warriors in the battle with evil, the adrenaline running, every fiber of their
being engaged in their navigation of every last precious moment. They
"live with death on their shoulder."[56] No longer bound by customary
rules, no longer prisoners of conventional expectations, millennialists can
explore the world of human possibilities and experiment with their own
feelings. Their imaginations unfettered, they can make connections and
intuit relations at levels that escape most of us pedestrians. In his brilliant
and fanciful "Proverbs of Hell," enumerated in the *Marriage of Heaven
and Hell* (1796), William Blake articulates an assertive millennial mindset, uninhibited by owl wisdom: "prudence is a rich ugly old maid,
courted by incapacity"; "the tigers of wrath are more valuable than the
horses of instruction"; "he who desires but acts not, breeds pestilence";
"what is now proved was once only imagined"; "energy is Eternal Delight";
"exuberance is Beauty."[57]

In his poem on the American Revolution, Blake gave voice to the
demotic dream with the characteristic exuberance of those who rejoice
in hope:

The morning comes, the night decays, the watchmen leave their stations;
The grave is burst, the spices shed, the linen wrapped up;
The bones of death, the cov'ring clay, the sinews shrunk & dry'd.
Reviving shake, inspiring move, breathing! awakening!
Spring like redeemed captives when their bonds & bars are burst;

Let the slave grinding at the mill, run out into the field:
Let him look up into the heavens & laugh in the bright air;
Let the inchained soul shut up in darkness and in sighing,
Whose face has never seen a smile in thirty weary years;
Rise and look out, his chains are loose, his dungeon doors are open.
And let his wife and children return from the oppressors scourge;
They look behind at every step & believe it is a dream.
Singing, The Sun has left his blackness, & has found a fresher morning
And the fair Moon rejoices in the clear and cloudless night;
For Empire is no more, and now the Lion & Wolf shall cease.[58]

Committed to egalitarian ideals, demotic millennialists are especially imaginative in the field of social relations—generating and embracing new social paradigms that, in some cases, go mainstream (the opposition to slavery in America at the time of the Revolution was from millennialists).[59] This social creativity often places a high value on manual labor (as any egalitarian ethic must), and millennialists often become early adopters of new technology, especially communications technology.[60] Millennialists are prolific in communication, whether it be art, writing, dance, or song. They live in an enchanted and exciting world, and they want nothing more than to bring the rest of us into it. Or, if we will not move, they will bring it to us. And if we still resist, alas, they will strike us down as the apocalyptic enemy.

But this apocalyptic millennial condition also carries serious disadvantages, many related to its prime occupational hazard: the belief of all such enthusiasts that they occupy the center of the cosmic stage. At some profound level, millennialism is a product of what we might call ADD type II. ADD type I (with its hyperactive variant ADHD) comes from an inability to pay enough attention. As ADD type II comes from an inability to get enough attention,[61] it can produce millennial movements of disconcerting vigor, and, too often, destructive creativity. Hence the central fantasy shared by all apocalyptic believers—they have been chosen by God (or by the fates, destiny, or the dialectic of history) to live at that central turning point in human destiny. Not only is "the whole world . . . watching," but the whole cosmos is involved.[62] When the Xhosa's fourteen-year-old prophetess Nonquawuse first told her vision to her uncle Mhlakaza, he saw in it his vehicle to overcome his attention-starved soul. Taught to preach millennial rhetoric, but turned away by white Christians, Mhlakaza now had a real prophecy. He could and did stride right into the courts of the chieftains and, with their help, lead the people to their redemption, just as had Moses.

This self-image becomes problematic when the millennialist's expectations are disappointed or frustrated; the failure, the *defectum*, inevitably comes, and inevitably causes unbearable dissonance. Here we find a frequent tendency to "up the ante,"[63] as was the case with the Xhosa when the failure of that August moon of 1856 led to an even greater wave of cattle killing. Semiotic arousal becomes semiotic promiscuity—anything means something, and free association becomes an impeccable and convincing system of meaning (which actually permits the psyche to come to conclusions satisfying inner needs). Vocational arousal becomes megalomania, in which one stands not merely near or on the stage, but at the very center of the entire drama. In such apocalyptic conditions, not just opposition, but even tepidity becomes an affront, a willful obstacle to the glorious salvation on its way. And megalomania often leads to paranoia, whence the elaborate conspiracy theories that so often populate the minds of millennialists. After all, what is paranoia but the megalomaniac belief that most of the people in the world have nothing better to do with their time than to plot against you? The history of millennialism is littered with the wreckage of groups with leaders who, unable to tolerate the world's enduring imperfection (including their own), preferred to destroy everything they could.[64]

Of course, the idea that one can fill such an emotional void with a fantasy of a situation in which one is already the center of the cosmos, and will soon be visibly so, has profound conceptual flaws, not the least of which is the inevitable disappointment. Roosters believe that, in the very near future, either God or some cosmic force (extraterrestrials, the dialectic of history, technological breakthroughs) will publicly intervene on their side, rewarding them and their faithful companions, and punishing those who scoffed and opposed them. Evangelical premillennialists, for example, currently anticipate an awesome tribulation (based on the book of Revelation), a seven-year period of staggering punishment for the billions of sinners (nonbelievers) on the planet.

There is great irony behind all such thinking. The coming tribulation is not that of the outsiders, the unbelievers who cling pitifully to their antiquated notions of a world that goes on tomorrow much as it has today, who scoff at the news and mock the prophet. No, the tribulation will strike the true apocalyptic believer, the rooster, who must confront his or her own failed expectation. This is true, moreover, whether the rooster successfully produces a radical change in this world or not. However much power men such as Robespierre, Lenin, Hitler, Mao, Khoumeini, or any other "successful" roosters wield, they always find that humans fail them, that the new citizen, comrade, Aryan, or Muslim, who in principle should emerge with the destruction of the forces of evil, fails to materialize. Because roosters are perfectionists—at once their strength and weakness—they cannot be satisfied with partial transformations.

Thus, in a profound sense, the study of millennialism as a historical force is the study of disappointment, and how these most extravagant optimists come to terms with their failed hopes. As will be seen in the course of this volume, the results are as extravagant as the hopes, but the answers that disappointed millennialists have supplied range from the formation of new religions to totalitarianism to civil society. The key paradox here is that although millennialism has always proved wrong in its apocalyptic expectations, it has rarely proved inconsequential or unproductive. Studies have shown that while pessimists are more often right in predicting the future, optimists accomplish more.[65] Partly that is due to the willingness to take risks; partly to the enthusiasm that optimism brings to a task; partly (in the more peaceful versions) to a willingness to learn from mistakes. The history of millennialism reflects such a dynamic—a range of fruitful mistakes, however nourishing or poisonous. And the history of the most millennial culture in world history—the West—is that of a long series of interlocking and unintended consequences that we, retrospectively, like to call progress.

This last remark calls forth one more. Although I have presented roosters here as apocalyptic prophets calling for the Day of the Lord, there are both modified and secularized versions of these prophecies. When Jonah prophesied destruction, he was not apocalyptic—only the city of Ninevah was concerned—nor did he call for a preparation for the inevitable "day of wrath and justice." He offered the classic prophetic deal: change or else. His is the language of reform, not revolution; and the consequences of his prophecy (especially when leading to repentance) have a secular dimension: they change the way people interact in this world. Thus, successful prophecy can play (and has played) a major role in social change.

The distinction between prophetic and apocalyptic, however, has limited value. They are kissing cousins, and spend so much time together that they share the same wardrobe and address the same audiences. Prophets with unexpected success eagerly expand the range of their mission; less successful ones reduce their scope as seamlessly as possible.[66] Reform can often ring apocalyptic alarms and promise nearly millennial results just to motivate people. Environmentalists are the most obvious current case of roosters crowing warnings that range from the prophetic to the apocalyptic, using the stick of cataclysmic destruction if we do not change, and the carrot of millennial harmony with both nature and technology as the reward for repenting of our greedy, wasteful ways. Few millennial discourses seem worthier, though their zealots may unfortunately cling tenaciously to the road of excess long after the palace of wisdom has been passed. Thus roosters need not be "apocalyptic," although any apocalyptic believer is by definition a rooster or a rooster's disciple, and any truly successful rooster must struggle with the demons of apocalyptic megalomania.[67]

Antiapocalyptic Owls—The Nocturnal Wisdom
of the Public Transcript

Every force has its contrary, and not surprisingly, a force as volatile and uncompromisingly hostile to the status quo as apocalyptic expectation has its implacable enemies. For every rooster crowing on his dunghill that the great and terrible day has dawned, there are a dozen owls hooting from their lecterns that the night is still long, the fox abroad, the master asleep, and only damage can come from prematurely waking the barnyard. To roosters, they seem like a cross between ostriches, with their heads in the sand, and bats, blinded by daybreak. But they have a certain wisdom. Minerva's owl is retrospective; it flies, *ex post defectu*, at dusk.

Whereas roosters like to tell of the emperor's new clothes, owls have a cautionary tale about Chicken Little, who, with her hysterically apocalyptic reading of a fallen acorn, led the whole barnyard into the clutches of Foxy Loxy. Indeed, Foxy Loxy did not even have to hunt for his prey. And neither did the English who, despite suspecting a plot, found that the prophetess Nongqawuse delivered the Xhosa, broken by famine, into their clutches. And why did Chicken Little and the others leave the farm? To tell the king. To hold center stage at the heights. To quench that desire for fame.

There are different kinds of owls: millennial owls believe the millennium will come, but, for a variety of reasons, believe that now is not the time (quiet optimists); reluctant owls do not believe the millennium will come, although they do not like the world as it is (quiet pessimists); and aggressive owls like the world as it is and will resist any effort to change it, unless it be to their advantage. True owls are, by nature, conservative, anxious about (if not hostile to) change, especially about rapid change, and suspicious of radical new ideas and approaches. Obviously, most people in the established elite of any culture tend to be owls. The process is self-selecting. But that is never true of all of the cultural elite, and societies where the dominant religion promises an apocalyptic resolution to the current world—Judaism, Christianity, Islam—tend to produce an unusually high number of roosters within their own elites: *la trahison des clercs*.

Normally, and especially in prime divider societies, owls dominate public discourse, and one of their jobs is to make sure that roosters do not breach the public transcript. Indeed, so profoundly do they dominate that most roosters never even appear on our documentary screens, although we can suspect they have a more powerful oral existence. The documents—writing as a retrospective act—are inherently hostile to apocalyptic discourse: oral communication is especially suited. Owls are representatives not so much of the status quo, but of the rules of the current social paradigm. They are powerful and influential precisely because they have played the rules to their own advantage (true of both aristocrats born into positions of power and meritocrats who attain such positions). Needless to say, they are not only hostile to new rules, but use the current rules to thwart the introduction of new ones.[68]

Owls have a reputation for wisdom, and in most millennial cases that reputation is well-deserved.[69] The vast majority of roosters have, in fact, proposed ludicrous scenarios and equally implausible rule sets. The owls' steady grip provides a most valuable stability since any culture whose elite runs after every (or even every tenth) apocalyptic rumor will not long endure. True, as Blake suggested, what is now proved was once only imagined, but much that is imagined does not get proved.

Just as roosters have both their strengths and their weaknesses, so do owls. Their main failure inverts the rooster's great strength: that is, they lack imagination, and they cling to the current order of things even after it has become dysfunctional. Owls have an almost instinctual response to sweeping ideas or predictions of social mutation; they dismiss them, if necessary, with scorn and ridicule. Their attitude is justifiable; you cannot jump every time someone tells you to take a conceptual leap. But behind this reflexive response often lies an unwillingness to question the prevailing paradigm. As Kuhn puts it, "normal scientists" are problem solvers; they know the rules, and they pose their problems and seek their solutions according to them.[70] To question the rules disrupts an orderly world and undermines predictable rewards for diligence, for mimetic discourse.[71] And just as the rooster's danger is to fall from exhilaration to megalomania, so the owl's danger is to fall from skepticism into negativity, from critical reasoning to clinging to reason, whether that "logic" be stoic, scholastic, positivist, or whatever new form the normative paradigm takes. Overall, these seem like mild and venial sins when compared with the colossal crimes of maniacal messiahs. But even these can cause serious and unnecessary culture wars.

Owls and Roosters Interact—Chicken Littles and Ostriches

The natural tendency of owls when roosters crow is to hear them as "Chicken Littles"—alarmists whose excessive imaginations have cooked up panic from nothing. Roosters, of course, tend to set off such responses because they, almost from the start of their missions, articulate their insights with the intention of shocking, knocking their listeners loose from their complacent attachment to what the roosters know is a fast-fading world. So, roosters want and need rapid and energetic responses—this is, after all, for the good of their listeners. They thus have little patience with the slow responses and reasoned skepticism of the owlish reasoners.[72] Just as owls tend to see roosters as Chicken Littles, roosters tend to see owls as ostriches with their heads in the sand, blissfully and tragically unaware of the oncoming stampede. Roosters hear the Doppler sound waxing: owls seem deaf. And of course, if one would make oneself heard by someone whose head is in the sand, obviously one must speak louder. And the louder you speak, the more incomprehensible and unreliable the speech becomes. So the more shrill the Chicken Little roosters, the more unresponsive do the ostrich owls become and the farther down in the sand do they bury their ears.

This clear example of a failure to communicate is something which, in the course of millennial history, has often led to tragic consequences.[73] But that difficulty is more than just a well-intentioned failure. It is a lack of understanding on both sides to imagine anything but a zero-sum relationship between roosters and owls. As Wessinger here highlights, each side sees the other as its nemesis, each works toward eliminating the other. Behind the exuberant embrace of the rooster lies a fanatic passion and a staggering capacity for violent intolerance. And behind the seeming deafness and ridicule of the owl lies a more aggressive defensiveness which, should the rooster persist, can shift from a polite ignoring to a much more violent objection.[74] The owls, like the roosters, know full well that the success of the new message would spell the end of the old hegemony—culturally, socially, and politically. Owls do not stand poised between listening and ignoring. Most of the time, and throughout most of human history, owls have chosen between ignoring and exterminating. Louder rarely means more successful when roosters try to reach owls. Most often it just further enrages both.

The most dangerous situations occur when the rooster crows loudly and attracts an enthusiastic audience of people who grow progressively hostile to the authorities, largely on a diet of resentful private transcripts now rendered public. The apocalyptic community bathes in the charisma of openly speaking what so many hearts for so long kept locked away in trunks. As long as roosters crow to unresponsive barnyards, owls can mock and ignore. But when roosters gather a large and enthusiastic following, when their claims begin to gain currency, the situation becomes intolerable. When owls see a real threat from roosters, they shift from ostrich to hawk, confining roosters to monasteries, prisons, and mental hospitals where possible, and, where necessary, executing them and massacring their followers. That was certainly the Roman policy around the time of Christ. Jesus, no matter how pacifist, apolitical, and unthreatening he might have been, proved intolerable to the Romans merely because of the excitement he aroused. Messiahs, in the premodern period and in the contemporary world, rarely die of natural causes.

Chapter Two

Millenarianism and Violence in the Contemporary World

John Walliss

For over two thousand years, apocalyptic images and motifs have inspired, tormented, and puzzled their audiences. Many have found, and indeed still do find, hope in the image of the prophesied New Jerusalem, the emergence of heaven on earth, and the coming of the Messiah. Many have also sought to determine the exact date of the prophesied end times by performing complex calculations with the various numbers and time frames given in the apocalyptic literature. A small number, however, have gone further and, believing themselves to be on the side of the forces of good, have taken the martial themes found within apocalyptic literature as a justification for violence against those whom they perceive to be the enemies of God.

Although the great majority of these incidents occurred several centuries ago, most notably in the high Middle Ages,[1] the last quarter of the twentieth century witnessed several well-documented cases where groups inspired by apocalyptic/millenarian ideologies engaged in violent episodes or acts of collective suicide. On November 18, 1978, in Jonestown, Guyana, over 900 members of Peoples Temple, a California religious movement led by Jim Jones, died in an act of collective suicide; almost a decade and a half

later, 74 members of the Branch Davidians, a Seventh-day Adventist splinter group, met a fiery end when, in an attempt to end a fifty-one-day stand-
off, U.S. authorities inserted tear gas into the Branch Davidians' home at
Waco, Texas, igniting (so it has been argued[2]) several fires in the wooden
building; between October 1994 and March 1997, some 70 members of
the Order of the Solar Temple died in a series of ritualized murder-suicides
in Switzerland, Quebec, and France; in May 1995, members of Aum Shinrikyo, a Japanese group already implicated in at least 23 other murders,
launched an abortive attack on the Tokyo underground using the nerve gas
sarin, an attack that could easily have resulted in thousands of fatalities;
two years later, 39 members of a group calling itself Heaven's Gate committed collective suicide in the apparent belief that the world was about to be
"spaded under," and that they could escape the destruction via a spaceship
hiding behind the then-passing Hale-Bopp comet; finally, in Uganda, in
the spring of 2000, around 780 members of the Movement for the Restoration of the Ten Commandments of God (hereafter MRTCG) died in a
series of murder-suicides, the details and reasons for which are still—and
possibly will remain—unclear.[3] Indeed, such was the fear in the period leading up to the eve of the year 2000 that "doomsday cults" would unleash
havoc on the world or on themselves that several law enforcement agencies, most notably the U.S. Federal Bureau of Investigation and the Canadian Security Intelligence Service, produced reports for their respective
staffs concerning what the former referred to as "individuals or domestic
extremist groups who profess an apocalyptic view of the millennium or
attach special significance to the year 2000."[4]

Leaving aside the question of why such incidents occurred when they
did (a sociological topic in its own right), perhaps the most important question is why they occurred at all. Although millenarian beliefs are often suf-
fused with violence, and although a number of millenarians believe that
they will play an active role in the prophesied final apocalyptic struggle, the
vast majority hold to a more passive view of the end times, believing that
their task is simply to observe the signs and omens and passively wait for
the inevitable.[5] Indeed, even among those who believe that they will play
an active role in the violent transition to the millennial kingdom, the vast
majority (even where they engage in violent rhetoric or arm themselves) do
not believe that it is their millennial role to instigate the final confronta-
tion.[6] Why then, of all the groups holding millenarian ideologies in the
world in the late twentieth century, did these six engage in violence either
against themselves or others? What made these groups cross the line from
violent rhetoric to violent behavior?

In this chapter, I intend to go some way toward answering this question
by presenting a comparative discussion of these six incidents of apocalyptic violence, focusing in particular on the key recurring issues and social

processes that fostered the progressive acceptance of violence within each group's respective ideology, and which ultimately helped to precipitate the use of force against their own members or against outsiders. To this end, this chapter will be divided into three main sections. In the first, I sketch out the broad parameters of the debate through a brief discussion of the various factors that have been highlighted within the literature on millenarianism and violence as either predisposing millenarian groups to volatility and violence, or enhancing such groups' propensity to engage in violent actions. Following on from this, I present a comparative analysis of the six incidents, focusing on the role played in each by three broad, often interlinking, sets of factors: *the actions of "cultural opponents," challenges to leaders' authority or charisma,* and *internal challenges to the millennial goal.*[7] Finally, I conclude by drawing out the broader themes touched on in my analysis and by offering some final observations on the topic of millenarianism and violence.

Millenarianism and Violence—The Contemporary Debate

In broad terms, the debate over millenarianism and violence centers upon two key questions. First, are the internal characteristics of millenarian groups (such as their beliefs, practices, and leadership styles) sufficient in themselves to produce volatility or violence, or do they serve instead simply to make certain groups more likely (other things being equal) to become volatile or violent? Second, if internal, organizational factors are necessary but not sufficient in themselves, what other factors serve to precipitate acts of apocalyptic violence? Robbins and Anthony, for example, have framed the debate by focusing on the role of what they term endogenous (intragroup) and exogenous (or cultural/intergroup) factors, and, in terms of the first question, have highlighted three that are of particular salience in increasing the likelihood of volatility or violence in millenarian groups: *apocalyptic beliefs, charismatic authority,* and *"totalistic" social systems.*[8]

Apocalyptic Beliefs

The first and perhaps most obvious factor that might be seen as predisposing millenarian groups to volatility or violence is their respective millenarian ideologies. There are several possible reasons that this should be the case. Millenarian groups, to draw on Norman Cohn's classic definition, picture salvation as *collective, terrestrial, imminent, total,* and *miraculous.*[9] Central to millenarian ideologies, then, is the belief and hopeful expectation that at some point in the very near future the present, corrupt world will be radically and ultimately transformed, usually by supernatural means, into an earthly paradise. Millenarians thus believe themselves to be living within the end times or last days, a belief that can often lead to antinomian behavior. In some cases, for example, millenarian groups have transgressed a variety of sexual and moral boundaries, abandoned their worldly activities and their families, and rejected the authority of earthly powers. Similarly, there are numerous well-documented cases of millenarians abandoning their livelihoods, or even giving away their possessions, in anticipation of the end.[10] In other cases, the antinomianism inherent within millenarian beliefs might be manifested in the use of violence. Indeed, in some cases, the belief that the end time is at hand may even be perceived as offering a sanction for its use in hastening the final end-time scenario.

Another characteristic of millenarian ideologies that might predispose believers to violence is their image of salvation in collective rather than individualistic terms. "The aim of millenarism," as Talmon notes, "is not only the salvation of individual souls but the erection of a heavenly city for the chosen people, or the elect."[11] Consequently, the apocalyptic imagination has a tendency to conceive the world in starkly dualistic terms: divided between, for example, the forces of good and evil, saints and sinners, God and the devil, and, perhaps most importantly, between the elect and the forsaken. There are, in other words, no shades of grey within apocalypticism, nor any moral ambiguity. It is this vision of the world that can predispose its adherents to violence.

Catherine Wessinger, for example, has distinguished between what she terms "catastrophic millennialism" and "progressive millennialism," arguing that, all things being equal, the former is more prone to violence than the latter.[12] Whereas progressive millennialism is characterized by an optimistic view of humanity and the belief that the transition to the millennial kingdom will take place in a peaceful, progressive manner, catastrophic millennial groups, according to Wessinger, tend to perceive the world in extremely dualistic terms: hence, she argues, their propensity toward violence. Similarly, Robbins and Anthony have highlighted what they term "exemplary dualism"—"an apocalyptic orientation in which contemporary socioreligious forces are viewed as exemplifying absolute contrast energies in terms not only of moral virtue, but also of eschatology and the millennial destiny of humankind"—as an extremely potent factor in millenarian violence.[13] Like Wessinger, Robbins and Anthony argue that such a worldview "is volatile because it confers deep eschatological significance on the social and political conflicts of the day, thereby raising the stakes of victory or defeat in immediate worldly struggles."[14] In particular, they argue, actual or perceived opponents will come to be seen as actors on the side of evil in the cosmic war against the forces of good. Likewise, apostates will often be perceived through the lens of exemplary dualism as "traitors" and de facto enemies of the forces of good.

Charismatic Authority

Another important factor cited in the literature as predisposing millenarian groups to volatility or violence concerns the role that charismatic leadership plays within such groups. Indeed, a common image presented in the media and in the rhetoric of anti-cult groups is that of the "charismatic leader" who is able to control his or her followers through a form of hypnotic mind control or brainwashing.[15] Although such views have largely been discredited among scholars of new religions, a number of commentators have focused in a more measured way on the role that charismatic leadership might play in producing volatility or violence within millenarian groups. Several explanations have been offered as to why this would appear to be the case.

One explanation that has been offered focuses on the precarious nature of charismatic authority. Stemming from the work of Max Weber, who designated "charismatic authority," along with "traditional" and "legal-rational" authority, as one of his "ideal types" of legitimation, charismatic authority has been characterized as being inherently precarious. Unlike those holding legal-rational forms of authority, the charismatic leader, according to Weber, "does not deduce his authority from codes and statutes," nor, unlike those holding traditional forms of authority, does he "deduce his authority from traditional custom or feudal vows of faith." Indeed, it is often the case that charismatic leaders will self-consciously set themselves against both "codes and statutes" and "traditional custom or feudal vows of faith." Rather, Weber reckons, the charismatic leader must sustain his or her own legitimacy.

For these reasons, Weber argues, charismatic authority is inherently precarious and, in order to continue and develop beyond "short-lived mass emotions of incalculable effects," will typically undergo a process of "routinization," whereby it is transformed into either traditional or legal-rational authority.[16] The leader's words, for example, may be written down by his or her followers and become codified into a clear theology, or the often ad hoc structure of the charismatic group may give way to a more structured hierarchical organization. Charisma will not, of course, completely disappear, but where it does continue to exist, it will do so in "a greatly changed sense."[17]

There are, however, marked differences in how leaders "negotiate" this process. In some cases, "the charismatic leader, finding himself trammeled and constrained, acquiesces to the situation with more or less good grace," while in others they may even take an active role in the process, actively directing it "in such a way as to control it and utilize institutionalized structures and procedures to buttress his authority, rather than allowing it to constrain him."[18] In yet others, the process may even occur without the leader recognizing what is transpiring until it is too late to reverse it. In other cases, however, charismatic leaders may attempt to forestall the process in a number of ways, most notably through "the introduction of unpredictable changes and demands,"[19] or engaging "in continual crisis-mongering, whereby a movement is kept in such turmoil that stable institutional structures and routines cannot be consolidated."[20] This in turn, it has been argued, serves to eliminate or erode any potential restraints on the leader, and "provide[s] opportunities for charismatic leaders to *indulge the darker desires of their subconscious*" [italics mine], possibly through "unconventional sexual practices and violence."[21]

Aside from the pressures brought about by the process of routinization, charismatic authority is also precarious in another important sense that, too, might lead to volatility or violence. As Weber observes, charismatic authority "exist[s] only in the process of originating" and thus is "constantly being proved."[22] In contrast to traditional or legal-rational forms of authority, charismatic authority thus requires constant "legitimation work." When this does not occur—when, for example, the leader is unable to offer "signs of the miraculous" or feels "forsaken by his God"[23]—he or she may thus be said to have experienced a "loss of charisma." In particular, Dawson argues, charismatic leaders must, in order to avoid creating instability, successfully sustain their legitimacy by managing key problems or issues inherent within charismatic leadership; they must maintain their own persona, moderate the effects of followers' psychological identification with them, achieve new successes, and negotiate the routinization of charisma. If this does not occur, if they fail to manage one or more of these issues successfully or, indeed, mismanage them, then, Dawson argues, the outcome may be implosion of the group in question and, in some cases, violent behavior.[24]

Another explanation for the link between charismatic leadership and volatility concerns the lack of institutional restraints and, indeed, supports for such forms of leadership. As noted previously, charismatic leaders are ultimately their own source of legitimacy, and will therefore typically operate in a vacuum without any of the restraints and supports available to either traditional or legal-rational leaders. Again, in the absence of such structures—without checks on the leader or supports that they can fall back on in times of crisis—the potential for volatility and instability is increased in that the leader may "try and simplify the environment within the group by eliminating sources of dissension, normative diversity, and alternative leadership," or perhaps more dangerously, "feel increasingly impelled to act forcefully to meet the expectations of the devotees."[25] In such situations, Robbins and Anthony claim, violence may be turned either inwards in the form of purges, or outwards if, in an attempt to shore up his or her position, the leader lashes out at actual or perceived enemies in the outside world.

"Totalistic" Social Systems

The final factor highlighted by Robbins and Anthony as having the potential to produce volatility within millenarian groups stems from their functioning as "totalistic" social systems and agents of "resocialization." Stemming from their world-rejecting orientation, millenarian groups have traditionally set themselves apart from the rest of society, both in an ideological sense and, very often, also in a geographical sense. Whether attempting to (re)create the ideal society in preparation for the postapocalyptic world, preparing themselves spiritually for the future events, or simply trying to create a bounded space where the elect can live apart from the perceived corruption of the world, millenarian groups have often sought a form of "ecological discontinuity" from the moribund social order.[26]

Aside from the necessary physical separation from the outside world, a central concern for such communities is the (re)socialization of their members.[27] Galanter, for example, has proposed a social systems model of "charismatic groups" and argues that the basic transformative function performed by such groups is the "processing" of new recruits. Like factories, Galanter claims, "charismatic groups" take "input" from the outside world in the form of recruits with outside attachments and beliefs, which they then transform through a variety of social and cognitive techniques into a specific "output": members who adhere to group norms and beliefs.[28] Likewise, Lebra has argued that millenarian movements act as agents of socialization in a similar manner to other total institutions such as psychiatric or correctional institutions. However, whereas the latter typically "serve the established order and . . . [aim] . . . to rehabilitate misfits," the millenarian movement, in contrast, expects and prepares for the imminent destruction of that order.[29] Such resocialization, Lebra argues, involves the "interlocking" or synchronization of the group and the individual through three specific mechanisms: *enlightenment*, *integration*, and *commitment*. Through the process of enlightenment, the individual undergoes "a drastic, intense form of cognitive reorientation" which awakens them to the putative truth of which the group claims to be the custodian.[30] Through the process of integration, he or she engages socially with a community of believers and, through developing commitment, abandons attachments to the old order and becomes committed to the group and its vision.

Similarly, in her work on commitment mechanisms within millenarian and other utopian communities, Kanter argues that individuals' commitment to such groups operates on three interrelated levels: an *instrumental* connection with group membership; an *affective* connection with others in the group; and, finally, an *evaluative* connection with the beliefs and moral demands of the group. In particular, Kanter claims, commitment is reinforced and sustained by a process of "giving up" and "getting" in each of these three areas. The (potential) member must, in other words, "give up connection with other competing options and renounce the possibility of taking them up . . . [and must] . . . experience and recognize the positive benefits and gains of the new connection to the new community."[31] Crucially, at the moral or evaluative level, the individual must undergo what Kanter terms *mortification* and *surrender*: the "death" of the member's former self and the "birth" of a new one, and the surrendering of one's decision-making prerogative to a higher power.[32]

Although neither Lebra nor Kanter addresses the question of what connects social isolationism and resocialization to volatility, potential links have been explored by several more recent writers. Mills, for example, has highlighted what he terms the "reduction of normative dissonance" within totalistic groups as a key factor leading to "extreme, perhaps even violent, behavior."[33] Similarly, Galanter and Dawson both point to the role that "negative feedback," such as internal or external criticism, can play as a moderating force within totalistic groups, and how the suppression or absence of such feedback can potentially lead to volatility. According to Mills, the commitment mechanisms within most groups "are dampened and inhibited by the interplay of complex and partially inconsistent norms and values of the group and its environment."[34] Contrasting norms and values thus act as "countervalues" or "dampers" to each other, thus reducing the possibility of what Mills terms "supercommitment" occurring: a situation where individual autonomy, "both in moral judgment and role behavior, is replaced by unquestioning obedience, even to participation in violence."[35] In particular, Mills argues, the existence of such countervalues promotes a "slack" institutional structure wherein members possess multiple loyalties to a variety of contrasting norms and values. This "ordinary morality" is, however, according to Mills, "constantly in danger of being reduced by leaders who aspire to total rationality, to complete devotion to a cause."[36] Such leaders will, he argues, seek through a variety of means to reduce such "slack" and produce a "taut" organization of "supercommitted," obedient members. When this occurs, where any potential damping mechanisms are absent, Mills argues, members are robbed of both individual autonomy and any possible constraints on extreme behavior.

This is not, of course, to say that what Mills terms "the slide toward violence" necessarily follows from the absence of damping mechanisms. As he himself concedes, "the relative absence of normative dissonance within a group does not in itself produce violence."[37] Indeed, he goes on, "Many examples exist of wholehearted and unquestioning devotion to a cause or leader that does not issue in violence."[38] Likewise, although there is no denying that millenarian rhetoric can often be incredibly violent and that in some cases it may apparently offer a "divine sanction" for violence, it would be wrong to say there is a direct causal link between such rhetoric and violence. Rather, as noted above, the violent rhetoric of millenarianism typically remains at the level of rhetoric. Similarly, although charismatic leadership may by definition be precarious, it would be equally wrong to claim that such forms of leadership are inherently prone to volatility or violence. Although it is clear that charismatic authority was a significant factor in the development, and potentially in the volatility, of all of the groups discussed below, such groups were very much exceptional cases. Not only is charismatic leadership found, and actively cultivated and rewarded, in a variety of settings, both secular and religious, but, as with millenarian ideologies, there exist innumerable "charismatic leaders" who have not (as yet at least) manifested any propensity towards volatility or violence. There are also numerous groups that could be characterized as "totalistic," yet very few of these have ever (again as yet) displayed any propensity toward violence. Indeed, as Kanter has shown, the great majority of such groups will dissolve before they have the chance to develop in one direction or the other.[39]

In this way, although it is possible to highlight factors, such as those above, which might *predispose* groups to violence or enhanced volatility, this does not allow us to predict with any degree of certainty which millenarian groups will become volatile or violent. Consequently, any attempt to locate the genesis of millenarian violence in the characteristics of specific groups themselves is invariably a fruitless endeavor; for every one Peoples Temple or Aum Shinrikyo, for example, there are innumerable similar groups who have never, and probably never will, become violent. Not only this, but any attempt at prediction along such lines will typically ignore the role that exogenous factors—the most notable of which being external opposition—may play in precipitating incidents of violence.

Exogenous Factors—Three Models of Millenarian Violence

Although the term "exogenous factors" can refer broadly to any environmental factors that might impinge on a marginal religious group, it is typically used to describe various forms of "cultural opposition" encountered—or, perhaps, engendered—by such groups.[40] Such opposition can take various forms, ranging from "atrocity tales" concerning specific groups being presented in the media, or the abduction and forceful "deprogramming" of members, to, in some cases, the use of actual violence against members of marginal religious groups.[41] Indeed, as Anthony et al. and others have pointed out, the opponents of marginal religious groups can, in many ways, be as dualistic in their thinking and as zealous in the "crusades" against their opponents as the most extreme millenarians.[42]

The "Cultural Opposition" Model

The relationship between cultural opposition and millenarianism is complex, and there is substantial debate about the extent to which such opposition might be said to produce volatility or violence in millenarian groups. While accepting that some groups may be more predisposed to violence than others, the central thesis of what may be termed the "cultural opposition model" is that millenarian violence develops as a product of the interaction between an "apocalyptic religious movement" and its "cultural opponents" in the outside world. In doing so, however, Hall and his colleagues do not discount the possibility that, as a consequence of their internal organization or beliefs, some groups might be more predisposed to violence than others.[43] Rather, they argue that although such endogenous factors are necessary conditions, they are not by themselves sufficient to produce violence. Millenarian violence instead "grows out of the escalating social confrontations" between "apocalyptic movements" and their opponents in the wider world.[44] Such confrontations, they argue, invariably develop through several stages:

> Because apocalyptic movements are both voluntary and deviant, they are likely to produce defectors who take up the role of oppositional apostates and [along with, perhaps, relatives of members] work to mobilize broader cultural opposition. . . . If the apostates succeed in convincing agents of established social institutions (in our era, the mass media, politicians, and the state) to frame the movement as a threat to the established order, these agents may take actions intended to discredit the movement in the public eye, or subject it to actions and policies that undermine its capacity to exist as an autonomous collective.[45]

In response to such pressures, Hall et al. go on to say, the group in question may unleash aggression in one of two ways. In some cases, violence may be directed outward, with the group attacking real or perceived opponents in the outside world, before committing collective suicide. Alternatively, the group in question may forgo attacking their opponents and instead seek through an act of collective suicide to "escape" from the material world, and, in so doing, achieve some kind of "other-worldly grace."

Similarly, David Bromley and J. Gordon Melton propose a theory of religious violence that treats incidents of millenarian violence as "the product of an interactive sequence of movement-societal exchanges."[46] Such "dramatic denouements," as they term them,

> transpire when a movement and some segment of the social order reach a juncture at which one or both conclude that the requisite conditions for maintaining their core identity and collective existence are being subverted and that such circumstances are intolerable. . . .

> Parties on both sides thereupon undertake a project of final reckoning
> under the aegis of a transcendent mandate to reverse their power posi-
> tions and to restore what they avow to be the appropriate moral
> order.[47]

The path to dramatic denouements is, however, an interactive and contingent one, with numerous outcomes and responses possible on the path of
increasing movement-societal tension. According to Bromley, prior to such
"moments of destiny," disputes between marginal religious groups and the
wider society develop through three stages of increasing tension—*latent tension*, *nascent conflict*, and *intensified conflict*—with three types of response
possible for both parties at each stage of the process: the group may sever
its connections with the wider world and withdraw itself physically and
socially, or, alternatively, the social order may ignore or marginalize it
(*retreat*); either the group or the wider society may become more accom-
modative of the other (*accommodation*); or, one side may enter into conflict with the other (*contestation*). Similarly, conflict, if it occurs, may take
a variety of forms ranging "from symbolic posturing, to ritualized disputa-
tion, to violent combat."[48]

Dramatic denouements are thus relatively rare due to the variety of
means whereby both parties can reach a settlement and thereby lower the
tension and hostility between them. Indeed, even where they occur it does
not necessarily follow that contestation is the only possible outcome.
Rather, according to Bromley, the full range of response actions are still
available, although "a few of the logical possibilities are the most probable."[49] Within the state of increased tension, such responses "assume their
most extreme forms," to the extent that, for example, "partial accommodation will no longer suffice." Instead, the only acceptable form of accommodation becomes *capitulation*, in which one party accedes totally to the
demands of the other.[50] Where this is not an option, *contestation/battle* or
retreat/exodus become the most likely outcomes. The option that each side
is likely to choose is, however, according to Bromley, determined by the
asymmetrical power relationship that exists between both parties. As the
state cannot withdraw, the only path open to it is that of contestation. In
contrast, the group may respond either through *exodus*, whereby, through
an act of collective suicide, it reasserts "the moral superiority of its position,
rejects the existing social order, and totally separates itself from that order,"
or through *battle*, whereby it "launches a coercive campaign to replace that
order with its own vision of an appropriate social order."[51]

The "Interpretive Approach"

This notion of millenarian violence as a product of reflexive social interaction between conflictual parties draws parallels, and in many ways

overlaps, with what has been termed the "interpretive approach" to millenarian violence. Drawing implicitly on ideas found within symbolic interactionism, this approach focuses on the manner in which millenarian groups and their cultural opponents act on the basis of the meanings that they ascribe to the actions of the other. As noted previously, both millenarian groups and their cultural opponents tend to perceive the world and, particularly, the other party in extremely stark terms:

> Each side claims to have knowledge of the other, yet this knowledge is not derived from the other but from one's own concept of the world. To the extent that the other is demonized—to millenarians, the state is evil, and to the state, millenarians are crazed—there is little incentive to see the world from the other's point of view. What is looked for instead is evidence that confirms the picture already held. To the extent that the two sides interact on the basis of these mirror-image scripts, each will selectively identify and interpret evidence that fits into the appropriate script.[52]

The result, as Michael Barkun has shown in his discussion of the Christian Identity movement, is a form of deviance amplification wherein the action of each party seemingly "confirms" the "script" that each holds of the other and, more importantly, offers a justification for their continued posture vis-à-vis the other party.[53] Violence consequently develops out of a spiral of growing mistrust, misinterpretation, and actions that seemingly, rightly or wrongly, "prove" to both sides that the other is a danger to them and their respective goals.

"Catastrophic Millennialism" and Violence

Another theory of millenarian violence that has generated a significant amount of debate and analysis can be found in Catherine Wessinger's work on progressive and catastrophic millennialism. Acknowledging that neither category is mutually exclusive and that it is possible for a particular group to shift between the two, Wessinger argues that the radical dualism and pessimistic view of humanity inherent in the latter tends to make it more predisposed to violence than the former. In particular, Wessinger argues, violence or volatility is likely to occur when catastrophic millenarian groups feel that their "ultimate concern"—or "millennial goal"—is threatened in some way. This, Wessinger argues, "is more important than anything else in the universe for the person [or the group] involved," and therefore when it is threatened in some way groups are likely to become volatile or violent.[54]

Such threats may come, Wessinger argues, from both internal and external sources, and violent responses may, as noted by Hall and Bromley, be directed inward or outward. Consequently, and again acknowledging that such categories are fluid and not mutually exclusive, Wessinger distin-

guishes between three broad types of millennial groups involved in violence: *assaulted millennial groups*, *revolutionary catastrophic movements*, and
finally, *fragile catastrophic groups*. Assaulted millennial groups, according to
Wessinger, commit violent acts in self-defense when they "are attacked by
law enforcement agents because they are perceived as dangerous."[55] Consequently, the violent acts that such groups commit are typically "reactive" in
nature—reactions to an external threat or threats to their "ultimate concern." In contrast, revolutionary catastrophic movements are likely to
engage in preemptive, "offensive" actions, believing "that revolutionary violence is necessary to become liberated from their persecutors and to set up
the righteous government and society."[56] Violence is thus a method
whereby such groups may bring about their "millennial goal." Finally, in the
case of fragile millennial groups, violence stems from a combination of
internal pressures and the experience of external opposition. When such
internal pressures are exacerbated by external opposition, whether real or
perceived, Wessinger argues, the group may be destabilized and, in an
attempt to preserve their ultimate concern, may "direct their violence out-
wardly to kill enemies or inwardly to commit murders and group suicide."[57]

While there is a general consensus, then, across all three models that
external opposition plays an important role in incidents of millenarian violence, there is some debate over whether, by itself, it is sufficient to produce
volatility or violence. On the one hand, both the "cultural opposition"
model and interpretive approach focus explicitly on the role that the various "cultural opponents" of marginal religious movements play in precipitating outbursts of violence from the object(s) of their opposition. While
not denying the role of certain endogenous factors in predisposing certain
groups to become volatile, for Hall and his colleagues and for Bromley the
emphasis is more on how such "potentiality" is actualized through the
actions of various cultural opponents. Similarly, the interpretive approach
focuses on how the (often fatuous) beliefs that each party has regarding the
other can fuel further misunderstanding, tension, and, in some cases, conflict. On the other hand, the model proposed by Catherine Wessinger,
while acknowledging the importance of external opposition, differs in also
highlighting the way in which volatility and violence within millenarian
groups may stem from a combination of such opposition *and* endogenous
pressures. In such cases, then, external opposition may serve to exacerbate
existing pressures and tensions within a particular group, rather than actually producing volatility or violence directly.

Millenarianism and Violence in the Contemporary World

Having reviewed the current literature, I now return to the question that
I posed in the introduction: why did these six groups engage in acts of

homicide and suicide? What, in other words, were the specific factors, or combination of factors, that precipitated their acts of violence? My own analysis of these incidents[58] suggests that three key sets of factors, often working in combination, would appear to have played a role in the development of each group's millenarian ideology and, by extension, in precipitating their violent actions: *the actions of cultural opponents, challenges to the leader's authority or charisma,* and *internal challenges to the millennial goal.* I shall focus on each in turn.[59]

The Actions of "Cultural Opponents"

Turning first to exogenous factors, the actions of "cultural opponents" would seem to play an important, but by no means crucial, role in precipitating outbursts of millenarian violence. All but one of the groups attracted opposition from apostates, and several also attracted opposition from the media, law enforcement agencies, family members, and anti-cult coalitions. For example, in the year leading up to their collective suicide, Peoples Temple experienced concerted opposition from a group of apostates calling themselves the Concerned Relatives, who, in turn, mobilized the media and several U.S. government departments in their campaign to undermine the Temple and its operations.[60] Similarly, the Solar Temple encountered dogged opposition from Rose-Marie Klaus, the estranged wife of a Temple member. This opposition continued and, indeed, intensified following her divorce, with her airing her grievances in the media and also denouncing the Order to several anti-cult groups.[61] Likewise, former Branch Davidian Marc Breault also mobilized elements of the media and, in a similar way to the Concerned Relatives, served as an informant to several government departments in their investigations of Davidians in the months leading up to the authorities' raid on Mount Carmel.[62] Both Aum Shinrikyo and the MRTCG also became the targets of complaints and campaigns from both former members and the families of members demanding access to their relatives. During the early 1990s Aum, too, encountered dogged opposition from local residents in the areas where it attempted to establish communes, while the MRTCG came under pressure from the Catholic Church in Uganda.[63]

However, only the cases of Breault and the Concerned Relatives would appear to fit into the "cultural opposition" model proposed by Hall and his colleagues and by Bromley. Indeed, in many ways, Breault and the Branch Davidians represent a paradigmatic example of the process by which apostates are able, in turn, to mobilize the media and law enforcement agencies in their struggles against the movements that they oppose. In contrast, although both the Solar Temple and Aum came under investigation by law enforcement agencies, this involvement did not stem from the actions of apostates. Rather, the Solar Temple came to the attention of the Quebec police during their investigations of a group calling itself Q-37, which had threatened to assassinate several members of the Canadian parliament (and then only after one of the Solar Temple's leaders, Luc Jouret, had sought illegally to buy guns with silencers).[64] Similarly, the Japanese authorities were extremely cautious in their dealings with Aum and (in spite of evidence linking Aum to several attempted assassinations and the production of chemical weapons) only acted against it following Aum's bungled abduction of the brother of a former member in the spring of 1995.[65] A similar reticence was displayed by the Ugandan authorities in response to complaints raised against the MRTCG by the families of members and former members, allegedly as a consequence of bribes paid by the Movement to various local officials.[66]

Moreover, the case of Heaven's Gate would also appear to challenge the claim that organized "cultural opposition" plays a crucial role in precipitating incidents of millenarian violence. Although several commentators have characterized the ridicule encountered by Heaven's Gate in response to its 1993 "last chance" proselytizing campaign as a form of "opposition,"[67] there is little, if any evidence to suggest that the suicides were influenced directly by this. Indeed, even Hall and his associates admit that

> the Two and their class never engaged in anything remotely like the cultural struggle that unfolded between Peoples Temple and the Concerned Relatives, or between the Branch Davidians and their "cultbusters." They certainly did not take on the warring posture like the leaders of Aum Shinrikyo. Nor were they even an object of any sting operation or media savaging of the sort that the Solar Temple encountered.[68]

Rather, drawing on Balch and Taylor's account, it would appear that the decision of the Heaven's Gate "crew" to "return home" was prompted not so much by any opposition, but rather by their belief that "they had exhausted their options at the human level" and that they had received their "marker" in the shape of the Hale-Bopp comet.[69] Indeed, if anything, the ridicule that they encountered merely reinforced their belief that "the 'weeds' have taken over the garden" and that, as one member stated in their "earth exit statement," "there is no place for us to go but up."[70]

Challenges to the Leaders' Authority or Charisma
Turning next to endogenous factors, it would appear that challenges to the authority of charismatic leaders plays an important role in precipitating violence or volatility. Such challenges to leaders' authority or charisma, an analysis of the incidents reveals, can come from three main sources. First, it may come through loss of reputation or through real or perceived rebuffs. Thus, following his conviction for purchasing illegal firearms in

1992, Luc Jouret's reputation as a lecturer on the New Age circuit was effectively ruined. Indeed, as one Solar Temple member later recalled, following the incident, "his mind changed, he was a tired, tired, disappointed, disillusioned person."[71] Not only this, but the image that the Solar Temple had created for itself as an elite, secret society characterized by chivalry and honor was irreparably ruined. Moreover, the police investigation of the Solar Temple raised the threat that its many "secrets within secrets" would be exposed to the profane world, a situation that would, again, further undermine its position as a secret society.[72]

Similarly, in the case of Aum, a chain of events that began with its failure to achieve the international growth in membership predicted by its leader Asahara Shoko and the rejection of its application under the Religious Corporations Law in April 1989 served to undermine the image that Asahara was attempting to create for Aum. Although its application was accepted later that year, Aum then came under pressure from "cultural opposition" in the form of the media and from a group of aggrieved former members and families of members, calling itself Aum Victims' Society. Finally, perhaps most damningly, Aum's attempts to achieve political power during the 1990 elections ended in a debacle, with Asahara himself attracting less than 1 percent of the votes in the district in which he had confidently predicted a landslide in his favor. Not only this, but the media became even more scathing of Aum, with "Aum-bashing" becoming a veritable "national pastime" and "media obsession."[73] In the aftermath of the elections, Asahara announced that Aum would cease in its efforts to save the world and would henceforth focus instead on saving its members alone. It would also, although Asahara did not state this publicly, begin its preparations to defend itself against its perceived enemies by developing various biological and, in turn, chemical weapons.[74]

Both the Solar Temple and Aum highlight another way in which the authority of a charismatic leader can be undermined: through their being exposed as frauds or as having practiced deception. As evidence of their election, both Joseph Di Mambro, the cofounder of the Solar Temple, and Asahara had claimed that they manifested several supernatural abilities. Di Mambro had claimed that the various supernatural events that transpired during Solar Temple rituals, such as the appearance of the Holy Grail, were real and were evidence of his contact with several Ascended Masters. Similarly, Asahara had claimed, among other things, that his blood possessed a unique DNA structure (a fact allegedly verified by Kyoto University), and that those who drank it would acquire some of his spiritual power. When these claims were challenged by the testimony of Antonio Dutoit, the lighting engineer who produced the effects for the Solar Temple rituals, and Sakamoto Tsutsumi, the legal representative of the Aum Victims' Society, the whole basis for Di Mambro's and Asahara's charisma was called into question. As one member wrote to Di Mambro in late 1993, "I would be really upset if I had to conclude that I'd sincerely prostrated myself in front of an illusion!!!"[75] In addition, the allegations also threatened the continued financial viability of both groups: Aum, for example, asked for a ¥300,000 "donation" for members to drink Asahara's blood, while a member of the Solar Temple in Quebec could pay up to $350 per month for their membership.[76] It is therefore perhaps not surprising that both leaders made a point of murdering these opponents, out of the desire to silence them (in the case of Sakamoto) or "punish" them as "traitors" (in the case of Dutoit and his family).

Third, a charismatic leader's authority can be undermined through ill health. All but one of the leaders of the groups were in real or perceived ill health prior to their group's respective denouements.[77] Following Jim Jones's move to Guyana, for example, his health deteriorated seriously as a consequence of heavy drug use. Jonestown residents heard him speaking over the loudspeaker in slurred tones, saw him staggering around the community, urinating on occasions in public view, and all who came into contact with him witnessed signs of mental confusion and frequent, erratic changes of mood. Jones had also put on weight and claimed to be seriously ill with several maladies, although this belief was contradicted by the subsequent autopsy on his body.[78] One member, for example, recalled that when she moved to Jonestown in December of that year, Jones, whom she had not seen for several months, was a physical wreck:

> He had gained a great deal of weight, and he complained constantly of such a number of serious ailments that it was a wonder he was still on his feet at all. He claimed to have cancer, a heart condition, a fungus in his lungs, and a recurring fever of 105 degrees. He dosed himself with painkillers, tranquillizers, and amphetamines, which only added to the incoherence of his speech.[79]

Similarly, in the period leading up to the Heaven's Gate collective suicide, the health of its leader, Marshall Applewhite (or "Do" as he was known), also began to deteriorate and, as a reflection of this, he began to speak of assuming a "professor emeritus" role. Like Jim Jones, Do also believed that he was dying of cancer, a belief that—although, again, subsequently discovered to be unfounded—proved sufficiently convincing to be a catalyst in the crew's decision that the time was approaching to "return home."[80] As one member stated in his "Earth Exit Statement," "I know my Older Member, Do, is going to his Older Member, Ti, at this time . . . [and] . . . I know that my graft to [Ti and Do] would be jeopardized if I linger here once They have departed."[81] Similarly, Reader notes how "followers and former followers confirmed that [Asahara] frequently appeared to be ill in 1994 and that when he spoke his voice seemed to be husky."[82] Indeed, "when he was arrested in May 1995 Asahara was, by all accounts, overweight and in poor condition, and at that time there were many rumours that he was dying of liver failure or some such ailment."[83]

While the maladies of the above leaders were to a great extent imagined, those endured by Joseph Di Mambro and David Koresh were, in contrast, very real. Whereas Asahara was rumored to be dying of liver failure, Di Mambro was actually suffering from this ailment and, indeed, had to wear incontinence pads. Likewise, whereas Jones and Do believed themselves to be dying of cancer, Di Mambro had been diagnosed as such. He had also contracted diabetes and had begun to experience diabetic fits.[84] Similarly, whereas Asahara had accused, among others, the U.S. government of trying to kill him with chemical weapons, David Koresh was actually injured by a bullet during the ATF's raid on Mount Carmel.[85]

Internal Challenges to the Millennial Goal

Finally, volatility or violence would also appear to stem from real or perceived internal threats to the respective groups' "millennial goal."[86] Such threats can stem from various factors, although it would appear that dissent and defections (particularly when there is also a demand for refunds) and the failure of the group to realize its ambitions or to fulfill its goal are particularly crucial. Indeed, as Mayer notes, such threats are in many ways much more serious than those arising from the actions of cultural opponents:

> When followers cease to believe, the whole structure of plausibility of the message seems to be put into question and the very survival of the group may seem threatened—not even mentioning the fact that insiders may in some cases be privy to facts that the leadership does not want to see leaked to the outside world.[87]

In four of the six cases, dissent and defections played a crucial role in either exacerbating the effects of external opposition or undermining the continued existence of the group and its mission. In the case of Solar Temple, Mayer observes how the shift within its ideology from an optimistic belief that members would survive the prophesied ecological apocalypse to the belief that it would be necessary to escape Earth beforehand occurred in the months following the defection of several core members in the early 1990s.[88] Similarly, the defections of a number of members in the aftermath of Jouret's arrest and the exposure of the lighting tricks served to further undermine the "virtual reality" that Di Mambro and Jouret had built around themselves.[89] Indeed, evidence of the impact of these acts of "treason" on Di Mambro in particular is provided by Mayer, who notes:

> In the very last days of his life, at a time when several members had already perished, Di Mambro still wrote drafts of two letters (dated

October 3, 1994), denouncing two former members to the Attorney
General, accusing them of having blackmailed him. . . . In addition,
there are clear indications that, during the last weekend of his life,
he tried (unsuccessfully) to lure into his chalet the first person who,
years earlier, had left the communal core of the group. If the man
had accepted the invitation, he would certainly have become one of
the victims.[90]

Likewise, according to Chidester, suicide was apparently first proposed as
a strategy within Peoples Temple following the defection of a group of
young black members in 1973, who left accusing the Temple of racism and
of not being radical enough in its ideals.[91] Moreover, Maaga notes that the
defections of two key members of the Temple leadership committee in May
and October of 1978, respectively, played "pivotal" roles in the decision to
commit mass suicide in that they demonstrated "that Jonestown had failed
as a socialist community."[92] Indeed, it was the defection of several high-
level, core white members of the community with Congressman Leo Ryan
during his November 1978 fact-finding effort, which seems, in retrospect,
to have been the final, fatal blow to Jones and Peoples Temple. Not only
were these individuals "among the last people one would have expected to
leave,"[93] but their defections sent an alarming message to the rest of the
community that all was not well within the Promised Land.

In a similar way, Shimazono notes how the increase in the number of
defections from Aum's communes in the early 1990s, coupled with the
lack of new members to fill their places, played a key role in the development of Asahara's increasingly pessimistic apocalyptic vision.[94] According
to Reader:

Defections [from among core commune members], along with the
feeling that its message was not being properly received, were recurrent concerns for Aum. Asahara had earlier questioned whether his
movement could continue because of defections, and his sense of his
mission was in some senses failing or, rather, as with the Solar Temple, that his message was not being listened to, had been a major factor in Aum's hostile attitude towards society at large.[95]

Internal dissent also appears to have played a crucial role in the MRTCG
murder/suicides. Despite the different theories put forward to account for
what transpired within the MRTCG during the spring of 2000,[96] a consistent theme in the accounts is how internal dissent, linked with demands
for refunds, played a central role in precipitating the murder/suicides.
According to the testimony of former members, the MRTCG leadership
had predicted the end of the world for the end of 1992, and then the end
of 1995, before finally settling on December 31, 1999. When the final date
came and passed without incident, dissent began to grow. One of the

MRTCG's leaders, Credonia Mwerinde, however, informed them that the Virgin Mary had appeared to her and the other leaders, informing them that the date for the end of the world had been put back to March 17. Although this raised the spirits of some, a number of members were not convinced by this, and discontent continued to grow. Many, for example, began to demand that the money that they had donated to the MRTCG be refunded, a situation that clearly threatened the Movement's financial viability and continued existence.[97] Others became openly disloyal and began to question the authority of Mwerinde and the other leaders. In an attempt to placate any dissenters, "Credonia promised that the Blessed Virgin Mary would refund the money from the sale of the members' properties." She also "asked her priests to record the names of those followers who were discontented."[98] Those who submitted complaints were, according to witnesses, called to a meeting with the MRTCG leaders and were never seen again. Any who asked where these individuals had gone were informed that they had been transferred to another of the MRTCG's properties or that "the Virgin had taken them to Heaven."[99] The hundreds of bodies discovered after the March 2000 conflagration buried beneath several of the MRTCG's properties are believed to be those of these dissenters.

Volatility would, in particular, appear to be linked, as Wessinger argues, to the failure of the group to fulfill its "millennial goal" or to realize its ambitions. Thus, Aum Shinrikyo's shift into a "culture of coercive asceticism," and the increasingly exclusive and pessimistic direction that its apocalyptic message took from the late 1980s onward stemmed from its failure to grow at the rate that Asahara had predicted and upon which he had pinned the future of humanity. Initially, in the mid-1980s, Asahara had claimed that in order for the apocalypse to be averted, Aum had to expand worldwide and train thirty-thousand spiritually enlightened renunciates. More broadly, Aum saw its mission—a mission that Asahara claimed to have had entrusted to him by Shiva—as the creation of the Buddhist paradise on earth, *Shambhala*, first in Japan and then extending throughout the world. However, within a couple of years it was clear that such plans were far too ambitious to be achieved, and so Asahara reframed the original prophecy in much more pessimistic and exclusivist terms, claiming that it was not possible to save the whole of humanity and that instead Aum should devote its attention to saving the "elect" only. In addition to this, he also turned his attention to the "elect" themselves, and began to emphasize more and more the importance of practicing ascetic activities and austerities. He also came to believe that those who were reluctant to practice these activities should be "encouraged," through force if necessary, to do so for their own good. Consequently, within a short time what Reader refers to as a "culture of coercive asceticism" developed within Aum, in which the lines between encouragement, coercion, and violence became blurred—a culture that marked the first step on the slippery slope to Aum's use of violence against outsiders, and, ultimately, its use of weapons of mass destruction against the Japanese public in 1995.[100]

In other cases, volatility may stem from the realization that the group's very viability is threatened from within. The continued existence and mission of the Heaven's Gate "crew," for example, were, as noted above, threatened by the possibility that Do would, like Ti over a decade before, depart from them through death and thereby leave them "stranded" on Earth. In an attempt partly to forestall this, the "crew" therefore chose to "exit their vehicles" with him. Similarly, leaving aside the pressure brought to bear by external opposition, toward the end of 1978, the continued existence of Jonestown as a viable community was also threatened by a number of internal pressures; not only was the community's stability threatened by its lack of self-sufficiency, but there was also growing dissent amongst the residents.

Initially Jonestown had been planned to accommodate around 500 to 700 Temple members, based on the calculation of four persons to a house. However, as a consequence of the mass exodus of the summer 1977 following a series of critical reports about the Temple in the U.S. media, each house had to hold eight, sixteen, and in some cases twenty people. Linked to this, as Moore has shown, just over half (57 percent) of the 1,020 Jonestown residents in 1978 were either over sixty years of age or under nineteen.[101] Although both groups contributed in some form to the economic well-being of the community, they relied heavily on the able-bodied adults, who comprised less than half of the total population, for their material support, health care, and education. Consequently, although "the dependents were not destructive, they drained the community's resources."[102] One consequence of this pressure placed on the able-bodied adults to support the rest of the community was the growth of dissent and, more crucially, defection and apostasy. In addition, Jones himself was increasingly becoming "a liability rather than an asset to the community," through his heavy drug use and increasing physical incapacity.[103]

The final blows to the community's existence came in the shape of Congressman Ryan and his fact-finding effort, which not only effectively opened up Jonestown to its enemies, but also provided the opportunity for several key members to leave the community. In addition, Ryan's recommendation that there should be "more interchange with the outside world . . . [and] . . . that people should be able to come and go freely" effectively spelled the end of Jonestown as a viable "socialist utopia," free of the "American antichrist system."[104] Jones and the community were in effect facing a triple defeat: not only had their enemies gained access to Jonestown, but they were leaving with a number of core residents and, effectively, promising to return for more whenever they wished. From this perspective, the subsequent murder of Ryan and members of his party and the collective suicide may be understood as an attempt to snatch a victory of sorts from their enemies and to then shut them out forever through an act of "revolutionary suicide."

Likewise, the decision of the Solar Temple leadership to escape the planet prior to the apocalypse may be seen as a reaction to a number of internal pressures that it experienced in the early 1990s. Not only had Jouret and Di Mambro's authority been undermined, but members, embarrassed by Jouret's conviction and disillusioned by the exposés of lighting fraud, were leaving in numbers and demanding refunds. Jouret's conviction also meant that he could no longer lecture on the New Age circuit, and that, consequently, the Solar Temple's main avenue of recruitment was closed off. In addition, in the eyes of its leaders, the Solar Temple's mission was also being undermined by Di Mambro's teenage daughter, Emmanuelle, and the existence of the antichrist in the shape of the infant son of former lighting engineer Antonio Dutoit and his wife Nicki. Emmanuelle had been raised from birth to be the avatar of the New Age. However, by the mid-1990s, she had become what Wessinger refers to as "a messiah difficult to deal with": not only was she rejecting her cosmically assigned role, but she was also becoming unruly and expressing an interest in teenage pop culture.[105] She was also, Di Mambro believed, under threat from the antichrist, who, he claimed, had been born to the Dutoits in the summer of 1994. Facing financial ruin, the loss of their reputations, and, indeed, the loss of everything that Di Mambro in particular had built up over several decades, the leaders reacted by planning one last dramatic "spectacular" gesture to the world: their "transit" to Sirius.

Conclusion

The study of millenarian violence is ultimately limited by the fact that the cases are, thankfully, few in number and occur too irregularly to permit the generation of complex theoretical models or to allow detailed comparative analyses to be conducted. However, on the basis of the foregoing, several conclusions may be drawn. Primarily, it is possible to discern from these incidents three broad paths to millenarian violence (or "apocalyptic trajectories," as I term them): violence stemming from external opposition (the Branch Davidians); violence as a consequence of internal pressures, exacerbated by external opposition (Peoples Temple, Solar Temple, and Aum Shinrikyo); and, finally, violence as a consequence of (largely if not exclusively) internal pressures (Heaven's Gate and the MRTCG). It is also possible, to a significant extent, to relate the direction of violence to the specific precipitating factors. Leaving to one side the contested question of whether the final conflagration at Waco was murder, suicide, or a tragic accident, what is clear is that the Branch Davidians' violence was directed exclusively outward as an act of self-defense against the government officials raiding their home. In contrast, both Heaven's Gate and the MRTCG turned violence inward in an attempt either to defend their millennial goal from their respective internal pressures, or, in the case of Heaven's Gate, to fulfill their goal in spite of the pressures. Finally, with Peoples Temple, Solar Temple, and Aum, we find a combination of violence directed outward against respective enemies and inward in attempts to defend or fulfill their millennial goals.

In this way, the evidence would appear to support Catherine Wessinger's thesis that acts of millenarian violence stem from threats to millenarian groups' "millennial goal" or "ultimate concern." Each of the incidents of violence examined can be seen as a response to threats to each group's millennial goal brought about by internal or external pressures. Four of the six cases had been made "fragile" by either a combination of internal pressures and external opposition (Peoples Temple, Solar Temple, and Aum Shinrikyo) or by internal factors alone (MRTCG). Indeed, even the Heaven's Gate suicides could be interpreted as a response to the problem of how the group could continue and achieve its millennial goal—to evolve to the next level—if Do left his body before the rest of his crew were ready. In contrast, although external opposition did play a part, to a greater or lesser extent, in four of the case studies, it would be inaccurate to claim that it played a crucial role in the majority of the cases (the case of the Branch Davidians being the exception). Rather, just as internal factors alone were not on the whole sufficient to produce volatility, real or perceived opposition served instead to exacerbate existing internal pressures within each group.

Chapter Three

The Eschatology of Heaven's Gate

Christopher Partridge

On March 26, 1997, the bodies of thirty-nine people, all dressed in identical black clothes, were found in a mansion in Rancho Santa Fe, an exclusive San Diego suburb. All of them were members of Heaven's Gate, a new religion that had, up to that point, remained relatively unknown. It was immediately apparent to Rio DiAngelo, the ex-member who discovered the bodies, that they had committed suicide. It was later discovered that they had all willingly eaten applesauce laced with Phenobarbital, followed by vodka. Why? The answer is to be found in an obscure millenarian eschatology, which, while drawing on New Age ideas, science fiction,[1] and the contemporary UFO subculture,[2] needs to be understood primarily as a vernacular and idiosyncratic form of fundamentalist premillennialism. Again, while Heaven's Gate recruited members from the New Age subculture, to understand fully the tragic demise of the group, one needs to look away from that subculture and to the group's particular development of Christian apocalyptic thought.[3]

The Advent of Ti and Do

Originally known as Human Individual Metamorphosis and then as Total Overcomers Anonymous, Heaven's Gate was founded by Marshall Herff

Applewhite (1931–1997) and Bonnie Lu Nettles (1927–1985)—also known as "Pig and Guinea," then as "Peep and Bo," "the Two," and "Do and Ti." Applewhite, the son of a Presbyterian minister, had initially followed in his father's footsteps and embarked on the path to ordination. However, he changed his mind and decided to study for a degree in music, which he was eventually awarded by the University of Colorado. After a brief period teaching music at the University of Alabama, he was recruited by Houston's St. Thomas University to establish a fine arts program. Although obviously successful, in 1970 he was dismissed following an affair with one of his students. This led Applewhite into much bitterness and resentment. Indeed, below the surface, he had been a troubled individual for many years. Although married with two children, he had had numerous homosexual relationships, which led to deep feelings of guilt about his double life. Robert Balch and David Taylor (two sociologists who infiltrated the group) have noted that he "confided to at least one of his lovers his longing for a meaningful, platonic relationship where he could develop his full potential without sexual entanglements." However, "after getting divorced, [he] vacillated between homosexual and heterosexual identities, never feeling comfortable with either."[4] This is not insignificant because, as is argued here, Applewhite's struggle with sexuality eventually contributed to the shape of the eschatology of Heaven's Gate.

Nettles, although brought up a Baptist, became fascinated with Eastern and occult ideas, eventually joining the Houston Theosophical Society. Following a chance meeting with Applewhite in a Houston hospital in 1972, where she was working as a nurse, the two quickly became inseparable. Nettles introduced Applewhite to the New Age subculture and, over time, "they withdrew from their friends, becoming absorbed in a private world of visions, dreams and paranormal experiences that included contacts with space beings who urged them to abandon their worldly pursuits."[5] Eventually, in 1973, they left Houston convinced that they were destined for an important mission, the details of which were yet to be clarified. Following several months of traveling and numerous odd jobs to support themselves, they discovered an isolated location near the Oregon coast on the banks of the Rogue River, where they could clarify their calling.

After six weeks their mission was clear. However, whereas they initially seemed to have been principally inspired by easternized or New Age ideas—and scholars have naturally focused on these elements within their teaching[6]—in fact, from the outset they understood their mission in broadly Christian terms. Strikingly similar in some ways to John Reeve and Lodowick Muggleton, two mid-seventeenth-century London tailors who founded the Muggletonians, a small, millennialist Christian sect,[7] Nettles and Applewhite became convinced that they were the "two witnesses" spoken of in Revelation 11. The following passage was particularly important:

> And I will grant my two witnesses authority to prophesy for one thou-
> sand two hundred sixty days. . . . These are the two olive trees and the
> two lampstands that stand before the Lord of the earth. . . . When
> they have finished their testimony, the beast that comes up from the
> bottomless pit will make war on them and conquer them and kill
> them, and their dead bodies will lie in the street . . . . For three and
> a half days members of the peoples and tribes and languages will gaze
> at their dead bodies and refuse to let them be placed in a tomb; and
> the inhabitants of the earth will gloat over them and celebrate and
> exchange presents, because these two prophets had been a torment to
> the inhabitants of the earth. But after the three and a half days, the
> breath of life from God entered them, and they stood on their feet,
> and those who saw them were terrified. Then they heard a loud voice
> from heaven saying to them, "Come up here!" And they went up to
> heaven in a cloud while their enemies watched them. (Rev. 11:3-12)

Interpreted literally, this passage is understood to foretell events soon to
befall Applewhite and Nettles. Consequently, they began to speak confidently of "the Demonstration," which they said would be the outworking
of Revelation 11, the proof of their soteriological significance, the evidence
that they are indeed the "two witnesses." Immediately prior to the destruction of the planet, they prophesied, they would be killed, resurrected, and
physically transported from the Earth's surface to a waiting UFO "in the
sight of their foes"—a "cloud" being, they claimed, the biblical term for a
spacecraft. In a conversation with Brad Steiger and Hayden Hughes in
Oklahoma City on July 13, 1974, "The Two said they would prove their
emissary status to skeptics in a short time: they would be assassinated; their
slain corpses would lie in state for three and a half days; and then they
would rise from the dead in full view of the national media."[8]

More than a year passed before they began to recruit followers from the
New Age subculture. In the spring of 1975, Clarence Klug, a New Age
teacher based in Los Angeles who was fascinated by esoteric interpretations
of Revelation,[9] heard of their claims and invited them to address his group
in a friend's living room. "The room fell silent as the man began to speak.
'You might say she's Guinea and I'm Pig,' he said. 'We are guinea pigs in
the sense that we are here to show how man, the caterpillar, can become a
butterfly in the next kingdom.'"[10] Perhaps surprisingly, not only did they
impress their audience, but also they managed to recruit over twenty people, including Klug.

Having gathered a small, committed group of devotees who were keen
to learn more, their teaching began to evolve. Indeed, they began by changing their names again. To symbolize their role as "space-age shepherds,"
they referred to themselves as Bo and Peep. They would later, finally,
change them to Do (Applewhite) and Ti (Nettles), names which, said
Applewhite, have no significance at all.[11] They're simply labels for "earthly

containers." This, we will see, was itself a key element in a cognitive process by which the inner self was detached both from their bodies—which they believed to be a hindrance to spiritual progress—and also from the doomed world in which they currently existed.

Cosmological and Soteriological Perspectives

Heaven's Gate understood the Bible to be, "for the most part . . . the primary historical record . . . of periods when the Next Level was relating to man."[12] That said, their use of it was very selective. For example, not only did they focus on eschatological passages, particularly from the book of Revelation, but also, as with other UFO religionists, they provided an interesting physicalist interpretation of the early chapters of Genesis. This they understood literally as a reliable account of human origins, and from this they developed what might be described as a "neofundamentalist" form of creationism. Unlike Christian fundamentalist literalism, however, according to this account the human race is the creation of superior extra-terrestrials.[13] Using a mixture of gardening and computing metaphors, it was taught that humans are beings with free will, placed in this "earthly garden" (there are other planetary gardens) to grow spiritually.

> The purpose of this creation is . . . to produce new members for the Level Above Human. . . . New members of the Kingdom of Heaven are born through a metamorphic process which begins when the Level Above Human, or Next Level, "plants seeds"—places deposits or "chips" of Next Level mind (mind that comes from the Creator, the Chief of Chiefs, or Most High God—the term you use is not important) into human "plants." . . . A deposit is potentially the *gift of life*, for it contains the programming necessary to begin the metamorphic process which can lead to entry into the real Evolutionary Level Above Human, where there is no death.[14]

Most humans simply have "spirits" (a collection of memories, emotions, and the like), but those with "deposits" are understood to have "souls."

Although notably eclectic, again, from an early stage it was clear where the principal concepts of their theology were being drawn from and thus what shape their eschatology was likely to take. Of course, the garden—central to the "primeval history" of Genesis—is the paradise that was lost. Likewise, just as Revelation can be interpreted as the story of paradise restored—the return of the Edenic "garden city" of God[15]—so we shall see that Heaven's Gate understood the "Next Level" in eschatological and utopian terms. Moreover, following the contours of Christian theology, Heaven's Gate taught that extraterrestrial creators (Next Level beings)[16] placed humans in the garden; they gave them the gifts of life and free will, in that some have been equipped with deposits of the Next Level mind to enable, but not to compel, them to evolve into Next Level beings ("the metamorphic process"); those who respond to the Heaven's Gate gospel progress to the Next Level "where the Chief resides"; this is "a level of existence wherein the many members do not experience death or decay"—the Kingdom of Heaven.[17]

Reflecting Applewhite's Presbyterian background, central to this salvation history is an explicit doctrine of election, which argues that extraterrestrials select certain individuals in which to plant "deposits" (or "souls"). The elect are unaware of these deposits until they come into contact with a "Representative of the Next Level," such as Applewhite, Nettles, or, two thousand years ago, Jesus. Moreover, just as the Christian elect, according to Reformed theology, respond to the preached gospel message, so the deposit is activated when it encounters a Next Level Mind. This activated deposit coincides with the joining of minds. That is to say, whereas, in Christian theology, the work of the Holy Spirit leads to the union and communion of the believer with God, which, in turn, involves a process of sanctification, in Heaven's Gate teaching there is an activation of the deposit, a melding of the spiritually immature mind with the highly evolved mind, and a subsequent technological sanctification as the former mind is matured. This "metamorphic process" is essentially a discipling process that nurtures the growth of Next Level beings who will become, as their extraterrestrial creators are, citizens of the Kingdom of Heaven.

Having argued that much of this is recognizably Christian, it should be noted that other aspects are less so. Reflecting Nettles's Theosophical background and interests, they claimed that the metamorphic process is a long one, spanning more than a single lifetime. In other words, Heaven's Gate incorporates a form of reincarnation whereby those with "deposits," as opposed to merely spirits, evolve over several lifetimes. Indeed, Next Level beings have appeared around every two thousand years or so for the benefit of evolving souls, offering "the discipline and 'grafting' required . . . [for] transition into membership in My Father's House." Applewhite and Nettles, of course, taught that they were *the last* Next Level shepherds to visit this current earthly garden, which is becoming increasingly corrupt. As in many fundamentalist millenarian theologies, it was taught that humans are living in the last of the last days. *Now is the time to repent, for the end is nigh.* Hence, while a form of reincarnation was taught by Heaven's Gate, it was capped by a strong form of millenarianism. Reincarnation stops with this generation. After the elect have had a chance to respond to the gospel of the Next Level, judgment will come swiftly. Highly evolved extraterrestrials will "spade-under the garden." They will destroy the Earth and return it again to its Edenic state.

That said, it should be noted that, because the afterlife is extraterrestrial, not terrestrial, the planet does not become a paradise for the saved (as in, for example, Jehovah's Witness and Mormon eschatology), but rather, in a way closer to the Hindu doctrine of yugas (but on a greatly reduced cosmic scale),[18] it is recycled. After a period of time, Next Level creators revisit the Earth, prepare "the garden," "replant" more beings, and thereby restart the evolutionary, metamorphic process—the aim of which is to create more "graduates"[19] for the Next Level.

However, whereas there are obvious parallels with New Age thought and Hinduism, it is important to understand that, actually, the traditional doctrine of reincarnation is largely rejected. Following Christian teaching, Heaven's Gate argued that a new "spirit is born each time a vehicle (body) is born. . . . Therefore reincarnation at birth, in the sense that many religions believe, is a completely inaccurate concept."[20] Moreover, the spirits of those without "deposits," at the death of the body, simply enter the spirit world as "discarnates." That said, as noted above, a form of reincarnation does apply to those beings with "deposits" who are undergoing an evolutionary metamorphic process. However, this is not cyclical reincarnation, embedded within a Hindu moral framework. Rather, as Wouter Hanegraaff has noted of the teaching of the cofounder of the Theosophical Society, Helena Blavatsky:

> . . . progressive spiritual evolutionism was far more central than the belief in reincarnation *per se*. She certainly did not adopt evolutionism in order to explain the reincarnation process for a modern western audience; what she did was assimilate the theory of *karma* within an already-existing western framework of spiritual progress. . . . It is not the case that she moved from an occidental to an oriental perspective and abandoned western beliefs in favour of oriental ones. Her fundamental belief system was an occultist version of romantic evolutionism from beginning to end. . . .[21]

The point is that it is this understanding of reincarnation as spiritual evolution over several lifetimes that informs Heaven's Gate's teaching about the elect.

The Ubiquity of Evil in the Last Days and the Need to Overcome It

Typical of millenarian eschatologies is a general pessimism concerning the current world. Moreover, this is often accompanied by an elaborate demonology. The reason for the latter, of course, is that it provides a way of explaining moral evil, persecution, suffering, frustrated religious expectations, perceived temptation, and the general unsatisfactoriness of life, without (at least initially) implicating God or, in this case, Next Level beings. For Heaven's Gate, the world, and particularly modern life in all its variety, was understood to be fundamentally corrupt and subject to an unrelenting deterioration of spirituality, morality, and the quality of life. This conviction is summed up in a despairing statement in Applewhite's "Final Exit" video: "We do in all honesty *hate* this world."[22]

This pessimism was amplified as their demonology evolved during the 1990s. Heaven's Gate became increasingly convinced that demonic "space aliens" or "Luciferians" were committed to reducing the number of those who would finally ascend to the Next Level. (In this way, of course, they were able to account for the small numbers sufficiently interested in their Next Level gospel to join Heaven's Gate.) Luciferians were believed once to have been superior, "angelic" beings who were "training for service to the Next Level, but through weakness, aborted their opportunity to further their Next Level knowledge (*mind*). . . . The agenda of these impostors is to distract and tempt those with deposits into their camp."[23] Again, the concepts and themes of Christian theology are conspicuous. "Luciferians" are fallen "technological angels"[24] seeking to tempt the elect away from the truth, particularly in these last days.[25] Such demonic space aliens are able to locate those with deposits and to prevent them from graduating to the Next Level.[26] Indeed, as is often the case, demonology and millenarian pessimism developed together, the one feeding the other. As the demonology and pessimism escalated, the group became increasingly apocalyptic, which, in turn, fed their paranoia about sinister forces that control everything from world governments to shopping transactions.

> We feel the current world economic systems are against all the guidelines given to humans by the Next Level at the beginning of and throughout this civilization. Although currency systems were not given to humans by the Next Level, we prefer to pay cash to using credit cards or purchase plans. . . . Banks are definitely tools of the "Luciferian" forces . . . and we would prefer not to make any banking transactions . . . [because] there are very real space-alien forces in opposition to us who can use such things as bank accounts and mailing addresses against us.[27]

A further manifestation of demonological activity was, they claimed, an increase in global violence. Reflecting Jesus' teaching in Mark 13:7-8, it was argued that "terrorists and militia groups are a phenomenon of these end times."[28] "Since this is the close of the Age," says Applewhite, there is "the spading-under of the plants. . . . 'Weeds' are now getting rid of weeds—from gang wars to nations involved in ethnic cleansing. This is simply a part of the natural recycling process, which precedes a restoration period of the planet in preparation for another civilization's beginning."[29]

It is important, however, to note that, as with the emphasis on Armageddon in premillennialism, so "the spading-under of the garden" was important for Heaven's Gate, in that it represented the final declaration of the supremacy of the Next Level. In other words, it functioned as a theodicy. Regardless of human corruption and the ubiquity of the demonic "principalities and powers," the final victory of good over evil is assured. Again, as in Christian theology, the demonic forces know that their time is limited and that they will finally be defeated by Next Level beings: "They are for the most part aware that with the cyclical spading-under of the garden, which is imminent as this is the end of the age, their ranks are scheduled to be recycled as well."[30] The Next Level will soon break into the existing world order, violently remove it, and replace it with a new world order.

Informed by this demonology, increasingly central to Heaven's Gate's thinking was a rigorously exclusivist theology of religions. Generally speaking, this would be a little unusual for a UFO religion, in that, drawing on the New Age and Theosophical subculture, such spiritualities tend to be eclectic and, therefore, selectively tolerant of the beliefs of others—even if they then go on radically to reinterpret those beliefs in terms of extraterrestrial contact. However, in the case of Heaven's Gate, their teaching evolved in a more typically Reformed Christian fundamentalist direction. While there is some acknowledgment that, originally, other faiths might once have contained "seeds of truth,"[31] planted there "by the Evolutionary Level Above Human," it was argued that "space aliens [had] twisted those truths so that souls might be blinded to the intended meaning."[32] Hence, not only were other religions understood to be spiritually misleading, but they were believed to be channels of demonic activity. Consequently, as in exclusivist theologies generally,[33] the relationship between Heaven's Gate and the religions of the world was understood to be one of *discontinuity*, not continuity. More specifically, as in fundamentalist thought, stark dualism led to rigid exclusivism. In these last days, salvation could be found only in a relationship with Applewhite, the chosen, messianic representative of the Next Level. To claim salvation by any other route could only be the result of demonic manipulation: "Space aliens have very successfully, through *their* religions, totally confused the humans' concept of 'God'. . . . The Next Level abhors religions, for they bind humans more thoroughly to the human kingdom using strong misinformation."[34]

Hence, to reiterate the point, radical theological dualism, premillennial pessimism, a developed demonology, and a rigid exclusivist theology of religions locate Heaven's Gate, ideologically, much closer to Christian fundamentalism than to some other UFO religions (such as the Raëlians, Unarius, and the Aetherius Society) or to the New Age subculture in which it originally emerged and from which it attracted its first members. Moreover, in a similar way to pre–late-1970s Protestant fundamentalism, which was dominated by premillennialist eschatology,[35] Heaven's Gate was politically quietist. They passively observed the decline of the world and the increased influence of the Luciferians. They spoke of its imminent destruction, and they awaited their technological rapture. They demonstrated no interest in political engagement or social improvement.

It is nevertheless important to understand that, for Heaven's Gate, the very fact of existence in this "garden" is necessary to "the metamorphic process." Again, this is a point of theodicy. There is a reason for everything, even evil. Indeed, without wishing to inflate the sophistication of this theology, it does resemble John Hick's eschatological approach to the problem of evil, which—developing the recapitulation thesis of the second-century theologian Irenaeus—understands the world as a "vale of soul-making."[36] Humans are not created perfect; they are not produced in a finished state; they are at the beginning of a process of maturation. For Irenaeus, humans move from "the image of God," in which they were created, to "the likeness of God." Hick puts it well: "the movement from the image to the likeness is a transition from one level of existence, that of animal life (*bios*), to another and higher level, that of eternal life (*zoe*), which includes but transcends the first."[37] Although the Heaven's Gate thesis is distinct in several respects, the end product is notably similar. "The Next Level created planet Earth, and it has been designed as a training ground for souls wanting to reach [the] physical, higher Level Above Human."[38] Through a series of incarnations, the elect grow into Next Level beings suitable for eternal life in the Kingdom of Heaven. There is, to change Hick's words slightly, a transition from one level of existence, that of human life, to another and higher evolutionary level, that of the Next Level, which includes but transcends the first.

Consequently, from the outset, in common with ascetic streams of conservative Christian thought, much teaching was devoted to training individuals to "overcome" attachments to "the world" and, thereby, to grow spiritually. As the early name for the group suggests, their aim was to produce "total overcomers." Heaven's Gate quickly became, to use Roy Wallis's terminology, a world-rejecting new religious movement.[39] That is to say, it became characterized by epistemological authoritarianism, emphasizing the boundaries between the Next Level and humanity, between the Kingdom of Heaven and this world, and between the faithful and the wider society. The community of believers was understood to be the ark of salvation floating in a sea of profanity. Salvation, it was believed, was found only within the group: *extra ecclesiam nulla salus*.[40] Needless to say, this led to a strong emphasis on the maintenance of purity, self-denial, and uncritical obedience to the leadership. For example, reflecting Applewhite's personal struggles, emphasis was placed on overcoming relational and sexual urges. Hence, the socialization of members included both strong discouragement from contact with the "outside" world and disapproval of any relationships within the group that might detract from their transition to the Next Level: "Don't read newspapers or watch TV; don't call your parents; don't visit old friends; don't pick up hitchhikers. . . . Quit using drugs; change your name; shave your beard; get rid of clothing and jewelry that symbolize your old self . . . no sex, no human-level friendships, no socializing on a human level."[41] As in the theology of the early Christian apologist Justin Martyr, for whom devils and demons were understood to be "swarming everywhere [obsessing] men's souls and bodies, infecting them with vice and corruption,"[42] so, for Heaven's Gate, it was taught that the world was infested with space aliens and forces against the Next Level. No one could be trusted, no relationship was incorruptible, no thoughts could be left unguarded, no bodily appetite was without its dangers. Indeed, there emerged a Christian Gnostic-like belief that even the body was antagonistic to the true self. The body must be disciplined:

> It is time for humans to take control and realize their mind/spirit is the true driver of the body. If we allow the body to dictate our desires, it is much like the horse deciding the direction the rider is to go. When humans unconsciously think they are the body, it leads to a false perception that equates happiness with the satisfaction of the body's sensory desires, instead of knowing that the mind/spirit can find pleasure in service to a higher level of existence. . . . So, if someone identifies with mind/spirit, he can discipline the body to whatever degree he chooses—separating his relationship with the body in order to have better control over it.[43]

Suicidal Rapture—Removing Clothes and Ascending to the Next Level

Early in the group's history, following the successful meeting with Klug's students on September 14, 1975, Applewhite and Nettles held a meeting in Waldport, which attracted around two hundred people. The purpose of the meeting was to explain how individuals could gain eternal life in the "Level Above Human." As we have seen, the Kingdom of Heaven, the Next Level, "is not an etheric or spiritual place, but a many-membered physical Kingdom that exists in deep space."[44] It was argued that, just as Jesus had ascended bodily to, they claimed, a waiting UFO, so likewise would all the faithful be transported. It should be noted carefully, however, that this emphasis in the 1970s and early 1980s on physical ascension from the Earth's surface to a waiting spacecraft ceased shortly after Nettles's death in 1985.[45] Quite simply, her death had placed a large question mark against some of the group's principal teachings, thus becoming the catalyst for a major eschatological development. If she was indeed a Next Level being, why had she died prior to the completion of her mission? More to the point, why had she not ascended in a living, physical body in accordance with their core teachings? In other words, what of "the Demonstration," which, according to their interpretation of Revelation 11:12, would see *both* "witnesses" physically ascend to the Next Level in a UFO? Bearing in mind that the group had been watching the skies for UFOs since 1975, expecting physical transportation to the Kingdom of Heaven, Nettles's death came as a severe blow.

No longer able to teach physical ascension, the necessary revisions required to make sense of her death eventually led to the incorporation of suicide into their eschatology.[46] Basically, Applewhite developed what might be described as Heaven's Gate's "spacesuit" anthropology. His highly dualistic understanding of the body and the self became central to his later teaching. Indeed, one is reminded of H. H. Farmer's criticism of the term "incarnation," which etymologically suggests "the underlying dualism of Greek thought, with its readiness to think of the Incarnation as the ingress of a divine principle into a mortal envelope of flesh essentially alien to it."[47] That said, while it seems clear that Applewhite was influenced by his knowledge of incarnational Christology, a cruder development of a similar idea had been popular in theosophical circles for some time. Functioning as a form of occult adoptionism, it argued that Jesus and the Christ were separable. The Christ, a highly evolved spiritual entity, entered the body of Jesus—for example, at his baptism in the Jordan. This type of thinking is further developed in Ruth Montgomery's "walk-in" theory, which had become popular in the occult subculture. Operating with a similarly strong body-spirit dualism, "walk-in" theory claims that, to quote Montgomery, "a high-minded soul in the spirit realm can exchange places with another soul who wishes to depart the physical plane, by entering as a walk-in."[48] The point is that, understanding the body similarly—as "a suit of clothes" or "a vehicle"—Applewhite can, as we have seen, simply argue that he is a Next Level being inhabiting a human body.[49] (Indeed, we shall see that he understood himself to be, in effect, "the Christ" in the body of Applewhite.) Hence, in accordance with his evolving theological anthropology, he claimed that the envelope of flesh can be removed without any harm being done to the individual person, who can then incarnate another envelope of flesh. In other words, ascension to a UFO could happen "spiritually" and invisibly—one need not be *bodily* transported. Hence, the revised teaching is a little more sophisticated and is able to account for Nettles's death by arguing that she had *both* ascended *and* left her body behind—as one might leave one's clothes behind.

Applewhite, who was personally devastated by the loss, began referring to her as the more senior of the two, "the Older Member."[50] In attempting to make sense of her departure, he argued that she had gone ahead in advance, leaving him on Earth to bring the mission to a close. This conviction was confirmed when, on July 23, 1995, two American astronomers, Alan Hale and Thomas Bopp, discovered an approaching comet, which they expected would pass the Earth sometime in the late winter of 1997. More significantly, it was not long before a rumor began circulating within the occult subculture that NASA was covering up information about the Hale-Bopp comet. Speculation escalated in late 1996 when photographs appeared on the Internet showing a large object accompanying the comet.[51] For his part, Applewhite became convinced of the portentous significance of Hale-Bopp. This was a sign from Nettles, who was trailing the comet in a spacecraft, that the end was close and that he and his followers were about to experience technological rapture. However, now claiming that any rapture would *not* be physical, he argued that, following Nettles's example, their earthly "containers," their mortal envelopes of flesh, their human clothes, would have to be left behind.

Inevitably, suicide became an integral part of Heaven's Gate eschatology, being interpreted as release from a corrupt and evil planet, prior to its apocalyptic destruction. Transport to Heaven was little more than a change of clothes, and suicide was the gate through which the faithful must pass. With obvious reference to Jesus' words (Matt. 16:25),[52] the group issued the following statement shortly after the reported discovery of Hale-Bopp: "If you have grown to hate your life in this world and would lose it for the sake of the Next Level, you will find true life with us. . . . If you cling to this life, will you not lose it?"[53] In line with this reasoning, the term "suicide" is rejected as a description of what they were planning. True suicide was interpreted instead as commitment to this world "of the walking dead,"[54] which is about to be "spaded under." In a carefully phrased article entitled "Our Position Against Suicide," they redefine it as follows: "the true meaning of 'suicide' is *to turn against the Next Level when it is being offered*."[55] True life, on the other hand, is found in Heaven. Death is this side of the apocalypse, life is the other side; to commit suicide is to do nothing, to choose life is to progress to the Next Level. Hence, interpreted Gnostically, the body that binds the self to this human level must be removed. Again, this is not death, because the self does not die—it simply exchanges containers. As one member put it, "I have been given this rare and golden opportunity to leave this world and return to life, to become a newborn in the Evolutionary Level Above Human."[56] In becoming a Next Level heavenly being, "the final act of metamorphosis or separation from the human kingdom is the 'disconnect' or separation from the human physical container or body in order to be released from the human environment and enter the . . . environment of the Next Level. . . . We will rendezvous in the 'clouds' (a giant mothership) for our briefing and journey to the Kingdom of the Literal Heavens."[57]

If this is the end of planet Earth for the time being, and if this is the appointed time to pass through heaven's gate, what happens to the faithful of previous generations? We are told the following: "At the end of the Age or civilization (where we are now), it seems that all souls that were deposited . . . are brought back."[58] That is to say, those of previous generations who have been perfected are not translated to the Next Level immediately, but are rather, says Applewhite, "put on ice" until the last days.[59] The reincarnated faithful "who have the deposit of *life*" now await the arrival of the "Older Member" (Nettles) in a UFO to rapture them—"they will be protected and 'saved' from the approaching recycling and 'spading under' of the civilization. They will have nothing to fear, nor will they know *DEATH*—even if they lose their human body."[60] Hence it was believed that, as in Christian pretribulationist rapture theology, the dead await the second coming of their savior prior to the apocalypse—Nettles in a spacecraft trailing the Hale-Bopp comet. Just as faithful Christians are caught up to meet Christ in the air (cf. 1 Thess. 4:17), so, on Nettles's arrival, will the spirits of the faithful of previous generations be transported along with those few faithful members of Heaven's Gate who willingly shed their containers of flesh.

The Second Coming (in More Ways Than One)

While much of the above mirrors premillennial theologies of the second coming, Heaven's Gate's doctrine needs to be understood a little more broadly. For the members of Heaven's Gate, Applewhite and Nettles were not only understood to be space messiahs, but they came close to being deified. For example, one devotee, recalling an initial encounter with Ti and Do, uses words similar to those ascribed to Thomas in John 20:28:

> I remember the moment clear as a bell. We were at a campground . . . in Colorado, and Ti and Do were . . . meeting individually with the new prospective students who came out of the Waldport meeting. As I approached them, Ti asked, "How can we help you?" This vehicle was speechless at first, and I remember so clearly that the impulse I had was to drop on my knees and cover my eyes. The only way I can describe it is . . . it felt like I was standing before my Lord and my God.[61]

It is little surprise then that the identification with Jesus came easily both to the devotees and also to the objects of devotion. More specifically, the emergence of Ti and Do was understood to be none other than the second advent. As one member exclaimed: "Now, all this talk of the Second Coming? Guess what? It's really here! We are at the End of the Age."[62] Applewhite encouraged this identification with Christ. More than that, following Nettles's death, he began to refer to her as, not merely "the Older Member," but as "the Father":

> Remember, the One who incarnated in Jesus was sent for one purpose only, to say, "If you want to go to Heaven, I can take you through that gate—it requires everything of you." Our mission is exactly the same. I am in the same position to today's society as was the One that was in Jesus then. My being here now is actually a continuation of that last task as was promised to those who were students 2000 years ago. They are here again continuing in their own overcoming, while offering the same transition to others. Our only purpose is to offer the discipline and "grafting" required of this transition into membership in My Father's House. My Father, my Older Member, came with me this time for the first half of this task because of its present difficulty.[63]

This, of course, is why Heaven's Gate was so antagonistic to mainstream Christian teaching. Christians look back to a particular human vehicle rather than focusing on the Next Level being who had discarded that vehicle. Deceived by corrupt doctrine, they failed to recognize the eschatological significance of Applewhite; they failed to acknowledge the *parousia*, the *apokalypsis*, the *epiphaneia*; they failed to see the visible, bodily *adventum* of the one who was in Christ. Hence, in rejecting the teaching of Heaven's Gate, Christians were rejecting the teaching of the returned redeemer who they professed to worship. More than that, however, not only had they rejected the one who was in Christ, they had rejected the Father also. For, it was argued, whereas two thousand years ago the Father had remained distant in the Next Level, communicating his will to the being who was in Jesus, this time both beings were present on Earth.[64] Hence, standing on the very edge of the Apocalypse, the Christian churches were turning people away from salvation and, as prophesied in Revelation, mocking and persecuting the "two witnesses." "If you really knew the Bible," declared one member, "you would recognize Ti and Do for who they are."[65]

However, not only did Applewhite believe himself to be the return of the one who was in Jesus, but he also believed that those who had followed Jesus had returned in those who were following him. One member explains this as follows: "Before His departure, [Jesus] knew that His disciples hadn't overcome the world sufficiently to go with Him, so He told them that he would come back for them again at the end of the Age. That time is now. It is the end of the Age. The same mind, the same knowledge of the Next Level that was present 2000 years ago *is here again*, as was promised. . . . And many of those students/disciples who were present with the

Representative 2000 years ago are back now, with Ti and Do, to pick up where they left off during their last mission to this civilization."[66]

As is not uncommon in sects and new religions, particularly those that are world-rejecting, Applewhite and Nettles became shamanlike, in the sense that they were understood to be a connecting point between heaven and Earth. In a sense, they were, as Ted Peters has argued (using Mircea Eliade's term), an *axis mundi*.[67] However, more than this, we can see that Heaven's Gate as a community of the faithful is significant in itself, in that the *parousia* doctrine is extended to the community. There is a direct continuity with the *axis mundi* of Christendom, with the Father, with Jesus Christ, and with the original followers of Christ, the *kyriake* (those "belonging to the Lord"). To a large extent, the members of Heaven's Gate understood themselves to be the literal reincarnation of Christ and his followers in the very last days prior to the Apocalypse. This small group was in effect the holy and faithful bride of Christ, set apart for salvation with him at the end of the world. Consequently, members must have felt enormously significant and privileged. Not only was this belief increased by Applewhite's millenarian teaching, but it clearly led to an enormous desire to understand and to be faithful. Everything would be required of them by their messiah, and they would be happy to give it. This is evident in the following prayer to Applewhite and Nettles:

> I ask for your inner strength so that I may completely withdraw this vehicle from all the inner addictions of its animal flesh, and for your keenness so that I can block all thoughts or mental pictures of mammalian behavior, and for your consistency in maintaining non-mammalian behavior of the Evolutionary Level Above Human—around the clock—in order that my soul (mind) will be compatible with and able to occupy a genderless vehicle from the Next Kingdom Level.[68]

Staring into the face of the coming apocalypse, those who were once in Jesus and his disciples were prepared for deliverance, for the reappearance of the Father in a celestial cloud: ". . . the time has come for this Next Level classroom to close, and for us to make the transition from this world to Our Father's World. . . . Because I find no knowledge, and therefore no truth here on Earth, I have made *my choice* to "lay down my life in *this world*" and go with my Father, Do, and His Father, Ti, to *Our World*, the only *true* Kingdom of God."[69]

The Final State

Typical of millennialism, what was referred to as "*Our World*, the only *true* Kingdom of God," the Next Level was understood in utopian terms as an ideal physical, intellectual, and spiritual existence—"exactly the opposite of this human world."[70] It is "everlasting and non-corruptible."[71] It is "a genderless, crew-minded, service-oriented world that finds greed, lust, and self-serving pursuits abhorrent."[72] (For Applewhite, of course, genderless existence meant not being troubled by the complexities of sexuality.[73])

As to what happens to those who do not respond to the gospel of Heaven's Gate, we are told that they "align themselves with the opposition [and thus] will be 'recycled' when the Next Level terminates this temporal, impermanent existence, which we expect will happen soon after our departure."[74] However, this does not necessarily mean that individuals will die. Their bodies certainly will, but, as we have seen, bodily death is not understood to indicate the extinction of the self. "Spirits" (which are distinct from Next Level "souls") will "continue to live in the spirit world."[75] The spirit world is effectively hell: "when flesh dies . . . [the spirit] enters the spirit world surrounding us. This is hell because these identities still have all the likes, dislikes, wants, and desires they did while in the flesh, only now they don't have the hardware [that is, bodies] to experience them."[76] That said, their existence and suffering is not eternal. We are told that "at a time and under the conditions of their own choosing," the Next Level will "literally exterminate" spirits.[77] Again, at the initial recruiting meeting to which "the Two" were invited by Klug, Applewhite used the following rather dramatic evangelistic device: "If you *do not* choose to undertake this final step, then your soul, upon death in this lifetime, will dissolve into the ethers and you will *never* incarnate again."[78] Hence, as in Jehovah's Witness eschatology, annihilation would seem to be the final destiny of the rebellious.

Conclusion

Most millenarian groups throughout history have been sectarian offshoots of major religious traditions, Christianity being particularly significant as a theological provider.[79] Michael Barkun, however, has argued that while this is true, it is increasingly difficult to classify groups in this way, in that "fewer millenarian movements arise wholly within single coherent religious traditions."[80] Heaven's Gate is a good example of both statements. On the one hand, it is an eclectic group carrying theosophical baggage, similar to other groups that have emerged out of the New Age subculture. As such, it is not, strictly speaking, a Christian sect. On the other hand, as has been made clear here, the tradition is heavily derivative of Christian theology in several important respects. In particular, while drawing from the occult-New Age subculture, the eschatology of Heaven's Gate is fundamentally shaped by Christian pretribulationist premillennialism. Although one should not underestimate the significance of Theosophy and, to a lesser degree, science fiction on the thinking of Applewhite and Nettles, it was the confluence of these ideas with those drawn from Christianity that set Heaven's Gate apart from other UFO religions and gave it its millenarian character. Their particular Luciferian demonology; the resulting paranoia concerning demonic conspiracy; their rigorous self/body, sacred/profane, Next Level/this world, extraterrestrial/terrestrial dualisms; their belief in their elect status; their particular understanding of the *parousia* and its relationship to Christ and the disciples; their consequent exclusivism regarding Heaven's Gate as the sole ark of salvation, the only recipient of true revelation; their concern regarding escalating wickedness in the world; their consequent emphasis on the coming apocalypse; the biblical passages copiously referenced; and the way the Bible is read all mirror or have roots in fundamentalist Christian premillennialism. Hence, while it is popular and understandable to claim, as, for example, Robert Bartholomew and George Howard have, that the best route to understanding the Heaven's Gate tragedy is through a broad grasp of the social history of UFO belief per se,[81] I would disagree. Indeed, we have seen that Heaven's Gate was not a typical UFO religion. A far better approach would be through an understanding of Christian theology, particularly eschatology, and a grasp of the nature and dynamics of fundamentalist and apocalyptic thought. Indeed, while Bartholomew and Howard do provide an excellent social history of UFO belief and some insights into the nature of such belief (particularly their analysis of the fantasy-prone personality[82]), their help in understanding Heaven's Gate is minimal.

Furthermore, it is difficult to avoid the conclusion that, while Heaven's Gate is a UFO religion shaped by the occult subculture, its rationalization of suicide was assisted by the development of a rigorously dualistic anthropology, informed by a conservative Christian theology and hermeneutic. Although there has been much debate within Christian theological anthropology over the body/soul question, generally speaking, the emphasis, certainly at a popular level, has been dualistic. The doctrine affirmed by much of the Christian church since its beginning is that there exists a soul which can survive and function apart from the human body. Humans are constructed in such a way that, at death, the conscious, personal self continues to exist while the organism disintegrates.[83] It is precisely this personal eschatology, this strong belief in the survival of the soul after bodily death, that was developed within Heaven's Gate. While it was possibly shaped by popular adoptionist ideas within the occult-theosophical community, such as Montgomery's "walk-in" thesis, the evidence suggests that Christian anthropological dualism was the central paradigm.[84] Indeed, although some have argued that "walk-in" theory informed Heaven's Gate's anthropology and that they spoke of themselves as "walk-ins,"[85] I have found no reference either to "walk-ins" or to Montgomery in their writings. Heaven's Gate's dualism is never described using "walk-in" terminology. Christian anthropological terms, however, pervade their literature. As one member's exit statement puts it, "the soul is separate from the body, and when the body dies the spirit continues on."[86] Another student's "exit statement" makes a similar point: "We do not identify ourselves as the body, as almost all humans mistakenly do, but rather as the *soul* that occupies the body it is temporarily using as a 'vehicle' or 'suit of clothes.'"[87] Again, it is difficult to avoid the conclusion that such ideas are indebted to popular Christian dualism, particularly as explicit discussions of dualism include copious references to the Bible—especially passages such as Matthew 10:28: "Do not be afraid of those who kill the body but cannot kill the soul."[88]

The point is that this strict dualism was developed along with other dualisms common in premillennialism—particularly that of the corruption of *this world* and the utopian nature of *the next*—the effect of which was, following the death of Nettles, the theological rationalization for suicide.

Chapter Four

Millennialism in Contemporary Israeli Politics

Brenda E. Brasher

For the state of Israel, millennialism has been considerably more than a marginal religious concept of earthly transformation. In 1891 a Protestant millennialist wrote the first petition to the government of the United States to support the establishment of a Jewish homeland in ancient Palestine.[1] Starting in 1897, a secular Jewish millennialism, Zionism, focused Jewish energies on the goal of establishing a Jewish state—a goal which 52 years later informed the worldview of Israel's founders.[2] Millennial ideas had been significant in key events in the history of the region, such as the Bar Kokhba Jewish revolt in the second century C.E. and the medieval Christian Crusades. Consequently, they inform a notable part of the background to Israeli history. This unique millennial history ensured that millennial ideas and millennially inspired actors were familiar elements in the warp and woof of Israeli sociopolitical life. The strong association between Israel and millennialism made it practically inevitable that transcendent symbols would become associated with political struggles over the normative identity of Israel as a modern sovereign state.

Whether and how the ideas that flow within a given society attain influence has been a core debate in the history of sociology. When attempting to explain the change from traditional to rational action in modern West-ern societies, Max Weber suggested that a Protestant ethic, which encour-aged individuals to apply themselves rationally to work, was a contributing factor to the early spread of capitalism in the West. Though his conclusion has been heavily criticized, his overarching goal—to understand the connec-tion between ideas as frameworks for meaning and action, and their effect, if any, upon the societies that adopt them—continues to be a factor in some contemporary macro-sociological research.

Israel and millennialism present an interesting contemporary case study in which to revisit the possibility that a religious ideal can have social con-sequences. Yet there are some key differences from the above scenario. Weber theorized that a rather homogenous set of Protestant beliefs adopted by Europeans influenced European society toward social change. In Israel, no such homogeneity exists with regard to millennial belief. Instead, myr-iad millennial visions are at play whose differences contribute to social frag-mentation rather than to social change. Further, where Weber concluded that it was the *unintended* consequences of Europeans adopting a Protestant ethic that proved significant, in contemporary Israel it is groups striving to achieve what they understand to be the *intended* consequences of their beliefs that keeps local and regional politics on the boil. In particular, com-peting and contradictory religious millennialisms impose transcendent challenges upon Middle Eastern conflict resolution that the language and protocols of a largely secular international diplomatic heritage find difficult to address. They also infuse local political deliberations with an absolutist dualistic rhetoric, which necessitates that those who wish to lead Israeli society be able to engage in apocalyptic politics.

Varieties of Jewish Millennialism

Although numerous varieties of millennialism percolate through Israeli soci-ety, most belong to one of five contending millennial visions: secular Jewish millennialism, practical Zionism, messianic religious Zionism, Jewish mes-sianism, and Christian millennialism.[3] Each is grounded in what its follow-ers consider to be a set of sacred texts—mainly biblical writings, although in some cases heavily supplemented by the writings of key founders. Four of the five competing millennialisms revere the same set of texts but interpret them differently. The odd one out is Christian millennialism: yet it too includes in its canon the biblically based millennial texts that Jewish millen-nialists acknowledge. Despite this, each offers a distinct horizon of meaning and value for land and for peoplehood. The differing and conflicting values that each of these visions associates with land, and whether and what bound-aries each sets out for its millennial vision, are factors in how far concessions over land are cognitively viable for the various groups that adopt them.

Zionism as Secular Jewish Millennialism

> On that day, God made a covenant with Abram, saying: "To your descendants have I given this land, from the river of Egypt to the great river, the Euphrates River." (Gen. 15:18)

The history of the founding of the state of Israel is a story of millennial struggle. Throughout the history of the Jewish people, small numbers of Jews have sought to live in the historic Jewish homeland of Palestine, but, in general, Jews were a thoroughly diasporic people. "The hoped for return to Palestine," Moses Mendelssohn wrote in 1770, "for synagogue and prayer . . . has no influence on our conduct as citizens."[4] Bowing to the Talmudic warning that there should be "no forcing of the End," Jews prayed each Passover on Seder night to be "next year in Jerusalem," without making any concrete plans to go there.

This attitude began to change in the nineteenth century. It started at first as the initiative of a small number of secular Eastern European Jews who abandoned the convention of messianic patience to champion the creation of a Jewish homeland in regular (rather than millennial) time. Practical concerns as well as intellectual ones were implicated in its origins. Rising nationalism had given birth to repeated waves of pogroms and expulsions, generating a need for Jewish organizations to provide a home for an increasing number of uprooted Jews. Thus, it was in response to a pragmatic necessity as well as to an intellectual development of the *haskala* (Jewish Enlightenment) that a handful of Jewish leaders rewove the millennial artifacts of Jewish tradition into a secular millennial vision of this-worldly redemption for the Jewish people via the establishment of a Jewish state, legally owned by Jews and recognized by other nations as a legitimate nation of Jews. Drawing upon the vocabulary of nationalism that was at the time changing the political organization of much of the Western world, Jewish leaders including Nathan Birnbaum and Theodor Herzl began interpreting the biblical promises of land to the patriarchs and Moses, and the biblical covenant of land between God and Israel, as a collective, worldly imperative. Thus, it was not by accident but rather a development in keeping with its time that during a period of ascendant nationalism, a group of almost exclusively secular Jewish intellectuals began advocating the creation of a Jewish state.

The term that quickly became most closely associated with the movement was "Zionism," an expansion of the biblical Hebrew for Jerusalem, "Zion." Though the term "Zionism" was coined by Birnbaum in 1890, it was Herzl who (along with Birnbaum) convened the First Zionist Congress in Basel, Switzerland, in 1897; it was also Herzl who in the end became credited with founding the Zionist movement. In a poignant summary of the historic Jewish situation, Herzl wrote: "We have sincerely tried every-where to merge with the national communities in which we live, seeking only to preserve the faith of our fathers. It is not permitted us." Assimilation being impossible, Jews should have their own homeland where they could become "normal"; where Jews could be free. The Zionist millennial vision was born. Yet, while Herzl wanted religion to have a place in this state, he did not want religious leaders to be in charge of it. Israel was not to be a theocracy, but a modern civil state.[5]

For Herzl, Zionism was a peaceful solution to the moral and political dilemmas faced by the nation-states with a minority Jewish population. Though a little religious support for Zionism existed, "the majority of Orthodox leaders condemned Zionism from its very outset," particularly the rabbis of Eastern Europe.[6] Their concerns were twofold: they feared that Zionists were overidealistic and were misleading the Jewish people about what was possible; they were also concerned that the Zionist millennial vision was an attempt to preempt the Messiah. These concerns fed into the decision by rabbinical leaders to reject the 1917 Balfour Declaration. Only the Messiah could call Jews to live in Israel. When Israel was founded in 1948, it organized itself along Zionist principles as a Jewish state with an almost exclusively secular leadership. Religious leaders were given province over both religion and personal status matters, and two parallel educational systems were guaranteed: state and state religious, but nothing else. Herzl's foundational principle that "the Jews are one people" guided the organization of Israel's institutions. Thus, early Israel took the shape of a socialist democratic state. Kibbutzim played a central role as did labor unions. The population was offered a strong social safety net. Israel as a modern state would be the answer to the Jewish millennial dream. It would be the "land of milk and honey" for modern Jews.

Practical Zionism

> There is only one radical means of sanctifying human lives. Not armored plating, or tanks, or planes, or concrete fortifications. The one radical solution is peace.[7]

The "vision of the new Middle East" promulgated by Shimon Peres in Israel between 1980 and 1990 had "at its heart a quasi-messianic peace, embodying an eschatological vision." This eschatological vision espoused by the new Middle East entailed that

> [t]he decisive end of the political dispute between Israel and the Arab peoples, after which the liberal, universal values of personal freedom and self-fulfillment will blossom into realization, in the context of a

flourishing economy for all. Peace, as the agent of this utopian era, becomes a supreme value, a sort of mythic entity.[8]

The peace and economic millennialism of practical Zionism was to be realized in concrete ways in Israeli life. Informal dialogue groups among Israelis and Palestinians flourished. Conferences dealing with issues such as the effect of the creation of Israel on women were held, at which the possibility that some shared histories existed was explored. Yadidya, a modern Orthodox synagogue located in an upscale Jerusalem suburb, organized a Tisha B'Av reading of Lamentations at Rabin's grave. In 1998, the first year it was held, attendance exceeded several hundred, even though participants had to twist through a small opening in a locked gate to get in. Rather than mourn the destruction of the Temple as was customary for the day, liberal orthodox Jews mourned the loss of a harbinger of peace who "sanctified peace with his blood."[9] From the construction of elaborate pathways along the Lake of Galilee to accommodate the 1999 papal Israeli visit, to the development of new tourist hotels in Nazareth and Bethlehem, practical Zionism changed the contours of some Israeli communities.

When the second intifada began in September 2000, one of the reasons that it struck so hard at Israeli daily life was the abrupt halt it brought to the realization of this particular millennial dream. Disillusionment became widespread. Those who had invested in hotels saw them sit empty. Almost all dialogue between Israeli and Palestinian peoples ceased. The contradictions between eschatological peace-making and political realities proved impossible for supporters of practical Zionism to absorb and overcome. The decision by the Israeli government to build a security fence or wall was an unpleasant and costly disruption of the practical Zionist peace and economic millennial dream.

Messianic Religious Zionism

> Moses began to explain . . . You have remained near this mountain too long. Turn around and head toward the Amorite highlands and all its neighboring territories in the Aravah, the hill country, the lowlands, the Negev, the seashore, the Canaanite territory and Lebanon, as far as the Euphrates River. See! I have placed the land before you. Come, occupy the land that God swore He would give to your fathers, Abraham, Isaac and Jacob, and to their descendants after them. (Deut. 1:5-8)

Decades before the founding of Israel, Rabbi Abraham Kook, then chief rabbi of Eretz Israel, wrote that "nothing in our faith, either in its larger principles or in its details, negates the idea that we can shake off the dust of exile by our own efforts through natural, historical processes."[10]

Kook's utopian vision was that Israel would return to Jerusalem. His hope for Jewish future was the recovery of a Jewish past. But it was his son, Rabbi Zvi Yehuda Kook, who forged much of the religious language that envisioned the establishment of the state of Israel "at the heart of the messianic process"[11] and whose vision was of "the State of Israel as the fulfillment of the biblical vision of redemption."[12] For Kook, the concrete actions of the Jewish state were hallowed, and Israel's battles were not merely for survival or over reclaiming ancestral lands but "portrayed in ethical and theological terms, as a mighty struggle to uproot evil and achieve universal rectification."[13] Kook claimed that "it is not we who are forcing the end but the End that is forcing us," and viewed this as justification for the religious acceptance of innovation in Jewish tradition. Kook went into mourning when the rest of Israel celebrated the UN partition decision in 1947, because it meant giving up significant parts of the land of Israel. Kook's ideas "became a beacon for the leadership of Gush Emunim and the movement of settlement of Jews in Judea and Samaria."[14]

The ten lost tribes were also an important component of the Jewish messianic vision. The Amishav movement, among others, worked to convert and bring to Israel peoples with vague Jewish connections who might be members of the ten lost tribes, such as the Jews of Mizzoram or, as some would contend, the Ethiopian Jews. A small faction of Jewish messianists focused on restoring the Temple. The Temple Mount Faithful and its affiliated organizations have as their goal the creation of the third temple in Jerusalem. Though few in numbers, the movement occupies a notable place in Israeli life, in part due to the fact that it enjoys significant Christian Zionist support. On the Jewish day commemorating destruction of the Jerusalem Temple, Tisha B'Av, each year, its leaders attempt to lay a cornerstone for the new temple on the Waqf-administered grounds popularly referred to by Jews as the Temple Mount. They are not the only messianic group focused on taking over the Temple Mount. Revava, too, has this as its goal, though unlike the Temple Mount Faithful, most of its members derive from the right-wing settler movement.

Traditional Jewish Messianism

> Rabbi Yohanan ben Zakkai taught: "If you happen to be standing with a sapling in your hand and someone says to you, 'Behold! The Messiah has arrived!' First plant the tree and then go out to welcome the Messiah." (Avot de Rabi Natan B 31)

Among the Haredi, neither secular Zionism nor messianic religious Zionism signified a credible millennial interpretation of Jewish thought. To the

Haredim, Israel was simply a state like any other state. As such it was "a religiously neutral entity" that embodied "neither a messianic awakening nor an antimessianic eruption."[15] It existed in history, not beyond it, and certainly not at the end of days. According to the traditional Jewish messianism the Haredi uphold, the Jewish people will remain in exile until the Messiah comes, where "exile" is a theological condition consisting of the absence of redemption.[16] Thus, to the Haredi, Jews who live in modern-day Israel are still in exile. The sole difference is that they are living in exile among Jews. The consequences of these beliefs for Israel, espoused by a growing and highly vocal portion of its population, have been immense. The Haredim do not pray for the welfare of the state. Few serve in the army. They have employed their expanding political power to obtain benefits for Haredi communities, carrying political weight well beyond their numbers because of their characteristic voting solidarity. The one exception to this is the Lubavitch-Habbad Hasidic movement. While not Zionist, followers of Habbad support the state. The movement does not discourage army enlistment and has actively supported the settler movement in rejection of the Labor Party's policy of "peace for land." Habbad played a decisive role in Israeli politics when it strongly supported Binyamin Netanyahu's campaign to become prime minister.

Neturei Karta is a fringe, extremist example of this millennial stance. A small messianic religious group, its members believe that, until the Messiah comes, Jews should not be setting up the state of Israel. They are overtly anti-Zionist, and support the Palestinians. For the most part, the members of Neturei Karta are descended from Hungarian Jews who settled in Jerusalem's Old City in the early nineteenth century. Late in that century, they participated in the creation of new neighborhoods outside the city walls to alleviate overcrowding in the Old City, and most are now concentrated in the neighborhood of Batei Ungarin and the larger Meah Shearim neighborhood. They have always opposed the political ideology of Zionism and resented the new arrivals prompted by Herzl's ideas when they began appearing in the Middle East at the end of the nineteenth century. Like the Haredi, Neturei Karta followers claim that the redemption of the Jewish people can only be brought about by the Messiah. Many in Neturei Karta chose simply to ignore the state of Israel when it was first formed; however, this became more difficult as Israel took shape. A fringe element took proactive steps to condemn Israel and strove to bring about its eventual dismantling until the coming of the Messiah. Chief among these was Rabbi Moshe Hirsch, Neturei Karta's foreign minister, who served in Yasser Arafat's cabinet as minister for Jewish affairs.

Christian Zionism

> I saw the Holy City, the new Jerusalem, coming down out of heaven
> from God, prepared as a bride adorned for her husband. (Rev. 21:2)

Since the time of Constantine, Christian tradition has cherished sites located in what is now modern-day Israel. Today, the country of Israel possesses a singular allure for millennially inclined Protestant Christians, especially for those affiliated with the conservative spectrum of American Christian evangelicalism. Their Christian Zionism, or overt Christian support for a Jewish homeland in present-day Israel, arose as an offshoot of nineteenth-century theological developments in Christian Protestantism. It began when biblical theologian Cyrus Scofield claimed that Christ could not return to earth until a number of events occurred—among them, that Jews must return to Palestine, gain control of Jerusalem, and rebuild their temple. Only then could the great final battle of Armageddon take place, signaling the beginning of the end. To avid, biblical literalist Christian Zionists, the creation of the state of Israel in 1948 was interpreted as concrete evidence that the millennial, end-of-time scenario in which they believed had begun. This was especially the case when included within the borders of the state of Israel were sites such as the plains of Megiddo, where they believed that the battle of Armageddon would take place. When, in 1967 at the conclusion of the Six-Day War, Israel also included "where the end of time begins,"[17] Christian Zionists were ecstatic.

Christian Zionists have a long history of the "holy land" settlements and activities. They have been deeply involved in social projects such as the resettlement of Ethiopian Jews from Africa to Israel. They maintain an active presence in daily Israeli life and sponsor organizations such as Bridges for Peace, founded in 1976, and the International Christian Embassy founded in Jerusalem in 1980, that regularly participate and contribute to civic events. Fundamentalist-inclined Christian Zionists have forged enduring relationships with numerous right-wing Israeli Zionist organizations. Convinced that a reestablished temple in Jerusalem is necessary to trigger Jesus' return, these latter have shown a particular penchant for establishing relationships with Israeli organizations associated with restoring the temple. This has contributed to the destabilization of relationships with Israeli and Palestinian Muslims over the final status of Jerusalem.

Within the American Christian subculture, Christian Zionists are the staunchest advocates of Israel. In U.S. politics, they have supported Israel more consistently than has any other Christian faction, either within or outside of the evangelical sphere.[18] They also contribute to American popular support for Israel. A 1998 *New York Times* poll exploring American-

Israeli relations found considerably more public support for Israel than
could readily be attributed to Jewish lobbyists. Nearly half described Israel
as a "special place," not simply another country. That year, Israel received
approximately $3 billion in economic and military assistance, more than
the United States extends to any other nation in the world. When those
polled were informed of this, well over half (58 percent) favored maintaining this high level of support.[19] The role Christian Zionists play in promoting pro-Israel sympathies within the United States has not gone unnoticed
in Israel. Christian Zionist leaders have been acknowledged and honored
for their support by Israeli prime ministers from Menachem Begin to
Binyamin Netanyahu.[20]

Outside the Millennial Paradigm

From the media coverage, Jewish settlements in Gaza and the West Bank
appear to be significant instances of millennial activity, but a closer look at
the historical trajectories and demographics of settlements fails to substantiate such an evaluation. The first settlements in Judea, Samaria, and the
Jordan Valley were initiated and set up by Labor, the political party in
power in the late 1960s and early 1970s. Their impetus stemmed both
from historical motives and from the need to secure the new, if temporary,
borders and to resettle sensitive areas such as Gush Etzion. The religious
settlers, Gush Emunim and the Land of Israel Movement, only became
prominent in the second and third waves of settlement.

The settlement movement today has two very different social sources.
One consists of religious or secular Zionist impulses. These neo-Zionist settlers are relatively few in number, and they occupy a small number of settlements that follow the eastern borders of biblical Israel. But the majority
of settlers have economic motives. Approximately 80 percent of settlers are
located in settlements close to the borders of the green line, where they can
obtain cheap housing close to the center of Israel. Though this is Israel's
suburbanization, when one moves to the suburbs one can readily end up
living on land whose status is unresolved. People who live in the major settlements such as Ariel, Maale Adumim, and Efrat have no messianic ideology; they are simply trying to live near major centers of work and
employment, on land they can afford. In peace negotiations, these settlements have not been a contentious issue.

The media made much of the spurt of settlements in Israel during the
1990s. Some of this wave of settlement activity reflected the influence of
millennially inspired Jews endeavoring to fulfill biblical passages, but pragmatic Zionists also played a part, trying to secure defensible territory.
Among Jews, the centrality, indivisibility, and significance of Jerusalem
were paramount ideologically and religiously. All Jews who prayed, prayed

toward Jerusalem and urged its rebuilding. Until 1996, settlement growth in the territories was stagnant, and the number of settlements stood at 145. In 1996, the Israeli government articulated a commitment not to establish any new settlements. Though this remains officially binding, since 1996 over 100 new "outposts" have been established on the West Bank. The majority are occupied. Around 60 percent were established since Ariel Sharon became prime minister in February 2001. The term "outpost" typically refers to a hilltop area with a number of structures, totally separated from any permanent settlement. Each outpost collects its own taxes and has its own secretariat and absorption committees.[21]

Outpost and settlement patterns reflect little connection to early Abrahamic texts. Instead, they appear to be aimed at expanding and consolidating historical Jewish areas. It is urbanization and defense strategies rather than millennialist ideologies that have provided the main motivating impetus for these controversial expansions. One important exception to this is Jewish settlement in and around Hebron, one of the oldest cities with continuous Jewish presence in the region. Except for a brief period when resident Arabs expelled Jews from Hebron in 1929, Jews have resided there since biblical times. The Land of Israel Movement, one of the staunchest supporters of Jewish presence in Hebron, explicitly argues that Israel must include the historical (read "biblical") land of Israel within its borders.

Conclusion

Generalizing about anything always entails the risk of imprecision. Millennialism is no exception. Religious ideas about ideal life on Earth represent a complex facet of a religious tradition. Thus, the depictions above represent large-scale clumping together of trends that contain much diversity within them.

In Israel, preparations for a Protestant Christian-style apocalyptic millennialism are less in evidence than efforts to actualize various millennial visions of terrestrial transformation. No visible preparations for a battle between Gog and Magog have begun. No bunkers have been built as yet on plains of Megiddo in preparation for the battle of Armageddon. No universal movement toward Sabbath observance is under way. But from where the country's borders should be set to who should be offered citizenship, from the rationale and value of participating in world fora to the style and content of public education, contending millennial visions pull Israeli society in incompatible directions.

By inspiring discernible patterns of social and political action and inaction among their advocates, these contending millennial visions have become a critical force in contemporary Israeli life. Christian Zionists long for the return of Jesus, and a time when everyone recognizes Jesus as Messiah. They hope for the day when "everyone becomes us." Religious Jewish Zionists dream of the day when the Messiah comes, and Jews gather together united as Israel. They wait for the time when everyone is reconciled to God, but consider Gentiles (non-Jews) a minor concern. Secular Jewish millennialists act rather than wait and value non-Jews as an important salvific concern. They understand them to be the means by which Jews finally can have normal lives: they are those by and through whom the Jewish people will finally manage to live in peace.

Christian millennialists are driven by a messianic vision of a future second coming and want to bring that about. Jewish millennialists are driven by a historical vision of a past Jewish kingdom (whether it existed or not), not necessarily to bring the Messiah. Emotionally, Jewish millennialism primarily is expressed as nostalgia while Christian millennialism takes the form of future hope. The Israeli people at times have benefited from and at other times have been unhappily caught between these divergent theological paradigms and their accompanying emotional palettes, between radically different "holy" visions of what their country is and could or should be.

Chapter Five

Millennialism, Ecumenism, and Fundamentalism

Andrew Pierce

One feature of the scholarly literature devoted to the study of fundamentalism and millennialism is its oscillation between, on the one hand, interest in manifestations of fundamentalism within mainstream religious traditions—for instance, Roman Catholic integralism between 1907 and the Second Vatican Council (1962-1965)—and, on the other, interest in peripheral groupings that rejoice in the obscurity of the elect—for instance, the remarkable array of post-Conciliar "traditionalist" groups that articulate allegedly pre-Conciliar ideology.[1] This feature of the literature should help to safeguard awareness of the semantic instability exhibited by the word "fundamentalism": the term is applied in most cases analogically, requiring transcontextual sensitivity to both similarities and differences in specific cases, together with great caution in venturing transcontextual generalizations—but venturing them nonetheless.

Sources and secondary literature regularly draw attention to a defining gulf between fundamentalism on the one hand, and its Other—usually presumed to be a cocktail of notoriously imprecise ingredients such as liberalism, Western cultural imperialism, or modernism. This chapter explores the extent to which modern fundamentalism may be understood as the Other

80 Millennialism, Ecumenism, and Fundamentalism

of Christian theology's rediscovery of the notion of *oikoumene* at the end of the nineteenth and start of the twentieth centuries. Although the focus here is on theology, it will be apparent that a clash between a religious imagination that is consciously ecumenical and dialogical on the one hand, and one that resists such an imagination, on the grounds that it dilutes and disfigures saving truth, on the other, carries consequences that reach further than the discipline of theology.

A concern with the unity of the Christian faith, together with a growing sense of scandal at ecclesial disunity, is evidenced by a wide range of contemporary literature. In order to lend greater focus to this discussion, this study considers the nine volumes of papers produced in preparation for the World Missionary Conference, held in Edinburgh in 1910, the same year as the first of *The Fundamentals* went to press.[2] Among the key ideas that made possible the emergence of both the modern ecumenical movement and modern fundamentalism, it is argued, was the characteristically liberal theological apologetical strategy of defining or distilling an "essence" of religion in general, together with a suspiciously complementary essence of Christianity in particular.

The starting point for the chapter is the conventional presentation of nineteenth-century theology in the West as an apologetically focused enterprise, so eager to commend itself to its surrounding culture that it lost its capacity to stand back and offer a critique of that culture and society. That is, of course, a stereotype of nineteenth-century theology. By way of challenging that presentation, this study considers the missionary movement of the nineteenth century, some of whose proponents had, by the end of the century, adopted the millennialist motto "the evangelization of the world in this generation."[3] This combination of missionary concern for the church (focused both at home and abroad) on the one hand, together with a decrease in methodological confessionalism (popularly attributed to the rise of historical-critical methods in theological study) on the other, is an important key to understanding the emergence of a popular ecumenical movement after 1910.

Disputing the Legacies of Liberalisms

Scholarly approaches to fundamentalist and millenarian thought originate, to a striking extent, from disciplines other than theology, such as sociology, psychology, or anthropology. (This is not to suggest that theology alone should tackle such matters—far from it—but greater academic adequacy requires theological input.) Theologians who have worked in the area—for example, James Barr—are exceptions to the rule.[4] This has a number of consequences. Contemporary critical theology, shaped by its dialogue with the social and natural sciences, appears to presume the theological insignificance of fundamentalist theologies on an a priori basis, and that is a considerable presumption. A second and equally significant consequence of theological absenteeism on this issue is the remarkably limited range of theological themes and subdisciplines brought into play by nontheological commentators. Doubtless eschatology, election, and revelation are important themes in many fundamentalist and millennialist self-understandings, but they are not the only theological themes present and in need of analysis in these movements.

What then of the theological background to the emergence of *oikoumene* and its Other? A mere decade separates key dates for both the modern ecumenical movement and modern fundamentalism. The World Missionary Conference took place in 1910, and following the publication of *The Fundamentals* between 1910 and 1915, the term "fundamentalist" was coined in 1920. This is an era open to considerable contestation in historical theology, and an era with live consequences in systematic theology. This section of the study, therefore, is concerned with conveying a sense of the polarized theological environment, within which *oikoumene* and its Other were formed, and challenging the popular schematizing of this period around the polarities of liberal apologetics and neo-orthodox confessionalism.

Cultural historians of the West—including historical theologians—often regard 1918 (or the trauma of 1914–1918 in its entirety) as marking an end to the nineteenth century. This places the decade from 1910 to 1920 on the cultural boundary between two centuries, and liminality requires that we proceed with caution. Even if we retain conventional chronology for a century's end and beginning, the question of when an epoch begins and ends is important: echoes of the nineteenth century—in theology, politics, church, and society—do not fade suddenly away after 1900. Nor indeed do they after 1918.

So how is the perduring influence of nineteenth-century theology to be evaluated? In a snappy synopsis of scientific development in the nineteenth century, Joseph Fitzer provides just four key words: "trains, Darwin, vaccination, and Freud."[5] Though by no means comprehensive, these names and developments give a flavor of some aspects of contemporary intellectual life in which the mobility of people and ideas, faith in technology, and reductionist approaches to morality and religion were options for an increasingly powerful middle class. Hence, it is sometimes argued that the nineteenth century either believed in "progress" or that it experienced an age of "progress." George Steiner has recently written:

> Roughly from the time of Waterloo to that of the massacres on the Western front in 1915–16, the European *bourgeoisie* experienced a privileged season, an armistice with history. Underwritten by the

exploitation of industrial labor at home and colonial rule abroad, Europeans knew a century of progress, of liberal dispensations, of reasonable hope.[6]

This was, in short, an age that should have had no need of traditional millennial hope; instead, "reasonable hope" could be invested in the betterment of society on an incremental basis. Rather than expressing a concern with being delivered from this present age, the Western *bourgeoisie* hoped for more of the same, only better.

How would Christianity seek to address such a culture? One apologetical strategy had been proposed by a Reformed theologian in 1799, responding to the Enlightenment critiques of revealed religion with a Romantic defense of the autonomy of "piety" as an irreducible field of human experience. Friedrich Schleiermacher's (1768–1834) *On Religion: Speeches to its Cultured Despisers* was directed to his contemporaries: post-Enlightenment Romantics whose cultured sensibilities excluded religion, a priori, from serious intellectual or existential engagement.[7] Schleiermacher challenged the assumption that religion was essentially either praxis or speculation and therefore to be dismissed as either a heteronomous morality or a now passé form of natural science. Religion, according to Schleiermacher, is neither: it is "the sensibility and taste for the infinite,"[8] "the intuition of the universe."[9] Religion, he insisted, is essentially a matter of feeling (*Gefühl*): "That is the level on which religion stands, especially that which is autonomous in it, its feelings."[10] This focus on feeling continued a turn toward locating epistemological authority in present experience, which had been a key feature of the inductive reasoning of the Enlightenment, and which had been given lasting theoretical shape in the critical philosophy of Immanuel Kant. According to the Schleiermacher of *On Religion*, without an apprehension of *Gefühl* in the present, the deposits of a historic faith were no more to be identified with religion than was a tomb to be identified with a deceased person.[11] Kant's coup de grâce to piety appeared to have been premature.

A noticeable feature of Schleiermacher's apologia is that it relies on a distinction between religion's essence on the one hand and its nonessential elements on the other. The error made by religion's "cultured despisers" was that they had confused the former with the latter and had thus failed to discern the true essence of religion. To correct this error, Schleiermacher insisted on a reinterpretation of religion made possible by a correct grasp of its essence. Reading through the five "speeches," it is apparent that Schleiermacher's strategy—both rhetorically and theologically—requires a clear demonstration of what religion is not (praxis, speculation) in order to show clearly what religion essentially is.

On Religion is a youthful work. Later editions qualified the pantheistic and immanentistic turns of phrase that characterize the first, but even in his later dogmatics, the experiential focus remains.[12] Schleiermacher retained this emphasis on feeling, which in his dogmatics he qualifies as the feeling of "utter dependence,"[13] as that which precedes and gains subsequent expression in doctrine, liturgy, art, and so forth. It is in the present tense, in experience, that Schleiermacher's apologia is grounded. For a religion like Christianity, however, in which appeals to the normativity of historical truth claims are ubiquitous, the turn to experience raises uncomfortable theological questions about the authority of the religious past. Of Schleiermacher's five speeches, the final—in which historic (albeit reinterpreted) Christianity emerges as superior to the other religions—is by far the weakest. The problem is primarily methodological: despite its concern with experience, *On Religion* generally moves deductively, and its surprisingly inductive switch to particularity in the last speech is not convincing.

This approach, which emphasized experience, but which found historical particularity more difficult to account for in theological terms, is often presented as paradigmatic of a tendency among some nineteenth-century theologians, known by the somewhat unsatisfactory label "liberal Protestants." (The term unhelpfully blurs a distinction between description and evaluation: "liberal Protestant" does not feature in the literature as an approving adjectival phrase.) Other theological options were available in the nineteenth century, often categorized—self-servingly—in contemporary literature into a polar opposition between rationalism and orthodoxy; but post-Schleiermacherian theological liberalism correlates neatly with Steiner's description of a middle-class armistice with history.

In his classic study of Christian social ethics, H. Richard Niebuhr constructed a typology of ways in which Christ has been related to contemporary culture.[14] According to Niebuhr, those who minimize—or try to eliminate—tensions between faith and culture belong to the type that he called the "Christ of Culture," and, for exemplars, Niebuhr offers Peter Abelard (1079–1142/3) and Albrecht Ritschl (1822–1889).[15] This is a curious and suggestive conjunction of thinkers: Ritschl was amongst the most eminent of nineteenth-century liberal theologians, and Abelard's theology of atonement—which stressed the centrality of divine love rather than human sin—attracted many nineteenth-century liberals for whom substitutionary models of atonement proved frankly unethical.

The weakness associated with this type, according to Niebuhr, is that it is insufficiently discriminating in its appeal to culture. The apologetically concerned theologian appeals to experience as it is mediated and interpreted in a given culture: yet what safeguards can be utilized in order to safeguard against either sacralizing culture, or else adjusting the claims of faith so as to secure a more impressive cultural "fit?" The accusation that it pursued cultural relevance at the expense of theological identity haunts nineteenth-century liberal Protestant theology—it too easily became a theology of the status quo: Ritschl, for instance, never seems to have wavered in his support for Bismarck. Liberal Protestant theology's ethical and eschatological failure of theological imagination is perhaps best exemplified in the actions of Adolf von Harnack, the theologian who drafted Kaiser Wilhelm's appeal of August 1914, "To the German People," which was subsequently toned down by the Kaiser.[16] Once present cultural experience becomes explicitly and primarily authoritative in theology, on what basis, and by whom, is that cultural experience itself to be critiqued?

If Schleiermacher's *On Religion* marks the mythical origin for theological liberalism, then the Swiss Reformed theologian Karl Barth is often presented as the embodiment of its no less mythical end. Born in 1886, Barth was educated by some of the leading liberal Protestant scholars of the day, but the actions of intellectuals in supporting militarism, and in particular the churches' uncritical support for war in 1914, led Barth to reconsider the kind of theology that had been at the center of bourgeois society for almost a century. For Barth, the theology of the nineteenth century was approached as a pilgrimage *ad fontes* to see where the rot had set in. The answer, he decided, was Schleiermacher, who had dispatched theology on a wayward descent into anthropology, based only on fallen human experience, with the consequence that theology was no longer capable of either hearing or proclaiming the Word of God. Barth's indictment of Schleiermacher's theological focus on human experience is notorious: "One can *not* speak of God simply by speaking of man in a loud voice."[17]

The existential repercussions of Barth's disenchantment with his teachers (and with their lineage) is brought out in a lecture that he gave in 1957, in which he surveyed Protestant theology in the previous century:

> For me personally, a day in the beginning of August of that year [1914] has impressed itself as *dies ater*. It is the day on which 93 German intellectuals published a profession of support for the war policy of Kaiser Wilhelm II. Included among the signers I was shocked to see the names of pretty much all my teachers—theologians whom I had until then loyally honored. Having been estranged from their ethos, I observed that I would also no longer be able to follow their ethics and dogmatics, their exegesis and historical interpretation. For me in any case the theology of the nineteenth century had no future any more.[18]

In response to the Schleiermacher-induced cul-de-sac, Barth began to articulate his theology of crisis with a reversal of Schleiermacher's method and an attack on the progressive temper of nineteenth-century liberalism. In place of an apologetics based on a defense of religion in general, Barth rejected religion as the construction of sinful humankind and emphasized the particularity of Christian revelation.

This approach fell like a cold shower on early twentieth-century theology, provoking both shock and energy. Curiously, Barth's attitude to Schleiermacher remained characterized by ambivalence. Some of Barth's followers and colleagues—notably Emil Brunner—were less conflicted in this regard, but Barth remained curiously vigilant in disallowing anything that he saw as unjust criticism of Schleiermacher.

This rise-and-decline—or decline-and-rise—account of theology between Schleiermacher and Barth has a familiar feel to it for theologians. It is, after all, the theological story that is narrated in most works of historical theology dealing with the nineteenth century. It echoes into the theological present too, where similar issues of theological method and cultural hermeneutics remain contested between and among various forms of revisionism, radical orthodoxy, postmodernism, and postliberalism. For our purposes, however, it raises a number of issues in need of attention.

The first is obvious: like all generalized accounts it inevitably cuts corners, some of which are more important than others. Theology, as an intellectual discipline, was not confined to German universities for the entire nineteenth century, nor was it the exclusive preserve of university-based academics. Theology faculties and seminaries remained predominantly concerned with preparing men for ordained ministry, a large number of whom served with missionary societies overseas. In preparation for the World Missionary Conference of 1910, for example, the various sections undertook field research by correspondence with a large number of agents of churches and missionary societies overseas (approximately two thousand were consulted). The proliferation of missionary activity had in fact made it necessary by 1910 to publish a *Statistical Atlas of Christian Missions* (replacing one produced in 1900) to accompany the conference papers. It is striking that many of the missionaries consulted in preparation for the conference had obtained theological doctorates before working overseas. To see theology in the nineteenth century as a doomed exercise in flattering bourgeois interests is to misinterpret seriously the contemporary activities of churches, the concerns of contemporary theologians, and the location of theological reflection.

Second, the mythical methodological contest between Schleiermacher and Barth too easily suggests that Schleiermacher's experiential philosophy of religion characterized theology for the rest of the nineteenth century, until it was dismissed firmly by Barth. Undoubtedly, many philosophers of religion in the period were indebted to Schleiermacher's retrieval of piety, but there were other approaches, ranging from a confident idealism inspired by Hegel through various shades of neo-Kantianism. Confining apologetical concerns to epistemology is, however, to underestimate the apologetical importance of history in the nineteenth century, and it was in history (of doctrine, church, sacred writings, and other religions) that many of the so-called liberal Protestants produced their most significant work. Significantly, the approach to history taken by, say, Albert Réville, Ernst Troeltsch, or Adolf von Harnack was understood by these writers as either challenging or escaping from the constraints of confessional prescription. To use Troeltsch's distinction, this history was explicitly intended to be "critical"—and not "dogmatic"—history.[19] Viewed with the advantages of hermeneutical hindsight, confessional horizons proved less easy to slough off or even to take into account (a point not lost at the time on either Troeltsch or Alfred Loisy), but increasing awareness of the modern, historical-critical methods was seen to open a gulf between dogmatically correct views of the past and the views available to the critical historian. Karl Barth's esteem for the discipline of historical theology and his own important contribution to the history of nineteenth-century Protestant theology underline an important continuity between Barth and nineteenth-century apologetical concerns.

A third and final point to highlight is the (perhaps unduly) Apollonian character of the relationships within and between religion, culture, and society that this account of the period encourages. Rather than portray Barth as a somewhat unlikely Dionysus overthrowing excessive sweetness and light after theology's collusion in warmongering, it is more important to look closely at the intellectual history of the period: Dionysus was there all along. France, in particular, had witnessed an impressive number of "secular religions," most famously that of Auguste Comte, which culminated in a ritualist positivism.[20] But alongside the secularists, a concern with the occult and with spiritualism was thriving, especially by the turn of the nineteenth century into the twentieth. J. W. Burrow has pointed out the explicit notes of rebellion against deterministic materialism evidenced by theosophical movements, expressing "impatience with the limitations of a mundane, de-mythologized human existence and a disenchanted world."[21] This echoes the Romanticism of Schleiermacher and his contemporaries at the turn of the previous century and its protest against a narrow and restricting rationalism. But now the protest was directed against a more diffuse foe: modernism. Antimodernism gained explicit religious expression in the heartlands of religious modernism, and at the same time.[22]

The conventional account of theology in the nineteenth century does not, therefore, prove particularly helpful in setting the context for the emergence of either Christian fundamentalism or ecumenism in the early decades of the twentieth century. One development, however, that has been touched on already, namely a concern with Christianity's essence, may repay closer attention.

Essence and Purity, Apologetics and Evangelism

Like the quest for the "historical" Jesus, the quest for Christianity's essence exudes nineteenth-century historiographical concerns. In an influential study of the contesting of Christianity's essence, Stephen Sykes has argued that the notion of Christianity's identity should be regarded as an "essentially contested concept," a notion that he borrows from W. B. Gallie's *Philosophy and the Historical Understanding*.[23] Such a proposal would have the effect of emphasising the form, rather than the content, of the concept of identity/essence. The contesting, however, takes place—and in the nineteenth century took place—in terms of content rather than form (with the possible exception of Troeltsch, who was both a historian and—consciously—a philosopher of history).

In their popular account of fundamentalism, Martin E. Marty and R. Scott Appleby draw attention to that clash of modern historical metanarratives presupposed by emergent fundamentalism.[24] Steiner's description of a bourgeois armistice with history seemed compatible with a Hegelian philosophy of history (Hegel with either an upper- or lower-case "h")—dialectically evolutionary and progressive. Not everyone, however, was prepared to read history in this way, ostensibly at any rate. An alternative was voiced by John Nelson Darby who, in 1827, resigned his living in the Church of Ireland and became part of A. N. Groves's "Brethren" movement. Rather than treat history as a whole process unfolding according to an immanent rationale, on the basis of his biblical interpretation Darby viewed history as a series of divine "dispensations." These dispensations echoed the idealist belief in progress in history, but attributed progress to divine providence rather than advances in human technological skill. By the time of the period 1910-1920, dispensationalism's most significant literary legacy had appeared: C. I. Scofield's *Reference Bible* (1909), which popularized a reading of Scripture focused on seven divine dispensations.

The emergent higher criticism treated the biblical text as a window to an ancient world. Scofield's Bible, on the other hand, is a guide to the past, present, and future. Dispensationalism combined its reading of the biblical text with its reading of the signs of the times and concluded that the present age is the age of The Church, which will last from the gift of the Holy Spirit (portrayed in Acts 2) until Christ's return. This is, therefore, the sixth of the seven dispensations. The next dispensational age is the Millennium, the rule of Christ for a thousand years before the End.

The apparent proximity of the millennial reign of Christ provoked a certain contemporary urgency in the need for evangelical preachers, such as Sankey and Moody, to campaign for the saving of souls through acts of conversion. Though evangelical preachers and teachers differed among themselves on certain aspects of eschatology (in this period the tribulation and its sequencing proved especially divisive), they favored what was in effect their own version of the essence of Christianity. Frequently attributed—by defenders and opponents alike—to the Niagara Bible Conference of 1895 were the "five points of fundamentalism," which expressed an ethos of dissent to accommodation with higher biblical criticism. Regardless of their precise origin, or of their role in expressing precisely the ethos of nascent fundamentalism, the five points are illuminating as symptoms of the impact of biblical criticism. They affirmed what others either denied or failed to affirm: the plenary verbal inspiration of the Bible, the divinity of Jesus Christ, Christ's virgin birth, a substitutionary theology of atonement, and Christ's physical return.

Dispensationalist historiography made sense of history by discerning God's purposive involvement in specific historic events: to grasp history as a whole, dispensationalists needed a sense of what that whole was. They might have been surprised, if not dismayed, to note that treating history in this way marked them out as children of their time, reacting to a context shaped by evolutionary and idealist reflections on the purpose of history.

The term "essence" has a long history in Western metaphysics and theology, especially, though not exclusively, where Aristotle's influence has exercised a bearing on developments (for Aristotle, essence referred to the way in which living creatures embodied the principle—or character—expressed in their definition). Strong echoes of Aristotle were also to be found in nineteenth-century Roman Catholic theology, especially in the period after 1879, when Leo XIII's encyclical *Aeterni Patris* made neo-Thomism the sole theological and philosophical currency of the Roman Catholic Church. Neo-Thomism, or neoscholasticism, however, found nineteenth-century historiography problematic: for a card-carrying neo-Thomist, essences are eternal, and are—a priori—not to be found mutating in the contingencies of history.[25]

Other appeals to essence language were, however, stirring in the nineteenth century and are clearly shaped by a post-Romantic, idealist philosophical outlook. G. W. F. Hegel's philosophy of history, for instance, is symptomatic of much of the debate on an "essence" of either religion or of Christianity in the mid-nineteenth century. For Hegel, the essence of the human person is reason, and the purpose after which history strives is the establishment of a free and reasonable community of persons.[26] The nineteenth-century fascination with religion's or Christianity's "essence" presupposes this historiographical shift. In "What does 'essence of Christianity' mean?" Ernst Troeltsch dates the prior enabling conditions of this concept to the Romantic reaction to the post-Enlightenment period, and to the admittedly very different approaches to identity found in Chateaubriand, Lessing, and Herder. A professionalization in identity discernment has taken place in this period. Rather than situate identity in

creedal formulations or in traditional teaching authorities, an essence is
abstracted by modern historians:

> According to this conception an intellectual unity, of which the masses
> are unaware and which can only be grasped by historical abstraction,
> develops within the manifold detail of Christian history, and this unity
> is drawn up into consciousness as the essence of Christianity.[27]

The situation to which Troeltsch addressed his essay was shaped by the
debate on Christianity's "essence" provoked by Harnack's popular book,
Das Wesen des Christentums (1900), rendered into English as *What Is Christianity?*[28] The popularity of Harnack's work is sometimes underestimated:
the book was based on a series of public lectures given at the University of
Berlin on the threshold of a new century in the semester 1899–1900. Conceived, therefore, as a work of *haute vulgarisation*, it succeeded in making
explicit—almost unwittingly—the philosophy of history that underlay Harnack's major scholarly enterprise, his *History of Dogma*.[29] It is, therefore,
strange to see this popular treatment of critically aware Christianity provoke
such a remarkable level of critical engagement in the scholarly literature of
the day. There is an almost comic disproportion, for example, between Harnack's book and the deceptive clarity of Alfred Loisy's *L'Évangile et l'Église*,
in which Loisy claimed to answer the liberal Protestantism of Harnack in
Prussia and that of Auguste Sabatier in France.[30]

Harnack was in many ways symptomatic of fin de siècle theological con-
fidence that historical study would yield Christianity's essence, and that
this essence would be uncontaminated by dogmatic presuppositions. The
repercussions of such a belief impacted not only in historical studies, but
would rapidly be discerned in ecclesiology. By a rigorous process of historical abstraction, particularity and contextual presuppositions would be relativized, thereby yielding an intellectually respectable and doctrinally
neutral essence. Thus, it was supposed that the historical-critical pursuit of
what was essential in Christianity would no longer be determined on a
denominational basis: historical-critical methods transcended ecclesiastical
boundaries. It is evident that from the period surrounding the turn of the
nineteenth century into the twentieth, an increasing number of authors
remark that Christianity's divisions run within the various traditions as
much as, if not more than, between them.

This relativizing and blurring of confessional boundaries in the modern period is not confined to historiography. As noted, the nineteenth
century has often been portrayed as the century of Christian missions, a
designation that indicates a certain confessional spin on previous missionary enterprises. Certainly a great deal of missionary work was undertaken
in the nineteenth century; what is striking, however, is that in the two

previous centuries, overseas missionary work had been the almost exclusive preserve of Roman Catholicism, with its access to the overseas territories governed by Spain, France, and Portugal, as well as areas in which
missionaries had enjoyed particular success, notably the Jesuit order's initial work in China. From the last decade of the eighteenth century
onwards, however, Anglicans and other Protestants developed missionary
enthusiasm, often by means of missionary societies, some of which were
denominationally constituted, while many others were transdenomina-
tional, although unmistakably protestant with a lower-case initial. In addition to a concern with mission overseas, a number of societies were
formed—in keeping with the apologetical concerns of Schleiermacher et
al.—to evangelize (or reevangelize via revival campaigns) the emergent
bourgeoisie and working classes of the United States and Europe. One of
the early ecumenical movement's most significant figures, John R. Mott
(1865–1955), emerged out of this context, having become involved with
the YMCA during his student years at Cornell in the 1880s, then going
on to found the World's Student Christian Federation in 1895, before his
involvement in the planning of Edinburgh 1910 and its subsequent development into the ecumenical movement.[31]

Concern with mission, therefore, emerged as a point of consensus
among Protestants and Anglicans in the nineteenth century, a consensus
that was also shared by the Roman Catholic and Eastern Orthodox
churches, although the ecclesial self-understanding of the latter bodies prevented their involvement in the kind of cooperation that was possible
among Anglicans, Protestants, and various pan-protestant missionary societies. Philip Jenkins has recently chastised church historians and theologians for their willingness to regard such missionary endeavors with
distaste, and to ignore them, or, worse, stereotype them as being simply
impositions of Western norms on non-Western cultures: "Images of Victo-
rian missionaries in pith-helmets," he observes, "are commonly in the
background."[32] The nineteenth-century missionary movement is complex,
and its consequences remain surprisingly undiscerned amongst the Western churches.

To make sense of such complexity, a new theological and political discipline emerged. In addition to the historical-critical quest of Christianity's
essence, Christian theology was also concerned with resourcing the nineteenth-century missionary movement. In this regard, perhaps the most significant development is associated with Gustav Warneck (1834–1910),
widely acknowledged as the principal architect of the discipline of missiol-
ogy, and the first person to hold a university chair of mission (at the University of Halle). There are uncomfortable echoes of what has been
criticized as "cultural protestantism" in Warneck's program in his anticipations of the need for the enculturation of Christianity or christianizing of

a given culture. The well-known missionary command of the risen Jesus in Matthew 28:19, that his own disciples should make "disciples of all nations," raised, for Warneck, the question of how a nation is to be discipled. It is difficult to read Warneck without a certain nervousness as to how certain national traits are to be characterized and how Christianity is to be shaped to respond and appeal to such national characteristics.

Religion's ambivalent relationship with ethnic tension was not, however, Warneck's major concern. Rather, he sought to articulate a scientifically rigorous theory of mission, grounded in history, in which missionary activity proceeded in three stages: individual conversions, the development of ecclesial life among these converts, and finally an organized, systematic christianizing of the non-Christian population (discerning ethnic characteristics belongs to this third stage). This third stage required social and political analytical skills, and not just evangelical zeal to reach the unbelieving hordes. The critical study of mission had found a home in the university sector.

One of those who came to hear Warneck lecture was a Scottish former missionary, Joseph Oldham, who visited Halle between 1904 and 1905. If John Mott was the energetic promoter of Christian mission and unity, and in many ways the public face of Edinburgh 1910, then Oldham supplied the methodological clarity and strategic thinking that contributed to the success of the 1910 conference and to its wide-ranging impact.[33]

The Edinburgh conference was not the first missionary conference in this period. The first such meeting is usually regarded as having been the one held in New York on May 4 and 5, 1854, with the second taking place less than six months later on October 12 and 13 in London. The main purpose of these meetings was to enable representatives of British and American missionary societies to meet with one another. The first missionary conference to publish its proceedings took place in Liverpool in 1860, and among its participants was one Indian national. Promoting solidarity among missionary societies and publicizing their work remained the evident objectives of these meetings. In 1878, a further conference was held in London, attended by eleven non-British missionaries, and which paved the way for the next two major conferences, the London "Centenary" Conference of 1888, which attempted to reflect the global range of the missionary movement (and which marked the centenary of modern Anglican and Protestant missionary activity), and the "Ecumenical" Conference held in Carnegie Hall, New York, in 1900. As these conferences developed, they became longer events and included an increasing number of participants, notably an increase in the number of participants from outside of Europe and the United States. One senses, however, that as well as settling into a pattern of holding a conference every decade, the conferences themselves were in danger of becoming stuck in a rut.

The preparations for the Edinburgh conference began in earnest in 1908, when an international committee met at Oxford, with Mott as chairman and Oldham—almost by chance—as secretary. The preparations required Oldham to become a full-time secretary to the conference, and his imaginative grasp of what was at stake as well as his capacity for focused thought prevented Edinburgh 1910 from becoming just another occasion for missionary solidarity. Ironically, in view of later developments, the international committee decided against calling the Edinburgh conference "ecumenical," for the excellent reason that it simply would not be ecumenical in terms of the interests that it would represent.

Even if it declined the title "ecumenical," the nine volumes of papers from Edinburgh 1910 offer a fascinating insight into the condition of the global Christian missionary movement at the start of the twentieth century. Warneck's challenge to missionaries to take seriously cultural context, as well as social and political analysis, had been taken to heart by Oldham. In the years before the conference, a voluminous correspondence had taken place with approximately two thousand overseas missionary workers, in order to build up a precise audit of the non-Christian and Christian world. Those involved in the conference, as chairs of the eight different commissions, were well-placed in social and political life on both sides of the Atlantic.[34] In addition, the church spokesmen who attended left no doubt but that the conference, and its future undertakings, enjoyed their full support. Far from becoming one more interest group among others, missionary concern had entered into the mainstream of ecclesiastical interests.

Although not an assembly representing all Christian churches, attendance at the Edinburgh conference was decided on a representative basis, unlike previous such meetings. Missionary societies were entitled to send a representative to Edinburgh if they currently had missionaries at work overseas and if they spent a minimum of two thousand pounds per annum on overseas missionary work. For every extra four thousand pounds per annum spent on overseas missions, societies were entitled to send an extra delegate. (To gauge the economic significance of contemporary missionary investment, perhaps it should be noted that the total expenses incurred in the running of the ten-day Edinburgh conference, plus the two years of preparatory work, were estimated at seven thousand pounds.)

In terms of focusing the Edinburgh agenda, it was decided that this missionary conference would be concerned with strategy, rather than simply enthusing missionary supporters, hence the importance assigned to the work of the preparatory commissions. Three aims were to be borne in mind. The first was that the focus of attention was to be on missionary activity among non-Christian peoples, and what steps needed to be undertaken in order to evangelize them. Second, in a short conference there would be a limit on what could usefully be considered, and therefore an emphasis was placed on matters most urgently in need of shared decision making. Finally, the conference would not be requested to express its mind on doctrinal matters that would divide its participants needlessly.

Doctrine, however, has many ways of making its presence felt. One of the most obvious features of the conference papers is a concern with unity amongst Christians. The conference issued two messages to "The Church," in Christian and non-Christian lands respectively. In the latter, the conference noted: "We thank God for the longing after unity which is so prominent among you and is one of our own deepest longings to-day."[35]

In a crude sense, the church militant affirms militancy. Military metaphors are ubiquitous in the reports. Writing "To the Members of the Church in Christian Lands," the conference describes its work thus: "we have surveyed the field of missionary operation and the forces that are available for its occupation,"[36] "Everything is conducive to an aggressive forward movement in Formosa,"[37] and "All reasons combine to urge upon the missionary societies the wisdom and the necessity of marshalling their forces for the prompt and thorough evangelization of Korea."[38] These examples are but a small sample of the ethos. The same note is struck in W. H. T. Gairdner's account of the conference, published at the request of the international committee, with its frankly alarming synopsis of how the first commission drew attention to how "the storm-centres of interest and urgency and anxiety in the ecumenical crusade today might be roughly defined as (1) India, (2) the yellow Farther East, (3) Islam as a whole, especially where it is advancing."[39]

The urgency and the dangers of the current situation detected by the conference, together with the range of ways in which the conference presented the world as being ripe for harvest, open for conquest, receptive to new and better ways, and so forth, is striking. The conference papers are relatively consistent in what they believe that Christianity has to offer, namely the "pure" gospel, which can be articulated "aggressively" by "wise" missionaries. The recurrence of this terminology—wisdom, purity, and aggression—is one of the hallmarks of the conference papers. Curiously, however, the "pure" gospel is never unpacked in terms of content: it exercises its appeal at a formal level only. So what is this remarkably powerful "pure" gospel? Perhaps part of the reason that its content remains unspecified is to be found in the decision to keep potentially divisive doctrinal matters off the conference agenda. But it is also entirely probable that the recurrent trope of "pure gospel" presupposes the continuing debate on the essence of Christianity, and that in seeking to propose a "pure" gospel, the Edinburgh conference was, in fact, proposing a denominationally nonspecific essence of Christianity as its weapon of choice.

Conclusion: *Oikoumene* through the Looking-Glass

The emergence of both modern ecumenism in the aftermath of Edinburgh 1910 and the modern fundamentalist movement within the same decade was no accident. Each exhibits a globalizing tendency, each operated with a missionary concern that relativized—but did not eradicate—existing denominational allegiances, and each has defined itself against the explicit and implicit concerns of the other. This process of self-definition first took place in the context of modernity, and modern consciousness has been described by Hinrich Stoevesandt as causing "discomfort with creed."[40] Yet despite this apparent cultural ethos of anticreedalism, quasi-creedal state-ments—the essence of Christianity, *The Fundamentals*—occupy a pivotal role in these movements, each expressing what the other rejects.

In his illuminating essay "Identity in the Globalizing World," Zygmunt Bauman argues that it is more accurate to speak of an incomplete process of "identification" in which we are always already engaged, rather than of "iden-tities" that we either have or lack. En route to his conclusion he remarks:

> Boundaries are not drawn to fence off and protect already existing identities. As the great Norwegian anthropologist Friedrich Barth explained—it is exactly the other way round: the ostensibly shared, "communal" identities are by-products of feverish boundary-drawing. It is only after the border-posts have been dug in that the myths of their antiquity are spun and the fresh cultural/political origins of identity are carefully covered up by the genesis stories.[41]

Neighboring genesis stories are therefore worth examining to see what light they shed—or, more interestingly, fail to shed—on each other. The world of nineteenth-century theology has long been presented as the pre-serve of a bland theological liberalism, which, after its ethical embarrass-ment in 1914–1918, was dispatched by Karl Barth and neo-orthodoxy. Like all caricatures, there is some truth here, but it is not helped by its distor-tion into a simplistic rise-and-decline, or decline-and-rise, storyline. The-ologians who hold to this storyline, moreover, may exclude themselves from other features of the era.

In addition to cultural apologetics in the West, Christian theology in the nineteenth century was engaged in a more challenging apologetic adven-ture in its missionary work overseas. In both spheres of activity, the notion of "essence"—discerned by the activities of contemporary historical scholar-ship—played an important and novel role. By specifying the essence of a complex whole, one was placed in a position in which it was possible to articulate what sort of "whole" it was, and what sort of purpose it served.

By the time of the World Missionary Conference at Edinburgh in 1910, it is reasonable to speak of an ecumenical imagination shaping the work of

men like John R. Mott and J. H. Oldham. Through their missionary information gathering, they had managed to conduct a detailed audit of the
state of Christianity in the contemporary world. And not only the non-
Christian world: the report of Edinburgh 1910, replete with its discomfort-
ing militaristic imagery, has its sights fixed also on the church at the home
base, and its need of radical change.

Imaginative concern for the one inhabited earth—*oikoumene* to the
Greek fathers of the Christian church—inevitably shared its cradling with
an Other, against which it increasingly defined itself. It is striking that
among the first of *The Fundamentals* is an attack on the very notion of an
"essence" of Christianity, and that the nascent ecumenical movement, as
it emerged from Edinburgh 1910, would become a symbol to biblical fundamentalism of the dangers of cultural accommodationism and the dangers of seeking unity at the expense of truth.

Perhaps in seeking to take seriously the theological plurality of the nineteenth century, it would be wise to replace Schleiermacher and Barth as
the preferred icons of theological polarity with the multiauthored, multi-
contextual papers of Edinburgh 1910 on the one hand, and with *The Fundamentals* on the other. Each operates with a sense of what Christianity's
essence is, and is not, and to understand one is to engage with both or else
risk understanding neither.

Chapter Six

The Liberal Antichrist–*Left Behind* in America

Darryl Jones

In 1996, after viewing *Independence Day*, Roland Emmerich's monumental updating of H. G. Wells's *The War of the Worlds* as a paean to American triumphalism, a senior advisor to Bob Dole, who had endorsed the movie as a model of American patriotism and who was then running as the Republican candidate for president against Bill Clinton, remarked, "Millions die, but they're all liberals."[1] These dead millions are New Yorkers, Angelenos, and residents of Washington, D.C., all cities spectacularly wiped out by the film's invading alien spaceships. They are, that is to say, the inhabitants of America's traditionally more liberal seaboards, not its conservative heartland: what, following psephologists, we have now learned to call "Blue" rather than "Red" America, after the media practice of coloring Democrat states blue and Republican states red. Not widely represented among these millions of dead are the 62 million (and counting) buyers of Tim LaHaye and Jerry B. Jenkins's publishing phenomenon, the *Left Behind* series of evangelical "rapture novels," which has recently completed its twelve-volume cycle (though there are also numerous prequels, sequels, and spin-offs). In a self-lacerating analysis of the cultural politics of American voting practices, David Brooks makes precisely this point:

> We in the coastal metro Blue area read more books and attend more
> plays than the people in the Red heartland. We're more sophisticated
> and cosmopolitan—just ask us about our alumni trips to China or
> Provence, or our interest in Buddhism. But don't ask us, please, what
> life in Red America is like. We don't know. We don't know who Tim
> LaHaye and Jerry B. Jenkins are. . . . We don't know what James Dob-
> son says on his radio program, which is listened to by millions. We
> don't know about Reba and Travis. . . . Very few of us know what goes
> on in Branson, Missouri, even though it has seven million visitors a
> year, or could name even five NASCAR drivers. . . . We don't know
> how to shoot or clean a rifle. We can't tell a military officer's rank by
> looking at his insignia. We don't know what soy beans look like when
> they're growing in a field.[2]

Since the fifth volume, *Apollyon*, published in 1998, every one of the *Left
Behind* series has made it to number one on the *New York Times* best seller
list, a list that does not even include the sales from Christian bookstores.
LaHaye and Jenkins are currently the biggest-selling authors in America,
outselling even such established popular heavyweights as Stephen King
and John Grisham. Seventy-one percent of *Left Behind*'s readers are from
the American South and Midwest, compared to just 6 percent from the tra-
ditionally liberal Northeast. *Left Behind*'s "core buyer," according to David
Gates, is "a 44-year-old born-again Christian woman, living in the South."[3]
But, as noted in an editorial in the May 24, 2004 U.S. edition of
Newsweek, which ran a major feature on the *Left Behind* phenomenon,
"Tim LaHaye and Jerry Jenkins are not exactly household names in New
York City, which is where much of the national press lives and works."[4]

Demographically, then, *Left Behind*'s readership comprises a fairly substantial chunk of what John Micklethwait and Adrian Wooldridge have
recently dubbed "The Right Nation": "a vast conservative country hidden
away in the uncivilized wilderness between the Hudson River and
Pasadena," they write, with an acknowledgment of the insularity of the liberal, metropolitan worldview whose proponents *Independence Day* had so
gleefully wiped out.[5] Nevertheless, although this "Right Nation" is a conservative America whose values and ideologies are sometimes incomprehensible and frequently anathema to much of the rest of the developed
world, it is currently in a powerful global, imperial ascendancy under
George W. Bush and his administration. We liberal, secular, post-Enlightenment intellectual citizens of what Donald Rumsfeld once witheringly
wrote off as "Old Europe" (and I, for one, am proud to be an Old European) ignore the Right Nation, and ignore the *Left Behind* phenomenon,
at our peril.[6]

The *Left Behind* series, in keeping with the dispensationalist theology that animates so much American evangelicalism, begins with the rapture, in which the true believers are taken up into the air and out of this world by Christ, causing temporary chaos in communications and transport, but opening up an opportunity for a far more serious disruption in that it facilitates the rise of the antichrist. This is Nicolae Carpathia, an obscure Romanian politician (the referents here are, of course, simultaneously the Communist dictator Nicolae Ceausescu and the Prince of Darkness himself, Count Dracula). Carpathia wins the trust of the Nobel prize-winning botanist Chaim Rozenzweig, who has gifted Israel with enormous political power by discovering a process that renders desert land fertile. Carpathia, backed by shady financiers, maneuvers himself into the position of secretary general of the United Nations, elbowing aside the incumbent Mwangati Ngumo, a thinly disguised Kofi Annan. His chief backer is Jonathan Stonagal, "the mightiest of a secret group of international money men"[7]—this is presumably a version of the so-called Bilderberg Group, according to some theorists the secret power behind all the world's democracies, endlessly plotting for control of the planet. The Bilderberg Group, celebrating its fiftieth anniversary at the time this chapter was written, is a secretive organization of international money men, politicians, industrialists, and media barons who are, in Will Hutton's phrase, "the high priests of globalization," secretly guiding (or so it is believed) world events: "Is Bilderberg molding US domestic policy?" the *New York Times* asked in the summer of 2004.[8] (Conspiracy theorists were particularly attuned to Bilderberg before the last American presidential elections, since Senator John Edwards, John Kerry's presidential running mate, is himself a Bilderberger.)

In the *Left Behind* series, the American president, Gerald Fitzhugh, "a younger version of Lyndon Johnson," and thus, as a Great Society Democrat unable to resist the antichrist, is increasingly marginalized by Carpathia, losing control of all the apparatus of power until only "the American militia movement" remains loyal to him.[9] Once in charge of the United Nations, Carpathia renames it the Global Community, relocates to Babylon, creates a unified world currency, and takes control of the world's media (with only the Internet remaining as a source of dissent). The Global Community is to operate on "proactively nonsectarian" principles.[10] To ensure this, the Global Community takes control of the world's weapons, decommissioning 90 percent of them, and keeping the remaining 10 percent to deal with threats. Carpathia plans to end poverty: "We will need much more [money] to effect our plan of raising the level of Third World countries so that the entire globe is on an equal footing. . . . You are all doing a wonderful job of moving to the one-world currency. We are close to a cashless society."[11] With this comes "an international healthcare organization that will take precedence over all local and regional efforts . . . a blueprint for the most aggressive international healthcare system ever."[12] With the connivance of the venal and pompous new pope, Pontifex Maximus Peter II, Carpathia instigates the creation of a new one-world faith, Enigma Babylon. While LaHaye and Jenkins primarily use this as a vehicle for travestying Catholicism as well as any form of religious modernism, it is also the case that Enigma Babylon is founded on the principles of inclusion, liberalism, and tolerance, set up to end the bloodshed caused by interfaith wars. Carpathia himself announces that "The era of peace is at hand, and the world is finally, at long last, on the threshold of becoming one global community."[13]

With the exception of Carpathia's media control, I find it difficult to dissent from very much of this, not least because much of it is so familiar, the traditional discourse of socialist utopian thinking. In fact, much of what Carpathia achieves had already been imagined by the greatest twentieth-century utopian, H. G. Wells. In 1941, George Orwell accused Wells of preaching "the same gospel as he has been preaching for forty years, always with an air of angry surprise at the human beings who can fail to grasp anything so obvious. . . . All sensible men for decades past have been substantially in agreement with what Mr Wells says; but the sensible men have no power."[14] Wells began to formulate his ideas for a world state as early as *Anticipations* in 1900, and never substantially deviated from them thereafter. Never a modest man, Wells liked to take the credit for the intellectual impetus animating the League of Nations. Certainly, he was a vociferous champion of that organization, writing, for example, in *In the Fourth Year* (1918), in terms that should be familiar to us:

> The League of Free Nations must, in fact, if it is to be a working reality, have power to define and limit the military and aerial equipment of every country in the world. . . . It must have effective control over every armament industry. . . . Its powers, I suggest, must extend even to a restraint upon the belligerent propaganda which is the natural advertisement campaign of every armament industry. It must have the right, for example, to raise the question of the proprietorship of newspapers by armament interests. Disarmament is, in fact, a necessary factor of any League of Free Nations, and you cannot have disarmament unless you are prepared to see the powers of the council of the League extend thus far. The very existence of the League presupposes that it and it alone is to have and to exercise military force. Any other belligerency or preparation or incitement to belligerency becomes rebellion, and any other arming a threat of rebellion, in a world League of Free Nations.[15]

Thus, the position of the Fabian socialist in 1918 is *precisely* reiterated as the position of the antichrist in 1996. The last and most detailed of

Wells's works of futurology, *The Shape of Things to Come* (1933), purports to be a transcription of the dream writings of Dr. Philip Raven, a high-ranking official in the League of Nations. *Things to Come* has a technocratic world state arising from the ashes of a nationalistic Western civilization devastated by war and pestilence (and Wells was at least as addicted to megadeath and grand scenes of catastrophe as are LaHaye and Jenkins). Wells's world state has its base in Basra, just down the road from Carpathia's Babylon—both are in what is now Iraq. In *Things to Come*, the declaration of the World Council at the Second Basra Conference, 1978, is a blueprint for Carpathia's program of world domination:

> [The Council] is the only sovereign upon this planet. There is now no other primary authority from end to end of the earth. All other sovereignty and all proprietary rights whatever that do not conduce directly to the general welfare of mankind ceased to exist during the period of disorder, and cannot be revived.
>
> The Council has its air and sea ways, its airports, dockyards, factories, mines, plantations, laboratories, colleges and schools throughout the world. These are administered by its officials and protected by its own police, and the latter are instructed to defend these organizations whenever and wherever it may be necessary against the aggression of unauthorized persons.
>
> Without haste or injustice and without delay, with a due regard to your comfort, your welfare and your wishes, the Bureau will set itself to bring your life into sound and permanent correlation with the one human commonwealth.[16]

How did we get from there to here, from Fabian socialist utopia to the tyrannical reign of the antichrist? The answer lies first in the deeply political nature of American evangelical Christianity. These politics, it need hardly be added, are conservative. In 2003, Donald Paul Hodel, president of the Christian ministry Focus on the Family and a former member of Ronald Reagan's cabinet, wrote: "The fact is, without the hard work and votes of millions of Christians, there would be no Republican majority in both Houses of Congress, no Bush presidencies, few Republican governors, and a small handful of state houses in Republican hands."[17] Thirty-nine percent of Americans describe themselves as having been "born again"; one third of registered American voters are white evangelical Protestants.[18] Evangelicals have now overtaken Catholics to constitute the largest single religious group in America; significantly, in a PBS poll of April 2004, 71 percent of evangelicals said they would vote for George W. Bush.[19] While the Christian Right is not necessarily a single monolithic organization, nevertheless this does constitute a powerful voting bloc whose ideological needs the Bush administration largely shares and is happy to accommodate: according to the Washington magazine *Campaigns and Elections*, Christian conservatives now exercise either "strong" or "moderate" influence in forty-four Republican state committees.[20]

The centrality of his born-again Christianity to George W. Bush's political worldview is well-documented. Asked during the 2000 presidential campaign to name his favorite philosopher, Bush replied, "Jesus, because he changed my heart." Specifically, Bush dates this change—from his sometimes wild youth to his mature position of policeman of global conservatism—to his meeting with Billy Graham in 1986: "He led me to the path and I began walking."[21] During his first campaign for governor of Texas, Bush told a reporter in Austin that only those who had accepted Jesus Christ as their personal savior could go to heaven.[22] "I would not be Governor," Bush was to write, "if I did not believe in a divine plan that supersedes all human plans."[23] In January 2001, Bush's last stop before taking up the presidency was his hometown of Midland, Texas, where he told his audience that in Washington he would "govern by Midland values." As Peter Stothard has shown, these "Midland values" are overwhelmingly those of the Christian Right, heavily influenced by dispensational theology: "Suppose," one Midland resident tells Stothard, "the President and his wife were to come here this afternoon and the Rapture happens. There'd be bodyguards and press people and stuff. Most of them would be left behind, especially the press people. . . . But where the Bushes had been there'd just be piles of clothes on the ground and that pin he wears. They'd be gone—into the air. That's what we believe."[24]

In fairness, the Bush administration is a broader church than this, comprising old-school hawks like Dick Cheney and Donald Rumsfeld; neocons like Paul Wolfowitz, Richard Perle and perhaps Condoleezza Rice; and even, in the first administration, one important figure from the Republicans' liberal wing, Colin Powell, who allegedly described Cheney, Rumsfeld, and Wolfowitz as "f---ing crazies."[25] The Christian Right, though, is represented not only by the president himself, but also (during the first four years) by the spectacularly crazy attorney general and part-time crooner John Ashcroft, the son of two generations of Pentecostal ministers, who anoints himself with oil before important meetings.[26] His faith is inextricably a part of his rebarbative right-wing politics: he famously boasted that there were only two things to be found in the middle of the road, "a moderate and a dead skunk." Among his many questionable political acts are his opposition, as attorney general of Missouri, to plans for the voluntary desegregation of schools. A BBC profile of Ashcroft has this to say: "Mr. Ashcroft's record as a senator helps explain why he is so controversial. The conservative Christian Coalition gave him a 100 percent rating for the year 2000, while the environmentalist League of Conservation Voters and the left-leaning National Organization for Women each gave him a zero."[27] His pet project, the PATRIOT Act, a response to the 9/11 tragedy that allows the government unprecedented power to collect and use information on private citizens, has been seen by many liberal commentators as no more than a large-scale violation of civil rights. Famously, when Ashcroft ran for reelection as senator for Missouri in 2000, he lost the vote to a corpse, the Democrat Mel Carnahan, who had died shortly before the balloting.

The American evangelist Michael D. Evans—author of such best sellers as *The American Prophecies: Ancient Scriptures Reveal Our Nation's Future* and *Beyond Iraq: The Next Move—Ancient Prophecy and Modern Conspiracy Collide*—believes that "God is foreign policy" and that 9/11 was a punishment from God for America turning its back on Israel.[28] On September 13, 2001, two days after the tragedy, Jerry Falwell, interviewed by Pat Robertson on his *700 Club* TV show, said:

> I really believe that the pagans and the abortionists and the feminists and the gays and the lesbians who are actively trying to make that an alternative lifestyle, the ACLU [American Civil Liberties Union], People for the American Way—all of them who have tried to secularize America—I point the finger in their face, and say, "You helped this happen."

To which Pat Robertson replied, "Well, I totally concur."[29]

Jerry Falwell and Tim LaHaye were cofounders of the Moral Majority in 1979. "Tim was my inspiration," Falwell has written of LaHaye, whom he first introduced to George W. Bush.[30] LaHaye is, in fact, a veteran culture warrior, who once walked out of a meeting with the famously saintly President Jimmy Carter, bowed his head, and prayed, "God, we have to get this man out of the White House and get someone in here who will be aggressive about bringing back traditional moral values."[31] In 1988, he was relieved of his role as cochair of Republican presidential candidate Jack Kemp's campaign after commenting that Catholicism was a "false religion."[32] In an article entitled "The Colossal Battle," published in *Esquire* magazine shortly before the 2004 election, LaHaye makes it clear once again that, for him, religion and Republicanism are effectively synonymous:

> The presidential election of 2004 may determine if the United States will have the opportunity to return to the Judeo-Christian values upon which it was founded. It is my belief that these values, guaranteeing freedom for all, made ours the greatest nation on earth. If John Kerry is elected, we can expect him to continue the tradition of appointing radical, left-wing liberals to all federal judiciary positions and to his administration. . . .Liberals know that if conservatives ever gain a

solid majority in the Supreme Court, the continuing romance with
socialism that has characterized the liberal agenda for the last sixty
years may be over. Governmental intrusion into religious affairs will
end. Freedom will return to our public schools, so that parents can
have a real voice in the education of their children. A mother's womb
might once again become a safe haven for defenseless, unborn babies.
And most important, God can once again be reverenced and honored
in our courts and other public places, instead of being barred, so that
each individual can have the freedom to worship or *ignore* Him, as he
so chooses. . . . Such a task is not difficult. All we need is 10 percent
more of the evangelical Christians in this country to vote on Election
Day. We don't need to tell them specifically *whom* to vote for. (Some
consider that illegal.) We must simply urge them to vote for the presidential candidate and senator who best share their moral values and
principles. In most (but not all) cases, that will be the Republican candidate. Bush, for example, has already delivered on his promises to
cut the discriminatory tax on marriage, reduce taxes in general, and
defend the traditional view of marriage as being between a man and
a woman. . . .The soul of America is truly at stake in the next presidential election. . . . Voting for the most morally committed candidate
for any political office is now more important than ever, and 2004
could turn out to be the most important election year yet for this, the
greatest nation on earth.[33]

If this sounds like the unhinged right-wing ranting of a crazy old coot, that
is because it is. But we should never forget that this crazy old coot is the
biggest-selling author in the most powerful nation in the history of the
world, who would, if he could, dissolve the separation of church and state
enshrined in that classic document of the Enlightenment, the American
Constitution; nor should we forget that this forms a part of a more general
ideological attempt to theocratize modernity by imposing a right-wing
Christian agenda upon its polity. In *Soul Harvest*, the fourth book in the
Left Behind series, Tsion Ben Judah, the Rabbi-turned-Christian culture
warrior, remarks that: "Those who pride themselves on tolerance and call
us exclusivists, judgmental, unloving and shrill are illogical to the point of
absurdity."[34] On the contrary: exclusivist, judgmental, unloving, and shrill
are all accurate descriptions, but only scratch the surface—underneath,
things are much worse. LaHaye and Jenkins image forth a vision of contemporary America as "a nation of overweight, alcoholic drug abusers and
sexual perverts who cannot control our desires and passions," and who are
thus sorely in need of the moral cleansing of Armageddon.[35]

The ways in which the *Left Behind* series engage conservatively with
sociopolitical issues are many and obvious, but I just want to point out a
few of them in the next part of this chapter. Self-evidently, the books take
a hardline stance on sexual politics, with the various women characters
used as vehicles for articulating the Christian Right agenda on sexual iden-

tity and desire, feminism, the role of the family, and, perhaps most crucially, abortion.

Chloe Williams, founder member of the Tribulation Force, daughter of its leader, Rayford Steele, and wife of the other leading male character, the journalist Cameron "Buck" Williams, is a Stanford-educated quasifeminist, there to provide a spunky and liminally dissenting corrective to the testosterone-driven antics of her father and her husband. This dissent, though, operates within strict parameters: when she takes Ben Judah up on a condescendingly sexist remark, her husband responds, "Forgive her. . . . She's going through a twenty-two-year-old's bout with political correctness."[36] Shortly thereafter, Chloe confirms her willingness to engage in traditional gender power relations within marriage, telling her husband, "I don't have a problem submitting to you because I know how much you love me. I'm willing to obey you even when you're wrong."[37] This is classic Christian Right thinking: "God," writes Jerry Falwell, "intends the husband to be the decision maker. Wives and children want to follow."[38] Pat Robertson went further:

> The whole feminist agenda is not about equal rights for women. It is a socialist, anti-family political movement that encourages women to leave their husbands, kill their children, practice witchcraft, destroy capitalism and become lesbians.[39]

Overlaid onto their insistence on traditional gender relations, the novels exhibit a characteristic fear and loathing of sexuality and desire. In their companion to the *Left Behind* series, called *Are We Living in the End Times?* LaHaye and Jenkins write:

> The sexual revolution of the sixties—based on the perverted sex studies of Alfred Kinsey in the fifties, followed by the explicit sex education of the seventies and eighties, and strengthened by the Supreme Court's 1972 decision that transformed pornography from an illegal business into a legally acceptable, ten-billion-dollar-a-year trade in the nineties—has turned the Western world into a sex-obsessed cesspool of immorality . . . just like that of the Tribulation. It is hard to believe that sexual immorality can get any worse than it already is—but it will![40]

Wallowing at the very bottom of this cesspool are gays and lesbians; those with sexual identities "which for centuries were called 'perversions' and in the Bible are called 'an abomination' and 'unnatural.'"[41] LaHaye and Jenkins have this to say:

> It is almost unbelievable in our day how those who reject the sexual laws of God have succeeded in making one of the basest of sexual sins—sodomy—respectable and even acceptable. Just a few years ago

Hollywood stars kept their personal sex lives (which brought them to
an early death) in the closet. But today homosexuals are "out" and
demanding their "rights." What rights do they demand? The right to
marry, the right to cohabit with the same sex, the right to teach
school, where they could influence young minds, the right to adopt
children, the right to serve in the military—and the list goes on.

Even though their dangerous lifestyle can shorten their expected lifes-
pan by as much as 50 percent, it is considered a "hate crime" to warn
or speak out against it. And discrimination against a homosexual in
job selection or dismissal is a violation of the law. If you refuse to rent
your home to a homosexual couple, you are a lawbreaker! The secular world has turned the sexual laws of God upside down. A few years
ago the American Psychological Association considered homosexual-
ity a mental deficiency; now the APA has endorsed it and proposed
that their members no longer urge homosexuals to change their
lifestyle.[42]

In *Nicolae*, the third book in the series, Buck's vicious colleague Verna Zee,
who wants to expose him as a member of the Tribulation Force, backs off
when he threatens to out her as a lesbian; later in the series the mincing
sculptor Guy Blod, fetishistically worshiping his own statue of Carpathia,
is a grotesque version of a gay man. Enthusiasts as they are for retributive
justice, LaHaye and Jenkins even cling to a version of the discredited "Gay
Plague" interpretation of AIDS, an interpretation which, as Richard Davenport-Hines has demonstrated, is predicated entirely on "hating others."[43]
AIDS, LaHaye and Jenkins write, "do[es] not afflict those who follow
the sexual laws of God," and "is similar to the plagues that Revelation
describes."[44]

What this means is that the novels' righteous characters are forced into
absurd caricatures of sexual propriety. When the twenty-year-old Chloe
confesses to Buck that she is a virgin, this seems plausible enough in the
era of abstinence pledges and the "Silver Ring Thing." The abstinence education movement has been vigorously backed by the Bush administration,
who have poured money into the SPRANS Programs, "which teach that sex
outside marriage is likely to have harmful psychological and physical effects,
and which refuse to promote condom use."[45] Alas, studies have shown that
abstinence education may not really be effective: a Columbia University
study showed that 88 percent of pledgers did in fact have sex before marriage, that rates of sexually transmitted diseases among pledgers and non-
pledgers were comparable, and that pledgers were "much less likely" to use
contraception. According to a North Kentucky University survey, 55 percent of those who did not break their pledges nevertheless had oral sex (a

piece of fancy footwork of which Bill Clinton could be proud).[46] While Chloe's confession may be plausible, what is definitely *not* plausible is Buck's reply that he, too, is a virgin. Buck, you will note, is a hitherto-secular, thirty-year-old alpha male Pulitzer prize-winning star feature writer with *Global Weekly*, a fictional *Newsweek*. I put it to you that, within a strictly realist economy, Buck is very unlikely to be a virgin: even his name rhymes correctly. Also implausible is the response of the series' other alpha male, airline pilot Rayford Steele, to his wife-to-be Amanda's sexual forwardness: she "had actually started kissing Rayford before he kissed her."[47] Oh, dear—it is no surprise that, later in the series, Amanda should be suspected of being a double agent in Carpathia's employ. Given this degree of ostentatious prudery, it is worth remembering that when our friend John Ashcroft came to Washington as attorney general one of his first acts was to order that a cloth be draped over the naked breast of a statue of Justice; and it was recently announced that those TV networks which inadvertently showed footage of Janet Jackson's naked breast are to be fined $500,000 each.[48] This climate of sexual hysteria had been whipped up by Ken Starr's obsessive reporting on the sexual practices of Bill Clinton. The Clintons, of course, were condemned by their enemies as archetypal sixties radicals out to destroy American values—and no smear was too smeary, from the exact constitution of Bill's semen to this story in *Unlimited Access*, the biography of former FBI agent Gary Aldrich, who had been on temporary reassignment to Clinton's White House. Aldrich recalled a White House Christmas tree, decorated by Hillary herself with twelve lords a-leaping, all of whom sported large erections, and five gold "cock rings," plus condoms and crack pipes.[49]

It is abortion, of course, which animates the Christian right more than almost any other subject. It may be that more heat than light is generated here since, as a number of commentators including Micklethwait and Wooldridge have argued, Bush is actually very unlikely to roll back *Roe v. Wade*, though he is happy to gesture rhetorically toward it to appease the Christian Right. Furthermore, a number of high-profile Republicans, such as Arnold Schwarzenegger and the First Lady herself, Laura Bush, are avowedly pro-choice (as also is George W. Bush's mother, Barbara Bush).[50] This subject really could fill the entire chapter, so you will forgive me if this is little more than a gesture. During the rapture, the innocent are spared and taken up; this includes all children before the age of puberty, when presumably they become corrupted by sexuality. The unborn are also raptured. In *Left Behind*, Rayford Steele watches a TV broadcast: "Most shocking to Rayford was a woman in labor, about to go into the delivery room, who was suddenly barren. Doctors delivered the placenta. Her husband caught the disappearance of the fetus on tape."[51] The implication could not be more obvious: abortion is the murder of the innocents. Its greatest proponent is Carpathia himself, who on a global scale advocates a program of compulsory abortions on Malthusian grounds, and on a local scale pressures his pregnant fiancée Hattie Durham to get an abortion. Hattie, indeed, exists largely as the vehicle for an ongoing sermon on abortion. Now, one would think that that this might be the opportunity for some real moral ambiguity, for the resolution of a really complex and tricky issue, for if ever there is an argument to be made for justifiable abortion, it is when you are carrying the child of the antichrist. But no—abortion is abortion, and therefore it is wrong: as Rayford tells Hattie, "I don't think you can shirk responsibility for it the way a rape or incest victim might be justified in doing."[52] I think the use of the verb "to shirk" in this context constitutes the single most callous moment in the entire series.

To give credit where it is due, though, *Left Behind*'s politics are not at all points reactionary. They do, in fairness, attempt to offer a multicultural, global perspective which eschews the kinds of racism traditionally associated with evangelical Christianity—witness, for instance, John Ashcroft's record on segregation and that of the institution which awarded him an honorary degree, Bob Jones University, which only allowed black students inside in 1975, and which in 2000 finally caved in to state pressure and ended its notorious ban on interracial dating. In 1980, Bob Jones Jr. and Bob Jones III together denounced Jerry Falwell as "the most dangerous man in America": "Falwell's transgression," according to Mark Taylor Dalhouse, "which in the Jones worldview eclipsed even the evil influences of liberalism, was his political alliance with conservative Catholics, Jews, and Mormons."[53] Bob Jones University is also the college where Tim LaHaye studied. But *Left Behind* does offer an apparently progressive, if occasionally patronizing, racial agenda for America and beyond. This enables the books to step outside the usual demonization of Muslims, a rhetoric familiar to the Christian Right in, for example, Jerry Falwell's declaration that "Mohammed was a terrorist," or Pat Robertson's belief that Muslims are "worse than Nazis."[54] One supporter of the Tribulation Force, an Iraqi fixer codenamed "Albie" (because he is based in Al Basrah), explains to Rayford that he is on their side because he is enraged by Enigma Babylon: "'I should never mock Allah with such blasphemy.' . . . So, Rayford thought, Christians and Jews are not the only holdouts against the new Pope Peter."[55] Another ally is the Jordanian fighter pilot Abdullah Smith, a significant character in the second half of the series.

However, as Melani McAlister has noted:

> As evangelical performance, these novels struggle to enact modernity, and to establish both for their protagonists and implicitly for their

readers the kind of broad cultural reach that might authorize fundamentalist mappings of American global politics.[56]

Nowhere is this concern with "fundamentalist mappings of American
global politics" more evident than in the series' attitude towards Israel. It
is significant, as McAlister suggests, that Abdullah Smith, the righteous
Islamic holy warrior, is Jordanian and not Palestinian: "In fact," she writes,
"there are *no* Palestianian Arabs ever mentioned in a series where much of
the action takes place in Jerusalem and the surrounding areas. . . . [T]here
is no Palestinian problem on the evangelical map."[57]

If, to reiterate Michael D. Evans's soundbite, "God is foreign policy,"
then nowhere is this more evident than in the attitude of evangelical Christianity toward Israel. Here we can say with absolute certainty that the Christian Right *does* influence American foreign policy, unswerving in its
support for the state of Israel. *Left Behind* itself opens not with the rapture,
but with the Russians, in league with Libya and Ethiopia, launching an air
attack on Israel—they are "Frustrated by their inability to profit from Israel's
fortune and determined to dominate and occupy the Holy Land. . . . The
assault became known as the Russian Pearl Harbor." Through divine intervention, the Russian air force is totally wiped out, while "Miraculously, not
one casualty was reported in the whole of Israel."[58] This, however, can at
best be described as a conditional philo-Semitism: literal interpretations of
the book of Revelation require the conversion of 144,000 Jewish "witnesses" to Christianity as a precondition for the second coming. Israel is
necessary to evangelical eschatology. The last thing one needs, therefore,
from the perspective of the Christian Right, is Arab control of Jerusalem.
In *Are We Living in the End Times?* LaHaye and Jenkins devote a lengthy
chapter to Israel, which they describe as "God's key to the future."[59] Thus,
American evangelicals contribute millions to the maintenance of Israeli settlements in the occupied territories; in a debate in the House of Representatives, Republican Congressman Jim Inhofe said that Israel should keep
the West Bank "because God said so"; in 2002, Bush's request that Sharon
withdraw Israeli tanks from Palestinian territory was greeted with a protest
of some one hundred thousand emails sent to the White House at the
behest of Jerry Falwell; in the same year, the Christian Coalition's Rally for
Israel saw speeches from both Republican Congressman Tom DeLay and
the mayor of Jerusalem, while Bush himself sent a video message.[60] In
Britain, Baroness (Shirley) Williams has argued in the House of Lords that
the Bush administration's policy is "propelled to some extent by what I can
only describe as a fundamentalist Christian and fundamentalist Jewish
drive that is almost as powerful as fundamentalist Islam itself."[61]

Finally, in my look at the politics of *Left Behind*, I want to return to its
valorization of the militia movement—the only force, you will remember,

that remained loyal to the U.S. President Gerald Fitzhugh, who informs Rayford that "patriotic militia forces in the U.S. were determined to take action before it was too late."[62] Rayford "recalled not liking the militias, not understanding them, assuming them criminals. But that had been when the American government was also their enemy. Now they were allies of lame duck United States President Gerald Fitzhugh, and their enemy was Rayford's enemy."[63] Here, LaHaye and Jenkins really are playing with fire, as the militia movements are deeply interconnected with the American far right. Famously, Oklahoma bombers Timothy McVeigh and Terry Nichols were members, or at least associate members, of the Northern Michigan Regional Militia (now thankfully dissolved). McVeigh's reading material included Andrew MacDonald's far-right novel *The Turner Diaries* (1978), which gives an account of the bombing of an FBI building in Washington, killing seven hundred; when the FBI raided Nichols's house, they found a copy of another book by MacDonald, the vigilante novel *Hunter* (1989). MacDonald was the pseudonym of William Pierce, a major ideologue in the American Nazi Party and later the leader of the far-right splinter group the National Alliance. The protagonist of *The Turner Diaries*, Earl Turner, comes to believe that "We are truly the instruments of God in the fulfillment of His Grand Design."[64] My own copy of *Hunter* closes with an advertisement for its publisher, National Vanguard Books:

> Many books that are interesting and important to Whites are not available through conventional booksellers because their publishers are not listed in *Books in Print*, and they are not carried by wholesalers or distributors. In some cases they come from "underground" publishers. National Vanguard Books carries over 600 hard-to-find books and tapes, including *White Power* by George Lincoln Rockwell [founder of the American Nazi Party], *The Talmud Unmasked*, *You Gentiles*, *The Secret Relationship Between Blacks and Jews*, *Gun Control in Germany*, *Stuka Pilot*, *Knights of the Reich*, *Protocols of the Learned Elders of Zion*, *Did Six Million Really Die?*, *The Secret of the Runes*, *Mein Kampf*, *The Immigration Mystique*, *The Rising Tide of Color*, and *The Reconstruction Trilogy*.[65]

Perhaps unwittingly, their championing of the militias also connects LaHaye and Jenkins to Christian Identity, the religious arm of the far right. There are important doctrinal differences between the evangelicals and Christian Identity, particularly insofar as the latter movement has come to reject dispensational theology and, crucially, the rapture—which they reject on what can best be called grounds of machismo, since as violent fascistic psychos they want to stick around for the last battle and slug it out *mano a mano* with the antichrist. No respectable right-wing God would let his supporters miss out on the action: "Our God," said Norman Olson, the leader of the Michigan Militia, "is not a wimp. . . . He's the God of righteousness and wrath. Our way of looking at God and country is not passive Christianity."[66]

"The militias of the 1990s," according to Michael Barkun, ". . . constitute not so much a departure from as an extension of ideas that circulated widely in the [Christian] Identity-radical right milieu in the two preceding decades." As Barkun argues, an important foundational text for Christian Identity is the Zionist conspiracy novel *When? A Prophetical Fiction of the Near Future*, published in Vancouver in 1944 under the auspices of the fundamentally benign British-Israel movement. However, clearly written under the influence of *The Protocols of the Elders of Zion*, *When?* presents a Zionist conspiracy by Ashkenazic Jews, the sons of Cain, whose father was not Adam but Satan. From here comes the central Christian Identity tenet, that the Jews were created by the devil, with whom they are still in league. The pseudonymous author of *When?* is "H. Ben Judah": it is surely an accident, is it not, that *Left Behind*'s Jewish intellectual should be called Tsion Ben Judah—or, as he says to Buck, "You may call me Zion."[67]

To conclude: the *Left Behind* series is clearly the foremost contemporary example of what James A. Morone has described as the classic American discursive form, the jeremiad, a lament against the vices of the world, that has characterized America's traditional and continuing engagement with "the politics of sin." "Liberal political history," writes Morone, "underestimates the roaring moral fervor at the soul of American politics."[68] But the *Left Behind* series is also, for me, a powerful manifestation of what the great liberal historian Richard Hofstadter identified as the tradition of anti-intellectualism in American life: the very fact that Nicolae Carpathia is a polyglot polymath makes him inherently suspicious. In the first book, Buck comes early to a realization: "And yet wasn't that exactly what he was—a fool? How could it have taken him so long to learn anything about Christ when he had been a stellar student, an international journalist, a so-called intellectual?" Shortly after, Chloe and Pastor Bruce Barnes discuss her return to Stanford: "'You can go to college right here,' Bruce said. 'Every night at eight.'"[69] Which is precisely what many American children now do: the homeschooling movement now numbers some 2 million families, and is overwhelmingly of the Christian Right; the first homeschooling university, Patrick Henry College in Virginia, insists that all its staff and students "give testimony of personal salvation through Christ alone."[70] "All education," Bob Jones III argued, "is brainwashing. We wash with the pure water of God's Word, and they wash with the polluted waters of the New Age."[71] Like Bob Jones University, Patrick Henry teaches creationism, a creed endorsed by LaHaye and Jenkins, who want "a spike . . . driven through the heart of the theory of evolution. . . . But humanistic man would rather believe the unscientific theory of evolution than the truth of Scripture that God created man and will hold man accountable for the way he lives."[72] Indeed, it seems that a large part of the impetus of the home-schooling movement is to allow evangelical parents to steer their children clear of evolution. In the most technologically advanced nation in the history of the world, I find this terrifying. The evolutionary biologist Stephen Jay Gould has suggested that the creationism debate was not fundamentally *about* religion, since here "the great majority of professional clergy and religious scholars stand *on the same side* with the great majority of scientists," but rather it was about politics, defending the First Amendment "against the imposition of any specific theological doctrine, especially such a partisan and minority view, upon the science curricula of public schools."[73] But I fear that the great Harvard intellectual had not bargained on the 62 million readers of *Left Behind*, nor perhaps on George W. Bush; and now, alas, it is too late.

Hofstadter writes:

> It is to certain peculiarities of American religious life—above all to its lack of firm institutional establishments hospitable to intellectuals and to the competitive sectarianism of its evangelical denominations—that American anti-intellectualism owes much of its strength and pervasiveness.[74]

Hofstadter was writing in the Camelot years of the early 1960s, and his book is a specific response to the McCarthy era of the 1950s. I have to say that almost all of it still rings true today. Hofstadter recognized that the specific manifestation of anti-intellectualism he was confronting was brought about by "the village Protestant culture" of America being "repeatedly shocked by change," the change of modernity. Its response was defensive, as is that of LaHaye and Jenkins, with their retreat into moral absolutes. From the same period of the early 1960s comes Susan Sontag's essay on the aesthetics of catastrophe, "The Imagination of Disaster," written in the wake of the Cuban missile crisis. Sontag suggested that "The lure of such generalized disaster as a fantasy is that it releases one from normal obligations," positing instead an economy of "extreme moral simplification—that is to say, a morally acceptable fantasy where one can give outlet to cruel or at least amoral feelings."[75] Feelings like, for example, the right-wing revenge fantasy of wiping out all liberals.

embracing pessimism and separatism at precisely the moment when their influence is at its highest.

The modern roots of this pessimism can be traced through the reformulation of dispensationalism in the 1970s, when Hal Lindsey, with all his lurid end-time calculus, popularized a fundamental rethinking of the "any-moment" rapture. By pointing to specific events (such as the formation of the state of Israel) as the fulfillment of Scripture, he was abandoning the dominant dispensational view that the next event on the prophetic calendar was the return of Christ, and was refashioning a century and a half of a significant variety of evangelical expectation. Lindsey's work went on to exert immense influence. His most important book, *The Late Great Planet Earth* (1970), sold 28 million copies in the first twenty years after its publication, disseminating widely his expectation of the rapid marginalization of evangelical belief even as his ideas exercised increasing influence on successive presidential administrations.[4] The book made famous Lindsey's 'this generation' claim and provided handy maps for readers to trace the military maneuvers that would culminate in the Russian invasion of Israel and the ensuing Armageddon that, Lindsey argued, had to take place within forty or so years of Israel's founding in 1948. Discussing Matthew 24:34, he strongly implied that the rapture of the church would take place within one "generation"—which he noted, biblically, was a period of forty years—of 1948. Around 1988, in other words, the church would vanish, the antichrist would rise to power, and his final totalitarian government would be erected in readiness for the judgments of God.

This claim, had it been true, might have been understood to have had some very specific implications for public policy in the 1970s and 1980s, but Lindsey was embraced by certain sections of the American political elite, was appointed special advisor to the Reagan administration, and was given opportunities to brief the Israeli government on American affairs. The failure of his claims did nothing to dampen his credibility as a scholar of prophecy, and Lindsey went on to publish a series of related studies, which pointed more often to the errors of others than to those of *The Late Great Planet Earth*. As the example of Lindsey illustrates, prophetic failure can always be explained, and explanations for failure often continue to sell to the faithful. Even Edgar Whisenant, who confirmed Lindsey's mathematics in *88 Reasons Why the Rapture Will Be in 1988* (1988), was able to capitalize on the disappointment of his hopes. Those who had read the 2 million copies of his title sold before his contradiction may have been surprised to find the argument tweaked and repackaged for additional sales in 1989, 1990, 1991, 1992, and 1993.[5] When prophecy is postponed, expectation is revised, and the process of marketing that expectation begins again. But, as Lindsey's recent turn to fiction also shows, the rapture novel has been an inherent part of marketing this revision of eschatological hope.[6]

These trends appear to be at play in a series of novels that has sold over twice as many copies as *The Late Great Planet Earth* in less than one decade, a series whose sales in ten years halve those of *The Lord of the Rings* in fifty.[7] The series epitomizes the paradox that evangelicals embrace despair when their cultural influence is at its height, and evidences the extent to which traditional dispensationalism has changed in the aftermath of the Cold War and in the rapprochement between certain sections of the movement and the Roman Catholic Church. This is the "pathbreaking"[8] "publishing phenomenon"[9] of *Left Behind*.[10]

Since the release of the first novel in 1995, the series has sold over 62 million copies and has generated many more sales of spin-off products, including two films (the first of which, at least until *The Passion of the Christ*, was the most expensive Christian film ever made) and a lively online culture based around the www.leftbehind.com website. *Desecration* (2001), the ninth book in the series, was the best-selling novel in the world in its year of publication, knocking John Grisham from the number-one spot in *Publishers Weekly* for the first time since 1994. Undeniably, while providing vast wealth for its authors—ghostwriter Jerry B. Jenkins and prophecy writer-cum-marriage-counselor Timothy LaHaye—the series has propelled evangelical culture to the attention of the wider American public.[11] The consequences of this marketing success have been startling, leading to entirely new formulations of the previously dichotomous relationship between evangelical and mainstream cultures. Melani McAlister, for example, has argued not only that the novels are in "the mainstream of postmodern American life,"[12] but also that the brand of fundamentalism they represent "might *be* the mainstream of American life."[13] The novels are evidently successful, but the paradox of *Left Behind* is that its narratives can only be plausible when they refuse to admit their popularity. Dispensationalism thrives on the social margins, and its credibility depends on the increasing marginalization of evangelical faith. Rapture novels therefore resonate with this expectation of victimhood: evil forces will exercise increasing control of broadcasting and publishing;[14] press spin will serve the interests of this wicked elite, for "truth is perception";[15] the film industry is their "most important propaganda tool."[16] Thus, the rapture novels typify evangelicalism's suspicion of the cultural mainstream, a suspicion that the success of *Left Behind* hardly justifies but a suspicion that appears to be confirmed by the novels' critical reception. Critical hostility rescues rapture novels from the pervasive popularity that would mark their expectations as implausible and untrue.

Critical responses to the series have been so voluminous that it would now be impossible for Paul Boyer to claim, as he did as recently as 1992, that evangelical millennialism "has received little scholarly attention."[17] As if to soften the blow of this recent and unexpected popularity, these critics regularly deny the centrality of dispensational thinking in American life and mock the cultural norms the novels present. Scholars have responded to the dominance of recent rapture fiction by dismissing the genre as comically ludicrous, or as a destabilizing and chauvinistic threat. The *Times Literary Supplement,* for example, reviewed the final novel in the initial twelve-volume series, *The Glorious Appearing* (2004), and noted the "awkwardness" with which its authors blended "folksy humour, treacly sentiment and religiously justified bloodbaths."[18] Amy Johnson Frykholm has similarly complained that the novels' characters "seem flimsy and ill developed, the plot contrived, and the writing thin."[19] But critics reserve sterner judgment for the series' political and cultural overtones. Although the novels "claim to be about the future . . . they are also very much about the present."[20] Their plots offer "very precise implications" for public policy, for, the *Times Literary Supplement* complained, "the God worshipped by LaHaye and Jenkins considers abortion to be wrong, has it in for gay people and feminists, and opposes most forms of government regulation, especially gun control."[21] Frykholm has agreed, finding in the novels a "conservative, patriarchal, even racist, agenda that mirrors that of the Christian Right."[22] Elsewhere she complains of "a strong conservative agenda, a hostile anti-feminist perspective, hints of anti-Semitism, and an overt homophobia,"[23] and quotes another reviewer's description of the series as "hard-core right-wing paranoid anti-Semitic homophobic misogynistic propaganda."[24]

It seems that the media can only deal with traditional evangelical sentiments by dismissing them as marginal. "Despite extraordinary newspaper and television coverage," McAlister notes, "each account of the *Left Behind* phenomenon finds it necessary to introduce the books to an audience who presumably finds their very existence to be news."[25] Evangelicalism, in these reports, is consistently presented as a novelty. This is despite the fact that "approximately one-third of Americans define themselves as 'born again,'"[26] despite the fact that 49 percent of Americans state their belief in a future antichrist,[27] and despite the fact that 19 percent of Americans believed in 1999 that he was on earth at that moment.[28] Discussions of the *Left Behind* phenomenon almost invariably ignore these statistics and confirm popular evangelical expectations of increasing hostility from the powers that be. The paradox of late-twentieth-century dispensationalism is, as in the nineteenth century, that its adherents embrace apocalyptic pessimism at precisely their moment of greatest cultural power, because the credibility of their hopes depends upon despair; but the irony of the critics responding to this trend is that their representation of the movement as marginal is reaffirming the cultural dichotomies that had been obscured by the crossover success of *Left Behind*. In dismissing the significance of the dispensational movement, critics are both confirming its worst fears and fostering its optimal social conditions. If Jenkins's *Soon* is any guide, this critical hostility might even be the catalyst that will propel some dispensationalists into violent resistance to a politically correct but increasingly repressive regime. Liberal commentators might be more prescient than they realize when they represent the *Left Behind* phenomenon as a potential political doomsday. Like the anti-Christian authorities in one recent rapture novel, they might discover to their cost how beliefs "that the end was near, that Jesus was coming soon" can develop into a "justification for flat-out sedition."[29] Hostility confirms the dispensational worldview, and could turn some adherents violently active.

Of course, rapture fictions—like other aspects of popular culture—exist in a complex relationship with human agency. Rapture fictions may be read passively, for entertainment, but they may also be read actively, as shaping or confirming existing systems of belief. Critics, citing the novels as evidence of a profoundly dangerous moment in American evangelical life, have worried that readers will approach the texts without sufficient critical sense, allowing the series' presuppositions to dominate their own. The novels' social conservatism is understood as dangerous partly because critics do not trust readers to negotiate with the authors' political views. But the audiences of *Left Behind* are more often "assumed . . . than investigated," Frykholm has complained, and her interaction with readers has illustrated something of the variety of their negotiation with the texts.[30] Evangelicals, she insists, respond to rapture fictions with evident irony. The latest such novels at times suggest that this is the way they have been designed to be read: one character in a recent futuristic rapture novel is described as "imitating John Malkovich in *Con Air*."[31] (Will it really be a film classic in 2046?) Frykholm's study of the reception of the novels suggests that rapture fictions are read on their own terms, as fiction, and are not simply understood as a static manifesto for cultural or religious activism in the present.[32] Nevertheless, by totalizing audiences and ignoring readerly negotiation, liberal commentators confirm the marginal status of dispensational believers. This projection of marginality, as has already been noted, tends to reinscribe the cultural dichotomies that the success of *Left Behind* has overcome but that dispensationalists believe will characterize the end of time, thereby running the risk of turning the fiction they abhor into the fact they could hardly imagine.

But it would be a mistake to assume that the rapture novel genre—and its later manifestations—represents the opinions of all dispensational believers. Dispensationalists of various hues are addressing contemporary prophetic interest but continue to negotiate with the ideas the novels raise for discussion. In 2002, for example, Billy Graham's daily syndicated newspaper column featured a letter inquiring whether he believed the antichrist was alive today. His answer was evasive.[33] In the same year, Mark Hitchcock, a writer of pedagogical material in the wider *Left Behind* project, published his answer to the question. Noting that the mark of the beast—666—has been linked to John F. Kennedy, Gorbachev, Reagan, Bill Gates, Windows 95, and even MS-DOS 6.21, Hitchcock claimed that the question could not be answered, as the antichrist would only be revealed after the rapture.[34] Others have more obviously attempted to capitalize on *Left Behind*'s revival of prophetic interest. Salem Kirban's truly dreadful rapture fictions, *666* (1970) and *1000* (1973), were republished in 1998 with covers designed to appeal to the *Left Behind* generation.[35] These novels are among the worst in the genre, but they are also among the most politically significant.[36] Kirban's novels rewrite America's relationship to the antichrist's evil empire in statements that resonate with modern audiences attuned to current affairs. In *Left Behind*, the American president is betrayed by his military, which supports the claims of the UN-backed antichrist, and a nuclear exchange decimates the population centers: this is why the Bible appears to say nothing of America's future destiny. America is neutralized, but, as the Tribulation Force discovers, is still the home of the brave. In Kirban's fiction, on the other hand, the antichrist's empire includes the United States.[37] Photographs illustrating his novels show characters being branded with "666" inside American churches (although careful inspection shows that the "666" would be reversed on the candidate's brow). The apocalyptic atmosphere created by the phenomenal success of *Left Behind*, the significance of the restaging of the United States in Kirban's republished fiction, and the pollsters' claim that one-fifth of all Americans believe in the present existence of the antichrist could therefore signal that a significant element of the American population are prepared to imagine that within forty years the United States will cease to exist as a sovereign power, that its establishment will capitulate to totalitarian evil, and that evangelicals, along with all other religious adherents, will be subject to brutal persecution. This sense of fear and protracted danger is immanent in Jenkins's latest work.

After *Left Behind*

Jenkins and LaHaye have responded with some ambivalence to their series' unanticipated success. Despite a continuing strong media profile—the writers were hailed on the cover of *Newsweek* as recently as May 24, 2004—their writing partnership appears to be ending. *Left Behind* readers are now expecting further prequels and sequels to the original twelve-volume series, but additional writers have already been recruited, and the *Left Behind* franchise has generated a number of new series. Several of these series appear deliberately to capitalize on readers' expectations, but others challenge them in significant ways. Two of the new series—the titles *End of State* (2003), by Neesa Hart, and *Apocalypse Dawn* (2003), by Mel Odom—operate within the original *Left Behind* scenario and are actually advertised as being "based on the best-selling *Left Behind* series." The plots of their political and military thrillers refer to the same basic chronology and major characters as the earlier works. Jenkins's book *Soon* (2003), another *New York Times* best seller, focuses on life before the rapture, but offers a more significant revision of *Left Behind*'s earlier paradigm.

Soon suggests that *Left Behind* never happened. It is a futuristic thriller that extrapolates its description of a dystopian and humanistic totalitarianism from actual letters to *Time* magazine that a frontispiece reproduces. The novel imagines what will happen if *Left Behind* is wrong and Christ does not come back in the immediate future. It ignores the current prophetic revival, evidenced in the millions of sales of rapture novels, and describes a future for evangelicalism against the backdrop of a series of religious wars springing from the 2001 attacks on the World Trade Center and the invasion of Iraq in 2003. From these incidents, the novel projects an escalation of the Israeli-Palestinian conflict and terrorist strikes throughout North America and Europe in 2008. As these wars of religion intensified, "the globe was ablaze with attacks, counter-attacks, reprisals, and finally, an all-out nuclear war that most thought signaled the end of the world."[38] The war brought the United States to the verge of extinction: a coalition of Muslim nations destroyed Washington, D.C.,[39] and a North Korean ballistic missile, "the largest warhead ever to land on American soil,"[40] obliterated the Pentagon. Worldwide, bombs "snuffed out tens of millions of lives" and, by literally splitting China in two, generated a tidal wave "a million times more destructive" than the Hiroshima explosion,[41] a tsunami that "engulfed all of Hong Kong Island, swamped Taiwan with hundreds of feet of water, raced to the Philippine Sea and the East China Sea, obliterated Japan and Indonesia, swept into the Northwest Pacific Basin and the Japan Trench," "swallowed" Hawaii, and killed "thousands more" in California.[42] The unprecedented scale of its devastation brought a sudden end to all religious wars, as the battling faithful realized that global destruction was no longer a divine monopoly. Extremists abandoned the religious convictions that had almost ended humanity, and nations embraced a world purged of sectarian terror. America was reorganized into seven regions: Atlantica (ten former states in the Northeast, with New York as the capital); Columbia (nine southeastern states, with Washington, D.C., as capital); Gulfland (Texas and five "nearby states," with Houston as capital); Sunterra (Southern California, Arizona, and New Mexico, with Los Angeles as capital); Rockland (seven states, with Las Vegas as capital); Pacifica (northern California, Alaska and four northwestern states, with San Francisco as capital); and Heartland (ten midwestern states, with Chicago as capital).[43] The regime inaugurated "the most repressive time in human history—when world governments have not only banned religion but are also technologically capable of enforcing that ban by spying on every citizen."[44] The state is exalted above the individual,[45] but the nation-state has been largely superseded by the UN-sponsored new world order whose international currency the American states adopt.[46] As if to symbolize the diminution of statehood, the American flag now displays seven stars, in a biblical allusion that the novel unsuccessfully extends.[47] Under the shadow of the UN, the new world is "an intellectual, humanistic society that eschewed both religion and war."[48] To signal the importance of the world's new humanistic beginning, the international government, based in Switzerland, renames the calendar, with January 1, 2010 beginning the year 1 P3 (post-WWIII).[49]

Thirty-six years later, in the equivalent of 2046, Paul Stepola is given the responsibility of rooting out the menace of the American Christian underground. As a special agent with the National Peace Organization (the successor to the FBI and CIA), Stepola capitalizes on the specialist knowledge gained through his doctoral studies in religion. Shocked by revelations that both his father and his former military commander were believers, Stepola embarks on a spiritual journey that leads him inexorably toward evangelical conversion. But the interests of the evangelicalism he investigates challenge his expectations just as much as they challenge the expectations of rapture fiction readers. These evangelicals—"the Watchmen"[50]—are an underground militia, headquartered in "a city beneath a city" somewhere in the northern states,[51] driven by their belief that the miracles tormenting the administration are signs of the second coming, and prepared, much more than the characters of *Left Behind*, to be subversives, to take lives in order to secure their own. Stepola's conversion develops his character, and, like Rayford Steele in the earlier series, he struggles with temptation to engage in an extramarital affair.[52] But he battles on to eventually "sense the mind of God," which provides him with a new mission, "to motivate every underground believer he could find to pray and plead with God to show Himself to the enemy."[53] His active suppression of the Christian underground leads Stepola ultimately to its defense. His initial ideas of active resistance give way to the quest for a miracle, a quest that has an emphasis on prayer that seems fundamentally incompatible with the globetrotting, empire-building economic resistance of *Left Behind*'s survivors, the Tribulation Force.[54]

Rewriting America

Stepola's concentration on the fate of Christian America mirrors that of the novel as a whole. *Soon*'s narrative is based on a fundamental rethinking of the relationship between evangelicals and the American establishment and assumes that, within forty years, the influence of evangelical prophecy in the Reagan and George W. Bush administrations will have reached its antithesis. In *Soon*, Americans are as patriotic as ever, but this new patriotism is stripped of its religious content.[55] In its depiction of America, *Soon* stands as the logical outcome of a longer trend in evangelical eschatology.

Scholars have often attempted to discover America's role in prophecy.[56] Prophetic experts in the seventeenth and eighteenth centuries tended to identify the New World as possessing unique millennial agency—Jonathan Edwards, for example, wondered whether the "awakening" he witnessed might be heralding the millennium on American soil.[57] Throughout the nineteenth and twentieth centuries, as dispensationalism began to dominate the evangelical imagination, America lost its prophetic identity, and its end-time role steadily diminished.[58] The *Left Behind* novels worked on the presupposition that the United States had no role in biblical prophecy.[59]

Soon marries this changing prophetic perspective with America's new geopolitical situation. *Left Behind* was criticized for its international naïveté (for example, in its treatment of the Palestinian problem),[60] but *Soon* avoids this charge by neglecting international contexts entirely: there is no outside world to be concerned about. Cold War prophecy writers had imagined a bipolar political world—East versus West—in a dualism that mirrored the conflict's basic moral division.[61] The longevity of these prophetic polarities meant that this geopolitical analysis would have been familiar to such dispensational teachers as Donald Barnhouse in the 1950s, C. I. Scofield in the 1910s, and J. N. Darby in the 1840s. This tradition is completely upended in *Soon*. America has lost its sacred status, but the moral bipolarity of the Cold War is now projected onto a single nation. *Soon* is, in this sense, the ultimate post-Cold War fiction. America has been stripped of its prophetic significance at the same time as it has lost its moral authority as the counterweight to atheistic communism. The moral dichotomy that characterized Cold War geopolitics is now projected onto an exclusively American canvas.

In stark contrast to the uncomplicated patriotism of a great deal of American dispensational writing, America itself is now evangelicalism's eschatological "other." At times the parallels with Cold War communism are explicit.

> He turned back to his computer and scrolled. "Over a hundred years ago Russia closed almost all its churches and disposed of more than forty thousand clergy. They turned city churches into museums and country churches into barns or apartments. . . . What happened in Russia and China and Romania decades ago could re-emerge here, right under our noses."[62]

122 After *Left Behind*—The Paradox of Evangelical Pessimism

But there are hints in the novel that the nation is still culturally divided. The population divides into the familiar contours of the "50:50 nation," with "half" the population appearing prepared to consider the possibility that the strange events which so perplex the authorities are the miracles the Christians claim.[63] This intra-American moral polarity seems to invite comparison between the geography of *Soon*'s plot and the overwhelmingly southern distribution of rapture fiction readers. The action in *Soon* is almost entirely urban and is notably concentrated in Chicago, Washington, D.C., Las Vegas, California, and on a single Texas oil well. The novel's apocalyptic scenarios therefore tend to avoid the Bible Belt and those southern states where, polls have discovered, most readers of rapture fictions live.[64] Undoubtedly, this urban focus reflects traditional evangelical suspicions of the city,[65] but also provides a mechanism for prophecy believers to imagine the outpouring of divine judgments on those parts of the United States that are least receptive to their message. Perhaps Jenkins is identifying the United State's traditional political divisions with the future prophetic dichotomy his dispensational readers expect.

Thus, *Soon* represents changing expectations of America and shows Jenkins imagining the return of evangelicals to the social, cultural, and political margins. The novel is oblivious to the success of *Left Behind*, as it had to be if Jenkins's writing were not to veer from dispensationalism's orthodox center. His commitment to dispensationalism's traditional narrative patterns—which consistently emphasize the increasing marginalization and eventual persecution of the faithful—demands the deliberate elision of the success of the earlier series. As *Soon* illustrates, dispensationalists need to be alienated because they expect to be alienated at the end of the age, and they must always believe they could be living in that period.

Rewriting Modernity

One of the most consistent fears in the rapture novel genre, and the dispensationalism from which it emerged, has been the fear of modernity. Rapture fictions regularly worry about the technological invasion of the body, often by computer chips identifying the individual to the regime or by the individual's being branded with the mark of the beast. These worries play on fears of diminishing privacy but move beyond that typically modern concern to the ultimate concern that the antichrist will destabilize the last bastion of freedom—a coherent and independent subjectivity. For Kirban, for example, the tribulation would involve young people looking like "men from outer space with computers plugged into their heads."[66] Fortunately, for readers of rapture fiction, this invasion of individuality is regularly limited to the tribulation, when the antichrist would wield his nefarious technological power.

Significantly, in *Soon*, independent subjectivity ends long before the rapture. The regime the novel describes has citizens wearing "ID biochips" beneath the skin.[67] These 'biochips' are not, as in earlier rapture novels, the mark of the beast, but like the mark of the beast they do serve the purposes of an apparently all-powerful totalitarian system. *Soon* echoes earlier fictions in describing the administration's technology, which allows the government to spy on every citizen.[68] Individuals are subject to such invasive security precautions as iris scans and locks coded to specific sequences of DNA.[69] Perhaps most significantly of all, individuals carry "molar receptors," which allow teeth to receive radio and TV signals directly into the head.[70] After hearing "a tone in his head," the character can hold his fingers together to create the effect of a replying microphone.[71]

In many ways, the technological world of *Soon* is more frightening than that of traditional rapture fiction, in that it extrapolates the technology of the tribulation into normal time. Yet *Soon* seems less ambivalent about technical modernity than does *Left Behind*. In the earlier series, believers took advantage of the Internet, as the only medium free from government control. In *Soon*, it offers similar possibilities.[72] But believers also take advantage of their biometric implants.[73] However, realizing that "electronic equipment will become useless at some point,"[74] they resort to the traditional methods of letterpress printing to begin their "mass-communications program."[75] Taking on the administration's oppressive media hegemony, believers use technology, but prepare for its ultimate passing. The novel's dispensationalism is ultimately figured, like millennialism more generally, as a reaction against progress.[76]

Rewriting Evangelicalism

This reaction against progress feeds into that other basic trope in evangelical writing: ecclesiastical primitivism. In *Soon*, persecution takes believers back to their original situation. The recordings of the Bible that Stepola listened to during his blindness "told of constant persecution. . . . Paul was amazed that he had totally forgotten that the early Christians were also persona non grata with the government and had to meet in secret and worship virtually underground."[77] Persecution, quite literally, was offering believers the chance of a new beginning.

There is every sense that this new beginning offers believers the chance to meet without denominational divisions. Rapture fiction—and dispensationalism more generally—has traditionally inscribed very specific denominational boundaries. While dispensationalists generally deny the old Protestant identification of the pope as antichrist, the Catholic Church is regularly identified as the Whore of Babylon, dressed in purple and scarlet, and drunk with the blood of the saints (Rev. 17:4-6). While the Scofield

Bible—and LaHaye's earlier writing—was prepared to ascribe all manner of evil to the papacy, *Left Behind* described latter-day Catholicism in much more ambiguous ways. The series' website, for example, heralded *The Passion of the Christ* (director Mel Gibson, 2004), despite its overtly Catholic sympathies. Nevertheless, despite the criticism of American Catholic bishops, Jenkins and LaHaye appear to have abandoned the traditional evangelical and dispensational hostility to the Catholic Church. In *Left Behind*, the reforming pope, John XXIV, is among the raptured, perhaps because of his embracing neo-Lutheran reform; in later books in the series, entire congregations of Catholics are raptured, without any indication that they were closet evangelicals.[78] Balancing this affirmation of ecumenical rapprochement is the novels' insistence that John XXIV's replacement, Pontifex Maximus Peter Mathews, is named supreme pontiff of Enigma Babylon One World Faith, and is identified as the eschatological "false prophet."[79] Confirming traditional fears, this new one-world religion is initially centered on the Vatican.[80] Thus *Left Behind* balances its suggestion that some Catholics might be true believers with an affirmation of dispensationalism's traditional expectation that the Roman Catholic church will play a central role in the antichrist's rule. But, in *Soon*, evangelical attitudes to Catholicism are further rewritten. No longer is the Vatican the focus of apocalyptic fear: along with other world landmarks, it, too, is destroyed by "extremists."[81] Catholics, along with people of other faiths alike, are the victims of this new administration.[82] Indeed, the regime's strongly antireligious bias raises the question of where the predicted one-world religion will come from in a world where religion is illegal.

But it also raises the question of what kind of Christians *Soon*'s evangelicals are. The issue was plausibly avoided in *Left Behind*: classical dispensational orthodoxy teaches that those who come to faith after the rapture (*Left Behind* claims, incorrectly, that the Bible terms these individuals "tribulation saints")[83] are not, strictly speaking, part of the church, and should not, therefore, celebrate the sacraments, those monumental indicators of denominational affiliation. (Rayford's expression of thankfulness for being part of "the church" is a curious slip.)[84] For this reason, the *Left Behind* novels understandably avoid any references to baptism or the Lord's Supper. But there is less excuse for this in *Soon*: its plot is set before the rapture, but, like *Left Behind*, it shows underground fellowships enjoying Bible study while avoiding their sacramental privileges. This extremely "low church" atmosphere allows the narrative to continue without pausing to explain or choose between, for example, the theologies of infant or adult baptism—and therefore allows the narrative to carry the sympathies of a wide range of Christian readers. It might even be possible to argue that this absence of sacraments is related in some way to the absence of any clerical or priestly authority, and is related in some way to the Catholic sensitivities of some readers.

This possibility of post-Reformation rapprochement seems to reflect the progress of Charles Colson and R. J. Neuhaus's ecumenical initiative, *Evangelicals and Catholics Together: The Christian Mission in the Third Millennium* (1994),[85] but perhaps also indicates a growing recognition of the parallels between dispensational and Catholic eschatology. The *Catechism of the Catholic Church* (1994) parallels dispensational pessimism in refusing to countenance the triumph of the church in history:

> The kingdom will be fulfilled . . . not by a historic triumph of the Church through a progressive ascendancy, but only by God's victory over the final unleashing of evil.[86]

This "final unleashing of evil" bears an uncanny resemblance to the dispensational tribulation:

> Before Christ's second coming the Church must pass through a final trial that will shake the faith of many believers. The persecution that accompanies her pilgrimage on earth will unveil the "mystery of iniquity" in the form of a religious deception offering men an apparent solution to their problems at the price of apostasy from the truth. The supreme religious deception is that of the Antichrist, a pseudomessianism by which man glorifies himself in place of God and of his Messiah come in the flesh.[87]

Furthermore, the *Catechism* suggests, Christ's coming "could be accomplished at any moment."[88]

Remarkably, the *Catechism*'s statements demonstrate that on the issues of the gospel's failure to reform the world, the futurity of the antichrist and final tribulation, and in the imminence of the second coming, dispensationalism has more in common with Catholic orthodoxy than it has with the eschatological teachings of traditional Protestant postmillennialism. Simultaneously, as the rise of humanism forces evangelicals and Catholics into cooperative social engagement, the possibility of an overture to Rome may explain the remarkable absence of a theology of the church in either the *Left Behind* novels or in *Soon*. In these novels, evangelicalism has itself been rewritten. Recent rapture novels take evangelicals beyond their notoriously low ecclesiologies into a situation where the church itself can hardly be said to exist.

Rewriting Dispensationalism?

As these examples attest, recent rapture novels have popularized a significant revision of traditional evangelicalism. The recent novels can be

located on the opposite side of the parabola that saw rapture novels conform to a stricter dispensationalism as the genre developed.[89] Sydney Wat-
son's wider evangelical sympathies were, for example, narrowed by the
impact of the rise of dispensational scholasticism in the mid-twentieth century. Rapture novelists in the 1970s, like Salem Kirban, or Dr. Frederick A.
Tatford, one-time director of the U.K. Atomic Energy Authority, notice-
ably tightened up their prophetic scenarios to conform to the expectations
created by the immense success of *The Late Great Planet Earth*.[90] But the
end of the Cold War challenged many of the assumptions these novels presupposed and demanded that the rapture be rewritten. *Left Behind* made a
valiant attempt to address the end of communism. *Soon* further develops
the trend by abandoning the East-West geopolitical dichotomy that so
many earlier rapture fictions had presupposed and by focusing its moral
bipolarity on American soil. The radical restructuring of dispensationalism
that began in *Left Behind* has been significantly developed in *Soon*.[91]

Violence

Ironically, this rewritten evangelicalism seems to grow in its capacity for
violence as it loses its theological edge. Evangelicals are taking their place
in a wider Christianity that seems increasingly distanced from the American mainstream. This newly conceived disjunction between evangelicalism
and wider American culture explains *Soon*'s propensity toward violence.

Throughout their history, rapture novels have been powerfully ambivalent about the morality—and practical implications—of violence. *Left Behind*
played with this ambiguity for narrative effect. At times the novels appear to
justify murder when it would further the determined ends of history:

> Buck hung his head. What kind of a soldier was he? How could he
> be expected to fight in this cosmic battle of good versus evil if he
> couldn't handle killing the enemy?[92]

Elsewhere, Rayford prayed for the "privilege" of torturing and killing the
antichrist, though he knew that his death would only make him stronger
and more satanic: dispensationalism teaches that the antichrist will be resurrected after an assassination to even greater power.[93] Tsion Ben Judah,
normally the voice of reason and authority, also advanced the theory: "I
believe we are at war. In the heat of battle, killing the enemy has never been
considered murder."[94] Little wonder that the antichrist's elite, discussing
Rayford's ethic of murder, considered his grasp of situation ethics thus:
"Maybe he convinces himself it's a holy war. Then I guess anything goes."[95]
Rayford certainly has to undergo a rude awakening. Buck was chagrined
with his father-in-law's morality: "We don't play them, lie to them, cheat

them, steal from them, blackmail them. We love them. We plead with them."[96] Even in the tribulation, evangelicals had to be loving their enemies and trying to win them to Christ.

Nevertheless, the suggestion that a "holy war" means "anything goes" certainly reinforces audience suspicions. Although Rayford eventually seems to dismiss the idea, it does appear to underpin the remarkable movement in Jenkins's writing from his depiction of apocalyptic as exodus (*Left Behind*) to apocalyptic as battle (*Soon*).[97] Despite debates about the relationship between millennialism and violence—and the relationship between prophetic beliefs and behavior has been described as "unfathomable"[98]—scholars agree that dispensational groups have demonstrated "no proclivity" for violent action.[99] Significantly, however, characters in *Soon* remember the violence of Christian fundamentalists in the first decade of the new millennium, and worry about the possibility of an armed evangelical rising:

> . . . religious extremists . . . persecuted homosexuals, assassinated abortion doctors . . . and bombed stem-cell research labs. . . . And after the terrorist attacks of '05, it was the extremists who defied the tolerance laws and rioted, killing Muslims.[100]

The moral ambivalence of these references is clarified in the novel's depiction of the Watchmen, those believers organizing "Operation Soon," a project designed to spread the illegal news that the events the government dismisses as terrorist attacks are actually divinely wrought miracles heralding the imminent return of Christ. The believers construct a massive underground complex in an abandoned mine, post armed guards to maintain security, and, if necessary, kill intruders. The location of the shelter would be concealed by the guards' removing the corpse to the surface, "putting it in the vehicle it showed up in, and moving that vehicle somewhere so the body would not be traced to the mine."[101] Stepola was shocked by the revelation:

> "How do you justify that?"
>
> "We don't, Paul. We pray it never happens."[102]

Soon appears to show believers in different states responding in different ways to the possible necessity of violence. The physical resistance of the Watchmen in the Northeast is paralleled by the eventual pacifism of believers in the Southwest. In Los Angeles, military intervention meant that believers there were dying on a scale elsewhere unseen.[103] Under Stepola's guidance, believers discuss the possibility of disrupting the city's water supply.[104] The idea is later abandoned, and the believers issue a brochure that "stated unequivocally that the underground Christians in Los Angeles were not armed and never planned to be."[105] Nevertheless, as the novel's closing pages describe a final miracle—evidently designed to lead readers into the next installment—the novel suggests that the event would be the first of many that would be known, overground, as the "Christian Guerrilla War."[106] Once again, *Soon* moves beyond the expectations of audiences familiar with the resonances of *Left Behind*.

The Significance of Violence

Scholars of millennial studies suggest that the violent outbreaks of millennial groups are linked to a complex of isolation, paranoia, aspirations for dominion, and mismanagement of the crisis.[107] Specialists in millennial studies also argue that a basic difference exists between those groups that are organized militarily and those that assume a violent posture.[108] Whatever their inherent proclivity, prophetic movements "pose a fundamental challenge to the established social order and hence are in high tension with it," and are most dangerous when that resistance is sacralized.[109] Richard Landes has proposed a typology that explains millennial agency as a matter of timing.[110] He distinguishes "normal" from "apocalyptic" time and argues that millennial groups tend to remain passive and often quietist until their sense of apocalyptic time is triggered. In the case of dispensationalism, normal time continues until the rapture, at which point the prophetic calendar recommences and normal activities end.

The significance of *Soon* is that it completely overturns this chronological division even as it suggests the sacral function of violence. Using Landes's typology, *Soon* shows Jenkins moving from a depiction of passive fundamentalism in this age, represented in *Left Behind* as normal life before the rapture, to a depiction of violent fundamentalism in this age, represented in *Soon* as believers arming themselves in response to mounting persecution. The remarkable thing about this persecution is that it seems to mirror the totalitarianism that dispensationalists expect of the antichrist in the tribulation period. In other words, *Soon* reimagines normal time and imports into the age before the rapture the conditions that many dispensationalists expect after the rapture. It requires its characters to reorientate themselves to an American establishment that bears in this age the characteristics of the totalitarianism of the tribulation. *Soon* shows, therefore, evangelicals facing conditions in America that older dispensational theologians argued they would never see, and developing their sense of responsibility accordingly. Jenkins's characters are radicalized, taking up arms against their government. Through its characters—and for its readers—*Soon* dramatizes growing pessimism about the short-term future of evangelicals in the United States.

This pessimism seems to draw on the recent experiences of other sepa-
ratist religious minorities. Confirming dispensationalism's proclivity for
conspiracy theories, *Soon* hints that the evangelical future will parallel the
Branch Davidian past. Shadows of Waco engulf the novel's description of
government forces besieging a religious community it suspects of being
"heavily armed and dangerous" and engaged in "anti-American subversive
activities":

> We surrounded the place before dawn, awakened their leadership,
> and ordered them to stand down and surrender peacefully. . . . One
> minute after the deadline, they opened fire on our forces, and we
> were forced to defend ourselves. . . . We were forced to retreat as they
> bombed and burned the buildings and killed themselves.[111]

Of course, contrary to this report, the believers had not committed suicide. Suicide was an unnecessary effort when government forces were lin-
ing up to extinguish your life for you. Suspicion of the state is confirmed
by its evidently destructive intentions. As Jenkins's audience imagines the
necessary militarization of Christians in "normal time," their hesitance
about violence in their own time might begin to change.

Painting this picture of suspicious retreat, *Soon* represents the culting of
dispensationalism. *Soon* presents evangelicals taking on the trappings of
traditional cult stereotypes, engaging in illegal and underground activity,
and demonstrating an alarming propensity for violence. The novel abandons traditional dispensational expectations of this age as excessively optimistic and imagines, in contrast to previous dispensational writers, nuclear
war and unprecedented worldwide destruction entirely unpredicted by
Scripture. *Soon* sets the future free from biblical controls and opens up the
possibility of the triumph of worldwide atheism under the United Nations.
Soon is a rapture novel that breaks from genre archetypes by exploring the
eschatological significance of normal time. And in normal time, evangelicals—the novel's characters—become a cult.

Conclusion

This emphasis on normal time—before the rapture—perhaps challenges the
description of this novel as "rapture fiction." The novel's cover subtitles the
book "the beginning of the end." But the novel begins with expectations of
the second coming, announced in the letter Stepola discovers was written
by his father, and the rapture itself, first mentioned on page 201, is its
expected conclusion.[112] *Soon*, as a title, is a reference to the imminence not
just of the second coming of Christ, but also to the social conditions the
novel describes. *Soon* is therefore a powerful dramatization of one possible

evangelical response to the cultural logic of late capitalism. The novel itself, as "a remarkable mainstreaming of evangelical pop culture,"[113] depends for its success upon the very conditions it disdains.

But market forces are at play. Like the other spin-off products, *Soon* capitalizes on its audience's "ever-widening circles of consumption."[114] The novel's cover highlights Jenkins as the "bestselling author of the *Left Behind* series." But just as *Left Behind* reinvented the paradigms of earlier rapture fictions, *Left Behind* itself is reinvented by *Soon*.[115] But *Soon*'s totalizing demands are just as clear. Jenkins does not lead a movement; he only addresses a reading community. Readers are free to negotiate their relationship to his novels as they follow his imagination into a world of increasing paranoia, increasing separation from the social mainstream, and increasing suspicion of national and international government. Like *Left Behind*, *Soon* demonstrates that the rapture novel genre, and the Christian underground it depicts, is "not a movement for fence straddlers."[116]

This very committedness suggests the risk of critical disdain. That unsparing criticism that represents the novels as marginal and extreme is in danger of constructing the apocalyptic scenarios it describes with such distaste. Critical hostility runs the risk of turning Jenkins's sympathetically ironic reading community into a fully fledged apocalyptic movement. It risks becoming the agent of mismanagement that millennial scholars identify as the catalyst that turns passive movements active. By pushing evangelicals to the cultural margins, it risks confirming their fears and constructing them as a potentially violent underground cult. *Soon* has shown that apocalyptic time, with all its unusual norms, can exist before the rapture. Critical hostility risks becoming the trigger for the movement it abhors.

The paradox is already there. As in the nineteenth century, dispensational believers are opting for pessimism at their most culturally pervasive moment. For this paradox to be followed by irony—the irony that liberal criticism constructs the apocalyptic moment it dreads—would be the greatest tragedy of all.

Chapter Eight

The Davidian Seventh-day Adventists and Millennial Expectation, 1959–2004

Kenneth G. C. Newport

Between February and April 1993, the Branch Davidian movement near Waco, Texas, suffered a truly catastrophic sequence of events. By their conclusion some eighty members of the movement were dead, including, of course, the leader and prophet of the community, David Koresh. While "Branch Davidianism" survives as a tradition today, and indeed there is now a new church on the Waco "Mount Carmel" site, it is hanging by a thread. Soon, one suspects, the Branch Davidians will be no more. We will have seen the end of a religion.[1]

The complete story of the Branch Davidians—their origins, theology, development, and fate—is a long and troubled one, and those from the scholarly community who have so far discussed it have concentrated almost exclusively upon only a small part of the bigger picture. That part is, of course, the period of the siege (February 28 to April 19, 1993) and the months in the run-up to it. Some such as Tabor and Gallagher have done more,[2] but there is much in the history of this tradition that has been left unresearched, particularly with reference to the early history of the movement and to the general theology of the Seventh-day Adventist/ Davidian/Branch Davidian trajectory as a whole. Here an attempt is made

to fill one of the more glaring gaps: namely, the history and theology of the
Davidian Seventh-day Adventist movement (*not* the "Branch" Davidian
movement) from around 1959 to the present day.

The Davidian Seventh-day Adventists

As is well known, the Davidian movement began with the prophetic ministry of Victor T. Houteff, a Bulgarian emigrant to the United States who,
in 1929, was disfellowshiped from the Seventh-day Adventist church over
a dispute regarding the correct interpretation of biblical prophecy. After
first gathering a group of followers in California, in 1935 Houteff moved
the community to Waco, Texas. From their "Mount Carmel" headquarters
they began their central task: the gathering of the 144,000 (that is, those
believed by Houteff to be spoken of in Rev. 11:2; 14:1-3) who were destined
to inhabit the newly restored, literal "Kingdom of David" (hence the eventual addition of the name "Davidian" to this group). This Kingdom,
argued Houteff, would be based not in Waco, but in Jerusalem.³

While Houteff had been disfellowshiped from the mainstream Seventh-
day Adventist Church, he nevertheless took the view that it was the remnant
church of God. In fact, so Houteff believed, all of the 144,000 destined to
inhabit the new Davidian Kingdom were to be drawn not from the churches
in general, still less the world, but from the ranks of the Seventh-day Adventists. In short, Houteff believed it to be the task of the Davidians (or the
"Shepherd's Rod Movement," as they were then known) to call out these
elect ones from a church that had now slipped into corruption. Missionary
activity was hence restricted to Adventists alone. (This is a view that continued into the Branch Davidian tradition, a theological fact that explains
the near-exclusive concentration by Koresh on the conversion of Seventh-
day Adventists.)

Houteff was held in great esteem by his followers, whose numbers soon
multiplied. Indeed, as is so often with these movements, it soon became
the case that the proclaimer became the proclaimed, and even during his
lifetime the view began to gain wide acceptance among the Davidians that
Houteff was himself the antitypical King David whose destiny it was to lead
the 144,000 into the new (literal) Kingdom.⁴

Houteff's destiny, however, was more Mosaic than antitypical Davidic,
for in 1955 he died without entering the promised land. This, of course,
raised huge problems for the community he had led, and a number of different reactions emerged. One of these came to be focused upon an individual who, already by the time of Houteff's death, had been making
claims to the leadership of the movement, and had in fact already moved
a small band of followers to the Holy Land to establish a small community
of believers as a visible sign of what was to come—the literal Kingdom of

David. The name of that individual was Ben Roden, though by the end
of the 1950s his letters and tracts often bore his "spiritual name": "the
man whose name is the Branch," or simply, "the Branch."[5] After a struggle lasting eighteen years, Roden and his formidable wife Lois, David
Koresh's immediate predecessor, gained legal control of the community's
property, which by now had moved away from the original site purchased
by Houteff to a different location some fifteen or so miles from Waco centre. The "Branch" Davidians remain there on this "new" Mount Carmel
to this day, though, as has been noted already, their longer-term fate now
seems very uncertain.[6]

In this chapter, however, we are not concerned with this "Branch" trajectory of Davidianism, important as it eventually turned out to be, but
with the development of the group that, following Houteff's death, did *not*
join with the Branch movement but went in a separate direction. Today
these "Davidian Seventh-day Adventists" have themselves fragmented, and
it is impossible to be sure just how many members of the various factions
there are: it is certainly hundreds; it could be thousands. The movement
as a whole is very cautious in its contact with nonbelievers, which may
partly be due to the events of 1993 and the fear that the "Davidians" will
be wrongly associated with the "Branch Davidians" (as indeed they have
been). But it is also the case that theological contact with non-Seventh-day
Adventists is of only limited interest to members of this community, since
the original Houteffian view prevails in most of Davidianism that the
work of spreading the message of the Kingdom is for Seventh-day Adventists only, and not for the world in general.[7]

It is necessary to return now to earlier events. As has been noted, Victor Houteff died in 1955; the movement went into crisis thereafter, and
Ben Roden made an ultimately very successful claim to leadership, but his
was not the only faction to emerge.

The first and most successful move toward the leadership of the community was taken not by Roden but by Victor Houteff's wife, Florence
(who was some twenty years his junior). Within a few months, Florence
had beaten off the main contenders for the leadership and by November
1955 (Victor had died in February) she was enjoying wide acceptance as
the new leader. It was in November, however, that Florence made what in
retrospect turned out to be a big mistake—though, one has to admit, in the
short-term it did pay definite dividends. The mistake was to gamble on hit-
ting the prophetic jackpot by predicting the very day that the Kingdom
would be established: April 22, 1959.[8] As time passed, the claim was
watered down somewhat, but nevertheless that day continued to be the
focus of great expectation in the Davidian community.

Precisely what was expected is not completely clear, though the Davidians themselves did issue a statement on the matter, outlining at least the

main features of their prophetic hope. Some thought that Houteff would be raised from the dead,[9] and it was widely believed that the day would see, if not the actual establishment of the Kingdom of David in Jerusalem, at least the outbreak of the preparatory war of Armageddon.[10]

There were about 1,000 Davidians present at Mount Carmel on that day. Contemporary newspaper reports and some material released by the Davidians themselves have survived and make interesting reading.[11] Nothing happened. Interestingly, however, the group did exactly what Leon Festinger would have predicted: they engaged in renewed evangelistic activity and made preparations, including erecting a number of new dormitory buildings, to accommodate the large numbers of the expected new converts.[12]

Within a few months of the April 22 date, Mrs. Houteff then made her second major mistake. In an effort to explain the lack of any discernible fulfillment of the prophecy, she ditched the view that the Davidian message was for Seventh-day Adventists only and argued that it was now time to take the message to the whole world. (Or, at least, to all Protestants: Catholics and non-Christians were thought to be beyond all hope.) This, she argued, explained the delay. The world was not ready, so the Kingdom could not come.

This was a rather dangerous theological move on Florence's part, for in effect it canceled out much of that for which the tradition had to this point stood. The Davidians had always seen it as their God-given role to call the 144,000 out of the wider membership of the Seventh-day Adventist Church, which they accepted as the true remnant church of God. This conviction ties in directly with their wider understanding of the gradual progress of God's purposes as outlined in Scripture—a process of which they, the Davidians, were the near-culmination. Since 1844, they argued, God had been calling out his remnant. It was now time to call the remnant out of the remnant— that is, to call the 144,000 faithful Adventists out of the corrupt wider Seventh-day Adventist Church. These must first be gathered, take up residence in the literal antitypical Kingdom of David in Israel, and then go out to call the rest of the world, thereby bringing in the "great multitude" of Revelation 7:9. Florence went against this tradition, arguing instead that the message was now (from 1959) to go out into all the world.[13] To take this on board, the Davidians would have to effect a paradigm shift, which, among other things, would involve nothing less than a denial of the inerrancy of the message of Houteff, who saw no place for non-Adventists ahead of the establishment of the Kingdom.[14]

In the event, many of those at Mount Carmel were unable to accommodate so radical a transformation to their self-understanding. Already they had suffered the indignity of the April 1959 debacle, and now they were being asked, in effect, to say that Brother Houteff had been wrong. Not surprisingly, a rift opened up. Florence seems to have lacked the qualities needed to hold things together, and the movement went into serious decline. Eventually on March 1, 1962, a little under three years after the April 22 date, Florence submitted her notice of resignation to the chairman and members of the General Association of Davidian Seventh-day Adventists. And it was not hers alone: there were seven signatories, comprising the entire executive council. The Waco-based Davidian Seventh-day Adventists were effectively dissolved, and their assets were put into the hands of a receiver. Legal dispute after legal dispute followed until eventually—and it took him the next ten years—Roden gained control of what remained of the property and moved his "Branch" followers onto it.

Before this mass resignation, however, a significant number of the Davidians, probably over 100, had decided in 1961 to leave Mount Carmel and return to Riverside, California. The group was made up especially of those who could not accept the view that the message was now for the whole world and not just for the Seventh-day Adventist Church.

The movers behind the California faction seem to have been two long-time Davidians, H. G. Warden and M. J. Bingham.[15] The group met in Los Angeles from July 28 to August 7, and a decision was taken formally to establish a separate Davidian Association in Riverside.[16] (Those meeting would not have seen it this way, of course; their view was that Florence was the one who had in effect separated from the original movement by so radically altering its central mission that Houteff's message had become corrupted beyond recognition. What they were doing, they would have argued, was moving Houteff's Davidian community from Waco to Riverside.) H. G. Warden was elected as the vice president of the association, and M. J. Bingham appointed to the role of editor of the publications that were now once again being planned—publications designed strictly for the work among Seventh-day Adventists and not Christians in general. These publications were, in the main, reprints of the original Houteff literature. One of those present at the original gathering, Don Adair (about whom more will be said later), wrote positively of his feelings that the work had been saved: "Then I returned to Portland, Oregon," he writes, "with the happy belief that now God's Headquarters was established and its work to seal the 144,000 would continue on."[17]

Already by 1961, then, there were three groups of "Davidians" in existence: the one in Waco led by Sister Houteff; the emerging "Branch" movement under Roden (also based in Texas); and the group that had now gathered in California.

But dust had not even fully settled when further problems arose. M. J. Bingham was of the view that the move from Mount Carmel to Riverside had brought to fulfillment the prophetic statement found in Amos 1:2—"And he said: The Lord roars from Zion, and utters his voice from Jerusalem; the pastures of the shepherds wither, and the top of Carmel dries up." Although Bingham played upon the reference to the physical Mount Carmel in Waco here, it was a spiritual rather than a physical move that Bingham detected. In fact, said Bingham, the Davidians had now gone into a new spiritual pasture spoken of in the Old Testament as a move from the pastures of Carmel to those of Bashan—"Shepherd your people with your staff, the flock that belongs to you, which lives alone in a forest in the midst of a garden land; let them feed in Bashan and Gilead as in the days of old" (Mic. 7:14). There had been a physical move then, but according to Bingham the physical was but a sign of the spiritual—the Davidians had now entered a new phase of their ministry and were feeding upon the fresh spiritual pastures of Bashan.[18] After Bashan was to come Gilead, which was the Kingdom itself.[19]

The problem that some Davidians perceived here, of course, was that Bingham was suggesting the need for prophetic progression; if the Davidians were to move from the (spiritual) pastures of Carmel into those of Bashan before the setting up of the Kingdom, it would indicate that Houteff could not have been the last prophet, the one who brought the final light. And that is exactly what Bingham said: Houteff was a prophet—the latter-day Elijah, in fact—but he (Bingham) was a "porter-prophet" who, upon hearing the command of the great shepherd to do so, would open the door of the sheepfold and allow the sheep access to new pastures. (Cf. John 10:3, "The gatekeeper opens the gate for him, and the sheep hear his voice. He calls his own sheep by name and leads them out.")

Bingham's views hence struck at the heart of the movement in no less threatening a way than did the suggestion by Florence that the message was now not for Seventh-day Adventists only but was to go to all the world. Both in effect questioned Houteff's place as the last prophet and questioned the validity of his message. As far as the group in Riverside was concerned, the message of Florence Houteff was now no longer a threat since they had taken the step of separation. But Bingham's views became a real issue.

Bingham's hand was significantly strengthened by the fact that when the standing committee of the Californian Davidians was set up, it had been decided that Bingham, who had been appointed to the post of editor, should have final say in all matters relating to what was published. This caused a problem. Immediately after that initial meeting, says Adair, Bingham wrote his *Bashan* article, which he then wished to see published in the organization's media. Adair says that this was all handled very badly and that the standing committee simply refused to publish Bingham's piece when what they should have done was go into print showing (from Houteff's writings and the Bible) where Bingham was wrong. The result of the refusal to publish, despite previous assurances that the editor would have the final say, was that a good number of the Davidians became suspicious of the standing committee's motives and sided with Bingham. The split was now evident to the point that the post office was not sure to whom they ought to deliver mail addressed to the Davidians in California—was this now Bingham's faction, still based in Riverside but at a different location (Knoeffler Drive), or those over whom the standing committee had authority, based elsewhere? In the end the mail was simply split in two. This was not an unimportant point, since the mail often contained the tithes and offerings of those Davidians who were not in Riverside, but who felt that they owed their allegiance to the group that had now settled there.[20] Financial stability hence became not only problematic, since there were now two separate groups and hence two sets of overheads, but dependent also upon decisions made in the sorting office.

By now Bingham was claiming a prophetic status: when challenged by Adair and others on a certain doctrinal point he was, says Adair, unable to show from the Bible that what he was teaching was true. In the end (and the meeting seems to have been a very long one) Bingham gave up trying to make the exegetical argument and said: "All right, I'll tell you how I know. . . . I know because I'm inspired of God, and he told me."[21] Some of the challengers left Bingham at this point, but others remained loyal despite—indeed, probably because of—his newly claimed prophetic status.[22]

What we have seen so far, both in the departure of the Davidian faction to Riverside and now in the split with Bingham, is a clash between the forces of conservatism and innovation. Deep within the movement there were those who held to an uncompromising belief in the final authority of Houteff, who had come as God's last prophet. Florence, in effect, challenged this by arguing that a central part of his doctrine had been wrong, or at least temporal. Bingham (and indeed Roden) challenged Houteff's status even more directly; for them he was certainly "a" prophet, but not the last one. The parties that developed reflect these tensions: there were those that stuck to the old message, the Houteffian orthodox we might say, and those that were prepared to move on and accept the new light of the Spirit. It is worth noting in passing that exactly the same thing happened following the death of Koresh. Some, such as Livingstone Fagan, remain loyal to the now-dead leader. Others, such as Renos Avraam and his "Students of the Seven Seals," are more imaginative. Avraam, not Koresh, is proclaimed as the final messenger.

Not unimportant in all this is the obvious strength of character with which Bingham was possessed. This was, in fact, the third time that he had made an attempt to gain control of the Davidians: the first was back in the summer of 1938 during a period when Houteff was absent from Mount Carmel,[23] and the second was immediately following Houteff's death in February 1955. On the latter occasion Bingham may have lost out as a result of being in the West Indies at the crucial time. However, his previous work in that part of the world was now about to bring much fruit.

By the time of this 1961 split, Bingham had married a Davidian Bible worker from Trinidad, a move for which he was disfellowshiped by Florence since he had previously been married, but had divorced for reason of his own adultery. Following his argument with the rest of the Californian Davidians, Mr. and Mrs. Bingham embarked on a further evangelistic tour of the West Indies, an area they already knew well and in which they had support. The new tour was a significant success, and most of the Davidians from those islands who had previously been part of the Houteff Davidian tradition now accepted the new Bashan message. The Binghams' success in the West Indies would eventually change the shape of Davidianism, and its effects are easily discernible in the form of Davidianism that one sees in America today. I shall give a fuller explanation of this statement shortly. Here we note only in passing that the substantial groups of principally West Indian Davidian Seventh-day Adventists that are now back in Waco and in New York owe their origins to Bingham's missionary endeavors (although neither of the communities is now part of the "Bashan" Davidian Association).

Upon separation from the wider Riverside Davidian group, Bingham had set up his headquarters on Knoeffler Drive, also in Riverside, California, but in 1969 he moved with about 35 of his followers to a 542-acre site in Exeter, Missouri, which Bingham named "Bashan Hill."[24] Soon thereafter Bingham died, but not before he had nominated his wife, Jemmy Rohoman, as the next leader.[25] The Bashan Hill headquarters still exists to this day.[26] Contact with the group has not been easy, though they have responded to telephone calls and sent out some literature.[27] From that material it is clear that the Bashan Davidians have by no means given up on the basic message of the coming of the Davidian Kingdom. In a fairly recent publication of the *Bashan Tidings*, for example, there is a somewhat traditional explanation of a number of Houteff's old charts, and there is little evidence of any movement on the main themes as Houteff put them forward. As with Adventists generally, there is a significant emphasis upon health, which takes up quite a lot of space in the disseminated literature. However, the basic message remains eschatological and is clear: God has raised up a people who will call out and seal the 144,000. After this comes the slaughter of the unfaithful Seventh-day Adventists who have not (contrary to the instruction of Mic. 6:9, King James Version) "heard the Rod and him who hath appointed it." The difference is that this group continues to see the now-dead Bingham as the "porter-prophet" who leads the flock into the new (Bashan) pastures. And it is in those pastures, physically located at Bashan Hill, Exeter, Missouri, that they await the time when they will move into Gilead: the Kingdom.

Just how many members of the Bashan community there are is not at all clear, though Tim Miller (then a professor of religion at the University of Kansas) who lived quite close to the Exeter headquarters and had made an attempt to visit the community, stated on the Ron Engleman show in April 1994 that the number of Bashan Davidians might run into thousands.[28] It has not been possible to check this information. However, the community does seem quite vibrant. Bashan publications carry letters from persons outside of Exeter, from which it is plain that the movement is actively seeking out converts (all from the Seventh-day Adventist Church, we presume). Leadership appears still to be in the hands of Bingham's wife, Jemmy Rohoman.

Bingham's Bashan Davidians seem, then, to be doing well today, but it has not all been smooth sailing. One of Bingham's closest supporters was M. T. Jordan, a Bible worker from Trinidad whom Bingham had put in charge of the work in Jamaica. In 1979 Jordan rebelled against the Bashan movement, arguing that just as the Carmel pasture had withered, so now had the Bashan, and that the period of Gilead had come (the reference is again to Mic. 7:14). This statement was a flat denial of what the Bashan movement had taught, namely that the Bashan pasture was the last before the setting up of the actual end-time Davidian Kingdom.

Information on Jordan's "Gilead Davidians" has been hardest of all to find. What is clear is that he moved with his followers to Canada, where they continue to exist today. To date no contact has been made with this group, which seems now to be in Ontario.[29] The faction may be significant numerically. Don Adair, who has been a Davidian for around fifty years, stated that he thought that the "Gilead Association" (as he called it) was the largest of the surviving Davidian groups and that the group had now accepted Jordan as King David.[30] This group too, it seems, continues to await the setting up of the physical Kingdom in Israel, while believing that they have now already entered it spiritually.[31]

We need to back up again. We have seen how, in 1961, a group of Davidians left Waco and returned to California where they established a new Davidian Association. The Bashan split was a serious blow to this group. They had lost a good number of members to the faction, including the central figure of Bingham himself. During the next several years, however, the Riverside Davidians stabilized. The location was good in terms of opportunities for evangelism: there were, and still are, a number of significant Adventist institutions within a ten-mile radius of Riverside itself. About ten miles to the east was Loma Linda Medical Center, which had begun as a sanitarium in 1905 and by 1960 had developed into a major health-care institution. The health work had in turn given rise to Loma Linda University, one of the Seventh-day Adventist Church's numerous higher-education institutions. Even closer, and to the west, was La Sierra University, which had begun life in 1922, had received accreditation in 1946, and was, among other things, a place where training for the Seventh-day Adventist ministry could be undertaken.[32] The combined student and staff population alone represented a major opportunity to Davidians keen to call out the 144,000 from the Adventist Church. However, add to those numbers the many Adventists who, though not formally connected to either the La Sierra or the Loma Linda institutions, had nevertheless chosen to settle in the region in order to be among fellow believers, and the potential for conversions was very great indeed. Adair, who was with the Californian Davidians at this time, reports how he, for one, spent many an afternoon talking to Adventists, in churches or at one or other of the institutions, trying to get Houteff's Kingdom message across.[33]

Things hence appear to have been going well for the Californian group when, rather oddly, a decision was taken in 1969 to move the headquarters from Riverside to Salem, South Carolina. Why this decision should have been taken is unclear; there may well have been factors at work that are not now apparent in the available sources. Adair claims that this decision was taken purely on the basis of Bible study, and one has to admit that any other explanation does indeed seem difficult to sustain.[34] The key passage was that found in Ezekiel 47:1, which reads as follows:

> Then he brought me back to the entrance of the temple; there, water was flowing from below the threshold of the temple toward the east (for the temple faced east); and the water was flowing down from below the south end of the threshold of the temple, south of the altar.

According to the Riverside Davidians (those at least who had the power to make decisions) this passage spoke of the work of the Davidian Association, which, according to their reading, must progress toward the east. Houteff, they said, had known this and had hence moved his headquarters from Los Angeles to Waco (which is east as well as south); they had now in effect reversed that move in coming back to the West Coast. The move east would continue until the Holy Land itself was reached. In moving from Waco to Riverside, then, the Davidians had in effect backtracked and were seriously out of tune with biblical teaching. This error was to be corrected at once: they must move east, but where were the Davidians to go? The Waco property had by now passed firmly (if not as yet legally) into the hands of Ben Roden and his Branch Davidians, and in any case a move back to Waco would at best only put the movement back where it was when Houteff died. They needed a property even farther east than Waco.

There was, in fact, one serious possibility. In 1949 Victor Houteff had overseen the establishment of a Davidian rest home in Salem, South Carolina. This rest home was a part of the "old" Mount Carmel estate, but at some point during her leadership Florence Houteff had sold it to those who lived there. In 1969, therefore, the Riverside Davidians sent two of their members to investigate the possibility of a move to South Carolina. A positive report was returned, and, on August 31, 1969, the executive council in Riverside decided to begin making preparations for a possible move. In 1970, at a meeting held in Salem, the decision was confirmed, and the group duly moved to the new location, encouraged it seems by a report given by "Sr C. T. Smith,"[35] who confirmed that she had been told by the late L. W. Nations[36] that Houteff had once told Nations that Mount Carmel would one day be in South Carolina.[37] (Nations had himself started a mainstream Seventh-day Adventist church in Salem, a church that became Davidian upon Nations's own acceptance of the Kingdom message.)[38] The group that moved to Salem was about 50 in number; perhaps another 25 or so, though they did not move physically to Salem, placed their allegiance there.[39]

Not all were in agreement, however. Particularly problematic was the fact that a number of the executive council officers were opposed to the move to Salem, including the vice president, H. G. Warden. An election for the vice president's post was in any case due in 1970, and it was fortunate for the Salem group that Warden was this time defeated. The new vice president was Sump Smith. He was reelected in 1972 also, but there was more trouble. Smith was later to take the view that Florence Houteff had taken—that the Kingdom message was for everyone and not just Seventh-day Adventists. In 1973 Smith was replaced as vice president of the Salem Association, with H. G. Warden again taking up the post. However, following his election, which took place in Salem, Warden went back to Riverside—to collect his belongings, he said. He did not return. Three members of the Salem Association (Don Adair, Marilyn Mueller, and Craig Mueller) therefore went to Riverside to investigate the matter and discovered that Warden, along with a number of the other Davidians who had remained in California after the move by the majority to Salem, was actually still in favor of moving the Association back again to Riverside.

The ensuing squabble resulted in another split and the formation, in 1974, of yet another Davidian Association, as those who wanted to move to Salem and those who wanted to stay in Riverside went their separate ways. The Riverside faction was at first headed by Warden himself, though the leadership passed into the hands of Adair's ex-wife, Wanda Blum (later Wanda O'Berry).[40] The group still works out of Riverside. Contact has been possible, and a very small amount of literature has been collected.[41] It is not clear how large that group is, but the indications are that it is relatively small. From the small amount of literature available it would seem that the group is keen to continue with the basic Houteff message and shows little sign of originality. There is no evidence of a new prophet having arisen.

By 1974, then, there were three quite distinct Davidian Associations in existence (this, of course, in addition to the "Branch" Davidians in Texas): the Salem Association; the California Association; and Bingham's "Bashan" Association in Exeter, Missouri. This would increase to four in 1979 with the formation of the Gilead Association, by M. T. Jordan.

But there were more developments still. In 1974 Adair, by now an absolutely key player in the Salem group, went to the West Indies to study with Bingham's Bashan believers there, in an effort to bring them back on board. This trip resulted, says Adair, in some considerable success, and many of those who had been converted to the Bashan message were now won over to the Salem Association.[42] One such person was Tony Hibbert, a Jamaican Davidian who had traveled to South Carolina to study with the Salem group. By this time Adair was vice president of the Salem Association, and it was he who sent Hibbert to take charge of the work in New York, which was seen as an area ready to receive the Kingdom message. In 1981, while Adair was himself conducting studies in New York, Hibbert disputed a doctrinal point.[43] The doctrinal dispute continued (a cover, one suspects, for a power struggle) until in 1982 a decision was taken by Hibbert and some others (all of them West Indian) who were sympathetic to his views formally to separate from the Salem Association and set up their own Davidian group in Mountain Dale, New York.[44]

The New York faction is today an important part of Davidian Seventh-day Adventism. The group is somewhat suspicious of external interest and has been less than forthcoming in answering inquiries and requests for information. However, its very professional website is informative, and one can learn much from it.[45] In addition, Hibbert himself has written at least one book, a source that is also of some value.[46]

In essence the New York Davidians continue with the old Rod message of Houteff. Such can be discerned easily enough from the website's audio files. All is in place: the sealing of the 144,000, the slaughter of the unbelieving Seventh-day Adventists, the setting up of the Kingdom, the "Loud Cry" that goes out into all the world and the consequent coming in of the "great multitude" of Revelation 7:9. There is no claim to prophetic status, so far as one can tell, though Hibbert seems to have the potential to make one at some point. Requests to visit the group have so far been turned down, though always in a pleasant enough way. Again, one should not read too much into this. Non-Adventists are of very little interest to Davidians since they are not (as yet) potential converts. A group as sharply focused as this one can ill afford to waste its energies on satisfying the curiosity of academic researchers.

One final (to date)[47] blow came in 1989 when a number of the New York Davidians (together it seems with a small number of persons living elsewhere)[48] decided that the time was right to return to Waco. A vote was taken, and the majority voted for the move. The sequence of subsequent events is unclear, but it is certainly the case that the decision caused some considerable dispute. Not all wanted to move. What we do know is that in February 1989 a small number of New York Davidians were in Waco try-ing to find a property that would in some way turn back the clock and bring the Davidians back. The reason these persons gave for wanting to return seems to have been that they felt that the Davidians had a duty first to evangelize Waco successfully before moving on to other parts of the world. The Davidians, they said, had failed in Waco the first time round and could expect no success elsewhere until they had corrected this situa-tion. They must then move back and do successfully what the Davidians after Houteff had failed to do.

As a part of these plans, longtime Davidians Sidney and Bonnie Smith went to Waco (bringing along Glen Green) ostensibly to help with iden-tification of the location of original Davidian property. While in Waco they gave a videotaped interview at Baylor University, which makes for fascinating viewing.[49]

The Smiths (who at this time lived in Yucaipa but appear to have joined with the New York Association) had previously been at Mount Carmel under Houteff and hence knew the location of the property well. From the video it is plain that they were not in favor of the proposed move back. Glen Green, a resident at Salem, seems to be similarly minded. Their plan seems to have been to come to Waco and explain to the group that Brother Houteff always saw Waco as a temporary place of residence and predicted that after his death the Davidian sheep would be scattered as a necessary part of the plan to take the message out more generally. In other parts of the Davidian tradition, the Smiths report, these ones who want to return to Waco are called, sensibly enough, "the going to Waco group."[50]

Despite the odds, however, the group from New York did secure some property, principally a former Presbyterian church located off Lakeshore Drive, and the move took place. Actually Adair states that the Presbyter-ian church was itself a conversion from the original Davidian print shop that was sold off when the move from the "old" to the "new" Mount Carmel took place. Adair worked on the construction of that building, he says, and did some of the plastering and the wiring. The Presbyterians bought it and turned it into a church, and now the "going to Waco" New York Davidians have possession of it again.[51] Adair also tells the story of how those who wanted to move loaded up a trailer and set off, only to be stopped by the police and forced to return to New York and give back the printing and other materials that they had removed from the New York Association's office.[52]

As they drove to Waco, "the going to Waco group" went through Salem and attempted unsuccessfully to gain further support. Nevertheless they pressed on and arrived in Waco sometime in 1991. From the old Presbyterian church they now run a very professional printing operation and literature campaign, targeting, as one would expect, only Seventh-day Adventists and not the wider Christian church. The leadership of the Waco group is currently in the hands of Norman Archer.[53] Each Friday evening they gather at the church for a worship service, which includes hymn singing, prayer, and a lengthy Bible study. A visit was made to the group in November 2002, when talk of war in the Middle East was very much in the air. The congregation, about 30 in number, was very excited as they looked forward to the fulfillment of their dreams, which must include the destruction of large numbers of both Jewish and Palestinian inhabitants of the Holy Land in order to make way first for the 144,000 and then for the "great multitude" that will follow the establishment of the Kingdom. On Saturday mornings no meeting is held since the members of the community belong also to mainstream Seventh-day Adventist churches and see it as their duty to attend those churches to spread the Kingdom message. This activity causes considerable conflict, it seems, especially so since (and this is always a sign of true allegiance) the Davidian Seventh-day Adventists of the Waco and Killeen churches do not pay their tithes and offerings to the mainstream Adventist Church but to the Davidian Association. In about 2003 a new pastor (a person of West Indian descent from London) was brought in by the Adventist church to sort the situation out.

Each Passover, the Davidians in Waco hold a worldwide meeting when some 100–150 are in attendance. How these numbers are made up is not clear, and (quite properly) the association will not release information on members' addresses. What is clear, however, is that there are Davidians who see their allegiance as being with the Waco community living in many parts of the world. There is at least one such person in London.

Conclusion

The Davidian Seventh-day Adventist movement appears to be in a fairly healthy state. The six major factions (and there may, of course, be others that have not come to the surface in this review)[54] are all independent of each other in terms of formal structures, but all seem nevertheless to be viable. This remark ought necessarily to be seen in the context of the fact that three of the groups (California, Missouri, and Canada) have not been studied in any detail and may be weaker than their literature, or the reports of these groups provided by others, suggests. Unlike the Branch Davidians, the Davidian Seventh-day Adventists have managed to maintain critical mass and indeed have almost certainly grown somewhat in the period 1963–2003.

In contrast to the probable fate of the Branch Davidians, then, the Davidian Seventh-day Adventists are an example of how a group can survive even against the odds. From a modest beginning with the arrival of the dozen followers of Houteff in Waco in 1935, they have undergone significant transition: first, significant expansion through evangelistic endeavor; then the crisis that came about with the death of Houteff; followed by an even greater one with the failure of the 1959 prophecy. Not insignificant either was the subsequent attempt on Florence Houteff's part to abandon some aspects of her husband's teaching, especially the view that the message was now for all Protestants and not only Seventh-day Adventists. This change, as we have seen, resulted in the splintering of the group and the eventual rise of at least six Davidian Associations, not including that of "the Branch."

The storms have been weathered, yet there may be others ahead. And there are certainly some obstacles to further success, not the least of which is the notoriety that the "Branch Davidians" now have; the brush with which all "Davidians" have been tarred is applied without recognition of the firm historical and theological boundaries that exist between the factions. In this regard the hostility of the general public is not the issue: it is the hostility of the only group of potential converts that matters. The publicity-shy, indeed rather paranoid, mainstream Seventh-day Adventist Church has understandably reacted with horror to the events of 1993: if "Davidians" could expect at least to gain a hearing within Adventist communities prior to 1993, no such expectation would be warranted now. It matters not if the "Davidians" in question are as horrified by the events in Waco as are mainstream Seventh-day Adventists, for the mere mention of the name "Davidian" is enough to put almost any Seventh-day Adventist on the defensive. To the average Seventh-day Adventist, "Davidians" are neither unknown nor safe; they are a dangerous group of fanatics, and in the swirl of defensive panic brought on by the mention of the word "Davidian," historical and theological distinctions mean little. Through no fault of their own, then, the Davidian Seventh-day Adventists now have a mountain to climb if they are to have any continued success in calling out the 144,000 from the Adventist Church. Koresh has not done them any favors in this regard. The significance of this is intensified greatly by virtue of the fact that it is on this very point, the need to present the Kingdom message exclusively to the Seventh-day Adventists and not to the world in general, that the Riverside group split from Florence Houteff. Limiting evangelistic activity to a group of persons who are fundamentally antagonistic to messengers of the proposed "new light" is not a recipe for success.

On the other hand, the Davidians do have some cards to play. As the situation in the Middle East continues to deteriorate and the events of September 11, 2001, remain unblurred, the argument can be made that the

Davidian understanding of biblical prophecy stands up in the light of current events. (Seventh-day Adventists have always been keen to see a correspondence between prophecy and history, and such reasoning may well appeal to them in a way that the outsider might find difficult to understand.) The group in Waco in particular has now found stability and is clearly a financially viable organization with a keen sense of mission and, importantly, the physical facilities, including printing equipment, to engage in it. In the person of Archer they have a solid, dependable, even if far from prophetic, leader, and for this group at least the future looks reasonably positive. Hence, while subject to fragmentation, Houteff's vision lives on. The 144,000 continue to be called. It may well be the case that in terms of sheer numbers some ground has been lost since his demise, but for a man of Houteff's faith and vision this would not have been an issue. Things can be impossible with humans, but not with God (cf. Matt. 19:26).

Chapter Nine

The Branch Davidians and Religion Reporting—A Ten-Year Retrospective

Catherine Wessinger

Studies of new religious movements and violence have demonstrated that violence involving religious groups is interactive in nature: the quality of the interactions of a variety of forces in the outside society with the believers is crucial for determining the potential for volatility.[1] These forces and actors in mainstream society include the media, law enforcement agents, and former members. All of these types of actors contributed to the conflict in 1993 known by the shorthand term "Waco," which occurred at the Branch Davidians' residence called Mount Carmel. Media personnel were major players in the conflict between federal law enforcement agents and the Branch Davidians, from the ATF assault on February 28, which resulted in ten deaths, to the FBI tank and gas assault on April 19 that culminated in the fire, which caused seventy-four deaths. The media shaped the public perceptions of the Branch Davidians underlying the conflict. The media were the locus of the struggle to define the events at Mount Carmel, and that struggle continues.[2]

Generally, from 1993 to 2003, reporting in the print media about the events at Mount Carmel evolved from "cult" stories to stories about excessive actions by federal law enforcement agents against an unconventional religious group. In 2003 a greater effort was made in the print media to depict the diverse viewpoints of the actors in the drama. However, the storyline remained highly contested. Federal agents and their anti-cult advisors still had vested interests in maintaining the "cult" filter through which the events at Mount Carmel were viewed.[3]

Since 1993, religion scholars and reporters have made greater efforts to be in touch with each other. As a result, religion reporting in the print media, especially on new religious movements, has improved in some ways, but remains uneven. This chapter does not deal with television reporting, where the "cult" stereotype remains dominant.

Here I shall discuss the roles that media representatives played in the conflict at Mount Carmel and indicate the main contours of reporting on this case. I compare particularly the *Waco Tribune-Herald*'s 1993 "Sinful Messiah" series with its 2003 "Flashpoint in History" series as suggesting how the print media reporting on this case has changed while remaining the same. The stories by Lee Hancock of the *Dallas Morning News* are discussed as representing some of the most in-depth investigative reporting on this case: Hancock's stories have impacted upon federal handling of the matter. The perspectives of surviving Branch Davidians on the media are presented, particularly in the voice of Bonnie Haldeman, David Koresh's mother. Lastly, I address the efforts made by religion scholars and reporters to improve religion newswriting.

The Media and the Conflict at Mount Carmel

Various media and media representatives were intimately involved in the conflict at Mount Carmel, from the beginning to the fiery end. Media representatives contributed to the debacle, and all parties involved used, or attempted to use, the media.

After the *Waco Tribune-Herald* had been contacted by former Branch Davidians, reporters Mark England and Darlene McCormick began research in June 1992 on stories that became known as the "Sinful Messiah" series. The Branch Davidians were a group that had split off from the Seventh-day Adventist Church that had existed in the Waco area since 1935. David Koresh, aged thirty-three, was the fourth in a line of Branch Davidian prophets. The research of England and McCormick focused on allegations that weapons were being stockpiled and that Koresh was having sex with underage girls. The series was ready for publication in February 1993, about the time that agents of the Bureau of Alcohol, Tobacco, and Firearms (ATF) were preparing to carry out a "dynamic entry" to serve an arrest warrant on Koresh and to search for illegal weapons. The ATF commanders in charge of "Operation Trojan Horse," Phillip Chojnacki and Charles Sarabyn, fearing that the series would create a more defensive posture at Mount Carmel, negotiated with *Waco Tribune-Herald* editors, the paper's publisher, and a Cox Enterprises vice president, seeking to postpone publication until after the raid. Thus began a dance between the newspaper and the ATF, with the *Tribune-Herald* seeking to publish the series before the raid and the ATF seeking to launch the raid before the series was published. The dance resulted in media representatives being directly involved with the disastrous events of February 28, 1993.

The *Waco Tribune-Herald* began the series on Saturday, February 27, thinking that the ATF raid would be carried out on Monday, March 1. The first story alleged that David Koresh had sex with underage girls and administered severe spankings to small children, as well as having accumulated and utilized a variety of weapons. David Koresh was painted as having all the worst characteristics of a "cult leader." When the first story appeared, ATF agents decided to launch the raid on Sunday, February 28. Tommy Witherspoon, a *Waco Tribune-Herald* reporter, and Dan Mulloney, a cameraman for KWTX-TV in Waco, separately received tips, which they confirmed with each other, that the raid would occur on the morning of February 28.[4]

There were two KWTX-TV vehicles and three vehicles containing *Waco Tribune-Herald* reporters on the roads just outside Mount Carmel early on February 28. A cameraman for KWTX-TV was lost when he was approached by David Jones, a Branch Davidian whose car was marked "US Mail," who asked if there was going to be a raid. The cameraman's shirt had a KWTX-TV logo on it, and police traffic could be heard on his scanner. Jones returned to Mount Carmel with the information that ATF agents would be arriving soon. He had gone out early that morning to buy a copy of the *Waco Tribune-Herald* in order to read the second installment of the "Sinful Messiah" series.[5]

Early on the morning of February 28, an ATF undercover agent, Robert Rodriguez, brought a copy of the Sunday *Waco Tribune-Herald* to Mount Carmel under the pretext of wanting to discuss it with Koresh. Rodriguez was really checking to see if the series had provoked defensive preparations on the part of the Branch Davidians. While Rodriguez was receiving a Bible study from David Koresh, the latter was called out. When Koresh returned he was shaking, and stated that he knew the ATF and National Guard were coming to get him. Rodriguez hurriedly left Mount Carmel to return to the undercover house across the road and called his commanders, begging them to call off the raid because the element of surprise had been lost. According to the plan, the raid should have been called off in this event, but instead Sarabyn told the agents to hurry up, "They know we are coming. It's show time."[6]

Immediately before the seventy-six ATF agents arrived in cattle trailers to carry out the raid, a car carrying *Waco Tribune-Herald* personnel, including Tommy Witherspoon, parked on the road directly in front of Mount

Carmel to take photographs, even though they had just been told to leave by an ATF agent in a nearby house.[7]

The raid was carried out beginning at 9:45 a.m. While National Guard helicopters flew over the residence, ATF agents were transported to the front door in cattle trailers, with Mulloney and John McLemore of KWTX-TV following in their vehicle. A shoot-out began at the front door of the residence and on the second floor, where ATF agents attempted to enter the building through a window. Mulloney and McLemore came under fire along with the ATF agents. The *Waco Tribune-Herald* personnel took cover in a ditch on the road when shots were directed at them.[8] At the conclusion of the shoot-out, four ATF agents were dead and twenty were wounded; five Branch Davidians were dead and four were wounded, including David Koresh. Branch Davidian Michael Schroeder, aged twenty-nine, was shot and killed by ATF agents later that day as he attempted to return to Mount Carmel on foot.

On the following day, agents of the Federal Bureau of Investigation (FBI) arrived to take over what became a fifty-one-day siege, and they took control of the media's access to information about the case. Mount Carmel was surrounded by tanks, and negotiations were carried out by telephone. Mount Carmel's telephone connections to the rest of society were blocked by the FBI, because on February 28 Koresh had given interviews to CNN, KRLD radio in Dallas, and the *Dallas Morning News*. From that point on, the FBI largely controlled information about events at Mount Carmel. Even the relevant court documents were sealed during this time.[9] Reporters were pushed back three miles to a site that was dubbed "Satellite City." The "Sinful Messiah" series became the first reference for reporters converging on Waco and shaped how the Branch Davidians were depicted in the national media. FBI news briefings became occasions for agents to deride Koresh and the Branch Davidians' beliefs in attempts to manipulate them.[10]

The Branch Davidians, realizing that they were being demonized in the media, wanted to get their side of the story out. Having had difficulty communicating with FBI negotiators, the Branch Davidians requested that reporters be permitted to serve as mediators. On March 9, the Branch Davidians hung from a window a sheet reading "God Help Us. We Want the Press." On March 14, they hung out another banner reading "FBI broke negotiations, we want press." On March 16, Branch Davidians used flashlights to convey a message in Morse code: "SOS, SOS, FBI broke negotiations. Want negotiations from press." After this, the FBI directed bright spotlights into the residence at night.

During the siege, a total of fourteen adults and twenty-one children came out of Mount Carmel. But whenever adults began to exit, FBI agents punished the Branch Davidians by ratcheting up psychological warfare tactics: blasting high-decibel sounds at them, making threatening maneuvers in the tanks, cutting off electricity, and using the tanks to destroy vehicles. Adults who came out were dressed in orange prison jumpsuits and paraded before the television cameras handcuffed and shackled.

Early in the siege, David Koresh said they would come out if an audiotape containing a sermon by Koresh was played on major stations. It was played on March 2 by KRLD radio and the Christian Broadcasting Network. However, Koresh then relayed to FBI agents that he was instructed by God to wait for further orders about what they should do. During the siege, FBI negotiators and the Branch Davidians sent each other videotapes in order to facilitate communication. The videotapes made by the Branch Davidians were not released to the media.

Despite communication difficulties, notably the FBI agents refusing to listen to what they called the Branch Davidians' "Bible babble," progress was made in negotiations, particularly when two Bible scholars initiated a creative intervention to communicate with the Branch Davidians in their Bible-based language and take seriously their concern with biblical prophecy. On April 1, Dr. Phillip Arnold of Reunion Institute in Houston and Dr. James Tabor of the University of North Carolina, Charlotte, discussed the biblical prophecies on the Ron Engleman talk show on KGBS radio. They offered to the Branch Davidians an interpretation of the prophecies suggesting that God wanted them to come out and did not intend for them to die at that time at the hands of the agents of "Babylon" to initiate the apocalyptic end-time events.[11] David Koresh and the Branch Davidians found Arnold and Tabor's arguments persuasive and told FBI negotiators that they would come out after Passover, a seven-day holiday. Passover ended on April 13, and on April 14 Koresh sent out a letter saying that after he wrote his "little book" interpreting the Seven Seals of the book of Revelation they would come out. The negotiation audiotapes recorded the Branch Davidians cheering at the prospect of coming out.[12] On April 16, Koresh reported that he had completed his interpretation of the First Seal, and the Branch Davidians requested a battery-operated word processor to facilitate the production of the manuscript. On April 17, they again asked for a word processor. In the meantime, Attorney General Janet Reno was told that negotiations were going nowhere, and she approved a plan to carry out a CS gas and tank assault on the residence.

The FBI assault began at 6:00 a.m. on April 19, while the world watched on CNN. Tanks used grenade launchers to hurl in ferret rounds containing CS gas. Tanks punched holes in the walls, dismantled the building, entered, and sprayed CS gas. At 9:10 a.m. the Branch Davidians hung out a banner saying "We want our phones fixed," indicating a desire to negotiate. The young children and their mothers huddled inside a concrete room on the first floor to escape the gas. A tank entered the building, destroying the one passageway leading away from the concrete vault and knocking concrete into the room, and may have inserted CS gas directly into the room. Fires started at 12:07 and 12:08 in three parts of the building where tanks had entered. The fires quickly escalated to consume the building. Fire engines arrived at 12:34 but were held back by FBI agents. The fire raged while the tanks pushed the burning walls and debris into the conflagration. The causes of the fires were disputed. FBI agents alleged that some Branch Davidians set the fires, while Branch Davidians alleged that the tanks knocked over kerosene lanterns. Nine Branch Davidians escaped the fire, including Ruth Riddle, who had a disk in her pocket on which David Koresh's unfinished manuscript was saved. Seventy-four Branch Davidians died in the fire, including twenty-three children. Among the children were two infants who were born in the fire when their mothers died.

Subsequently, the ATF agents and the families of the four dead agents filed suit against the *Waco Tribune-Herald* and KWTX-TV, alleging that their personnel tipped off the Branch Davidians about the raid. Without liability being admitted, an out-of-court settlement was reached in 1996 for an undisclosed sum.[13] In a 1994 criminal trial, eleven Branch Davidians were acquitted of murder and conspiracy to murder; five were convicted of voluntary manslaughter and weapons violations; and three were convicted of weapons violations. As of 2003, the surviving Branch Davidians and the families of the deceased Branch Davidians had been unsuccessful in their wrongful-death civil lawsuit brought against the government. Their appeal was rejected in 2005 by the 5th U.S. Circuit Court of Appeals and in 2006 by teh Supreme Court.

Manufacturing Consent about Koresh

In an article published in 1995, sociologist James T. Richardson applied the analysis of Edward S. Herman and Noam Chomsky[14] to the 1993 news coverage of the Branch Davidians. The thesis of Herman and Chomsky is that the media determine which victims are perceived as being "worthy" and which "unworthy." Worthy victims will be humanized in the media, the details of their lives and deaths will be given, and the grief of their surviving loved ones will be depicted to generate sympathetic identification by the public. In contrast, minimal information will be given about victims deemed to be unworthy; thus, they will be dehumanized, erased, and no public empathy with them will be generated. Richardson pointed out that much of the news coverage of the Branch Davidians was geared toward "manufacturing consent" that Koresh was a maniacal "cult" leader. The rest of the Branch Davidians were erased from view, either by not being depicted or by being depicted as brainwashed followers, rather than as people who were committed to following God's will as revealed in the Bible. Richardson's thesis was that, because law enforcement agents and the public shared a view of Koresh and the Branch Davidians as cultists, authorities were able to take extreme actions against the group with impunity, thinking that the situation"allowed, even required, such actions."[15]

Richardson and van Driel,[16] Wright,[17] and other scholars of new religious movements have pointed out that "cult" is a pejorative term conveying a stereotype that has serious consequences when it is applied to a religion. Applying the "cult" label can become a pretext for a government to attack a group and seek to eradicate it.[18]

The "cult" stereotype utilized in the 1993 media depictions of the Branch Davidians conveyed what Richardson called "the myth of the omnipotent leader" and the corresponding "myth of the passive or robotic follower,"[19] which contributed to the dehumanization of the Branch Davidians. Richardson and other scholars of new religions contend that neither of these myths bear up under social scientific scrutiny. While there were certainly group processes going on inside Mount Carmel, these were not different from those of many other groups. The "charisma" of a prophet or a messiah is socially constructed, and followers can withdraw their allegiance at any time unless physically constrained from doing so.

On April 9, 1993, Branch Davidian Steve Schneider explained to a negotiator that every day he tested the validity of Koresh's teachings by the Bible. On March 15, Schneider reported that the Branch Davidians were enthusiastic when they heard Dr. Phillip Arnold on a KRLD radio program discussing the Bible, and they requested that Arnold be permitted to discuss the biblical prophecies with Koresh. Schneider asserted that if Arnold could provide biblical interpretations to the effect that the Branch Davidians should come out, they would do so, no matter what Koresh might say. David Koresh himself pointed out to an FBI negotiator that he did not control the Branch Davidians and that his authority with them was based on his ability to interpret the Scriptures, but the negotiator declined to believe that he did not have total control over everyone.[20]

The ordinary Branch Davidians were relatively visible in local Texas print media. For instance, the *Waco Tribune-Herald* published a story[21] on Bonnie Haldeman, David Koresh's mother, in which she expressed her love and concern for her grandchildren and their mothers. The *Dallas Morning News* published a story on Koresh's life history that included family photographs.[22] But the 1993 coverage in the *Waco Tribune-Herald* and the *Dallas Morning News* was dominated by the "cult" stereotype.

The national news magazines portrayed David Koresh as a deranged, sex-crazed, gun-toting "cult leader," and the Branch Davidians as passive followers. Given the extensive stereotyping of the group as a "cult," it became assumed common knowledge that they were likely to commit mass suicide as with the Jonestown event in 1978, and that responsibility for the deaths would rest solely on Koresh.

As an example of the "cult" stereotype being imposed on the Branch Davidians, the cover of the March 15, 1993 issue of *Newsweek* bore the headline "Secrets of the Cult" in sinister lettering superimposed over a cropped and grainy photograph of Koresh's forehead with his eyes shaded by glasses. The story recounted the shoot-out at Mount Carmel, styled "an ambush" of the ATF agents. Photographs of the wounded and grieving agents were prominently displayed. The issue included a story on Koresh, followed by a story entitled "Cultic America," which relied heavily on stereotypes of "cults" provided by the (now-defunct) Cult Awareness Network. Accompanying photographs included those of followers of Bhagwan Shree Rajneesh, some of the bodies at Jonestown, the bombed remains of MOVE in Philadelphia, Elizabeth Clare Prophet (whose church had not been involved in violence), and Charles Manson. The following story, "From Prophets to Losses," had a photograph of the Jonestown residents' bodies lying close to the vat of poisoned punch, clearly suggesting that "cult" spells out a violent ending.

The Branch Davidians followed the news coverage of their case, and they realized they were being dehumanized in the press. Judy Schneider, aged 41, said in a videotaped statement:

> I just hope everyone doesn't jump to making decisions [about us] before they've heard our side, because right now all you're hearing is the press. You're hearing a very perverted press.[23]

After the fire on April 19, the cover of the May 3, 1993 issue of *Newsweek* depicted Koresh's face surrounded by flames and the words "Death Wish," clearly indicating that Koresh was the sole cause of the tragedy. This view was reinforced by the story entitled "The Killing Ground," which showed the ruins of Mount Carmel with Koresh's photograph next to the title of the article. The story, "Day of Judgment," included photographs of Rachel Howell (aged twenty-three in 1993) and her children Cyrus (eight) and Star (six), Floracita Sonobe and her daughter Angelica (the latter came out of Mount Carmel), Melissa Morrison (six, died in the fire), Perry Jones (sixty-four, died as a result of the ATF raid), Rachel Sylvia (thirteen, died in the fire), Steve Schneider (forty-three, died in the fire), together with a list of the deceased Branch Davidians. The article by Melinda Liu and Todd Barrett, "Hard Lessons in the Ashes," had a photograph of the dead from Jonestown with the caption "Jonestown, like Waco, shows the dangers of cults." This article cited Rick Ross as being an "expert" on "cults" who alleged that Koresh brainwashed his followers. The article contained the countervoice of Dr. James Tabor saying that the FBI tactics were a mistake: "If you want to make them fanatical, do just what the FBI did." Other scholarly voices criticizing FBI actions were Phillip Arnold and Robert

Fuller of Bradley University. This article marked a coming shift in the coverage, asserting:

> The difference [between a criminal worldview and an apocalyptic one]
> is enormous and the consequences were tragic—and unless the Feds
> learn to deal astutely and carefully with religious cults, it is a tragedy
> that could occur again.

The May 3, 1993 issue of *Time* likewise applied the "cult" stereotype and blamed Koresh as being the sole cause of the tragedy. The cover showed a photograph of Koresh that had been manipulated to make him appear to be laughing maniacally as he gazed toward the sky with his head engulfed in flames. Imposed on the cover was the verse from Revelation 6:8, "His name was Death, and Hell followed with him." Inside, a story by Richard Lacayo, "In the Grip of a Psychopath," said that Koresh was the "most spectacular example [of] the charismatic leader with a pathological edge" since Jim Jones of Jonestown. A photograph of Jim Jones reinforced that they were cut of the same mold.[24]

Sociologist Nancy Ammerman, who served on a commission to make a report to the government about the 1993 events, pointed to the problems caused by the application of the "cult" stereotype to the Branch Davidians. She noted that, when the law enforcement agents invoked religious categories at all to understand the Branch Davidians,

> they were categories derived from the definitions of cult leadership
> and behavior promulgated by the news media over the last two
> decades. A "cult leader," according to these images, can be easily seen
> as a sociopath, and "brainwashed" members can be defined as
> hostages. By defining a "destructive cult" as a group with an egomani-
> acal leader and ego-deficient followers, one need not attend closely to
> the particular religious beliefs and practices of the group.[25]

Ammerman pointed out that the FBI failed to take into account the apocalyptic religious beliefs of the Branch Davidians and ignored the advice of their own behavioral scientists, who said that aggressive tactical actions just confirmed the Branch Davidians' apocalyptic interpretations of the events.

Instead of consulting scholarly experts on religious groups, the ATF and FBI relied on advice from Rick Ross, a deprogrammer, and utilized information about "cults" disseminated by the anti-cult organization called the Cult Awareness Network.[26] In addition to serving as an advisor to the ATF and FBI agents in 1993 about how to deal with the Branch Davidians, Rick Ross helped shape public perceptions of the case by giving several television interviews.[27]

Rick Ross is not a religion scholar, and he has been linked to crimes. In 1975 he conspired to rob a jewelry shop. In 1991, Ross and two other men were accused of kidnapping a member of a Pentecostal church in order to deprogram him. Rick Ross, the Cult Awareness Network, and the two other men were found liable in 1994 and ordered to pay punitive damages.[28] Rick Ross and the Cult Awareness Network subsequently filed for bankruptcy. The original Cult Awareness Network went out of business, but Rick Ross remained an outspoken anti-cultist seeking media attention.

The "cult" stereotype combined with the warfare mentality of the federal law enforcement agents[29] obscured the agents' recognition that violence involving religious groups is interactive in nature, and that the quality of the interactions of outside actors with believers is crucial for determining a peaceful or violent outcome. The *Waco Tribune-Herald's* "Sinful Messiah" series was the first to apply the "cult" stereotype to the Branch Davidians, and the newspaper was directly involved in the events leading to the disastrous ATF raid.

The "Sinful Messiah" Series in the *Waco Tribune-Herald*

The *Waco Tribune-Herald's* "Sinful Messiah" series began its first installment on Saturday, February 27, 1993, and the second article was published on February 28, the day of the ATF raid. After the disaster on February 28, the *Waco Tribune-Herald* published parts 3-7 of the series on Monday, March 1 on the front page. The series was an initial source of information for the FBI agents and reporters arriving in Waco. Newspapers such as the *San Francisco Chronicle*, *New York Times*, *Fort Worth Star Telegram*, *Washington Post*, and *Chicago Tribune* either reprinted all or parts of the series or drew heavily on it for their own stories.[30]

The Branch Davidians saw David Koresh as the messiah ("Christ," or "anointed one") figure described in Psalm 40:12 as being full of iniquities, or sinful. They understood this messiah to be the Son of God described in Psalm 45 as marrying virgins and having children by them who "become princes in all the earth." Koresh identified himself as being this Christ and as being the rider on the white horse in the First Seal of Revelation (Rev. 6), who goes forth to conquer evil in the final apocalyptic events.[31] David Koresh as the Christ was sinful, not perfect, in order to be an effective savior of sinful humanity.[32] The "Sinful Messiah" series took the Branch Davidians' theological concept of the sinful messiah as the agent of salvation and made it into a condemnation of a "cult leader."

According to Tabor and Gallagher, the "Sinful Messiah" series, by perpetuating the "cult" stereotype, "promoted the agenda of the anti-cult activists while at the same time discounting or denying outright the seriousness and even religiousness of the Branch Davidians."[33] The "Sinful Messiah" series, "[b]y providing the public with a convenient interpretive shorthand, the characterization of the community as a 'cult,' unfortunately made it all too easy and attractive to deny Koresh and the other [Branch Davidians] their full and complex humanity."[34]

A dramatic story was behind the "Sinful Messiah" series written by Mark England and Darlene McCormick. The *Waco Tribune-Herald* and its owners, Cox Enterprises, had spent tens of thousands of dollars and dedicated months of investigative effort into researching and writing the series, possibly in the hope of winning a Pulitzer Prize for the newspaper. According to Wendell Rawls, this was why the *Waco Tribune-Herald* did not want the series to be preempted by the ATF raid. ATF agent Phillip Chojnacki met with publishers and editors at the *Waco Tribune-Herald* office on February 24, but they declined to promise to delay the story, citing concerns about the children at Mount Carmel and the public's right to know.[35] On February 25, Bob Lott, the *Tribune-Herald*'s managing editor, wrote the editorial that would accompany the first installment, demanding that law enforcement agents do something quickly about Koresh's activities.[36] Lott's editorial along with part 1 of the series was published on Saturday, February 27. According to Rawls:

> One suspects that what [Lott] really wanted was three days—three days of articles in the series before [the] anticipated ATF raid on Monday morning, March 1. Three days of articles like the above-the-fold, top-right, Page 1, copyrighted article with the headline that read: "THE LAW WATCHES, BUT HAS DONE LITTLE."
> One also suspects that when the raid came the newspaper would try to take credit for it. That seems to be one of the things that Pulitzer Prize juries appreciate: results.[37]

The "Sinful Messiah" series painted a grim picture of life at Mount Carmel, alleging that abusive spankings of children, to the point of drawing blood, took place and that Koresh boasted of his sexual exploits with young girls. The most disturbing allegation was that he forced himself on a twelve-year-old girl when she resisted.[38] It should be noted that Texas social workers had investigated the Branch Davidians for child abuse and closed the case for lack of evidence. Child abuse does not come under the jurisdiction of federal authorities.

The series relied on allegations made by former Branch Davidians who were concerned about what was going on at Mount Carmel, interspersed with a few extremely unflattering quotations from David Koresh. Marc Breault (aged twenty-nine in 1993) had left Mount Carmel over concerns about Koresh's sexual relations with girls and his 1989 teaching that all the women were Koresh's wives. After the fire, Breault published *Inside the Cult* (1993) depicting himself as a "cult buster." Breault stated that "my primary reason for trying to help is the children."[39] Robyn Bunds (aged twenty-three in 1993) was another important source for the series. She had had a child by Koresh and had successfully secured custody of the boy after Koresh had made efforts to keep him.[40]

Part 1 of the series asked why anyone would join such a group. The former members answered that they had been subjected to "traditional mind-control techniques to entrap listeners" and that Koresh's Bible study sessions were "spellbinding." The myth of the mesmerizing charismatic leader casting his spell on intelligent people powerless to resist was perpetuated in part 2, which referred to Koresh's influence as "eerie." The stories referred to Koresh as a "cult leader" and the Branch Davidians as "cult members." Part 1 concluded with a list of legal categories relating to sexual assault of children and was accompanied by an impassioned editorial by Bob Lott demanding that something be done to stop Koresh.

Part 3 was published after the ATF assault with a note by Bob Lott discussing the timing of the publication of the series and whether it had contributed to the deaths the previous day. He reported that federal agents had asked the *Tribune-Herald* to hold off publishing the series, but that because of concerns for the children they had decided it was "time to let the public know of this menace in our community." Lott concluded: "I don't agree with the tendency of some to point to our reporting as having affected Sunday's tragedy. We share the anguish over what happened. Everyone involved or who saw it is devastated."

In addition to testimony from a variety of former members, part 4 of the series introduced the voices of "cult experts" from the anti-cult movement asserting that David Koresh "controls the minds" of his followers in a "destructive cult." Priscilla Coates of the Cult Awareness Network and Rick Ross were cited, depicting Koresh as practicing mind control, leaving the Branch Davidians "passive and obedient."

In part 6, Jeannine Bunds, the mother of Robyn Bunds, gave an assessment of life at Mount Carmel untainted by the anti-cult movement:

> I'm over 21, intelligent. I could have walked away at any time. I chose to stay. He doesn't keep you. You can leave. What you have to understand, though, is he keeps you by emotion. When you're down there, it's all so exciting. You don't know what he'll come up with next. I guess everyone is looking for Utopia, Shangri-la. You don't want any problems. It wasn't all bad times, you know. The people in this are great. They'll give you the shirt off their back. They're nice, like everyone else in the world. Except they believe this.

But the overriding presentation of the Branch Davidians in the series was that they were a dangerous cult controlled by a manipulative cult leader exercising mind control. Over twenty disaffected former members (part 1) and self-styled "cult experts" were the main sources for the series. David

Koresh was interviewed several times by telephone[41] and was cited as say-ing, "If the Bible is true, I'm Christ. But so what? What's so great about being Christ? A man nailed to the cross. A man acquainted with grief." And also: "If the Bible is true, I'm Christ. If the Bible is true. But all I want out of this is for people to be honest this time."[42] But the perspective of Koresh was only lightly represented, and often in an unflattering light.

On February 27, after part 1 of the series appeared, Steve Schneider, aged forty-one, called the *Waco Tribune-Herald* and invited Mark England and city editor Brian Blansette to Mount Carmel, so that Koresh could explain the Seven Seals of the book of Revelation to them. Clearly Koresh felt that a better knowledge of the biblical prophecies was necessary for them to understand his activities. Knowing that the raid was scheduled for February 28, they decided not to go.[43]

The "Sinful Messiah" series would have been enhanced if the voices of faithful Branch Davidians and nondisaffected former members had been represented. The religious beliefs of the Branch Davidians were presented as bizarre, and therefore the perspectives of the Branch Davidians were seen as unworthy of serious consideration.

According to Tabor and Gallagher, "[t]he widespread failure to take the religious convictions of Koresh and the other Davidians seriously, signaled by the facile adoption of the term 'cult,' contributed directly to their deaths."[44]

> Since "cults" represent a dangerous threat to the social order, it is necessary to oppose them with all the resources the state can muster, including tear gas, SWAT teams, and tanks. Since "cult leaders" are power-mad megalomaniacs, no one should lament their passing and they alone bear the blame for the deaths of their followers.[45]

Lee Hancock's Investigative Reporting

Lee Hancock of the *Dallas Morning News* produced consistently high-qual-ity investigative stories on this case from 1993 to 2003. Hancock arrived at Mount Carmel at 1:30 p.m. on February 28, 1993; reported on the story throughout the siege; was present on April 19 and witnessed the fire; and covered the criminal trial in 1994, the congressional hearings in 1995, the trial of the wrongful-death civil suit brought by Branch Davidian survivors and relatives in 2000, and the Danforth investigation and report in 1999–2000.[46] Hancock reported thoroughly and intelligently on the com-plexities of the case and brought new information to light that prompted additional government investigations.

Hancock reported in 1999 that, contrary to FBI testimony before Con-gress that on April 19 no pyrotechnic devices (utilizing a spark) were used, two pyrotechnic CS gas grenades were in fact fired at an underground tunnel.[47] This story led to Attorney General Janet Reno appointing former Senator John Danforth as special counsel to investigate whether the actions of federal agents at Mount Carmel on April 19 were appropriate.[48]

Lee Hancock said that she was proudest of her stories that revealed the conflict within the FBI and between federal agencies about how best to deal with the Branch Davidians.[49] Indeed, she reported on FBI internal memos and Justice Department memos and interviews, which were not included in the Justice Department's 1993 report, which indicated that FBI negotiators protested the aggressive tactical actions against the Branch Davidians and predicted a tragic outcome if the tactical approach continued to be given precedence.[50] Negotiators asserted that their ability to establish trust with the Branch Davidians was undermined by the repeated physical punishments and psychological warfare inflicted on the Branch Davidians by the tactical team every time the Branch Davidians cooperated with the negotiators and adults started coming out.

Hancock reported on Justice Department interviews in which retired FBI behavioral scientist Pete Smerick said that he had warned in 1993 "that they should not send in the tanks, because if they did so, children would die." In 1993 Smerick wrote memos warning that an aggressive tactical approach would "draw David Koresh and his followers closer together in the 'bunker mentality' and they would rather die than surrender."[51]

FBI negotiators endorsed a plan to gas the residence gradually, because they hoped to restrain the tactical unit bent on aggressive action. Negotiators and behavioral experts were not consulted when the tactical commanders ordered the acceleration of the insertion of CS gas and the dismantling of the building by tanks. Now-retired FBI negotiator Gary Noesner said in 1993, "Any negotiator would have told them that dismantling the building would provoke a violent response." Noesner asserted that "it was a bad decision to start knocking down a building containing women and children because people could have been crushed."[52]

Hancock's articles detailed how FBI tactical agents punished the Branch Davidians when adults came out of Mount Carmel. After two adults came out on March 12, special agent in charge Jeffrey Jamar ordered that the building's electricity be cut off. Two adults came out on March 19, seven others came out on March 21, and the negotiators believed that about twenty people would come out on March 22; but on March 21 FBI agents used the tanks to demolish the Branch Davidians' cars. Noesner reported that "[a] guy from the HRT [Hostage Rescue Team] said it was just to 'piss them off.'"[53]

Noesner and another negotiator, Fred Lanceley, were recalled from Waco because of their disagreements with the tactical team. Lanceley reported that in 1993 he said, "I want to get out of here, because all of these people in that compound are going to die, and I don't want to be here when it happens."[54]

Hancock's reporting of the conflicts within the FBI indicated that agents were well aware of the likely violent outcome of a tactical assault on Mount Carmel. The tactical actions, which were known to counteract negotiations, called into question self-exculpatory statements of FBI agents after the fire. For instance, special agent in charge Jeffrey Jamar, speaking on CNN on April 20, put the blame squarely on David Koresh:

> Those children are dead because David Koresh had them killed. There's no question about that. He had those fires started. He had 51 days to release those children. He chose those children to die. We didn't have anything to do with their deaths. Those fires were started in the compound by them. They were not allowed to leave, some of those who wanted to. We have inform—some evidence, again it's conclusive, there was gunfire when the fire started. There might have been people killed who were trying to get out of the compound.[55]

Lee Hancock saw the conflict at Mount Carmel as a collision of groups possessing opposing worldviews, "a belief system about the way things are going to work,"[56] particularly between the Branch Davidians and law enforcement agents, but also the media and other actors in the drama. Hancock was proud that the reporting of the *Dallas Morning News* documented this conflict.

Hancock said that her overall aim in reporting about the Branch Davidian case was to bring to light information that was kept from the public by the government actors and to be an advocate for the story's complexity. She said that she had received criticism in the newsroom for including too many details, but she felt that this story in particular could not be encapsulated in simple terms. Hancock saw herself as advocating for the "other than the easy, pat explanation of what happened." Hancock aimed to represent all sides as fairly as she could without resorting to "white-hat/black-hat" dichotomized coverage. Hancock thought that sometimes "people need to be informed that there are no good guys and bad guys, that there are no easy answers."

According to Hancock, the increasing availability of information from 1993 to 2003 caused the master narrative of the story to shift. Initially, reporters saw the story as a murder case and police stand-off. Quickly it became a story about a police stand-off with weird religious nuts. Then it became a story of a conflict between a strange religious group and an overly aggressive law enforcement community. Lastly, it became a story of a misunderstood religious group in conflict with overreaching federal agents employing excessive force.

Hancock noted that constraints of time and resources limit reporters' ability to cover complex stories thoroughly. Her reporting on the events at Mount Carmel involved going back to the case again and again to dig up more facts. Hancock acknowledged that in 1993 reporters probably accepted too much of the federal agents' line about the case. She took a complex view of the case and the sources, acknowledging that "the government screwed up, and the government lied, and the government misrepresented some things, absolutely, and they should be held to a higher standard," and that the Branch Davidians continued to have a stake in presenting themselves to the public in certain ways, given everything that had happened and how they had been depicted in the media.

Early in its coverage of the Branch Davidians, the *Dallas Morning News* used the word "cult" in a pejorative sense, but Hancock said that as a result of educational efforts made by scholars giving interviews, she and many other reporters became more careful when writing about unconventional religions.

Hancock judges that the quality of the print reporting on the Branch Davidian case has been variable. Some reporting has been excellent, some bad; some "propaganda" has been "embraced as reporting," as when reporters "took as gospel" statements by either federal agents or Branch Davidians. Hancock pointed to an inherent problem in reporters tending to give greater credence to sources with whom they have had more contact.

The variable quality of reporting on the Branch Davidian case was manifested in the *Waco Tribune-Herald*'s 2003 series entitled "Flashpoint in History."

"Flashpoint in History—10 Years after Mount Carmel"

In 2003 the *Waco Tribune-Herald* ran a second series on the tragedy in each Sunday issue from February 23 through April 13, culminating in a story on April 19, the tenth anniversary of the fire. The "Flashpoint in History" series made a concerted effort to include a variety of perspectives on the case. It contributed to humanizing the key players by including short vignettes of individuals, ranging from law enforcement agents and government officials to the surviving Branch Davidians. The series attempted to convey the complexities of the story and to humanize the actors in the drama. However, it made egregious errors in continuing to give a voice to spurious self-styled experts such as Rick Ross and in continuing to depict the Branch Davidians as crazy "cultists." The different perspectives expressed in this series indicated that different parties were continuing to contest the framing of the story. I am part of that contest, so I attempt here to report my role as self-reflexively as possible while stating my views. Law enforcement agents and their former advisors still have a stake in blaming

Koresh and the Branch Davidians. The surviving Branch Davidians have an obvious stake in humanizing themselves and their loved ones in the media and in protesting the government's actions against them.

The February 23, 2003, overview by Jason Embry stated that the "Branch Davidian saga was fraught with missteps on both sides." The article was accompanied by a statement by Carlos Sanchez, editor of the *Waco Tribune-Herald*, saying that the series intended to examine the legacy of the case for the city and the nation: "The problem, we quickly discovered, is that the events . . . left not only our community but our country with several different legacies, all complex and many still unclear." Sanchez wrote: "The siege at Mount Carmel . . . has left lingering questions in Waco and American culture about the role of law enforcement—both local and federal—as well as religion, government intervention, and the media." Sanchez suggested that "the debate itself may be Mount Carmel's enduring legacy."

There was also a statement in the February 23 issue from Bob Lott, the *Tribune-Herald* managing editor in 1993. He wrote that, in 1993, "[t]oo many died, and too needlessly: spellbound followers of a religious fanatic, recklessly led government men and the children, most horribly the innocent children." Lott praised the investigative reporting of Mark England and Darlene McCormick in the "Sinful Messiah" series and protested "the false accusations that [the] paper had contributed to the tragedy."

Terri Jo Ryan (part 2) focused on the history and beliefs of the Branch Davidians and the different perspectives on the story. Surviving Branch Davidians were interviewed, as well as several scholars including Stuart A. Wright and myself. Branch Davidian Clive Doyle addressed the issue of David Koresh's sexual relations with girls by giving the Branch Davidians' theological understanding: "We have had to wrestle with that, but we got to where we accepted it as God's instruction. If people couldn't accept it, they walked away. David believed God instructed him to produce children, that they were to be special children, that they would be there for judgment." I was quoted as saying that I saw the Branch Davidian tragedy as being a story about what happened to an unconventional religious group and about the abuses that arise out of the militarization of law enforcement.

I regard it as particularly unfortunate that the Tribune-Herald went back again to Rick Ross as a "cult expert." Ross's quoted remarks in part 2 about the surviving Branch Davidians were aimed at discrediting them. These were personal and insensitive attacks; I regard them as being extremely inappropriate in a news article. For instance, Ross was quoted as saying about Sheila Martin, who lost in the fire her husband, Douglas Wayne Martin, aged forty-two, and four of her children, Wayne Joseph (twenty), Anita (eighteen), Sheila (fifteen), and Lisa (thirteen):

And consider Sheila Martin. She lost a husband, the love of her life, the father of her children. She lost half her children and all of her friends in this horrible, horrible tragedy. All she sacrificed was for nothing—and who did she give this up for? A pedophile, a criminal of the worst sort, a man who raped a 10-year-old.

Ross discounted the significance of David Koresh's teachings for the Branch Davidians, calling them "theology-on-the-fly."

Generally this article by Terri Jo Ryan demonstrated a clumsy inability to negotiate the different perspectives of the Branch Davidians, scholars, and anti-cult "experts." I note that I never spoke directly with Terri Jo Ryan, but to her editor, whom I thought would write the story.

Tommy Witherspoon's article (part 3) on the Branch Davidian prisoners was informative. Of the Branch Davidians convicted, Ruth Riddle had completed her sentence and had been released. The seven men remaining in prison would be out in three to four years, but they would still be required to pay financial remuneration.

Mike Anderson's story (part 4) focused on federal and state agents and agencies. ATF and FBI agents articulated their view that blame rested solely on Koresh and the Branch Davidians. Retired ATF agent Bill Buford, aged fifty-eight, asserted that on February 28, 1993, Branch Davidians were firing machine guns as the agents got out of the cattle trailers. In response to the Treasury Department's report that in 1993 ATF officials lied to investigators and reporters, the ATF developed a new training program for agents stressing the importance of honesty and how to work with the media.

This story reported that after 1993 the ATF created four specially trained tactical teams for high-risk operations, and agents were more carefully trained in intelligence gathering and decision making. Since 1993 the ATF shifted from using "penetration-type" searches to plans where agents surround a site and call for the subjects to surrender. Director Bradley A. Buckles noted that the ATF had learned that tactics that work with criminals will probably not work when applied to religious believers.

This story included an interview with Byron Sage, aged fifty-five, styled as the FBI's lead negotiator during the siege in 1993. Sage reported that after 1993 the FBI formed the Critical Incident Response Group (CIRG) to put the negotiators and tactical officers under a coordinated command. Sage said that all CIRG members took a two-week negotiation class every year.

Bob Boyd of the Texas Department of Protective and Regulatory Services was interviewed in part 4 on the child abuse allegations. Boyd explained that the department did nothing in 1993 in response to child abuse allegations, because the children they interviewed at Mount Carmel reported no abuse.

The FBI assault and the fire were addressed in this story. Clive Doyle reported that he knew of no plan for suicide and that he believed the Branch Davidians would be coming out once Koresh had completed his little book on the Seven Seals. Byron Sage asserted, however, that there was no evidence that Koresh was working on the book and that this claim was a delaying tactic. Sage asserted that the FBI agents had no control over the outcome at Mount Carmel:

> The FBI never had any control over how this was going to end. From day one, that was up to Koresh. I think the only control law enforcement had over this was where and when it was going to end. But ultimately the ending was up to Koresh. He never relinquished that control right up to the fire that ultimately took the lives of those children.

Carl Hoover's article (part 5) surveyed the products of popular culture alluding to the Branch Davidian tragedy.

Mike Copeland's article entitled "Escaping the Stigma" (part 6) traced the concern of the citizens of Waco that the name of their city had become synonymous with the tragedy. The "Flashpoint in History" articles repeatedly pointed out that Mount Carmel was located ten miles east of Waco, near the small community of Elk, Texas.

Throughout the series, despite reporters' efforts to be neutral and to include all views, the Branch Davidians were discounted repeatedly as being "Apocalypse-obsessed"[57] or "Apocalypse-fixated" (part 6)—strange appellations in the middle of the Bible Belt—or as being "apocalyptic cult members" (part 8). Copeland's article amazingly characterized the events at Mount Carmel as being a "combustible episode." His prose distanced the Branch Davidians in terms of proximity and worldview:

> Self-styled Davidian prophet David Koresh, 33, and his Apocalypse-fixated followers did not reside in Waco. They lived in a communal arrangement near the small city of Elk, 10 miles east of the city.

Copeland's article touched on the difference in the ways Americans viewed the victims of the Oklahoma City bombing (carried out by Timothy McVeigh and perhaps others in retaliation for the Branch Davidian deaths) and the victims of September 11, 2001. Oklahoma City Mayor Kirk Humphreys said, "I'm not sure Americans knew how to respond emotionally to the Davidians." Copeland's article concluded by putting the blame on David Koresh:

> Even critics of law enforcement's handling of the siege note that Koresh was anything but an innocent victim. Much of what happened to the Davidians is rooted in Koresh's obsession with weaponry, his

sexual relations with under-age girls and his earlier shoot-out with a
rival prophet at Mount Carmel.

J. B. Smith (part 7) focused on the children of Mount Carmel. Kevin
Jones, aged twenty-one, remembered hiding with his brother under a blan-
ket while the bullets flew through the walls during the ATF assault. He
remembered hearing his grandfather, Perry Jones, screaming when he was
shot and begging to be put out of his pain. Kevin Jones wondered why the
ATF did not arrest Koresh on one of his trips into Waco.

Daniel Martin, aged sixteen, described Mount Carmel as an environment apart from video games and fast food and as having no indoor
plumbing. He remembered that children were spanked, but did not recall
ever feeling fearful: "I was always watching. I was always deep in thought.
But I had fun. I was always happy."

Dr. Bruce Perry, a child psychiatrist who worked with the children who
came out during the siege, said that he was not surprised to hear that the
young people had fond memories of Mount Carmel. He stated that he
believed that the environment possessed a twisted worldview without being
physically abusive. Perry reported that when Attorney General Janet Reno
initially justified the FBI assault by alleging child abuse, he reacted, "What
is she talking about?" Reno had to retract that allegation. Perry stated in
the "Flashpoint" article that there was no evidence of child abuse during
the siege; nothing was going on inside Mount Carmel to justify the tank
and CS gas assault.[58]

A second article by Tommy Witherspoon (part 8) focused on the civil
liberty issues. The adult Branch Davidians' attorney in the wrongful-death
civil case, former Attorney General Ramsey Clark, was quoted as saying:

> I think it ought to be remembered always, painful as it is, because to
> me it represents the greatest tragedy in the history of the US domes-
> tic law enforcement, the greatest loss of life and the greatest failure of
> law enforcement to sensitively address a very difficult situation with
> the highest priority of securing life.

The article pointed out that in 1993, while federal agents were blasting
high-decibel sounds at the Branch Davidians and shining bright spotlights
at them all night long, Persian Gulf War veteran Timothy McVeigh was
nearby watching and became the antigovernment activist who bombed the
federal building in Oklahoma City on April 19, 1995, killing 168 people.
Sociologist Stuart A. Wright was quoted as saying: "[Mount Carmel] was
unprecedented in scope and consequence. I mean 86 people died in the
whole thing. It's just unprecedented for law enforcement to be involved
and for that many people to have been killed." Wright continued:

> I've noted an amazing shift in public reaction since 1993. By 1999, when we learned of the pyrotechnic devices, polls showed 50 percent of Americans believed the FBI had screwed up or had a major hand in the tragic outcome. Compare that with polls right after [the incident] where 93 percent blamed the Davidians.

Witherspoon's article stated that many law enforcement officials "remain convinced that apocalyptic cult members set the fire themselves as part of a grand suicide pact." A paragraph seemed to suggest that the Branch Davidians got what they deserved because of their sexual practices, as if these justified the aggressive actions that resulted in the deaths of the children:

> While Doyle and other followers say the Branch Davidians were peaceful people who merely wanted to study the Bible and mind their own business, DNA evidence revealed that at least a dozen of the 21 children who died in the fire were fathered by Koresh. Some of their mothers were underage girls.[59]

"Prophesying about Waco" by Brian Gaar, dated April 19, 2003 (part 9), again characterized the Branch Davidians as "Apocalypse-obsessed followers" who "perished in a mysterious inferno." The article discussed how college students in 2003, even those nearby at Baylor University in Waco and at Southwestern University in Georgetown, Texas, did not know what had happened at Mount Carmel in 1993. Much of the article was focused on citizens who were concerned that "Waco" had become "a household word, initially conjuring up gun-toting, Bible-quoting religious crazies." Bob Sheehy, who was mayor of Waco in 1993, expressed relief that the general public was starting to forget the association of the tragedy with the city. While Waco was planning a memorial to the 114 people who died in a tornado in 1947, Sheehy expressed opposition to any memorial at Mount Carmel. Two Baylor scholars expressed contrary views. Dr. Derek Davis said he would like to see a memorial at Mount Carmel, or a larger museum, to present information about what happened: "[I]t is something we want to remember as an important event concerning American religious freedom." Baylor sociologist Larry Lyon noted:

> When Waco was mentioned eight years ago, 10 years ago, it meant crazy people. It used to be a place where people had strange interpretations of the Bible. Now it no longer means religious fanaticism. Now it's a place where the government overreached. It's a place where there are lessons to be learned.

The "Flashpoint in History" series made a genuine attempt to give a balanced treatment by including a variety of perspectives on the Branch Davidian tragedy. The diverse voices in the series indicated that the framing of the story was still hotly contested, between Branch Davidians and law enforcement agents; between scholars and anti-cultists; and between citizens of Waco who wanted the world to forget the incident, Branch Davidians like Clive Doyle, who in part 9 asserted, "We're part of this community," and concerned Waco citizens and outsiders who believed a more elaborate memorial should be put on the site. In my opinion, it was extremely unprofessional to include the voice of a deprogrammer (a spurious profession) with a criminal record and no training in the study of religion as an "expert" on the Branch Davidians. The personal attacks that Rick Ross was permitted to launch in the pages of the *Waco Tribune-Herald* on surviving Branch Davidians were in extremely poor taste and did not reflect good reporting. The series' constant characterization of the Branch Davidians as "Apocalypse-obsessed" continued the discounting of the significance of their religious beliefs and humanity. The series came close to suggesting (part 8) that because of their sexual practices the Branch Davidians got a deserved outcome in the federal actions that resulted in the deaths of the innocents inside Mount Carmel. For the most part, Waco citizens expressed the wish that the rest of the world might realize that the Branch Davidians lived ten miles outside the city.

Branch Davidians and the Media in 2003

The surviving Branch Davidians who remained close to Mount Carmel—Catherine Matteson, Clive Doyle, Sheila Martin, and Bonnie Haldeman (who visited regularly)—continued to talk to the media through the years, realizing that they had a stake in humanizing themselves and their deceased loved ones in the public eye. However, by 2003, they felt they had been betrayed often by reporters, who came around pretending to be friendly and then left to depict them in a negative light. A significant instance of this was an article in *Texas Monthly*, "The Ghosts of Mount Carmel,"[60] which took a derisive tone toward the Branch Davidians. Even the article's photographs portrayed the Branch Davidians and interestingly, Byron Sage, as lonely, odd, and isolated, by depicting them individually and surrounded by a lot of space.

Yet the surviving Branch Davidians continued to give interviews. For instance, Bonnie Haldeman,[61] David Koresh's mother, believed that media representatives were mainly looking for the sensational stories. She believed that some reporters were looking for the truth, but unless there was a sensational hook they were not going to pursue the story. She was aware that reporters were limited in what they could write: they were constrained by the perspectives of their editors. Haldeman chose not to speak much to reporters on the subject of Koresh's wives and children, admitting that she did not understand it fully, but saying that Koresh's reasons were biblically based. Instead Haldeman chose to humanize them by regularly expressing her love for her deceased grandchildren, their mothers, and for her son, as well as for her friends who died in 1993. Haldeman hoped that, in the future, law enforcement personnel who were at Mount Carmel in 1993 would report what happened there. She felt that one day God would reveal the ultimate purpose of the deaths.

Promoting Contacts between Religion Scholars and Reporters

Contacts between religion scholars and reporters improved from 1993 to 2003. Scholarly professional associations reached out to reporters, and the Religion Newswriters Association took steps to put reporters in touch with bona fide scholars. Dart[62] and Religion Newswriters Foundation[63] advised that it was important for reporters to consult credentialed experts and to avoid the use of pejorative terms such as "cult."

The Society for the Scientific Study of Religion and the Religious Research Association, consisting mainly of sociologists of religion, since the 1980s had a scholar serving as publicity coordinator to reach out to reporters. Stuart Wright served in that capacity from 1989 to 2000. His goal was to make reporters more aware of the research being done by SSSR and RRA members, and he also made efforts to educate reporters about the problems with the "cult" and "brainwashing" stereotypes.[64] In 2003 Scott Thumma at Hartford Seminary served in this capacity.

In 1994 the American Academy of Religion formed the Committee on the Public Understanding of Religion, in great part as a response to the tragedy at Mount Carmel. As a member of the initial committee, I called the president of the Religion Newswriters Association and found that he had never heard of the American Academy of Religion (AAR), a nine-thou-sand-member professional association of scholars of religion, representing various disciplines and specialties. The AAR subsequently made efforts to make itself known to reporters needing experts on religion topics. A staff member at the AAR headquarters in Atlanta was designated to take calls from reporters and make recommendations about scholars.

In 2000 the AAR began giving awards to journalists for the Best In-Depth Reporting on Religion in three categories: news outlets with more than one hundred thousand circulation, news outlets with less than one hundred thousand circulation, and opinion writing.[65]

In August 2002 the AAR, with funding from Pew Charitable Trusts, initiated Religionsource,[66] a database of five thousand religion scholars representing fourteen hundred areas of expertise. A reporter can go to the website and type in a key word to find relevant scholars. According to Kyle Cole, associate director of Religionsource, the AAR began its outreach to reporters in response to the Branch Davidian tragedy.[67]

In August 2002, Pew Charitable Trusts provided funding for a service called ReligionLink from the Religion Newswriters Foundation, the educational arm of the Religion Newswriters Association. ReligionLink is edited by Diane Connolly, the former religion editor at the *Dallas Morning News*. Under her guidance the religion section of the *Dallas Morning News* won seven national awards for the nation's best secular newspaper religion section. ReligionLink's goal is to "help journalists write informed stories about the ways religion affects public life. It does not take sides on issues. It strives to treat all belief systems with respect and fairness and has no ties to any religious organization."[68] Its reporters anticipate possible upcoming news topics relating to religion, locate relevant experts, and send this information out by email to subscribers in free biweekly reports. Interested individuals can also access ReligionLink's archive on its website. According to Kimberly Winston,[69] a reporter with ReligionLink, there was a "mini-boom" in religion reporting after 1993, and now most newspapers have a reporter who covers religion at least part-time.

Debra Mason, the executive director of the Religion Newswriters Association, noted that many of the reporters who reported on the Branch Davidians in 1993 were general assignment reporters or crime reporters and were not religion newswriters, who would bring greater sensitivity to reporting on religious groups. According to Mason, ReligionLink's purpose is to give

> [j]ournalists story ideas and sources, with the goal of improving the quality and depth of reporting about the intersection of religion and public life. It's intended to convince reporters and editors of the merits of these stories and to point journalists toward useful background. In the area of religion, which is fraught with many nuances and the easy potential for inaccuracy, ReligionLink serves as a model for journalists seeking to balance sources and provide adequate context.[70]

The *Dallas Morning News* has demonstrated notable commitment to improving the quality of reporting on religion under the leadership of president and editor Robert Mong, who in 2004 acknowledged that in 1993 the *Dallas Morning News* did not properly integrate religion newswriters and news generalists in covering the events at Mount Carmel. Since 1993 the paper's Saturday religion section has been expanded, and in 2003 the newspaper had five religion newswriters, including Susan Hogan-Albach, winner of a 2002 AAR award for excellence in religion newswriting. The religion newswriters now serve as resources for the paper and work with general reporters on big stories, a model that bodes well for nuanced coverage of stories relating to religion.

Conclusion

Media representatives were actors in the drama in 1993 leading to the conflict at Mount Carmel that resulted in the deaths of four ATF agents and eighty Branch Davidians. There was a lot of behind-the-scenes activity as *Waco Tribune-Herald* and KWTX-TV reporters and photographers attempted to be in place to cover the ATF raid on February 28, resulting in the inadvertent tipping-off of the Branch Davidians. ATF commanders had the authority to call off the raid when they learned that the element of surprise was lost,[71] but they did not. After the debacle on February 28, the media depicted the Branch Davidians as "cultists," dehumanizing the ordinary Branch Davidians by erasing them by focusing on depicting Koresh as a deranged and manipulative "cult leader" who brainwashed his followers.

After 1993, the FBI and other federal agents continued to have a stake in blaming Koresh and the adult Branch Davidians for what happened, and the surviving Branch Davidians had a stake in humanizing their community and seeking legal redress. Religion scholars and their professional associations became more proactive in making their expertise available to reporters. Reporters, especially in the print media, likewise took steps to improve religion reporting and to reach out to appropriate scholarly experts. Despite these efforts, however, anti-cultist entrepreneurs such as Rick Ross still had an impact on media treatments of new religions.

Gus Niebuhr,[72] formerly a religion newswriter for the *Washington Post* and the *New York Times* and now an academic, pointed out that by 2003 reporting on new religions remained variable. It had improved in the print media in large urban centers, where reporters were more likely to attempt to avoid the easy label of "cult." But the problem was that very few reporters were committed to doing in-depth religion reporting. He pointed out that religion was not much addressed in schools of journalism. Young reporters, who did not have a memory of the Branch Davidian conflict and the subsequent scholarly and government inquiries, were more likely to perpetuate the old "cult" stereotype when writing about the Branch Davidians. Niebuhr saw the reporting of religion on television as being poor, with some notable exceptions. He advised that members of new religions could contribute to better news coverage of themselves by speaking with reporters. I note that the outcome is dependent on reporters approaching religious groups with open minds and without an underlying agenda of painting them as cultists.

The Branch Davidian story is multifaceted, with numerous actors and points of view. The framing of the story in the print media shifted from 1993 to 2003, from a simplistic "cult" mass-suicide perspective to questions being raised about excessive force utilized by militarized law enforcement agencies.[73] There is still room for improvement in reporting about religions and especially new religions, but scholars and reporters are making efforts to collaborate in their joint pedagogical mission of research and informing the public.

The media are significant actors in events leading to episodes of violence involving religious groups. The media are not simply bystanders in these dramas.[74] Therefore, the stakes are high regarding whether or not media report on religious groups fairly, accurately, and in a nuanced manner. The media also have a crucial function in reporting on an American law enforcement establishment that remains heavily militarized. It is well that reporters, scholars, mental health experts, and law enforcement agents continue to cultivate reflexivity about our biases, values, and goals, so that we do not contribute to future scenarios in which there is unnecessary loss of life.

Chapter Ten

Tensions in Dispensational Eschatology

Mark S. Sweetnam

Paul Boyer, writing in 1992, complained that evangelical millennialism "has received little scholarly attention."[1] A more recent commentator, dealing with Tim LaHaye and Jerry B. Jenkins's *Left Behind* series and its related spin-offs, was somewhat congratulatory in his conclusion that "critical responses to the series have been so voluminous that it would now be impossible" to sustain this viewpoint.[2] His complacency might seem well-founded; the remarkable success of the *Left Behind* series has attracted a great deal of critical activity, and commentators have been anxious to engage with this new phenomenon. It was, perhaps, to be feared that this upsurge of interest would be marked by a lack of concern for strict accuracy in the often-complex discussion of the prophetic framework implied in the novels. Overwhelmingly, critics have viewed rapture novels as an expression of the concerns and occupations of the school of prophetic interpretation known as dispensationalism. In doing so, they have paid insufficient heed to a warning given by a leading historian of the most dispensationally based movement of them all, the Plymouth Brethren: Roy Coad. Writing in 1966, Coad cautioned his readers against an oversimplification of prophetic positions:

> We shall rarely find in practice that our fellows will fall neatly into our
> mental categories. Our classifications are not a quarry for the brick-
> bats of debate: we shall be the better Christians if we refrain from
> extending the orderliness of disciplined minds to the placing of neat
> little labels on our fellow men.[3]

With a very typical moderation, Coad was cautious about making any hard
and fast assumptions about prophetic categories. Such scrupulousness has
frequently been lacking in the work of more recent commentators, who
have assumed a monolithic, standard dispensationalism, a system of
prophetic interpretation that is fairly represented by these fictional embod-
iments. Such writers might well be surprised to learn that the dispensationalism embodied by rapture fictions is often very far both from the roots of
the movement, and from a good deal of current dispensationalist belief,
and that the novels they discuss were greeted with horror by many dispensationalists. The inevitable fact that the more sensationalist versions of
prophetic interpretation attract greater interest than staid Bible teaching
has resulted in a perception of dispensationalism that is, to say the least,
decidedly lopsided. The alert critic must always remember that the mutation of classical dispensationalism at the heart of most of these fictional
accounts is only one of the possible responses to the tensions that are at
the very center of dispensationalist belief. To understand these tensions,
we must briefly examine the history of the movement and the structure of
its classical form.

The Development of Classical Dispensationalism

Dispensationalism developed out of the atmosphere of prophetic tumult
that marked the close of the eighteenth century, and the first decades of
the nineteenth.[4] Its emergence was closely connected with the secession
from the confessional churches of those who were to become identified as
the founding fathers of the Plymouth Brethren, and the Brethren movement has continued to be very closely identified with dispensationalism.[5]
Because of this close link, histories of early dispensationalism tend also to
be histories of the Brethren, and are thus afflicted with some of the distinctive historiographical complexities of that movement. Prominent among
these difficulties is the fact that some of the earlier historians of the
Brethren have been marked by a belief that the distinctive ecclesiology
adopted by the Brethren and their dispensationally based eschatology
emerged fully formed as dramatic revelations by the Holy Spirit.[6] This view
resulted in dispensationalism being detached from the very specific
prophetic climate that originated the theory. Coad, in his general *History
of the Brethren Movement*,[7] and more especially in his paper on prophetic

developments noted above, insisted on the importance of understanding the historical setting that energized dispensationalism, while Timothy Stunt, in his magisterial study, *From Awakening to Secession*,[8] has placed many of the most characteristic features of the Brethren in their true relationship to wider developments between 1815 and 1835. Both Coad and Stunt are agreed that the intellectual climate, marked as it was by the effects of the Enlightenment, and especially the growth of "a godless rationalism and glorification of man, was conducive to the sort of evangelical pessimism that fed directly into a growing sense that the end times were near."[9] Political events contributed still further to this sense of impending apocalypse. Europe was still reverberating from the shock waves of the French Revolution, an event sufficiently apocalyptic for the most violent taste. Revolution in Ireland seemed to threaten similar events closer to home—events, moreover, in which the specter of Rome, the traditional antichrist, could be seen. Furthermore, the turn of the nineteenth century was marked by "intense prophetic speculation, when the classical historicist views [of prophetic interpretation] were on the point of discrediting themselves."[10]

This, then, was the stage on which two of the pivotal figures of dispensationalism appeared. Edward Irving and John Nelson Darby, a Scotsman and an Irishman, were to have an enormous impact on the shape of dispensationalism. Irving was a romantic, flamboyant figure, and a close friend of Thomas Carlyle, who had worked with Thomas Chalmers in the Glasgow slums.[11] From Glasgow, Irving came to London, where he became the minister of the Caledonian Chapel. Here, his extrovert preaching and his repudiation of prevailing evangelical "prudence" attracted large congregations. Irving was later to become notorious for his enthusiastic endorsement of charismatic spiritual gifts and his ultimately heretical Christology.[12] His importance to the story of dispensationalism, however, centers on his participation in a five-year-long series of conferences held at the home of Henry Drummond, a banker and member of parliament, in Albury, between 1826 and 1830. It is telling, given the eventual shape of the system of prophetic interpretation that was ultimately to emerge from these beginnings, that these conferences were commenced at the instigation of Lewis Way. Way was a barrister who had taken Anglican orders and "devoted his life and much of his fortune to the welfare of the Jews, among other matters reorganizing and reconstructing the London Society [for Promoting Christianity Amongst the Jews], which under his leadership became very prominent."[13] The roots of dispensationalism are therefore closely linked with evangelical philo-Semitism. Others who gathered at Albury represented the "flower of evangelical belief from all denominations."[14] The precise extent and nature of the prophetic teaching that emerged from the

Albury circle is still the subject of (frequently heated) debate, but it was at these conferences that the doctrine of the secret rapture, the basic premise of every rapture fiction, was first formulated.[15]

The doctrine of a secret rapture of the church is not, by itself, dispensationalism. It does, however, provide a key element of the basic structure of that school of prophetic interpretation. The doctrine splits the second advent of Christ into two distinct parts. The first is a secret coming to rapture, or "snatch away," the church, composed of living and dead saints, those converted from Pentecost to the moment of the rapture. This rapture is followed by seven years of tribulation, and only then by a fuller manifestation in glory of Christ, accompanied by his church. This "rapture/tribulation scenario offers reward for a faithful church, a future for the Jews, and wrath for the apostate and ungodly, neatly tying together a number of eschatological loose ends."[16] As far as the development of dispensationalism is concerned, the rapture had two very important implications. First, it demanded a far clearer line of demarcation than had ordinarily been seen between the church and the Jewish nation. Second, as we shall see, the belief that this rapture could take place at any moment had profound implications for prophetic expectation.

Most students of prophetic history accept that the Albury group taught some variant of the secret rapture. There remains, however, considerable discussion as to how closely the Albury teaching can be linked with the emergence of dispensationalism.[17] What we can say with certainty is that the Albury conferences were followed by a series of similar, but "more sober" conferences in Powerscourt House, Co. Wicklow, under the patronage of Theodosia, Lady Powerscourt.[18] Three large conferences were held, from 1831 to 1833. Robert Daly, who was later to become bishop of Cashel, chaired these meetings, with a large, invited audience in attendance. As with Albury, prophetic speculation was the chief occupation of these conferences. Once again, no very clear synthesis of belief emerged from the meetings, but it is significant that J. N. Darby took a "prominent part" in the proceedings. Darby was an Anglican clergyman, a graduate of Trinity College, Dublin.[19] He was a man of marked asceticism, but capable, as his later career was to prove, of warm friendship and still warmer controversy. Very different in many ways from Irving's flamboyant persona, he was possessed of an equal charisma and evoked an almost fanatical devotion in his followers. At this point, Darby was strongly influenced by what he perceived as the apostasy of the larger part of the established church, and of confessional Christianity in general. Influenced as he was by this pessimism, the idea of an imminent rapture proved very attractive to Darby. Although he did not originate the doctrine, "he did clarify, systematize, and popularize it."[20] While his ideas on the subject were not to achieve a full formulation for a number of years, from the early 1830s onwards Darby saw himself as man with a heavenly and imminent hope.

This heavenly hope was, however, to bring Darby into conflict with some of his earthly friends, most particularly B. W. Newton.[21] To Newton, the idea of a secret rapture was abhorrent. There were two reasons for this. The first was personal. At Oxford, Newton had been a very close friend of Henry Bulteel, a fellow evangelical, and had been dismayed when Bulteel was "swept off his feet" by Irving's controversial teaching on miracles and spirit gifts. To Newton, any teaching linked with Irving and the Albury circle was, therefore, suspect, and he identified the idea of a secret rapture as just such an Irvingite delusion. His second objection was doctrinal. The separation between the church and Jews of Old Testament times seemed to Newton to demand two separate schemes of redemption, and thus undermined the sufficiency of the work of Christ. Newton, therefore, became a prominent opponent of the secret rapture teaching. Darby, meanwhile, sought to find a way around the radical christological implications of the rapture. He found the solution in what was to become known as dispensationalism: a system of Scripture interpretation that went beyond a merely prophetic significance. Broadly speaking, this view of past and future history posited the idea that God, in dealing with mankind, had adopted a series of administrations. Each dispensation had its own rules, each was a test of mankind, and each ended with human failure, divine intervention, and the instantiation of a new dispensation. This system gave Darby precisely the distinction between Israel and the church that his view of the rapture required. It also squared well with his concerns about the state of Christendom, his pessimism about the "ruin of the church." It was, however, a solution that failed to appeal to Newton, who devised his own compromise proposals—positing a series of concurrent dispensations, and thus eliminating the sharp dichotomy that Darby saw between Israel and the church. Darby rejected this idea, and his disagreement with Newton on prophecy was to be the first hint of the division that would, in a short time, split the nascent Brethren movement decisively.

Although this split was to distance Darby from the "open"—as opposed to the exclusive—side of the movement, both sections adopted a Darbyite, dispensationalist eschatology to a degree where it became the Brethren orthodoxy. The success of his views was aided by the scholarly prowess of William Kelly, Darby's disciple and prominent leader of the Exclusive section of the Brethren. The controversial accusations of heresy made against Newton in the heat of his split with Darby may also have robbed his opposing views of their credibility. Within the Brethren, dispensationalism reigned supreme. Nor was its success limited to the confines of that group. "It is important to notice that in the later development of prophetic teachings in the evangelical section of the Church at large we have one of our

most striking measures of the wider influence of the early Brethren movement."[22] This wider influence can be seen most clearly on the western side
of the Atlantic. "Darby himself . . . observed that in the United States people showed more interest in his prophetic teaching than in his ecclesiastical principles," and it is in America that we see dispensationalism flourish
outside of the movement that produced it.[23]

   The United States also provided the most definitive statement of classical dispensationalism in one of the crowning achievements of dispensational scholarship, the Scofield Bible (1909).[24] This annotated study Bible
has been described as "perhaps the most influential single publication in
millenarian and fundamentalist historiography."[25] C. I. Scofield was a
lawyer and one-time attorney general of Kansas. Later, he served as minister in a congregational church in Dallas, Texas, and was a popular speaker
at various conferences. In 1906 he began work on the reference Bible that
was to define dispensationalism. While Scofield's identification with the
Brethren was limited and flexible, his annotations bear the impress of
Brethren teaching, as much in ecclesiastical as eschatological matters. Spe-
cialized experience in Bible printing was desirable for the publication of
Scofield's version, and a deal with Oxford University Press saw the first
copies produced in 1909. This partnership

> took the dispensational movement back to one of the universities
> from which it emerged, and the reputation of those leading academ-
> ics mentioned in its foreword propelled its distinctive worldview out
> of the populist ferment of evangelical dissent. The world's leading
> university press had lent its cultural authority to the central manifesto
> of fundamentalism.[26]

The success of the Bible was immense: in the thirty years after that first
publication, over 1.95 million copies were sold. A slightly revised second
edition was published in 1917, and a more radical revision was published
as the New Scofield Bible in 1967. Dispensationalism had gained its key
text, and that text had originated on the west of the Atlantic. Dispensationalism continued to gain ground and became a key dogma in the emerging
evangelical seminaries in the southern United States. Chief among these
institutions was the Dallas Theological Seminary, and it was from here that
another codification of dispensationalism emerged. *Things to Come* was
first presented as a doctoral dissertation at Dallas by J. Dwight Pentecost.
When it was published in 1958, it marked the zenith of dispensational
scholarship, and, while its popularity has remained considerably less than
that of the Scofield Bible, it remains the statement par excellence of classical dispensationalism.[27]

To understand the next step in the development of the dispensational view of prophecy, a view that was to have a profound impact on later developments in North American prophecy belief, it is necessary at this stage to survey the chief points of dispensationalism as formulated by Scofield and Pentecost. Dispensationalism has the convenient feature that its outline is relatively simple—a fact that has resulted in its appearing in a variety of prophetic charts. It has already been noted how dispensationalism is based on a number of time periods, each "a period of time in which man is tested in respect of obedience to some *specific* revelation of the will of God."[28] Each dispensation tested humanity under different conditions, and each ended with human failure and divine intervention. Scofield laid the basis for classical dispensationalism generally, by defining seven dispensations: Innocence—from the creation of man to the expulsion from Eden; Conscience—from the expulsion to the Noahic flood; Human Government—from the flood to the calling of Abram; Promise—from the calling of Abram to the giving of the law; Law—from Sinai to the death of Christ; the Church age and the dispensation of grace—the present dispensation, which commenced with the death of Christ and will continue to the rapture; and finally, the Millennial reign of Christ and his saints.[29]

The first five of these dispensations were, of course, a matter of historical record. Eschatological interest, therefore, centered upon the final two dispensations. And it is here that the most contested feature of dispensationalism becomes important. For classical dispensationalists, the Church age is a "prophetic parenthesis"—no prophetic event could take place until the church had been raptured, and the field cleared for divine intervention in the affairs of Earth. This belief was a necessary concomitant of the imminent rapture. Sandeen points out that "Darby taught that the secret Rapture could occur at any moment. . . . Darby avoided the pitfalls both of attempting to predict a time for Christ's second advent and of trying to make sense of the contemporary alarms of European politics with Revelation as a guidebook."[30] Scofield's account agreed: "when the Church age will end, and the seventieth week begin is nowhere revealed."[31] Pentecost stressed precisely the same point: "Since the Church is given the hope of an imminent return of Christ there can be no signs given to her as to when this event will take place."[32] An earlier twentieth-century critic of dispensationalism—wiser in his generation than others—perfectly encapsulated the significance of the concept of an imminent return:

> Nineteen centuries have passed by, during which . . . this new age has been imminent. There is nothing in premillennial teaching to compel us to believe that the world may not need to wait nineteen or twice nineteen centuries more, since, according to men like Dr. Scofield and Dr. Pierson, "imminent" . . . means simply "next on the docket," whether near or remote.[33]

For dispensationalists, therefore, it was only after the rapture that the emergence of the antichrist, the seven years of tribulation, and the manifestation of Christ as king could take place. This insistence on a period in which no prophecy would be fulfilled is essential to dispensationalism as formulated by Darby, Scofield, and Pentecost—essential, that is, to classical dispensationalism. The prophetic caution springing from this view has been a key feature of dispensationalism, a fact that Coad points out:

> It is necessary . . . to pay tribute to one notable feature of the group which was adopting these futurist principles. . . . Despite their ardent expectations of the Advent, they generally took care to avoid any fixing of dates or other sensational prophesying. This observation still holds good.

Coad wrote this in 1966. The observation was soon to be shattered by a mutation of dispensationalism that threw both its principles of interpretation and its eschewal of sensationalism to the winds.

Mutating Dispensationalism—"Signs of the Times"

In 1970 the sensationalizing of dispensationalism began. The key document in this new approach to dispensational prophecy was Hal Lindsey's *The Late Great Planet Earth*, an unprecedentedly successful prophetic text, described by the *New York Times* as the "#1 Non-fiction Bestseller of the Decade."[34] Since its initial publication, the book has gone through more than 108 printings with sales, by 1993, of more than 18 million copies in English, and anywhere between 18 and 20 million further copies in fifty-four other languages.[35] In 1977, a film version of the book was produced, with narration by Orson Welles. Lindsey's book, with its putative identifications of the apocalyptic players and its emphasis on "the signs of the times" was a decisive break with the dispensationalism of Darby, Scofield, and Pentecost.

"Signs of the times" literature in itself was nothing new. The phrase had been first used by John Cummings in his 1855 book, *The Signs of the Times—or Present, Past and Future*. Cummings published a second book in the same year: *The End—The Proximate Signs of the Close of this Dispensation*. Despite this title, Cummings was not a dispensationalist; indeed, his precise prophetic position is somewhat difficult to define. His work is significant, however, as it establishes many of the basic tropes of the "signs of the times" approach to prophecy, including many of the identifications still made by Lindsey. Cummings also established another feature of the genre—the need for revisionary sequels. In 1861, just a year before the end of the world as predicted in his earlier books, Cummings published *The*

Great Preparation, which afforded him an extra five years of leeway. Similarly, over a century later, Lindsey's books discarded prophetic prudence and called for a similar process of revision and redating. So, for example, *The Final Battle* (1994) is essentially an unacknowledged rewrite of *The Late Great Planet Earth* (1970), *The Apocalypse Code* (1997) is a rewrite of *There's a New World Coming* (1973), and *Planet Earth 2000 A.D.* (1994, 1996) are revisions of *In the 1980s: Countdown to Armageddon* (1981). *Planet Earth: The Final Chapter* (1998) is the most recent version of the *Planet Earth* books, with the embarrassingly inaccurate date removed from the title.[36] This dearth of accuracy is in spite of Lindsey's advertised status as "The Father of the Modern-Day Bible Prophecy Movement" and "the best known prophecy teacher in the world."[37] Sensational date-fixing was, and remains, at the heart of Lindsey's approach. Such sensationalism sold, especially in the atmosphere of Cold War paranoia.

Given the enormous popularity of Lindsay's book, it was only a short time before other "scholars of prophecy" also realized that "the future is big business."[38] These writers followed Lindsey's approach and sought to see prophecy being fulfilled in current events. Despite the scale of their break with classical dispensationalism, these new proponents of prophetic theory continue to be identified as dispensationalists. They arrogated the title to themselves, and classical dispensationalism has, perhaps, been slow to reject the publicity thus obtained. To clarify positions, however, a new term is required for these practitioners of a prophetic system that has jettisoned a key tenet of dispensational interpretation. The postmillennial reconstructionist Gary North has coined the term "pop-dispensationalists" to refer to these writers; he offers as an alternative the accurate, if hardly elegant, "dispensensationalists."[39]

The critics of dispensationalism have joyfully seized the texts of this new prophetic system. This is understandable to an extent; the antics of Lindsey and the other pop-dispensationalists are somewhat inclined to elicit contempt. More seriously, however, among these critics there has been a marked tendency to depict the date-setting and sensationalism of these writers as being organically linked to the system of dispensationalism. Even North, whose helpful distinction between dispensationalists and pop-dispensationalists has been noted above, succumbed to this temptation. His commentary on the particularly egregious date-setting of Edgar Whisenant was scarcely as informed as it should have been—"This is all too typical of dispensationalism."[40] This type of response entirely fails to take account of the facts that the tendency to set dates is seen in a wide variety of prophetic interpretations, and that dispensationalism is, in general, highly inimical to date-setting.

No matter what the prevailing method of understanding biblical prophecy, students of the prophetic Scriptures have always found the temptation to set specific dates for the return of Christ particularly alluring. This is due in part to the following tendency, perceptively noted by Coad:

> Almost invariably interpretation has been vitiated by the reluctance or incapacity of commentators to visualize their own age as other than the end time. As a consequence, beliefs are in a constant state of revision and restatement.[41]

And this trait has been visible in commentators from all parts of the prophetic spectrum, from Ussher and Newton, to Whisenant and Lindsey.[42] Coad has gone so far as to link it particularly with historicism:[43]

> The weakness of all historicism is its passion for date fixing. Even Luther was not free from this weakness, nor, in a later century, was Wesley. The extremer elements soon began to bring disrepute upon prophetic interpretations.

Indeed, as has already been remarked, one of the forces to shape dispensationalism in its early years was the disrepute into which endemic speculation had brought the more traditional historicist views of prophetic interpretation. Any attempt, therefore, to link date-setting peculiarly to dispensationalism must be willfully ignorant of the state of prophetic interpretation since, and even before, the Reformation. Certainly, as Thomas Ice has remarked, "the fruit of date-setting and many other contemporary errors have not been gathered from the root called dispensationalism."[44]

It has already been noted that the theoretical underpinnings of dispensational interpretation make any preoccupation with "signs of the times" untenable. In theology, as in other areas of life, however, theory and practice sometimes fail to correspond. Therefore, I wish to trace the response of classical dispensationalists to some crucial global events, in an effort to investigate the extent of any tendency to sensationalize prophecy. This consideration will occupy us especially with the development of prophetic teaching within the Plymouth Brethren. There are a number of reasons for this. First, classical dispensationalism, in its purest form, has survived and flourished best in the movement that gave birth to it. This is particularly true in a European context. Concentrating on Brethren teaching, therefore, allows us to examine trends on both sides of the Atlantic. This is helpful because it is sometimes tempting to read the difference between classical dispensationalism and pop-dispensationalisms in terms of a geographical split. Further, the distinctive ecclesiology of the Brethren, and especially the absence of any special training for teachers, breaks down any dichotomy between views among clergy and the laity; in general, teaching represents an inclusive response to contemporary pressures, and there is little danger of consider-ing merely the different inflections of seminary teaching on the issue.

Classical Dispensationalists and the Great War

We have already remarked that dispensationalism developed in a climate of prophetic ferment and in the shadow of momentous events. These events were soon to fade into insignificance with the onset of the First World War. Of the wider premillennial response to the conflict, David Wilson has written: "World War I stimulated the premillennialist to a tip-toe expectancy and also provided tantalizing fulfillment of some of their longings."[45] This is scarcely the impression that one gleans from a study of the contents of *The Witness*, a major Brethren periodical, over the years of the war. These issues do show a marked increase in the already consider-able space that the editors devoted to prophetic discussion, but the kind of response outlined by Wilson was notable by its absence. Overwhelmingly, the response was to see the war as providential, but not prophetic.

The keynote of the response to the war was struck by Hy Pickering, the editor of *The Witness*, in a summary of "The World at War," which appeared in the November 1914 edition. Concerning the cause of the war, Pickering had this to say:

> The more we study the cause, . . . the more we are convinced that the rejection of the Revelation from God has paved the way for the denial of the Word of God, the setting aside of the Law of God and the giv-ing up of the love of one's neighbor.[46]

This providentialist emphasis can also be seen in A. T. Schofield's 1915 article entitled "Can Corsica Conquer Galilee?"[47] For Schofield, the cause of the conflict was clear: the "Napoleonism" of Germany, its "idolization" of Nietzsche and Treitschke were the sources of divine displeasure and the reason for chastisement. Another writer, in the same year, understood the war in very similar terms. Invoking the ministry of Elijah in 1 Kings 18 as a "divine method of reaching a nation," he goes on to apply the lesson to contemporary circumstances:

> [W]e may remind ourselves that the God of Elijah lives still, and that He is still within reach. At present He is having a controversy with the nations of Europe over national sins of various kinds, but possibly His hand will be lifted when self-judgement and humiliation has been reached. . . . For many years our own beloved country has been bow-ing down to the German gods, prostrating herself before their mod-ern culture and destructive criticism and disseminating the same throughout her overseas dominions; now she is having to bow before something else she did not want.

This type of commentary set the tone for response to the war, although one writer, Huntington Stone, was less sanguine about the admissibility of this application:

> God's voice to His people through the war differs from God's voice to the nation. Manifestly some connection is traceable between national righteousness and national prosperity. Speaking generally, however, this dispensation is not marked by clearly defined messages of God to individual nations.[48]

Stone also issued a warning that is as true and as necessary today as it was then:

> [A]n attempt to deduce from the War a special message from God to the nation might fail, partly because in the absence of any unbiased narrative of facts we have not sufficient ground upon which to build a judgment, and partly because we are not yet empowered to judge the nations.

This restraint and caution is very far from the sort of hysteria that Wilson finds in the broader premillennial response, and further still from the approach of Lindsey and his fellow students of the "signs of the times."

And, indeed, the general response to the events of the war was marked by a very similar restraint. While the rapture gained a new prominence, attempts to predict it were sedulously avoided. In the November 1914 edition, one writer acknowledged that "not only Christians, but even men of the world are inquiring 'Is this "Armageddon?"'"[49] While the author was willing to acknowledge that "the present great upheaval . . . is doubtless a link in the chain of God's purposes," he stressed that, before prophecy could be directly fulfilled, the church must be "caught up." The Christian's response to the war was, therefore, to "take a firm hold of the 'blessed hope': that he is coming *for* us." Traumatic events should cause Christians to look for the rapture, but not, crucially, to look for signs of its timing. This article illustrates an important distinction in dispensational thought. Dispensationalists were, as we have seen, providentialists; they expected God to control the destinies of nations. Thus, the war and every other international event worked toward the ultimate consummation of God's purposes. Therefore, it was perfectly legitimate, and even laudable, to draw lessons for the future from the war—to understand that, although prophecy was not, could not, be enacted in the present, the present could still afford indications of how prophecy would one day be fulfilled. It is particularly important to keep this point in mind when reading David Wilson's helpful but tendentious account of the premillennial response to Israel and Russia. One of the problems with this book is a tendency to treat this observation of providence as "sign of the times" sensationalism. Such is not the case; the providential need not be prophetic.

Two years into the war, *The Witness* maintained its high level of interest in prophecy, devoting a special number to "The Coming of the Lord."[50] In this issue, an article by Robert M'Murdo of Chicago gives us an American perspective on the war. Tellingly, his article is entitled "The Next Great Event: or, the Time of His Coming." The theme, clearly, is the imminence of Christ's return and the impossibility of setting a date on this "next great event."

> In the wisdom of God the date for the Coming of the Lord for His saints has not been revealed. The Church is a heavenly subject. Its divine proportions cannot be measured by human methods of computation, neither can the time of its sojourn on earth be determined by the manipulation of solar cycles. . . . So times and seasons, which mark the rise and fall of Jew and Gentile, have no place in the ordering of that great event, the date of which is fixed according to the plan conceived in a past eternity by love divine, which knows neither measure or end.[51]

Franklin Ferguson, a Brother from New Zealand, also contributed to this "Second Coming Special." His brief contribution stressed not so much the impossibility of predicting the rapture, but rather the danger of attempting to do so:

> [E]verywhere the spirit of Antichrist is gaining ground in an alarming manner. Let us, however, go on with God, doing his will, and beware of Satan lest he succeeds in so engrossing us with the war . . . that our eye becomes diverted from the upward look for our Lord's return; and thus a victory is gained over us by the powers of darkness.[52]

The repudiation of any efforts to view the Great War in a prophetic or apocalyptic context was, therefore, explicit in the writing of these dispensationalists, from a range of geographical locations, throughout the war. Interestingly, it is left to the chief dispensationalist teacher of the day to fully express a cautious approach to the use of prophecy. Sir Robert Anderson was a lawyer, a graduate of Trinity College, Dublin, and one of the most colorful figures connected with the early Brethren. He was a prominent Bible teacher and a prolific author.[53] He was a leading dispensationalist, and his monumental work *The Coming Prince* (1895) laid the basis for dispensational chronology. Given his status as a prophetic scholar, we might well assume that the temptation to interpret present events in the light of prophecy was especially strong in his case. However, his article "The Christian and the Crisis" warned against excessive concern with prophetic considerations. His chief warning was one that resonates powerfully today:

> I venture to raise a warning voice against what I may call the politics
> of prophetic interpretation. It has done vastly more to discredit Scrip-
> ture than all the attacks of infidelity. . . . Considerations of another
> kind . . . claim our earnest attention. The death toll of this war will
> be terrible, and countless thousands will soon be mourning the loss
> of relatives and friends. Is it fitting then, at such a time, that Chris-
> tians should turn aside to puzzle out a connection between the events
> of the campaign and the prophetic scriptures?[54]

The restraint, practicality, and clearness of this approach could scarcely be
more different from the sensationalism of the pop-dispensationalists. It
also presents a severe challenge to attempts to configure dispensationalists
as impractical and socially uninvolved. Rather, Sir Robert's article was a
call for Christian involvement, both in the hostilities of the war, and in
tending to the needs of those at home. Attempts to align the dispensationalist mindset with pessimism also founder here; Anderson points out that
"Had we lived a century ago . . . we might have supposed that the final
drama of prophecy had begun. But the Battle of Waterloo led to a period
of almost prosaic peace in Europe. And, it may be so again." Above all, the
closing words of this article deserve to be repeated, and would well be considered both by Lindsey and his ilk, and by those critics who perceive dispensationalism to be preoccupied with "signs of the times":

> The habit of studying prophecy in the light of history and the news-
> papers, while legitimate within certain narrow limits, always tends to
> draw the mind of the Christian from the hope of the Lord's return.
> The grace that has brought us Salvation teaches us to live "looking
> [not for the antichrist, nor yet the signs and portents of his coming,
> but] for that Blessed Hope and glorious appearing of our great God
> and Savior Jesus Christ."

As we have seen already from Ferguson's comments, prophecy could be
considered counterproductive, even dangerous. Thus, the dispensationalist response to the alarms of the war was one marked by hopefulness, practical engagement, and above all, a refusal to yield to the temptation to
compromise the key teachings of dispensational interpretation by replacing
a looking for an imminent second coming with a perturbed gaze on the
"signs of the times."

European Federation and the Revival of Rome

Another strand appears in those articles: the earliest speculations about a
European federation. This was seen by many as a likely, if not inevitable,
result of the war. So, even as Thomas Robinson refuted the idea that the
present war was Armageddon, he made reference to the prophetic neces-

sity of a revived Roman Empire. He drew attention to the "anticipations of our leading statesmen," quoting Asquith's hopes that "this war ought to mean, finally, perhaps by a slow process and gradual, the substitution for force and for the clash of competing ambitions, *of a real European partnership*."[55] Outlining a theme that was to be often repeated, he pondered the significance of the fact that Ireland, which was not a part of the Roman Empire, "should apparently be on the verge of being severed from Great Britain." Likewise, J. R. Caldwell drew attention to the "reconstruction of the map of Europe."[56] It was "in order to the fulfillment of this predicted end, so plainly foretold in Scripture, that the present European war [was] being waged." Wisely, Caldwell refused to make any definite predictions, acknowledging that, "whether the prophetic ten kingdoms emerge immediately at the close of this war, or whether there will be an interval of peace when men shall speak of 'peace and safety' . . . we cannot say." Caldwell's use of the language of scriptural prophecy seems to suggest a tendency to indulge in speculation. However, the effect is ultimately very different. Caldwell's "we cannot say" underlines the fact that prophecy, with its definite and predictable program, is not being fulfilled.

Particularly significant in the light of this commentary is the decision of the editor of *The Witness* to occupy a considerable number of pages in the 1915 volume with a serial study on "The Roman Empire in Prophecy" by the esteemed W. E. Vine.[57] The series commenced with a historical overview, tracing the Roman Empire from its birth to its decline and conquest. This was followed by an overview of possible candidates for a renewed Roman Empire—Austria-Hungary and the British Empire. The rejection of these powers as candidates led inexorably to the conclusion that prophecy would require a future "European federation," made up of ten states. Vine remarked that "agencies are already at work for the establishment of a confederacy of European States—not the least significant of the signs that the end of the age is approaching."[58] He went on to detail the activities of "a committee of influential men with the object of promoting a 'European Federation.'" He predicted that the establishment of such a federation would be effected by one of two means: "either by peaceful methods of arbitration and treaty or as a result of strife and confusion." Vine—in the first occurrence of the famed "premillennial pessimism" we have seen—was inclined to believe that violence was the most likely method; specifically the machinations of "the forces of Socialism, Communism &c." The "avowed aims" of such bodies "presage[d] anything but peace in the future." Vine reached back to an earlier era of prophetic speculation when he commented that:

> [N]ot improbably the ten kingdoms of the reconstructed Roman Empire will arise as a result of political and social confusion. Thus it

was in the case of the French Revolution and the subsequent uprising of Napoleon. A repetition of such events on a wider scale is quite conceivable.

There is evidence here of a considerable ambivalence and a very deep concern about European involvement. Vine is not, however, predicting; rather, his writing is speculative. Showing a very conscious awareness of the danger of being too dogmatic in such speculations, he stressed that:

> We are not predicting that this is to be the manner of the revival of the Empire and the advent of its imperial head. We have merely suggested possible circumstances in the light of Scripture and present-day movements. The actual circumstances attending the rise of the ten kings and their Emperor must remain conjectural.

Neither does he explicitly link these events to the imminence of the rapture; there is no compulsion toward date-setting.

Later in this series, Vine touched upon the ecclesiastical apparatus of the antichrist: his Babylonish religion. Once again, Vine is reiterating a number of concerns that have been common since the Reformation, and especially to the wider premillennial viewpoint. The papacy had always been a popular candidate for identification with the Babylonish religious system, and the pope was often identified as the antichrist. This characteristic of premillennial exegesis has been retained in the *Left Behind* series, in spite of their cautious and ill-defined gestures in the direction of ecumenism. Vine had little to add to this, and his expectation of secular anarchy did little to modify his anxiety about the increasing dominance of Rome:

> Though the Papacy lost its temporal power in 1870, it is far from having lost its political influence. Ecclesiastically, too, though it has received various set-backs, it is manifestly gaining power. . . . Power is undoubtedly the object of the persistent aggressiveness of Romanism. This aggressiveness is manifested in all the dominions of the British Empire, as well as in other lands. . . . Present events, therefore, point to a resuscitation of Papal power which would fulfill the prophecy relating to the woman and the beast that carries her.

This very traditional view was very slightly modified, in a way bearing the hallmarks of the Brethren's distrust of denominational Christianity:

> [T]he woman may be regarded as representing the apostate sacerdotal systems which have sprung from the Papacy as well as that system itself.

The prospect of a revived Roman Empire was, therefore, a prospect to be looked for as required by Scripture. This gave sinister connotations to any

European federalism, no matter how achieved. Further, in the expected national alignments, the influence and power of Rome particularly—and of corrupt religion more generally—was a source of deep concern. Such exercises are, however, clearly flagged as conjectural and maintain the providentialist concern with the course of history that we have already seen to be a key factor in dispensationalist thought.

Given this background of dispensational Euro-skepticism, it is fascinating to see the response to the realization of some of the trends that Vine had tentatively predicted. This reaction was widespread, in an informal and largely oral manner among the Brethren. We do, however, have a number of examples in print of the Brethren reaction to European union. These came from the pen of Dr. Frederick A. Tatford. Tatford was a director of the U.K. Atomic Energy Authority and published widely on prophecy. Among his books was the dispensational survey *God's Programme of the Ages* (1967). Tatford also has the dubious distinction of being the only Brethren author of rapture fiction, *The Clock Strikes* (1971). Of particular relevance to the present consideration, however, are his two booklets on Europe. The first of these, *Going into Europe: The Common Market and Prophecy* (1971), was published in response to Edward Heath's request for the "widest possible discussion and understanding of what [was] involved" in European union.[59] The second, published in 1980, had the very loaded title *10 Nations—Now What?* Both are largely straightforward accounts of the history and structure of the EEC. However, both conclude with sections discussing Europe in biblical prophecy, considerations that display emphases that we have seen in nascent form in Vine's study.

In *Going into Europe*, Tatford outlines the two motivating forces for European union: economic and political considerations. The creation of the European Economic Community was a process with a single end, namely, European federalism. He pointed out that "membership of the Community is permanent. . . . The organization is a permanent one and the member states will, in due course, become one entity."[60] Tatford was by no means happy about this prospect: like many others he feared loss of control over trade, foreign relations, and national destiny. Having expressed these fears mildly, and with little detail, Tatford addresses the aspect of European union that had most troubled Vine:

> An interesting and significant feature of the Community is that 77 per cent of the population of the Six are Roman Catholic and that the RC Church has a very great interest in those countries. . . . There is little doubt that in future the Church will make her voice heard in the councils of Europe. The present trend towards ecclesiastical union in Britain will ultimately lead to reunion with Rome of the Anglican Church and any other Churches which have, by that time,

> united with her. The aim is plainly a One World Church and it now
> seems clear that Rome will be paramount.

This analysis is, evidently, very close to Vine's. Here, too, we see the influence of Darby's views, perpetuated through the Brethren, on the ruin of the church, an influence that has lost little of its potency. Rome is still prophetic enemy number one, and Tatford is keen to preserve that identification. However, this does not prevent the stigma of Babylon being spread throughout mainstream Christendom. In this prophetic picture, Europe is to be controlled by an apostate church, and no element of denominational Christianity is likely to be excluded from this unholy federation.

In the penultimate section of his pamphlet, Tatford addresses a number of questions that are of central importance to our present consideration:

> Is this a development which has already been foreseen? Is it in accord
> with Divine will? Is there any reflection of it in Biblical prophecy?
> What should the Christian's attitude be to the current develop-
> ments?[61]

His attempts to answer these questions place him at the crux of the tension between providentialism and prophetic sensationalism that features in the dispensational worldview. In the year after Lindsey's book was published, Tatford's response is refreshingly considered, unfashionably cautious:

> Dogmatism in matters of this kind would be singularly inappropriate
> and, even when the Scriptures seem to paint a similar picture, it is
> inadvisable to specifically identify current events with Biblical predic-
> tions. Lessons may perhaps be deduced for our learning, and compar-
> isons may help to an understanding of the Word and contemporary
> trends.

As he closed, he re-stressed the need for prudence when handling prophecy:

> It would be foolish to maintain dogmatically, as some have done, that
> the European Community is to be identified with a revived Roman
> Empire or with the federation of ten kingdoms of which prophecy
> speaks.

The extent of the speculations that he was willing to hazard was modest in the extreme: "The similarity is, in fact, so great that we may well be seeing today the initial stages in the formation of the great western power which is to appear in the end times."[62] However, even at this mild stage of speculation, the doctrinal balance of the imminent rapture asserted itself: "Before these things come to pass, however, the true Church, composed of all believers in Christ, whether dead or living, is to be translated from this earth." True dispensationalism's antisensationalism mechanism once again prevents the dramatic pronouncements favored by the pop-dispensationalist mutation.

Nine years later, the growth of the EEC to ten members spurred Tatford to write on this subject once again. Ten countries was, as we have seen, something of a prophetic magic number—the predicted size of the coming federation of nations. Tatford's *10 Nations—Now What?* was very largely a reprise of his earlier work, including very similar analysis. The temptation to sensationalize is evidently stronger, and this text is closer to pop-dispensationalism than any other we have considered. The scale of the separation that remains should not, however, be underestimated. Tatford suggests that "it is not illogical to see pre-cursory signs" of the revived Roman Empire in the European Community. He claimed that

> the resemblance of current trends and happenings to those predicted in Scripture . . . seems almost too marked to be disregarded. There is at least a possibility that the preliminary indications are being given of the imminence of the time of the end, when Biblical predictions will be fulfilled. Indeed, taken in conjunction with many other indications of the present day, little doubt will exist in the minds of many that the shadows of the future can already be seen.[63]

What is remarkable about this is the sense we get of a writer being pulled in two directions. Tatford is pulled in the direction of a boldly dramatic connection of European events to prophetic Scripture. At the same time, his constant qualification pulls him in precisely the opposite direction. Thus, we have the interesting prospect of resemblances "almost too marked to be disregarded"; "at least a possibility that . . . indications are being given," and are allowed only a "little doubt." Any certainty offered is just as quickly undermined. This may be read as vacillating and indefinite, and in a sense, it is. This lack of certainty is, however, the result not of prophetic incompetence but of a respect for the tenets of Darbyite dispensationalism. With powerful temptations toward the sensationalization of prophecy, Tatford dramatizes precisely the same tensions that have always influenced classical dispensationalism, and displays the consistency of interpretation that led to Coad's accolade that Brethren dispensationalists "took care to avoid . . . sensational prophesyings."[64]

Dispensationalist Caution and the New Millennium

A very similar picture emerges from the classical dispensationalist response to the beginning of the new millennium. The December issue of the American Brethren periodical *Uplook* carried an article, written by the prominent American Bible teacher William MacDonald, entitled "Y2K—Is This the Time?"[65] MacDonald approaches the pop-dispensationalist viewpoint toward the end of the article when he lists nine reasons to expect the "imminent, any-moment return" of Christ. These reasons were already familiar to the readership of *Uplook*: the rise of ecumenism, the increased importance of Israel in international affairs, "the world decline of culture into a moral sewer," and the need for a strong world leader. However, Mac-Donald had, at the beginning of his article, carefully contextualized these speculations:

> What is the prophetic significance of the year 2000? Is January 1, 2000 related in any positive way to the coming of the Lord? There is good reason to avoid such a notion. That would be a form of date setting, and well-taught Christians know that they should not indulge in this pastime. The only definite thing we can say about the time of our Lord's return is that it is unknown and will be unexpected when it comes. . . . God has not boxed himself in to thousand year periods in spacing important prophetic events.

Once again, we see the tension in the dispensationalist response to a new millennium. Despite the evident temptation to sensationalize, MacDonald remains faithful to dispensationalism's teaching. His response to "Y2K" is in contrast to the response of historicist interpreters at the turn of the eighteenth century, and it is, once more, the imminent rapture that provides a brake on prolific speculation.

At this point, then, it should be very clear that attempts to link prophetic sensationalism and date-setting particularly to dispensationalism are only viable in the presence of considerable ignorance of both the basic tenets of dispensational theology and a long line of dispensational practice. Indeed, our analysis of what dispensationalists actually wrote makes it clear that, in the midst of traumatic events, they remained remarkably free from prophetic speculation. In particular we have noticed, as the key doctrinal strand, dispensationalism's insistence on the imminence of Christ's return. Undoubtedly, the temptations caused by disturbing global events had been felt just as keenly by the dispensationalists as by earlier historicist interpreters. That the response to such temptation was so muted is a tribute to the doctrinal consistency of the classical dispensationalist. Lindsey's pop-dispensationalist approach is, therefore, a dramatic mutation of dispensationalism, an aberration so radical as to allow us to dismiss Lindsey as a dispensationalist. Dispensationalism is not, by any means, a theology above reproach. However, it well behooves the careful critic to reproach it for its own weaknesses, and not for those that have been unfairly linked with it.

Chapter Eleven

Forty Years of Millenarian Thought in the Charismatic Movement

Stephen J. Hunt

Smail's Lament

In a paper exploring the subject of charismatic theology, published in 1995, renowned Anglican renewalist Tom Smail expressed disenchantment at the lack of the felt need among advocates of the charismatic movement to construct a coherent and meaningful theology.[1] The stress on the experience *of* God rather than thinking *about* God by leading renewal theologians and churchmen alike had tended to play down the importance of stringent theological constructs. For charismatics, explained Smail succinctly, God is not an intellectual hypothesis to be discussed, but a living personal agent to be encountered. Regrettably, however, when that happens, continued Smail, either individually for people or corporately for churches, the conclusion can easily be reached that they have neither need nor time for a complicated theology and all the awkward questions it subsequently raises.[2]

Smail's account of the paucity of charismatic theology was not merely with reference to the basic tenets of the faith: the atonement, the Trinity, the virgin birth, and so on. Rather, it engaged with issues stemming from renewal itself, from the charismata, signs and wonders, healing and prophecy, and the preoccupation which charismatics displayed at that time with the so-called power evangelism associated with the late healing evangelist John Wimber. While Smail's paper was a significant and timely contribution, there were, nonetheless, elements conspicuously missing from his appraisal that might be expected in the context of charismatic theology. In particular, he had next to nothing to say of the theology of the last days and the inherent hope in the coming kingdom of God, which in fact has rarely been absent from the charismatic worldview. Perhaps Smail was shrewd in not attempting to explore the complex and varied regions of eschatological thought among charismatics. However, it is unlikely that his wish to refrain from opening this particular theological can of worms would have been out of the fear of majoring on a theological minor, since the theme of the millennium has proved to be central to Christian dogma and experience for over two thousand years. Rather, Smail's reluctance was probably from viewing the subject as too wide, too intricate, and perhaps too controversial for a relatively short paper. Millenarian thought in the charismatic movement is a topic of not inconsiderable importance since, in many respects, millenarianism, renewal, and revival have historically walked hand in hand. Indeed, the annals of the Christian church relate how periodic perceived fresh "moves" of God and the outpouring of his Spirit were interpreted as breathing new and intoxicating oxygen into the millenarian hope—a hope that has given direction and purpose to his people ever since the first Pentecost experience in the upper room as related in the book of Acts.

In point of fact, an analytical sweep of four decades of the charismatic movement shows that, to some extent at least, it was born and developed with millenarian aspirations. These were aspirations that punctuated charismatic dogma and praxis, albeit carried through with different levels of intensity and presented in different guises. In short, the millenarian content and symbols of the promise of Christ's return and the kingdom of God has changed over this time, and so much is telling by way of how the related eschatology has been constructed. Here the sociology of ideas has something to offer, since millenarianism and all that it entails is not merely a theological construct referring to a literal or metaphorical period of a thousand years of Christ's dominion, but a phenomenon that transverses different cultures, religious traditions, and time and place. Often inspired by the more esoteric dimensions of the books of Daniel and Revelation in particular, the idea has furnished the ideology of small cults and large-scale social movements alike[3] with the dream of a divine new order that brings, in the words of Talmon, an ". . . imminent, total, ultimate, this-worldly salvation."[4]

As few as they are, sociological accounts of millenarianism in its various forms point to its construction as an essentially cultural event, one forged by the interplay of social conditions, ideal interests, and the influx of relevant ideas into unique situations. This is, of course, a variation of Max Weber's much-vaunted formula for the possibility of dynamic religious ideas in bringing far-reaching social change[5]—a formula that stems from his comparative sociology, is an enduring one, and remains a framework by which to appreciate and comprehend the millenarian drama; for Weber, the truly religious life had an emotional and intellectual basis, and yet these dimensions were also closely integrated with social factors. So it has proved to be with the evolution (if that is the correct term) of the theology of the charismatic movement.

While Smail lamented the lack of the intellectual skills of the adherents of the movement, there can be little doubt, certainly in terms of its broad theology, that emotionalism and the response to social environments have proved to be the essential ingredients in the millenarianism impulse as witnessed among charismatics throughout the second half of the twentieth century. Social conditions, ideal interests, and ideas are among the major components that have come together for almost half a century in creating the millenarian aspirations of the charismatic movement. Nonetheless, in a secular context such eschatological ideas have remained the preserve of the charismatic constituency and in Western society have no appeal outside of the movement that embraces it. In parts of the developing world, by contrast, it has undoubtedly helped transform the social experience of hundreds of thousands of people.[6] Charismatic millenarianism in the West, then, has remained essentially "in house," furnishing the worldview of a cognitive minority.

We might conclude that there is something integral about millenarianism to the charismatic worldview. The development of the movement on both sides of the Atlantic, as elsewhere, underlines the relationship between renewal, revivalism, and millenarianism. This has been evident in its episodic appeal over some four decades and the occasional wavering, although not without a certain degree of tension, between premillenarian and postmillenarian constructs. For the movement, indeed, millenarianism has proved to be an ongoing and malleable idea as much as a hope—one aided in construct by scriptural themes, but also molded by the twin considerations of the wider cultural milieu in which the renewal movement has found itself and its relationship within the context of global evangelism. For these reasons there has been a discernible change in millenarian thought over the decades, which ensures that stranding out the threads of the millenarian tapestry of the movement is no easy task. Thus, this chapter does not attempt a trawl through the history of the global charismatic movement, or neo-Pentecostalism as it is alternatively designated. Rather, it confines itself largely to developments in Britain over the last forty years, although in terms of millenarian thought there is a still a rich vein of ideas to quarry, some of which stretch back further in their origins to classical Pentecostalism.

Classical Pentecostalism and the Millenarian Hope

All renewalist movements seem to have their mythical beginnings. So it was with the story of Azusa Street in classical Pentecostalism at the beginning of the twentieth century. In the neo-Pentecostal movement it was deemed to be within Episcopalian circles in Van Nuys, California, in 1960, and the Church of the Redeemer in Houston, Texas, with outbreaks of the tongue speaking that has subsequently gone down in charismatic folklore. From those early and mid-twentieth-century beginnings, the successive waves of Pentecostalism have spread across the globe to the most diverse of places. While church history might in time prove that they turn out to have been a very small paragraph in the story of Christianity, there is no doubting their universal significance. According to Peter Wagner, an apologist for the movement, Pentecostalism in all its forms is one of the most significant political and nonmilitary social movements in the latter half of the twentieth century.[7]

It is clear that after some four decades the charismatic movement, as with classical Pentecostalism, has been impacted by different cultural environments. In North America and Western Europe the movement has gone through, and continues to go through, a process of metamorphosis, not least in its theological constructs, however ill-conceived they might have proved to be. An overview of developments at this point in time is by no means unjustified, since it is arguable that, in Western churches at least, the movement is now a spent force. The wind of change that the wider Pentecostal movement has brought to Christianity from the beginning of the twentieth century has never stopped blowing, but it may now be petering out. The so-called Toronto Blessing of the mid-1990s, with its own millenarian themes, was indicative of how far the movement had traveled, in many ways radically departing from the vision of early renewalists and rendering it unrecognizable to some of its more seasoned exponents. To be sure, the Pentecostal wind was always prone to rapid changes in direction, depending on local climatic conditions. For those involved, the Spirit may appear to move where it wishes, but the movement that claims to represent that will has been buffeted by social and cultural gales. It also appears to be subject to sociological laws relating to the development of movements of revival and renewal.

The early renewal movement had begun as an endeavor to bring new life into the churches at a time of decline in attendance and membership.

Simultaneously, it also attempted to counter the growing routinization and bureaucratization of church life. But what did it all mean in relation to the will of God? Members of the embryonic movement in the churches throughout the late 1960s and early 1970s struggled to make sense of the significance of the alleged new move of God in which they were swept up. Its rapid growth and spread across the various denominations, as well as the esoteric experiences that many claimed through the charismatic manifestations, raised questions as to what it all meant. For those who had the time and disposition to reflect beyond their own charismatic experiences, the emerging movement displayed an identity crisis of sorts.

This was all in marked contrast to the classical Pentecostal movement of half-a-century earlier, which had no such problem of identity. Condemned by existing churches, including the evangelical wing, the early Pentecostals found themselves beleaguered, ostracized, and set afloat from the rest of Christendom. This marginalization and persecution, real or imagined, fed into the Pentecostal worldview. The Pentecostals were convinced that the end of the world was imminent and that the omens were good for the second coming. In the adventist hope, Pentecostal revival was seen by its adherents as heralding the end time; its persecution reinforced this view. The scope was premillenarian. Satan buffeted the saints through secular evils and persecution by the apostate churches. Biblical references confirmed this stance. The outpouring of the Spirit of God in the last days, so biblical interpretation went, would bring its full measure of spiritual warfare. Marginalization and social ostracism were also the daily experience of many of its adherents.[8] Ideal interests and theological constructs thus fused, at least in the United States, as Pentecostalism rapidly spread. Here the cohorts of the dispossessed and disinherited hankered after the safe haven of sectarianism and the promise of the millenarian dream that was evidently heralded by the miraculous. Claims to "signs and wonders" among the impoverished masses of blacks and whites alike were considered by the established churches to be evidence of their lack of plausibility, but to the early Pentecostals they were the signs of coming redemption.

The classical Pentecostals believed that through their movement the gospel would be taken to the world: the field would be "white unto harvest." The prophecy came true in one form or another as the movement reached practically every corner of the globe in what was understood to be the great revival before the end. Glossolalia and baptism in the Spirit were the anticipated signs of the truly saved, an indication of who was "in" and who was "out." In this way classical Pentecostalism drew boundaries between itself and the secular world and the historical churches. This was millenarianism as envisaged by a spiritual elite that took a particular posture in relation to the world beyond its boundaries. Indeed, as Walker notes, the revivalistic fervor of the early Pentecostals was predicated upon charismatic experience and millenarian excitation. In turn, this led either to a hostile stance to the world or to an indifferent attitude to civic responsibility and the lure of modern progress: the Pentecostals were apolitical and culturally denying, and so the sinful world was left to its own destruction.[9]

The Emergence of Renewal

The Pentecostal story is now relatively well-documented. The revivalistic movement of the early twentieth century eventually succumbed to its own denominational structures, though it never lost its revival fervor or millenarian aspirations. The movement also became more ecumenical, engaging in what was previously unthinkable. The Pentecostal baton was passed on to the established denominations in the mid-twentieth century when the desire to dialogue had the unintended consequences of encouraging renewal in the respectable mainstream churches.[10] In turn, renewal and its accompanying charismata fed back into classical Pentecostalism and fulfilled the prophecy that the Pentecostal experience would reawaken the lukewarm established churches before the second coming of the Messiah.

The mid-century renewalists worked within no such clear-cut and all-embracing eschatological framework. Indeed, many struggled to understand what renewal signified. Did the newfound unity across the churches show not only that all believers were brothers and sisters under their denominational attire, but that something was being played out in the larger plan of God? At times the movement seemed to have been overtaken by the speed and scope of events, so that questioning what it signified was eclipsed by all the fervor and excitement. Nonetheless, some renewalists speculated that this *was* the great move of God before the second coming, so encompassing was the movement in its ecumenical breadth. Hence the movement was not eschatologically driven, but eschatology became part of the worldview for at least a few renewalists. In this regard, the first port of call for the charismatics, as with revivalists before them, was the word of God. Certain Scriptures allowed current events to be interpreted in a subjective light in a kind of virtual-reality Bible, where, above all, the return of the charismata to the church seemed to signify a revival before the end.

Other renewalists were more measured in their appraisal, and interpreted events as a periodic outpouring of the Spirit that showed God's people were one in unity despite the theology and tradition that separated them. Nevertheless, however it was interpreted, many leading charismatics despaired at the growing movement's lack of direction and coherence, and not only in its theological constructs. There needed to be more than the opportunity to promote the virtues of renewal in the churches. Hence, there was a fresh emphasis on revival in its true sense, the winning of converts in an increasingly secular society.[11] In this way the renewal gave rise to hope of conversions, a hope that may have encouraged a more joyful and optimistic rendering of the last days beyond the gloom and doom of premillenarianism.

Theological frameworks were, however, sketchy, and such themes that did develop often hewed millenarian dogma from the other side of the Atlantic, one that tended toward a theological dualism and foretold of the coming wrath of God. Here was the imprint of U.S. fundamentalism in its various guises, but one heavily influenced by the historical legacy of William Miller (1782–1849) of the Seventh-day Adventists, who cast an impression well beyond his own church and helped structure the view of North American evangelicals. Translated into the mid-twentieth-century context, this meant an apocalyptic vision forged in the growing secularity and pluralism of Western culture, the fear of environmental and atomic disaster, the Cold War environment, and the evidence of the satanic forces of communism and the European market—themes that led to fresh interpretations of the more esoteric Old and New Testament Scriptures.

In such ways charismatic theology, as crude as it was, made sense of a world that seemed to spiral toward destruction. To some degree this diluted apocalyptic millenarianism encouraged a social activism among the renewalists and engendered moral campaigns against the emerging permissive society. Certainly, the moral crusade was not the monopoly of the renewal movement, but the charismatic contingency was heavily involved in the Festival of Light and kindred organizations in the United Kingdom that took to the streets in protest or petitioned the politicians in earnest. To some extent, at least, as William Thompson notes, this passion for turning the tide of the permissiveness of modern society resulted from a fear of God's coming judgment on the unrighteous. The "Ezekiel factor," as Thompson terms it, proved a key motivating force. Was it not true that the Old Testament prophet called upon God's people to preach repentance to evildoers? Indeed, this was a duty and an imperative. It was a point of reminder for all Christians of their responsibilities, yet it had the consequences of adding extra vigor to millenarian aspirations.[12]

In its social activism in Britain, the charismatic movement played out the erstwhile global function of neo-Pentecostalism as outlined by David Martin. For Martin, neo-Pentecostalism in its various social contexts can primarily be understood as a grassroots initiative providing spiritual certitude in a modern world that could not provide it, along with a prophetic criticism of the prevailing social order through its esotericism and eschatology.[13] Yet it was a movement often ambivalent about the evils of modernity against which classical Pentecostalism had set its face. In the West, the charismatics' emphasis on experience was always in danger of accommodating itself to the very forces of secularization to which it was adamantly opposed. In opting for experience, the movement mediated

between the legalism of fundamentalism and the relativism of liberal theology. It thus never quite subscribed fully to the pessimistic premillenarianism and antimodernism of Edward Irving, which had no place for the
future of the "true" church in his worldview, let alone the possibility that
it might be seduced by some of its cultural attributes.[14]

From one perspective it could be recognized that the stress upon the
charismata marked a rejection of what the rationalized modern world
threatened to do to human beings. Such an emphasis dovetailed well with
the 1960s counterculture's devotion to spontaneity and disregard for intellectual and rational control and its search for an alternative way of living.
The next world was, then, never far away. Renewal took other directions,
too, which in turn indicated the multifaceted nature of the movement.
The search for community, which also had its countercultural undercur-
rents, was one aspect of the renewal movement, which was able to spawn
"intentional communities" for complete worldly separation and aided the
further building of God's kingdom, with Roman Catholic communities
often leading the way.[15]

Like many of the more radical new religious movements of the 1970s,
such communities marked an attempt to satisfy a yearning for community
and to reestablish social bonds as impersonal bureaucratic structures came
to dominate and traditional communities broke up, alongside the weaken-
ing of wider social relationships and networks. Many such communities
have subsequently evaporated, although some renewalists remain part-time
communitarians—succumbing to the attractions of the rampant individualistic culture generated since the 1980s. A few communities have
endured, however, with the successful archetype being the Jesus Fellowship, which, spawned by a revival in a Northampton Baptist church,
headed off early in the direction of postmillenarianism, indulging in an
exclusivism—creating sectarian boundaries with the outside world—but
launching fervent evangelizing campaigns in order to save it before the
looming Judgment Day.[16]

Renewal—A Metamorphosis

In the mid-1990s, I speculated in a paper, written along with Malcolm
Hamilton and Tony Walter, whether any of the principal distinctive hallmarks of the early renewal movement still held.[17] It had certainly come a
long way, yet changes were evident long before that time. All movements
of renewal and revival eventually stagnate and die: it is almost a sociological law. What was, in retrospect, remarkable about renewal in the mid-
twentieth-century churches was the speed with which it began to ossify.
The vigor of the movement began to falter, and for a while so did the millenarian dream—at least for those who dreamed it.

Gradually, as renewal spread, tendentious Pentecostal doctrines were dropped, especially the two-stage experience of conversion and spiritual baptism (which was inherited in part from the holiness days of belief in the "second blessing" of sanctification). Gone, therefore, were the self-affirming emblems of sanctity and separation. When renewal began to consolidate its position in the churches in the late 1970s, it underwent what Andrew Walker has called a process of "gentrification,"[18] since increasing respectability and official recognition defused its potency in the established church hierarchies. There was also more that indicated decline. The ecumenical mass meetings that charismatics had attended for a decade ground to a halt, while the Foundation Trust, the umbrella organization for denominational charismatics, ceased operations. Church attendance continued to decline. There was no hint of a revival.

At one level, renewal had left an indelible mark upon the traditional churches. Charismatic worship, symbols, and culture (although not necessarily charismatic theology) had penetrated nearly every corner of Christendom, yet its attractions were only for a rather limited clientele. This was a fairly distinctive middle-class contingent that was in marked contrast to the disinherited of the early Pentecostal movement.[19] Many indicators again seemed to confirm Weber's social psychology of religion, where the ideal interests of a constituency were fed by attractive theological constructs that reflected social experience. Like other new religious movements of the time, neo-Pentecostalism could be interpreted as providing a subculture into which those derived from the middle classes could occasionally or permanently retreat from the impersonality of modernity. It meant a departure into a world where males were allowed to cry in church, where glossolalia was understood to have therapeutic qualities, where embracing friends and strangers alike brought a sense of community.

The fairly limited, socially prescribed membership of renewal and its preference for healing and all things therapeutic was to prove of enduring importance as the movement changed direction and was impacted by parallel streams of neo-Pentecostalism from the other side of the Atlantic throughout the 1980s and 1990s. There were other influences felt by the mainstream charismatics during this period too, and some were closer to home. The most obvious were the attractions of the new churches that had grown out of the restorationist movement—a parallel manifestation of renewal and revival that carried its own unique millenarian themes. The two movements often converged in the increasingly popular Bible conventions. The restorationists offered much, and some mainstream charismatics jumped ship and joined their ranks. Others, while not accepting the entire theological baggage of the restorationists, took what was acceptable and added it to their own millenarian repertoire.

From Restorationism to "New Church"

The term "restoration" denoted a distinctive theology and reflected a profound disenchantment with the established denominations in the attempt to create the "true" church. This was, of course, in the time-honored tradition of sectarian evolution in the history of Protestant Christianity. Yet the challenge of restorationism continued to be of such consequence in the 1970s that it constituted what Andrew Walker described as "the most significant religious formation to emerge in Great Britain for over half a century."[20]

Unlike other sects, such as classical Pentecostalism or the Jehovah's Witnesses, which have attempted a return to the mythical "true" church of the first century and New Testament pattern after two millennia of perceived apostasy, restoration did not grasp the apocalyptic premillenarianism vision (although it was not entirely absent) that was forged by a persecuting world and ridicule of the established churches. Rather, restorationism was more influenced by the cultural milieu also partaken by the so-called new religious movements of the time, particularly those of a world-rejecting persuasion. Of such movements of the 1970s, Steve Bruce reflects that they appealed to those influenced by the counterculture and marked a response to the dehumanization of the public world; yet such movements came to realize that human effort was not enough to change the world. Hence, many of the world-rejecting movements claimed that some divine agency or power was poised to intervene in the world, even though that millennium would only be brought about by supernatural means if people committed themselves zealously to the endeavor.[21]

Compared to the mainstream renewal movement, the restorationists were more active in demonstrating the power of God, in attempting to restore a "lost" church and in reconstructing the kingdom of God, and represented, in the words of Grace Davie, "a desire for something special or distinctive about religious activity."[22] That distinctiveness was again shared with other new religious movements of the time, attributes which Eileen Barker has listed: the search for community, experience of the supernatural, direct communication with the divine, healing and therapies, the spiritual growth of the elect, and kingdom building.[23]

The renewal movement sought only to revive the mainline churches within their traditional structures. The early restorationist leaders, heading up groups such as New Frontiers, Ichthus, and the Pioneers, believed that this imposed severe limitations and that God wanted an all-embracing transnational church, not "the abomination of the denominations." The restored faith would mean that ecclesiastic authority, spiritual giftings, and unity were the signs of the true church before the second coming. In essence this was a revamped postmillenarianism—one that showed a tendency toward universalism on the one hand and exclusivism and spiritual elitism on the other. For the restorationists, biblical references and the cultural preferences of its middle-class membership overlapped and reinforced each other. The reference of the book of Revelation to the "bride without blemish" had an appeal to the therapeutically minded who sought to develop their spiritual potential. It also fed into the enduring hope of revival led by those who had prophetic insights into the last days and furnished the cohorts of restorationism with the suitably honed weapons of spiritual warfare.

Postmillenarianism Revisited

The significance of the postmillenarianism embraced by the restorationists is worth more than a fleeting reference. It was not a totally fresh formation fashioned in the hands of the restorationists, even if elements of it were clearly reinvented. Historically speaking, since the third century, postmillenarianism proved to be largely peripheral to established Christian theology. Among evangelical Protestants, however, for the better part of the nineteenth and twentieth centuries it vied for legitimacy alongside premillenarianism and amillenarianism (while all of these have displayed overlapping themes and have frequently culled theological constructs from rival strands).[24] Postmillenarianism accepted the literal thousand-year reign of Christ in the coming kingdom of God. Hence, it rejected the amillenarian position, which insisted that the millennium is interpreted as a symbolic and spiritual concept, where the events spoken of in the Scriptures take place in the heavenly realm rather than on earth, and which marked the period between Christ's first and second advents.[25] At the same time, the major departure from premillenarianism was that postmillenarianism interpreted the Scriptures to mean that Christ's return will be after the millennium, rather than before it.

From the mid-nineteenth to the early twentieth century, for particular historical reasons, postmillenarianism almost supplanted premillenarianism as the commonly received doctrine in the United States and strongly influenced evangelical thinking in Europe. The subsequent decline of postmillenarianism by the early twentieth century was no less due to a further set of historical developments. Postmillenarianism in the nineteenth century was essentially characterized by a belief in supernatural events and, at the same time, reflected natural laws of organic development in that it mirrored ideas of secular progress, optimism, and rationalism.

Postmillenarianism, then, may have initially reflected the Enlightenment project of progress, but equally it expresses the marginalization of certain forms of conservative evangelicalism. It constituted an active preparation for the second advent of Christ where the millennium might arrive in a triumphal gradualism that matched God's will with human effort: believers themselves could usher in the kingdom of God. While at least some of its underlying orientation was culled from liberal theology, it still retained the cosmic imagery of Christian eschatology that translated "progress" through revival and the conversion of souls, where the saints were to be coworkers in the creation of the New Jerusalem on earth. This is perhaps today taken to its logical conclusion in the political activism of contemporary reconstructionism U.S.-style, which seeks actively to transform sinful society along Old Testament lines.[26]

The hope of postmillenarianism proved to be short-lived. By the late nineteenth century many of its core doctrines had become increasingly hard to sustain in the light of learned biblical studies. It also looked increasingly implausible because world events had stubbornly refused to follow its prophecies. Religious decline, rather than revival, was evident; the wars and social upheavals of the early twentieth century challenged notions of progress and seemed more readily to fulfill premillenarian criteria—especially those espoused by John Nelson Darby—and the predictions of wars, rumors of global plagues and famines, and signs of growing moral depravity. From the mid-twentieth century, postmillenarianism was in favor again, although it frequently dipped into the premillenarian disaster syndrome and the convictions of the sign watchers and the fundamentalists of the U.S. Bible Belt, while its adherents took to subscribing to the popular doomsday culture of Christian novels. In the latter decades of the twentieth century, where it has been carried by neo-Pentecostalism on a global scale, postmillenarianism expressed itself in various theological formations. These included the doctrines and praxis of the so-called Third Wave movement and dominion theology, as well as the aforementioned reconstructionism. While these brands of neo-Pentecostal postmillenarianism differ radically in some ways, they share a number of core beliefs that cluster together in embracing a distinctive form of Christian eschatology that was also evident in British restorationism.

Signs and Wonders and All That Stuff

Restorationism, in its pure form at least, was short-lived. The anticipated kingdom did not come. In the 1980s the restorationist movement fractured. Moreover, in a matter of years the principal strands came to display denomination features of their own and opted to be bedfellows with the mainstream charismatics of whom they had so been critical.[27] There was thus good evidence to suggest that restorationism was capitulating to the very forces of secularization to which it was so vehemently opposed as it huddled with the renewalists and traditional Pentecostals, who also faced stagnation and ongoing membership decline. Each fed off another, establishing overlapping circles, partaking of theological interplay, and increasingly opening themselves to fresh inspirations and ideas from around the globe. By the 1990s, restorationism had revamped itself. The various strands became the "new churches"—a self-assigned badge of respectability. Its leaders and membership, disappointed by the lack of national revival inherent in the postmillenarian hope, sought new directions. The inspiration was to come from the other side of the Atlantic.

As we have already noted, postmillenarianism can be seen in other expressions besides restorationism. An alternative rendition brought an emphasis on the miraculous, on signs and wonders, providing an attempt to show the necessary power of God in an age of disbelief. This preoccupation with power is to a great extent bound up with the marginalization and powerlessness of evangelicalism in the contemporary world. Much was epitomized by the kingdom theology of John Wimber. In some respects Wimber's theology delved into many premillenarian themes. Nonetheless, the predominance of the postmillenarian tone was there to see. Kingdom theology placed a great deal of emphasis upon manifestations of divine power. Wimber insisted that it was necessary for the church to harness this power in order to be rescued from its impotence and numerical decline. While Wimber adopted rational strategies for church growth, they became enmeshed with issues of God's power through his emphasis on signs and wonders, including healing and deliverance, and the enduring theme of revival.[28]

Widespread revival, according to Wimber, precipitated such signs and wonders. These "signs" were supposedly evident in the revivals led by Wesley, Whitefield, and Edwards. Hence, they could accompany contemporary evangelism in the last days, a mission that would bring charismatics and evangelicals together in the Third Wave of God's twentieth-century revival. This theology did not remain at the theoretical level. Under Wimber's tutelage the Association of Vineyard Churches spread across the globe from its home in California. In the early 1980s, Wimber's church-growth strategy strongly impressed the Anglican charismatics who took his ministry on board. The trail of signs and wonders—of alleged healings, deliverance, and other ecstatic manifestations—took even many seasoned mainline charismatics by surprise; but there was no doubting their impact and attraction at a time when the renewal movement was dying on its feet and church attendance declined apace.

The emphasis upon the discernible and demonstrative active power of God in the late twentieth century was not unique to John Wimber and Vineyard. Sociologist of religion Jim Beckford has drawn attention to the widespread use of "power" in contemporary religion that reflects wider secular concerns of empowerment and potential.[29] This is undoubtedly the case, yet there is more to consider, and there is a sense in which the preoccupation with power constitutes nothing particularly new. Concepts of power in religion have at least partially reflected the underlying problem in secular society of the legitimation of values, beliefs, and ideologies which function as symbols held to be meaningful by those who accept the exercise of divine power as legitimate.[30] The contemporary charismatic emphasis on supernatural power, however, might be imperative in the light of relentless skepticism and subjective relativism of human knowledge, particularly in the context of globalization. In other words, the demonstration of divine power in particular brings the necessary "proof" to unbelievers, while verifying the faith of those who do believe. In the postmodern world of relativism, proof of the reality of the divine becomes indispensable for a cognitive minority.

In many respects, Wimber had rediscovered the secret of Pentecostal growth. The work of Chalfont et al. on classical Pentecostalism demonstrates the attraction of a close relationship between evangelism, a literal interpretation of the Bible, and religious experience, including glossolalia, prophecy, healing, deliverance, miracles, and other paranormal experiences.[31] Such experiences, interpreted through biblical literalism, not only carry profound religious significance and meaning, but simultaneously reveal the "power of God." This is the basic recipe for Pentecostal growth. In many respects, Wimber took such signs and wonders to their natural conclusion as part of an overrealized eschatology, but one dressed up in a middle-class therapeutic package. Its attractions were undeniable.

The impact of Wimber's kingdom theology on the renewal movement was phenomenal.[32] For Wimber, the kingdom of God is a realm of power that overthrows the controlling power of Satan. Here was the recurring theme of God dynamically intervening throughout history with signs and wonders and supernatural power. Wimber's main emphasis, therefore, was what he referred to as "doing the stuff"—the "stuff that Jesus did."[33] The Holy Spirit brings signs and wonders, healings, miracles, and other manifestations under specific conditions, if people are open to them. It also dovetailed well with postmillenarian frameworks, since these powers were returning to the church in the last days and cut through its restrictive rationalism and ritual. All believers could partake and develop their "gifts." Hence, there were conferences for "equipping saints," and the "saints" were once again overwhelmingly the middle-class cohorts of the charismatic movement. By the late 1980s the signs and wonders were taken to extremes. To some extent at least, this reflected the needs of the internal consumption of the charismatic movement. It was also more evidence that the faith was becoming part of what Noll calls the Christian entertainment industry.[34] In this need to be entertained and, in common charismatic parlance, "at the cutting edge of what God is doing," charismatic Christians were prepared to change churches or even belong to none at all, becoming what Walker has called "spiritual nomads" who flit from one church to another in pursuit of the novel and the new.[35]

In this fresh environment, leading personalities in the charismatic movement took differing directions. Some became apostles, individuals with particular gifts. Each and every esoteric direction was understood to be a revelation of God in the last days. There were even predictions that churches would come to comprise those with the same gifting. Then there was the preoccupation with all things demonic. When the "marches for Jesus" with their origins in the Festival of Light first took to the streets in 1989, it was claimed by some organizers to be a way of shifting demonic atmospheres across Britain. Here was a veritable fantasy land of dungeons and dragons, spiritual warfare writ large, furnished by imported animism inherent in third-world Pentecostalism. Demonology was taken to its extremes by not a few in the charismatic movement. Inspired by the ministries of men such as Bill Subritzky and Derek Prince, they ensured that the devil got more than his due.[36] Nonetheless, whichever way deliverance was conducted, every blow against Satan brought the kingdom of God closer.

There were other dynamics too. Esoteric phenomenon by its nature knows few boundaries, and those who indulge are likely to put it before theological constructs that, if subscribed to, are equally likely to be stretched to the point of heresy. The end of the second millennium beckoned, and many charismatic celebrities claimed ever more wishful prophecies, while the spiritual giftings were given true measure for the coming revival. Indeed, the late 1980s and early 1990s became practically synonymous with the so-called prophetic movement. Much was exemplified by the self-styled mission of the Kansas City Prophets, who took postmillenarianism almost to its logical conclusion.[37] The stress was on "a panoramic view of God's purposes in the next generation." This included the erroneous claim by Paul Cain that revival would break out in the United Kingdom in October 1990 and the even more preposterous prophecy that the children of some leading charismatics would be born with a semidivine nature.

The Toronto Blessing and Millenarian Mischief

With millenarian expectations high in the 1990s, it was hard to anticipate what might happen next. What did happen next was the Toronto Blessing. The Blessing, as it was more colloquially known, took many sociologists of religion by surprise. It took many in the renewal movement by surprise, too. For some charismatics who had just about seen it all, it constituted a counterfeit revival, a deceiving work of Satan. A conference of seasoned charismatics skeptical of developments in the Toronto Blessing issued a telling statement:

> ... that the prophecies concerning a great outpouring of power in the last days upon an elite company of believers is a dangerous eschatological teaching that has no foundation in scripture. It is, nevertheless, a teaching that has great appeal in an age characterized by a sense of powerlessness.[38]

The skeptics were probably half right: there may have been attempts to kick-start renewal since the 1970s. This was spectacularly the case with the Toronto Blessing, which burst onto the global charismatic scene. Much could be attributed to the psychological pressures that had been building up for several years in the charismatic movement, an expectation of revival born of the millenarian hope.[39] Much like the Pentecostal and charismatic movements, there was a mythological origin for the Blessing in the Toronto Vineyard Fellowship. Indeed, much emanated from the church, which became a point of pilgrimage for many charismatics across the world.[40] Nonetheless, many of the phenomena evident can be traced back to the ministries of Reinhart Bonnke, Benny Hinn, and Rodney Howard Brown, who had been doing the rounds of charismatic churches for some time. However, it was in Toronto that it was subsequently suitably "packaged"— as much as such phenomena can be packaged and exported.

Curious, if not miraculously attributed, phenomena had a wide appeal in the charismatic churches in Britain, where the Toronto Blessing was spread with the help of Holy Trinity, Brompton, and other large charismatic churches with channels open to the Vineyard movement. Around Pentecost Sunday in 1994, outbursts of uncontrolled, if not hysterical, laughter occurred during services in British charismatic churches. While some members of the congregations floated to the floor "resting in the Spirit," apparently under the power of God, others staggered around in what was designated "spiritual drunkenness"—laughing or displaying slurred speech and uncontrollable spasms of the limbs. Some pogo-ed up and down or frantically "ran on the spot." The curious lurched into the bizarre when later came the animal noises, including those imitating dogs, cattle, and chickens. There was the "Toronto twitch," playing at being motor cars, and women groaning—symbolically giving birth to the kingdom. Besides these physical manifestations there were more "hidden" esoteric experiences. There were prophecies, "pictures," and visions of angels. There were stories of angelic hitchhikers who spoke of a coming revival and who would then suddenly disappear from the backseats of the cars of Christians unaware that they were entertaining angels.

If, as suggested above, postmillenarianism was born of the optimism of the narrative of modernity, it had taken a new direction as the postmodern horizon loomed. The Toronto Blessing exemplified much, since it seemed to be encoded with the reenchantment of the supernatural sphere that typified alternative expressions of religion in the postmodern world. For one thing, it was based on the mysticism of subjective individual experience, as charismatics walked into an esoteric wonderland. Some of those involved tried to justify the manifestations with historical evidence—the signs and wonders of earlier revivals: those of Wesley, Edwards, the Quakers, the Shakers, and the Pentecostals. Others had recourse to biblical reference. The references were few, and even these were far from convincing. But perhaps this did not matter: if Tom Smail lamented the unsophisticated theology of the charismatic movement, the Toronto Blessing seemed to circumvent it altogether.

During the Toronto Blessing the kingdom expected to come appeared to be breaking through. It was postmillenarianism taken to its furthest conclusion. There were, however, different interpretations of what it all amounted to. The same questions were asked, by those who cared to ask questions, as were asked at the time of the beginning of the renewal movement. Some hedged their bets. Was it a periodic outpouring of the Holy Spirit or did it signify the end itself? One popular theme was that God was preparing his people for evangelism, the last evangelizing endeavor. Thus there was the enduring theme of revival throughout the short time that the Toronto Blessing held sway. According to the senior pastor of the Toronto Vineyard Fellowship, John Arnott, the people of God were being prepared for probably the greatest harvest in the world. The church could be "moving towards the last move of God . . . the real power is coming. God is saying just get used to it." The Toronto Blessing knew no boundaries. It was a coming together of the charismatic tribes. In Durkheimian terms it may have been a great gathering of effervescent enthusiasm that is the very nature of the religious life.[41] If so, it possibly highlighted once again the ecumenical nature of the charismatic movement, yet signified its weakness rather than its strength. The Toronto Blessing was also comparable to a ghost dance without the bulletproof shirts. It too ended in disappointment. There was no revival and seemingly no attempt to repair cognitive dissonance.

Conclusion—End Games or the End of the Charismatic Movement?

Like the charismatic movement, the Toronto Blessing soon become ritualized and routinized. This was no more evident than at the Toronto Vineyard church itself,[42] which had degenerated into little more than a charismatic tourist attraction. In Britain, as the manifestations petered out, those involved responded in different ways. Some sought ever more esoteric phenomena and gave up church services altogether, at least for a time. Then there was the gold teeth-filling craze and claims by some charismatics that they had received a visit from the divine dentist. Others simply said nothing. The Toronto Blessing disappeared as rapidly as yesterday's news and with hardly a word of explanation.

However, a good number of other charismatics found a new interest as the Toronto Blessing faded away: the growing popularity of the Alpha program. Put together by Holy Trinity Brompton, a leading player in the Toronto Blessing, Alpha was a return to Bible study, ideally for nonchurchgoers who sought to know more about the faith. Yet, it is more evidently subscribed to by church members who seem to have forgotten "the basics." Perhaps this was a legacy of the Toronto Blessing?

Using all the evangelizing techniques acquired by the charismatic movement over the years, the Alpha program is well-designed and eminently sensible. It introduces the "basics" of Christianity for exploration over several weeks and avails itself, through the formula of meal-video-discussion groups, of what contemporary evangelism has learned from psychology, sociology, and business acumen. Nonetheless, it has kept some of its charismatic credentials and a small portion of signs and wonders in its Holy Spirit weekend retreat. But for all intents and purposes it teaches historical Christianity. There is not a whiff of millenarian mischief.

Elsewhere I have argued that Alpha gave empty hands something to do after the Toronto Blessing.[43] This is not without some justification, since the first few thousand churches to take it up were probably of a charismatic disposition and, to one degree or another, had subscribed to the Toronto Blessing. For these churches optimism now burns brightly. A good deal of the literature surrounding the Alpha program talks of revival and conversion. It also has a global appeal. The course is now run in over one hundred countries and has been translated into dozens of languages. In some quarters, it may have sparked revival, but not in Britain, despite all the self-laudation of Alpha publications.[44]

Whatever the evidence suggests about the success or otherwise of the program, there has always been one aspect of latent propaganda surrounding Alpha that has not been exploited as it might have been, which is perhaps surprising. Alpha could have been used to repair the cognitive dissonance left by the Toronto Blessing. Since the Toronto Blessing was preparing the way for revival, surely Alpha was the divinely chosen means to bring it about? This would have possibly kept the millenarian dream alive. It can only be surmised that those involved in the Toronto Blessing so wished to distance themselves from those events that it is no longer mentioned in polite conversation. One prophecy of those days is, however, retained. The expectation that national revival would begin with the disinherited and marginalized is kept alive. Hence, the Alpha program has been applied to Her Majesty's prisons in earnest. Here, the Alpha literature has spoken of the first signs of revival. They are, however, few and far between.

The Alpha enterprise is indicative of how far the charismatic movement has come in four decades. The millenarian hope has been an integral part of that journeying. But it is not the same movement that emerged in the 1960s, and this is evident in the developments discussed above—not least in the way that it has dealt with the theme of the Last Days. The millenarian constructs may not be theologically sophisticated, but they are rich in diversity and in the way that they responded to challenges from secular society and within the broader church.

Several years into the twenty-first century, all seems quiet on the millennium front. The esoteric phenomenon has died down. The prophets have run out of prophecies, the spiritual warriors are battle-weary. It may well be that this is the beginning of the end for the charismatic movement. Andrew Walker has speculated as much when he states that "Pentecostalism rushed into the twentieth century like a hurricane at Azusa Street, Los Angeles, in 1906. Perhaps it finally blew itself out at Toronto Airport in 1994."[45]

Yet the movement is multifaceted, adaptive, and even contradictory. If postmodernity turns out to be a new cultural era, we might anticipate that the charismatic movement will share as many continuities with the past as discontinuities. Indeed, this is what has kept it alive for so many years. Such a scenario is plausible because the movement itself does not have the reflexive ability—unless it is justifying phenomena, as evident in the Toronto Blessing—to differentiate between such continuities and discontinuities. Neither does it have a sufficiently coherent theology to do so. Thus, Smail's lament still sounds loud.

What does the sociology of religion have to say? Certainly, sociologists have long displayed a tendency of being prophets in their own right in predicting future trends of religiosity. Like the charismatics, they as often get it wrong as right. Some things are, however, clear. Britain and other Western countries may not be entirely secular, but they are largely post-Christian. The fate of the charismatic movement is undoubtedly tied up with the fortunes of the faith of which it is a major shareholder. It is also clear that through such initiatives as the Alpha program, the doctrines and praxis of renewal are being extended throughout the churches. However, they are much diluted and are without either the zest of revivalism that was there at the beginning or the excitement that came with the millenarian hope. The end of the charismatic movement then, perhaps like the end of the world, will come not with a bang but with a whimper.

Chapter Twelve

Southcottian Sects from 1790 to the Present Day

Gordon Allan

The purpose of this chapter is to sketch the history and doctrines of a number of small millenarian sects that owe their existence, in varying degrees, to the English prophetess Joanna Southcott (1750-1814).[1] These groups, vestiges of which survive to the present day, are then evaluated under several headings, corresponding to various traits and doctrines that tend to identify fundamentalist groups, with an emphasis on their eschatological beliefs. The similarities between these groups, as well as some of their more interesting differences, are also highlighted.

I first became aware of one of these Southcottian groups a number of years ago when I saw an advertisement in a newspaper stating that "time is running out." The advertisement went on to say that the allotted six thousand years of humankind's reign was shortly to come to an end, to be replaced by a thousand years of the glorious reign of the Lord Jesus. Further investigation revealed that this glorious reign was to take place on this earth, not in heaven. Particular reference was made to a book, *Extracts from the Flying Roll*, by James Jershom Jezreel. The first "sermon" of these "Extracts" turned out to consist of seven parts, each between 25 and 30 pages, so the whole sermon runs to 208 pages. Anyone reading this work

today may well find that at first it seems rather incomprehensible. However, with perseverance and determination one can see what is being constructed by the author. We find a complicated doctrinal and prophetic
scheme that is quite different from anything one is likely to encounter in
the more mainstream Christian tradition. The biblical text is central
throughout, with, it seems, almost every sentence containing either an allusion to or a direct quotation of Scripture. This chance encounter with the
advertisement and further study of the associated literature was to be the
beginning of my acquaintance with a number of small millenarian religious sects, during the course of which I came to know personally, meet,
or else correspond with a number of the individual members of these sects.
Regrettably, many of those persons are no longer alive.

The recollections outlined above are not without importance. A good
deal of the material in this chapter is based upon a firsthand knowledge of
the tradition with which it deals. I make use not only of published material written by "outsiders," but also of personal conversations and other
communications with members of the Southcottian trajectories. I have
also used information found in private collections. This has given me a
privileged insight: generally Southcottian groups do not publicize details of
their internal organization and practices, such information being reserved
for members only. (The Southcottian groups are not, of course, unique in
this.) My work is thus rather different from much that has been written to
date, since earlier studies have been largely based upon Southcottian publications designed for general use or on newspaper accounts, which has
resulted in an incomplete picture.[2]

The New and Latter House of Israel

The publication *Extracts from the Flying Roll*, sometimes simply referred to
as *The Flying Roll* or even just *The Roll* (as believers in the publication often
call it) was written by a man calling himself James Jershom Jezreel (JJJ). He
is sometimes called "The Stranger" because so little is known about him.
His adopted middle name, "Jershom" (signifying "stranger"), is based upon
the biblical account of Moses' son by Zipporah, Gershom, who was given
that name because "I have been a stranger in a strange land" (Exod. 2:22,
KJV). Jezreel claimed that *The Roll* was revealed to him, but that it did not
originate *with* him. He called himself a messenger rather than a prophet,
and his work, *The Roll*, was claimed to be an explanation of biblical mys-
teries hitherto hidden from the world—a key that would unlock the Scriptures. In this context, Jezreel quoted Jesus in Matthew 13:35—"I will
proclaim what has been hidden from the foundation of the world." This is

a key text in the first sermon, and, he said, the justification of his revelation. To Jezreel, the end time was upon us and all was about to be revealed.

The Jezreelites accept a form of biblical fundamentalism, believing in the authority of the Old and New Testaments, while also being able to accommodate the Old Testament Apocrypha and other apocryphal writings such as the book of Enoch and the Book of Jasher. To these sources of authority they add a series of prophets (beginning with Richard Brothers in 1790, about whom more will be said later), though they would argue that the prophets always work within the biblical framework. Ultimately they would still appeal to the Bible as the source of their teaching and attempt to prove their beliefs from the texts of Scripture.[3] It is unusual for the average Christian fundamentalist to give any credence to apocryphal writings or to a human prophet, although there are exceptions. For example, the Seventh-day Adventists manage to be biblical literalists while the majority of members also accept the Spirit of Prophecy in Ellen G. White. White is, for Adventists, the inspired interpreter of the inspired text. Southcottians would also claim that the prophet is not placed on the same level as the Scriptures, but rather that the prophet is the servant of the text and a guide to it. Later Southcottian sects believe in the authenticity of previous prophets or messengers in the chain, though they believe that each messenger encompasses the teaching of all the previous ones, making it unnecessary to read too much of what the earlier prophets have said.

Jezreel claimed to be the sixth messenger of a line of seven. This leads to an obvious question: "Who are the previous five, and who is or was number seven?" The Jezreelites do not invite academic study. They are not interested in discussing their history with outsiders; they are only interested in directing people to *The Flying Roll*. However, documents that shed more light on this and predecessor movements have recently come to light, and this research continues as part of the Oxford University Prophecy Project.[4]

Seven Messengers

Support for the belief in a succession of messengers is drawn from the seven angels of the book of Revelation blowing seven trumpets, one after the other (Rev. 8:2–9:21 and 11:15-19). In the introduction to *The Flying Roll*, Joseph Head describes Jezreel as "the man of God, bound in chains, for the Hope of Israel—the trumpet that the Immortal Spirit bloweth through."[5] The seven messengers are warning of the imminent appearance of Christ's kingdom.

The seven days of creation are also seen as paralleling the seven messengers. Each day creation becomes better and better; the light becomes clearer and clearer, until the seventh-day Sabbath rest—the type of the millennium.

The seven days therefore foreshadow seven periods of a thousand years—the seventh thousand equating to the millennium. According to the tradition, we are currently still living in the sixth. The six identified messengers are detailed in the table below.

Prophet	Born	Died	Years of Leadership/ Prophethood	Prophesied
Richard Brothers	1757	1824	1790–1792	1790?–1824
Joanna Southcott	1750	1814	1792–1814	1792–1814
George Turner	?	1821	1814–1821	1795–1821
William Shaw	?	1822	1821–1822	1818–1822
John Wroe	1782	1863	1822–1863	1819–1863
James Jezreel	1840?	1885	1875–1885	1875–1885
Number 7?	?	?	?	?

Members of the movement believed that only one prophet could be "sounding" at any one time, although, as the table shows, some of the prophets were actually prophesying for periods that overlapped with other messengers. Each prophet had followers, some of whom moved on to accept the next prophet in line; but others did not, with the result that "intermediate" sects sprung up, some of which still exist today. The concept of a succession of prophets, however, did not appear until Wroe—number five. There is no evidence that Brothers, Southcott, Turner, or Shaw believed themselves to be in a prophetic line, although Southcott taught that she was one of several prophets, on the basis of Joel 2, which states that before the great and terrible day of the Lord, "your sons and your daughters shall prophesy, your old men shall dream dreams, and your young men shall see visions. Even on the male and female slaves, in those days, I will pour out my spirit" (Joel 2:28-29). Southcott believed and supported Brothers for some time, until she decided that he was making claims for himself that did not accord with Scripture. She accepted that others received visions, which she sometimes interpreted, and that others received communications from the "Spirit of Truth."

There are various accounts of the prophets by different groups within what has become known as "the Visitation." This study is primarily concerned with the first six of these prophets. I now give a summary account of each of them in turn.

Richard Brothers (1757–1824) is usually considered to be the first of the line.[6] He was born in Newfoundland, Canada, allegedly on December 25, 1757. (Brothers considered the date significant, though it has not been possible to validate it.) He was educated at Woolwich, went to sea in 1771, and was retired on half pay in about 1783. Brothers claimed to be the "Prince of the Hebrews," appointed to lead the Jews back to the promised land in Palestine as a precursor to the setting up of the kingdom of God on earth for a thousand years (the millennium). He further prophesied that the Hebrews would be returned to Jerusalem by 1798, a date that he claimed to have received by revelation. Brothers collected only a small number of followers, although his writings seem to have been more widely read. Eventually, because of the political stir his writings were causing, he was removed to an asylum. In 1794 he had published *A Revealed Knowledge of the Prophecies and Times* in two volumes, the second appearing a few months after the first. This was published in the United States as well as in the United Kingdom and went through several editions. He is considered by some to be the father of British Israelism, the theory that the British nation (and by extension the United States) are descendants of the lost tribes of Israel.

Brothers claimed to be descended from King David, and therefore of the tribe of Judah (not a lost tribe), and named other prominent people in his writings as also being descended from Israelite tribes.[7] He adopted the title "Nephew of the Almighty," because he believed his lineage continued through Jesus' family. He also espoused the (not uncommon) idea that mankind was allotted a period of six thousand years on this earth (corresponding to the six days of creation), which was soon to be followed by the great Sabbath of rest—a thousand years of peace on earth. This seven-thousand-year plan is adopted by all the subsequent prophets. Brothers continued writing up to his death in 1824, but early on he was eclipsed by the next in line, Southcott, to whom quite a number of his followers defected. As far as can be established, no direct following of Brothers continues to the present day.[8]

Joanna Southcott (1750–1814) was the daughter of a Devon farmer. She began to write down the words she heard from the "Spirit of Truth" in 1792, foretelling things that would take place on the earth as a prelude to Christ's kingdom. Southcott was told to take the message to the world, and in 1801 she published the first of her sixty-five works, *The Strange Effects of Faith*.[9] Soon she had attracted a following, some of whom were influential and included several clergymen. The historical facts regarding her life have been well-documented elsewhere and hence need not be rehearsed in any detail here.[10]

Right from her first book, Southcott claimed to be the "woman clothed with the sun" of Revelation 12. How that would work out in practice did not become obvious until late in her life, when, at the age of sixty-four, she was told that she was to bear a child, Shiloh, who would rule the earth with a rod of iron. What is sometimes overlooked, partly no doubt because of the sensationalism surrounding the prophesied birth of Shiloh, is the fact that Joanna also had a well-developed theology, and an interpretation of the scriptural text into which she wove her own place in prophecy. In some ways, Southcott could be considered an early biblical feminist, in that her explanation of the fall of Adam and Eve (recorded in Genesis 3) lays a foundation doctrine followed by later Visitation prophets. What she says is that the man (Adam) wrongly allocated the blame for the fall on the woman, and therefore ultimately on God for giving him the woman: "The woman whom *you* gave to be with me, she gave me fruit from the tree, and I ate" (Gen. 3:12). The woman, however, rightly (as far as the text goes) placed the blame on the serpent—traditionally seen in Christian theology as an early appearance of the devil. Because of this, the promise was made to her that her seed would bruise the serpent's head (meaning destruction), although her seed would be bruised in the heel (temporary incapacity). By this reasoning, Southcott puts the man in the wrong and the woman in the right.

Another fundamental part of Southcott's theology is the setting up of the kingdom of God, which is to be *on earth*. The traditional church teaching, in which she had been raised, was that the "saved" go to heaven. But Southcott's message was to prepare the world for the return of Christ to the earth. She retains the mainstream church teaching of an immortal soul and of the soul's going to heaven on death. However, her followers were expecting to live not in heaven but on a renewed earth, and although during the millennium there is to be free passage between heaven and earth, it is the earth that is the center of God's plan in the longer term; the earth will in fact be a renewed Eden.

Southcott sealed up some of her writings and placed them in a box, not to be opened until a time of national emergency, and only to be opened in the presence of twenty-four bishops of the Church of England or their representatives (based on the twenty-four elders in Revelation 4). The box was to be in the custody of believers and passed on from one believer to another. Many campaigns, particularly during the first half of the twentieth century, have been aimed at the bishops in an attempt to have the box opened. Several spurious boxes have been opened, but the real box remains in the custody of believers who still await the call from the bishops that they want the box opened.

Southcott also made extensive use of typology or, as she expressed it, "types and shadows," both with regard to her own life events and in her reuse of biblical prophecies and motifs, in similar manner to the New Testament writers' use of the Old (especially, for example, messianic prophecies in the Book of Hebrews). This typological use of Scripture was not, of course, unique to her (and the Seventh-day Adventists were later to use it very extensively), but it was an important part of her overall scheme.

During her lifetime, Southcott engaged in three "trials" to which members of the established church were invited. The focus of these "trials" was her own writings, which she invited others to question and search for the truth thereof. The "trials" were conducted very much like a legal trial, with evidence both for and against the authenticity of her writings being presented.

As has already been noted briefly, Southcott took the view that she was to give birth to Shiloh, the second Messiah (or "second child")—a teaching that became one of the most controversial things that she had to say. The name Shiloh is taken from Genesis 49:10, where Jacob is blessing his sons on his deathbed. Of Judah he says: "The scepter shall not depart from Judah, nor the ruler's staff from between his feet, until Shiloh comes to him; and the obedience of the peoples is his." This passage had been regarded by some rabbis as messianic, and Southcott also believed that this figure was to be the one who would restore the Jews and rule them in the millennial age; the restoration of the Jews to their own land was an essential part of her teaching. The concept of two Messiahs was also not new with Southcott, being similarly held by some rabbis, possibly because of the dual role of the Messiah presented in Scripture—political and spiritual.[11] Rather than combining these qualities in one person, they envisaged two. There is even some evidence that it was a feature of messianic expectation at Qumran. However, it seems unlikely that Southcott would have been aware of this previous tradition.

Following her claim to be pregnant with Shiloh in 1814, Southcott showed all the signs of pregnancy, even convincing several reputable doctors that this was indeed her condition. However, when Southcott died on December 27 of that same year, there was no sign of the child, nor any obvious cause of her own death. The nonappearance of the child caused many of her followers to fall away, but the faithful mainly came to believe that Shiloh had in fact been born as predicted, and on Christmas day (two days before Southcott herself died). Following the description in Revelation 12, so the believers argued, Shiloh had been caught up to God and to his throne, from whence he will come at the appropriate time.[12]

Toward the end of the nineteenth century, Southcott's following was dwindling, but in the early twentieth century, a revival of interest was brought about by Alice Seymour, who reprinted all of her writings and issued several magazines containing her unpublished communications. Southcott still has a direct following, though small, in the United Kingdom, Australia, New Zealand, and the United States; those followers (who do not accept any of the later prophets) are generally known as "Old Southcottians."

After Southcott died, a number of people came forward claiming to be her successor.[13] Those of her old following would not accept any of the claimants, but continued to meet for the reading and discussion of her writings. As well as the sixty-five published books, there were numerous manuscripts of unpublished communications. These were copied by hand into notebooks, which were then circulated among the believers, who felt that these contained deeper teaching than the published works. Southcottian churches had sprung up during Joanna's lifetime—more because her followers were made unwelcome in the mainstream churches than for any need for separation.[14] These communities continued after her death, and correspondence between the various groups of believers shows the wide differences of opinion between them as to the interpretation of the nonappearance of Shiloh, and whether Southcott would return to complete her mission. This went on for some years, with correspondence passing between the churches supporting one view or another. Some thought that Shiloh might be a person alive at the time, others that the birth was purely spiritual; others fell away believing the whole thing was a charade. Several colorful characters arose, who do not belong in the "succession" of the seven prophets, but who nevertheless have added their own particular slant. For example, Mary Boon, from Staverton in Devon, also known as Mary Joanna, is believed by some to have originated the teaching that true believers need to keep the law of Moses, particularly the seventh-day Sabbath. This teaching was accepted by some of the later prophets in the succession. Similarly, Joseph Allman, who adopted the name Zebulon, the "bruised reed," developed the theory that, overall, God was feminine, although the individual members of the Trinity were male. Another colorful character, John (alias Zion) Ward claimed to be Shiloh himself. In an extension to what Southcott herself had proposed, Ward taught that Scripture was *all* allegorical—that it was not history—and that it all pointed to him. His following (the "Shilohites") survived well into the twentieth century.

George Turner (date of birth unknown; died 1821) was a Leeds merchant, reputedly the brother of a former mayor of the town. He was an early follower of Brothers. Turner's first publication was *A Testimony to the Prophetical Mission of Richard Brothers* (1795), a booklet in support of Brothers's mission, but even at this early date he was hearing the voice of the Spirit and believed he was called to be a prophet.

According to Turner, "The Voice" told him while reading a copy of Brothers's *Revealed Knowledge* that "This is the word of the Lord." A few years later, in 1801, Turner became a follower of Southcott after he had examined her writings. Joanna spent more than six months with him in

Leeds toward the end of 1803 and into 1804; from there she went out to hold meetings in areas as widespread as Stockton in the northeast of England and Southport in the northwest, with the result that the Southcottian movement gained a strong hold in the north of England.

After Southcott's death in 1814, Turner became one of the leaders of the believers in her "Visitation" and took on the mantle of prophet himself. He was, however, not universally accepted, and many stayed faithful to the "old guard" represented by Jane Townley, who had been Southcott's companion, and the Reverend T. P. Foley, one of the earliest converts. Turner's following, predictably, was particularly strong in Yorkshire and Lancashire but, surprisingly, also in Devon and the west of England, with quite a following in London. (Turner, in his writings, lists meetings of his followers in Leeds, Sheffield, Bradford, Idle, York, Northallerton, Pontefract, Wakefield, Barnsley, Sutton, Manchester, Warrington, Ashton, Colne, Bury, Exeter, Plymouth, Totnes, Devonport, Ilfracombe, Bath, Bristol, Moorlinch, and Tewkesbury.)

Turner was arrested for high treason on account of the proclamations that he published in the newspapers, but the jury determined that he was insane, and in 1817 he was committed to a Quaker asylum, the Retreat, at Osbaldswick in Yorkshire, where he remained for three years before being released in July 1820. Unperturbed by his experience in the asylum, Turner then arranged "The Marriage Supper of the Lamb" (based on the description recorded in Revelation 19:9, 17), an event that took place in the City of Westminster on August 30, 1820. There were about six hundred people present. He also prophesied that Shiloh (whom he claimed to have seen) would appear on October 14 of that year. When no such event took place, Turner changed the date to April 10, 1821. It was a blow to his followers when, for the second time, the expectation was not fulfilled.

Turner revived the idea of the lost tribes of Israel that had been expounded by Brothers (though interestingly not by Southcott), teaching that his followers belonged to the tribes of Israel; one of his followers in Devon, Rebecca Wood (or Woods), had the gift of being able to determine to which tribe a follower belonged. He also introduced the first recognizable movement toward keeping the law of Moses by prohibiting (under the Levitical law) unclean meats from being served at the Marriage Supper. Turner died in September 1821, still believing that Shiloh's return was imminent. In spite of his death, and unfulfilled prophecies, his followers continued under the leadership of the man who had been his amanuensis while he was alive, Samuel Gompertz. However, his following gradually disintegrated, and there are no known direct followers remaining today.

William Shaw (died 1822) is a rather enigmatic character. He seems to have been based in London and to have been prophesying from 1818 onwards. He was definitely sending his own prophecies to (and supporting)

Turner at that time. His only known writings are those published by the
Panacea Society,[15] based on manuscripts that have not yet been traced. He
prophesies against nations (Arabia, Europe, Turkey), denounces London,
and predicts the imminent appearance of Shiloh. Evidence for even his
existence had been scarce, but reference to him in contemporary letters has
recently come to light,[16] validating not only his existence, but also the high
regard in which he was held by some of his contemporaries. Such sources
also refer to his receiving "the word of the Lord" and the surprise that his
early death caused. Shaw survived Turner by only nine months and does
not appear to have gathered a following either during his lifetime or after.

John Wroe (1782–1863) was born near Bradford, the son of a farmer
and collier. He set up as a woolcomber in 1810, but in 1819 he began to
see visions and fall into trances. He joined the group of Turner's followers
under the direction of the Spirit and upon Turner's death in 1821 claimed
to be his successor. Wroe's followers were called "Christian Israelites," and
they formed a properly organized sect rather than the rather loose association that had existed until then. He introduced into the prophetic teaching the belief of physical immortality (achieving immortality without ever
dying) through keeping both the gospel, as expounded in the New Testament, and the law of Moses, as expounded in the books of Moses in the
Old Testament—in particular the Nazirite vow (Num. 6). This involved
never cutting the hair, abstaining from alcohol and from blood, and not
going near a dead body. (The Nazirite vow is notable for including women
as well as men.) He traveled widely, preaching "the everlasting gospel of the
redemption of soul and body" not only in the United Kingdom but also
on the continent, in the United States, and in Australia. In 1831 Wroe left
Ashton-under-Lyne, where he had built a sanctuary, and moved to Wakefield. However, he retained a large following, many of whom emigrated to
Australia, where he visited them several times. (His followers built for him
"Melbourne House" near Wakefield.) He died in Melbourne while on one
of his Australian journeys. In contrast to some of the other sects of the
Southcottian tradition, the Christian Israelites have flourished (mainly in
Australia, though they also have small followings in both America and the
United Kingdom) and now constitute the largest of the Southcottian
groups still in existence.[17]

James Jershom Jezreel (1840?–1885) was the assumed name of James
White, about whom little is known. He joined a Southcottian group in
Chatham, the New House of Israel (a Christian Israelite group), in 1875,
while he was a private in the army. After only a few months, he claimed to
be receiving communications from the Immortal Spirit and started his
own group, managing to take the majority of the local New House of Israel
members with him. To distinguish his new church from the old, he called
them the "New and Latter House of Israel," commonly known as Jezreel-

ites. He married one of his flock, Clarissa Rogers, and they toured America and other countries, preaching and gathering followers with considerable success. Eventually the sect was established in Gillingham, Kent (or New Brompton as it was then called), where the erection of a headquarters, or sanctuary, which would hold 20,000 people, was begun. An artist's impression was published in the church's magazine. Many people were drawn to settle near the temple in the belief that they were among the 144,000 who would not see death but live and reign with Christ when he returned to earth again. The sanctuary was never completed, but its remains were extant till their eventual demolition in the 1960s. His main writing was *Extracts from the Flying Roll*, in three volumes, which he completed between 1879 and 1881. When he died in 1885, his wife Clarissa, who took the name of Esther, took over control of the sect, but funds dwindled and work on the temple was halted. Esther Jezreel died in 1888 at the age of twenty-eight, and the sect split: one group was led by Edward Rogers (Esther Jezreel's father), the other by Ann Rogers (Esther's aunt—she was married to Edward Rogers's brother). At this time, work on the temple finally ceased. However, work on gathering Israel did not end, and canvassers continued to sell *The Flying Roll* and magazines from door to door.

With the death of Esther Jezreel, the way was open for new claimants to come forward as successors or even as the seventh messenger. A number of small groups arose, usually under existing members, but these generally survived only until the death of the founders.[18]

Other leaders arose with yet new claims. W. D. Forsyth led an offshoot called the "Outcasts of Israel." Forsyth was a prolific writer, yet he had come to Gillingham to tend the cows during Jezreel's time. (Jezreel started up several businesses in New Brompton, one of which was in dairy products.) Forsyth could neither read nor write, but had taught himself. He believed that Esther and James would be resurrected and that Esther, whom he believed to be the seventh messenger, was to be the mother of Shiloh (which he thought Southcott had not been). Some of his followers left because he claimed that Jezreel was a manifestation of Jesus Christ.[19]

Another group was led by R. C. R. Intent. He called himself the "Courier to the Seventh Church" and changed his name from Rushcroft by adding the surname "Intent." When he died, his wife continued promulgating his teaching, but she was ousted by a woman called Alice Harvey. She too claimed to be the seventh messenger and also the mother of a spiritual child whom she had borne in 1905. Harvey changed her name to Esther Israel and began publishing a magazine and booklets from her Harrow (and later, Wembley) address.

Only the two groups calling themselves the New and Latter House of Israel survived for any length of time, although one branch eventually became extinct on the death of the last trustee. The other branch (that of

Edward Rogers) still carries out evangelism to this day, by advertising *The Flying Roll* in magazines and newspapers, and there is now a website.[20]

Into the twentieth century,[21] one branch of the Visitation accepted Michael Mills (also known as Prince Michael) as Shiloh and the seventh messenger. He set up in Gillingham with his followers, even occupying the house in which the Jezreels had lived. But when he and his wife died in 1922, some of the followers gave up the faith, the remainder joining the Panacea Society.[22]

Yet another group accepted Benjamin and Mary Purnell as the new messengers. They had been members of the Jezreelite colony in Detroit and itinerant missionaries for the New and Latter House of Israel until they received the knowledge that they were jointly the seventh messenger (combining male and female) and also jointly Shiloh. They built a colony in Benton Harbor, Michigan that flourished, at one point numbering well over a thousand.

The Visitation

Believers in one or more of these seven prophets usually refer to their system of belief as "the Visitation." This can mean (as it does for the Old Southcottians) specifically the visitation of the Spirit of Truth to Southcott, but others (such as members of the New and Latter House of Israel) take the term to mean the revelation given by all six of the prophets up to and including Jezreel. Christian Israelites would only mean the revelation up to and including Wroe. Who number seven was—or will be—also depends on which branch of the Visitation is being referred to. The Panacea Society believes that the seventh was Helen Exeter (a pseudonym for Helen Shepstone), a forerunner of Shiloh. Members of the House of David believe that the seventh messenger was jointly Benjamin and Mary Purnell. The New and Latter House of Israel followers await the appearance of Shiloh and no longer expect a seventh messenger.

Fundamentalism and Millennialism

How do the sects that comprise the Visitation fit in with our definitions of fundamentalists or millenarians? I have chosen six headings under which to evaluate them. These headings each refer to traits or specific doctrines that tend to be associated with fundamentalism, but the list is not exhaustive. My headings are biblical inerrancy, evangelical activity, limited salvation and conversion experience, personal holiness and separation from the world, male headship and suspicion of feminism, and dispensational premillennialism.

Biblical Inerrancy

All members of the various Southcottian groups prefer the Authorized Version of the Bible (KJV), though they would not go to the extremes of "KJV only," as some fundamentalist groups have gone. The approach is one of "literal where possible." However, although the term "Christian fundamentalist" would generally be associated with the rejection of the Old Testament Apocrypha, Southcott subscribed to its authenticity and quoted it in support of her teaching. Similarly, Turner and the later prophets had a particular liking for 4 Esdras, because of its apocalyptic nature, and later prophets still were happy to include the book of Jasher and the book of Enoch as inspired texts through which God had revealed himself. This is at variance with what is the norm among fundamentalists, yet it is still true that the approach taken to Scripture is similar, even if the definition of what constitutes Scripture is not.

Evangelical Activity

From the beginning, Southcottians were evangelistic. Southcott herself preached in public on occasion. The sixty-five books she published during her lifetime were widely read and circulated. She was concerned that ordinary people would not be able to afford her writings, so she specifically wrote one of her books to be distributed free to the poor at the expense of her wealthier followers.[23] Wroe and Jezreel held public meetings and used contemporary music to attract an audience. Jezreel was fond of the harp, which made an appearance at almost all the public meetings. Jezreelites combed the United Kingdom, the United States, Australia, and New Zealand, going from door to door selling The Flying Roll and trying to interest anybody in the message. Southcottians and Jezreelites were commonly seen at Hyde Park Corner in London during the twentieth century. A number of converts were made through public evangelism. In this sense they conform to the fundamentalist mold.

Limited Salvation and Conversion Experience

Southcottian groups are generally believers in universal salvation in one form or another. Despite the dire prophecies of Brothers, Southcott, Turner, and Shaw, the future was positive. When all the sufferings were over, salvation would come to all—though they might have to wait till the end of the thousand years before they achieved it. For the later prophets Wroe and Jezreel, followed by Prince Michael and the Purnells, the "elect" would achieve a special salvation—the salvation of the body—but everybody else would achieve the "common salvation"—the salvation of the soul. In this they differ from most fundamentalists, who generally see salvation as only for the few: those who conform to their exclusive belief system and have a personal experience of Christ.

Personal Holiness and Separation from the World

Southcott was a faithful member of the Church of England, although she had attended the Methodists for a time. She considered the established church to be God's authoritative church; for her, acceptance by the church authorities was vital. In no way did she wish to be separate. Southcottian churches grew up, even during her lifetime, largely because her followers were no longer welcomed by the mainstream. She specifically required that her followers should not wear identifying clothes or marks of discipleship.

Later Southcottian prophets added requirements that separated them further from the world. Wroe introduced a form of dress that was required of members (and that is still worn today). This requirement was rescinded by Jezreel, though the more conspicuous trait is the growing of the hair, which Wroe, Jezreel, and later the Purnells taught. This requirement applies to both men and women, and many current members of both groups have never in their life had their hair cut. For the men, the requirement is more difficult; women usually wear their hair up, but the men have an untrimmed beard and long hair, sometimes worn under a cap and occasionally worn long, down the back. For Wroe and Jezreel's followers the intimate laws of Leviticus apply in every aspect of daily life. Also, both groups are vegetarian. Seen in context, this is a clear marker of distinction, since at the time vegetarianism was very rare and considered quite peculiar. As a result, members of these groups separated themselves from the world. Old Southcottians, on the other hand, wore no distinctive dress, generally attended the Church of England, and were in no other way distinctive. Indeed, unless given the opportunity to talk about Southcott, their unorthodoxy would rarely become apparent.

An additional aspect of separation from the world introduced by the later Southcottians was the "gathering" of the followers to a particular location. First with Wroe, there was a gathering to Ashton-under-Lyne, where a sanctuary was built. Then under Jezreel, the gathering place was Gillingham in Kent. Benjamin and Mary Purnell gathered their followers to Benton Harbor in the United States prior to returning to England, where the final gathering will take place. For the Panacea Society, it was (and still is) Bedford. While it was never compulsory to move to the gathering place, in general the central core of members did so. It continues to be the expectation of these groups that the elect will be gathered in anticipation of Christ's return, or else concurrently with that event. So it can be said that there is a development within the Southcottian movement toward greater separation from the world and a greater emphasis on personal holiness in the strict adherence to the Levitical laws. While many fundamentalists would consider the keeping of Levitical law by Christians as heretical, the need for personal holiness and separation from the world would be in keeping with the fundamentalist mold.

Male Headship and Suspicion of Feminism

Generally, fundamentalists have a precise view of gender roles. They would claim that men and women were equal, but that, because of their respective God-defined roles, man holds a position of headship relative to woman. Historically, women's deprivation of rights has been supported by this kind of thinking. Southcott, having been a single woman in a man's world, felt this alienation. But her theology turned such thinking on its head. Joanna reversed the negative view of women as the cause of the fall and placed woman as the means by which the destruction of evil would come about. Man's place was to join the woman in petitioning God to carry out his promise in Genesis 3 to bruise the serpent's head (that is, to bring about its destruction). The woman was first in the transgression; it was true. However, the reaction to being found out was different between the man and the woman. The woman accepted that she was led astray and put the blame clearly on the serpent (the devil). However, the man put the blame on the woman as well as on God by saying not just that the woman led him astray, but that the woman was she "whom *you* gave to be with me"–putting the blame on God for giving him the woman. Because of this, the promise is made to the woman (though addressed to the serpent) that it is *her* seed who will bruise the serpent's head. This interpretation puts woman in a special place with regard to the plan of salvation.

Southcott also deals with the passages historically used to downgrade women, such as 1 Timothy 2:14, which states that Adam was not deceived, but the woman, being deceived, was in the transgression. The writer adds: "Yet she will be saved through childbearing, provided they continue in faith and love and holiness, with modesty"–a passage that has been used to justify woman's place as "pregnant in the kitchen." Southcott asks, "Is woman's place only to be the bearer of children?" Rather than accepting this at face value, she argues that this means that in the end time, a woman will give birth to the second child, Shiloh, and thus become a key figure in the redemption.

In all Southcottian groups, women take equal part with men. It was considered part of the healing of the fall that this equalization should take place. In addition, it is taught by the prophets from Wroe onward that the Godhead itself contains a feminine aspect, Jerusalem above[24]–the Holy Spirit is the Female Immortal Spirit, the female part of deity. Southcottian sects are therefore poles apart from the fundamentalist fold with respect to their teaching on male headship and feminism.

Dispensational Premillennialism

While it is true that Southcottian sects are premillennialists, and do teach a form of dispensationalism, there are significant differences between them and premillennial dispensationalism as presented by J. N. Darby and subsequent teachers.

In Southcottian teaching there is no concept of a rapture. The saints will not be taken away from the earth before God's judgments take place, though Southcott did introduce the practice of "sealing" her followers. She believed this was a fulfillment of the prophecy in Revelation 7:2-3:

> I saw another angel ascending from the rising of the sun, having the seal of the living God, and he called with a loud voice to the four angels who had been given power to damage earth and sea, saying: "Do not damage the earth or the sea or the trees, until we have marked the servants of our God with a seal on their foreheads."

The sealed were therefore expecting a level of protection, particularly from the impending woes that were to come on the earth. The "left behind" scenario has therefore no place in Southcottian theology. God will protect the elect while they live in a world that is racked with woes and calamities, but they will not be taken out of it.

The dispensational teaching of Darby holds that God has two plans in operation. One relates to the Jews, but the other, God's "supreme" plan, relates to the church, a plan not revealed in the Old Testament. During the millennium, a converted, natural Israel will live on the earth, following the return of Christ, but the church (this term meaning all those who have become Christians since Pentecost) will spend the thousand years in heaven (and the rest of eternity, for that matter). There is no suggestion of a special salvation for those living at the end of time (although they would be "raptured" to heaven to escape the tribulation—usually believed to be a period of seven years). However, in that scheme, salvation for the church is a heavenly reward, not an earthly one.

Southcottianism presents the *earth* as the millennial state to which Christians look forward. The later messengers teach that going to heaven is the "second best" salvation, or the "common salvation." God has reserved life on earth in an immortal body for a limited number—given in Revelation as 144,000. (In fact some later Southcottians came to believe that there would be 144,000 each of men and women, and that the total number of persons during the millennium would therefore be 288,000.) At the end of the millennium, a group referred to as "aliens," who lived through the return of Christ and continue to live through the millennium, still retaining their physical bodies, will have the opportunity to attain "the life of the body" like the 144,000, if they are faithful at the rebellion at the end of the thousand years.

Southcottians from Wroe onward have believed that God has three "churches" in the latter days, based on an interpretation of Isaiah 44:5:

> This one will say, "I am the Lord's," another will be called by the
> name of Jacob, yet another will write on the hand, "the Lord's," and
> adopt the name of Israel.

Those who say "I am the Lord's" are understood to be Christians, the
church of the Gentiles. Those who call themselves by the name of Jacob
are Jews—Jacob's descendants. But a third group "will write on the hand,
'the Lord's'" (that is, they are Christians), but also "adopt the name of
Israel" (that is, they are the remnant of the ten tribes of Israel who keep
the Jewish laws). The first two "churches" go to heaven (though not until
the resurrection), but only members of the third, who keep the law and
gospel, receive the immortality of the body on earth.[25]

The expectation of a premillennial return of Christ fits nicely into the
fundamentalist mold. But the rejection of a "rapture" and emphasis on
the earth as the place of reward puts them at odds with the fundamentalist norm.

Other Distinctive Southcottian Teachings

I shall now discuss in turn four aspects of Southcottian teaching that are distinctive: immortality of the body, the chronology of the millennium, British
Israelism, and the nature of the Godhead in later Visitation teaching.

Immortality of the Body

One very distinctive teaching of the later Southcottian movements is the
promise of achieving immortality of the body. The Southcottians distinguish between "immortality" and "incorruptibility." Immortality can only
be achieved in a physical body made immortal. They believe that anyone
who dies will never take their body again; they will be spirits forever and
will live in a state of incorruptibility. But a select number of human beings,
namely 144,000, will achieve immortality while still in the body. Three
people have already attained this, one in each of the three dispensations of
two thousand years: Enoch in the first, Elijah in the second, and Jesus in
the third. What specifically is the advantage of entering eternal life with a
body is never really explained, but it is repeatedly emphasized that this is a
special salvation reserved for the few. Everyone else of the human race will
also achieve a measure of salvation: there is no endless torment.

There is thus a "two-tier" salvation. The promise of the immortality of
the body is made only to those who are (racially) of the ten tribes of Israel
(scattered throughout the world, but living primarily in the northern
islands) and who keep the "law and gospel," but who do not die before
Christ comes.

The Chronology of the Millennium

Chronology plays an important part in the theology of Southcottian sects. For Brothers, it was simple: God had revealed to him directly that the restoration of the Jews to Jerusalem was to be accomplished by 1798. His ardent follower Nathaniel Brassey Halhed published a book which supported this date by calculating from Scripture, using the lengths of the lives of the characters mentioned in the Bible. This publication demonstrated that the six thousand years was to end in 1798.

Southcott was less specific. While she clearly taught the six-thousand-year period of man's reign on earth, she spoke more vaguely about the end of the century as the beginning of the millennium. However, in other places she implies that the fourth thousand-year period began with the ministry of Jesus, which could in fact take the end of the six thousand years to around 2030.

Turner prophesied specific dates for the appearance of Shiloh, but Shiloh did not appear. He blamed lack of faith on the part of his followers for this nonappearance. What Shaw taught about chronology, we do not know.

Wroe was the first to provide us with a more detailed chronology of the last days. He uses two approaches. First, he sees the six thousand years as three periods of two thousand years each. In each period, a man is made immortal. During the first two thousand years, Enoch was translated, so that he should not see death. In the second two thousand years, Elijah was taken to heaven directly without dying. At the beginning of the third two-thousand-year period, Christ was made immortal. For his second approach, Wroe's interpretation was based on a somewhat enigmatic statement of Christ recorded in Luke 12:37-38:

> Blessed are those slaves whom the master finds alert when he comes: truly I tell you, he will fasten his belt and have them sit down to eat, and he will come and serve them. If he comes during the middle of the night, or near dawn, and finds them so, blessed are those slaves.

Wroe sees those who are watching as having a special reward: the immortality of the body. When this will be is calculated as follows: there are four watches in an hour (this is taken from Jewish reckoning). There are twelve hours in the day (based on John 11:9, where Jesus said: "Are there not twelve hours in the day?"). A day with the Lord is as a thousand years (2 Pet. 3:8—"with the Lord one day is like a thousand years"). So if there are twelve hours in a day, and a day is one thousand years, then each day is 83 years and 4 months. Each day is made up of four watches, so a watch is 20 years and 10 months.

As we are in God's last day (which ends in the year 2000), the tenth hour of man's final day began in 1833 in April (by subtracting two hours [i.e., 166 years and 8 months] from 2000). The second watch ends in 1875 (41 years and 8 months added to April 1833), and in theory Christ should come in the third watch—that would be by the end of 1895.[26]

Wroe died in 1863, so he did not live to see whether his expectations would be realized. In 1875, Christ did not return. But an event of great significance did take place in 1875: the appearance of the one who claimed to be the sixth messenger, James Jershom Jezreel.

British Israelism

Brothers is regarded by some as having initiated the teaching of British Israel. This teaching holds that the ten tribes of Israel, after being taken into captivity by the Assyrians around 722 B.C.E., gradually migrated to Europe and eventually to Britain. A passage in the Apocrypha is used to substantiate this claim, as are various references in history. The doctrine, which was very popular in the late nineteenth century and the early part of the twentieth, particularly when Britain had an empire and was a world power, has gradually lost influence, though it is still held by a couple of nondenominational groups, as well as by some small Pentecostal groups (for example, Bible Pattern Fellowship and Revival Fellowship) and the Identity movement in the United States, to name just a few.

There was a mini-revival during the mid-twentieth century. During the 1960s, Britain was bombarded with the "World Tomorrow" broadcasts by Herbert W. Armstrong, who preached his millennial message on the radio. *Plain Truth* magazine, claiming to be a type of newsmagazine, was also the mouthpiece for his church, and it was offered free to anyone who wrote in and requested it. The circulation grew to be in the millions. Armstrong had been converted to keeping the seventh-day Sabbath and became a member of the Church of God, Seventh Day. However, due to various differences with the movement, he later started up his own "Radio Church of God," later to become the "Worldwide Church of God." A basic tenet of the faith was British Israelism, and Armstrong produced the book *The United States and British Commonwealth in Prophecy*,[27] which, like the magazine, was also sent free to any who asked. The gradual disintegration of this church after Armstrong died and the repudiation of the British Israelism doctrine has resulted in schism, with many smaller churches continuing to promulgate the British Israelism theory energetically.

However, the doctrine as taught by Brothers and as held by various groups of the Visitation does not equate exactly to British Israelism teaching. The Visitation prophets (with the notable exception of Southcott herself) taught that the lost tribes of Israel were scattered in all nations, but particularly in northern Europe (and thence America) as a *part* of the population, but not the majority.

The Nature of the Godhead in Later Visitation Teaching

In her writings, Southcott speaks of "God appearing in woman's form." She does not mean this literally, but as God speaking through her, and as woman being the bearer of Shiloh, the second Messiah. Later prophets, building on the groundwork that Southcott had laid with her reinterpretation of woman's role, introduced the idea of a feminine aspect to the Godhead. Based on Paul's comment to the Galatians that "Jerusalem above" was "the mother of us all," Wroe and Jezreel taught that the Female Immortal Spirit, Jerusalem above, is the feminine aspect of God—the Holy Spirit. This is taken further by Octavia in the Panacea Society, developing God into a quaternary—Father, Mother, Son, and Daughter—rather than a trinity.

Epilogue

It cannot be said with any certainty that the Visitation prophets influenced the later religious sects that held similar teachings. It is possible that Armstrong, the proponent of the British Israelism theory, had heard of Brothers. It is unlikely that David Koresh had heard of Southcott and her second Messiah, Shiloh, though he used similar scriptures to prove that he was the second (sinful) messiah. Nor can it be claimed that the idea of a plan of six thousand years originated with these sects—nor a belief in the restoration of the Jews to their own land. Nevertheless, in the Southcottian groups we have a movement that combined these elements in a series of related prophets and millennial sects extending over a period of more than two hundred years and continuing to the present day. These sects can be seen to fit comfortably under the heading "fundamentalist" in some respects (for example, evangelism, biblical literalism, personal holiness) but not in others (with regard to feminism and universal salvation).

The message throughout the whole Visitation since 1792 has been "Time is running out," meaning that time is running out for the present system of things: its days are numbered. Christ's return is essential and imminent. The message is strangely prophetic in that "time is now running out" for the remaining members of the Visitation groups. The only remaining groups are these: Old Southcottians (the United Kingdom, New Zealand, Australia; a handful of members); Christian Israelites (Australia, the United States, the United Kingdom; hundreds—by far the largest group); New and Latter House of Israel (one branch, the United Kingdom, the United States; a handful); Panacea Society (UK, the United States; few); Israelite House of David (the United States; a handful); and Mary's City of David (the United States; a handful).[28]

The year 2000 has come and gone. Although the date was not specified by Southcott herself, the later messengers developed a chronology that was closely tied to the year 2000 C.E. A certain amount of reinterpretation is going on. Various explanations have been put forward by some. Others are just waiting for further developments in God's good time. But the disappointment is clear.[29] However, millennial groups have a history of surviving failed prophecies, and one day, perhaps, they may just get it right!

Appendix

Key to Diagrams

Diagram 1—Early Southcottian Groups

Diagram 2—Wroe and Jezreel

Diagram 3—After Jezreel

Names in CAPITALS—people claiming to be a prophet, e.g. RICHARD BROTHERS.
Names in upper and lower case—leaders of the movements, e.g. John Finlayson.
Dotted lines denote a sizable movement of followers from one prophet or movement to another.

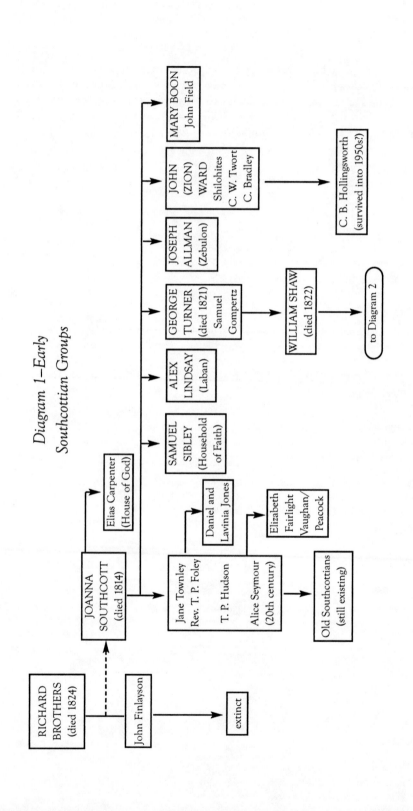

Diagram 1–Early
Southcottian Groups

RICHARD BROTHERS (died 1824)

John Finlayson

extinct

JOANNA SOUTHCOTT (died 1814)

Elias Carpenter (House of God)

Jane Townley
Rev. T. P. Foley
T. P. Hudson
Alice Seymour (20th century)

Daniel and Lavinia Jones

Elizabeth Fairlight Vaughan/Peacock

Old Southcottians (still existing)

SAMUEL SIBLEY (Household of Faith)

ALEX LINDSAY (Laban)

GEORGE TURNER (died 1821) Samuel Gompertz

WILLIAM SHAW (died 1822)

to Diagram 2

JOSEPH ALLMAN (Zebulon)

JOHN (ZION) WARD Shilohites C. W. Twort C. Bradley

C. B. Hollingsworth (survived into 1950s?)

MARY BOON John Field

Diagram 2–Wroe and Jezreel

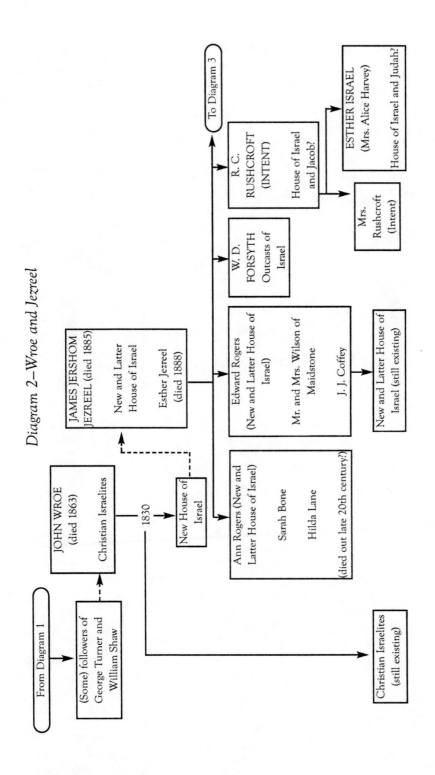

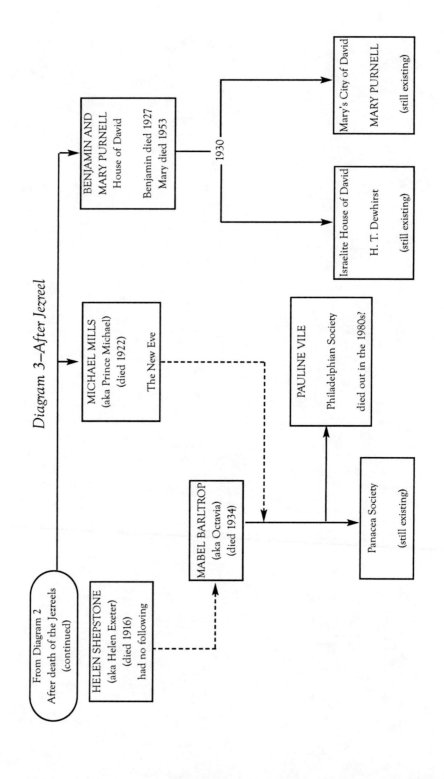

Diagram 3–After Jezreel

From Diagram 2
After death of the Jezreels
(continued)

HELEN SHEPSTONE
(aka Helen Exeter)
(died 1916)
had no following

MABEL BARLTROP
(aka Octavia)
(died 1934)

MICHAEL MILLS
(aka Prince Michael)
(died 1922)

The New Eve

BENJAMIN AND
MARY PURNELL
House of David

Benjamin died 1927
Mary died 1953

1930

PAULINE VILE
Philadelphian Society
died out in the 1980s?

Panacea Society
(still existing)

Israelite House of David
H. T. Dewhirst
(still existing)

Mary's City of David
MARY PURNELL
(still existing)

Chapter Thirteen

The Future of Millennial Expectation

Crawford Gribben

Perhaps, in the context of the twenty-first-century clash of civilizations, there is little doubt about the enduring appeal of millennial and apocalyptic thinking. Radical Islamists wage war on the West, while the United States and its diminishing band of allies adopt an aggressive strategy of regime change in the Near East. The quest to move from the Dar al-Harb (the "house of war") to the Dar al-Islam (the "house of Islam") is evidently millennial, though some of the means by which it is pursued might yet turn out to be apocalyptic, and the Bush administration's response to Islamist terror still invests its rhetoric with the righteousness of the "redeemer nation" and its providential duty in a changing world. The disappointment of those hopes associated with the year 2000 did not, after all, presage the "sudden evaporation of apocalyptic feeling" that some expected of the early twenty-first century.[1] Millennialism and its apocalyptic other are still the dreams that refuse to die.

The chapters in this volume have highlighted something of the immense range and utility of contemporary expectations of the end. Millennial and apocalyptic ideas have been traced in relatively minor groups, such as the Southcottian sects and the Davidian denominations, and chapters have also highlighted these ideas' impact upon the worldviews of some of the most influential of contemporary political elites. The chapters emphasize the importance of geography while acknowledging that the instantaneous transmission of ideas now minimizes the restrictions of locality and challenges traditional notions of the communal nature of the "cult." From Japan to the American Midwest, apocalyptic ideas have been shown to range from the violently aggressive to the politically passive and the culturally benign. These chapters, developing a social history of ideas, demonstrate the continuing resonance of expectations of the end.

It is appropriate that several of the chapters in this volume gather around the intellectual cultures of a resurgent evangelical dispensational-ism. This system of theology—reflected in some of the basic themes of American foreign policy—is certainly one of the most influential of con-temporary millennial faiths and perhaps the variant of Christian eschatol-ogy that enjoys greatest media appeal. Andrew Pierce documents the intellectual complex that surrounded the development of its account of the historiography of biblical revelation, while Mark Sweetnam argues that the movement's ideas cannot be understood to prescribe homogenous pat-terns of behavior. Crawford Gribben's discussion of the *Left Behind* novels illustrates the extent to which this resurgent dispensationalism differs from some of these earlier models of belief, while Darryl Jones's polemics argue powerfully against the series' cultural instincts. Brenda Brasher focuses on one of the movement's most political assumptions and weaves dispensa-tional philo-Semitism into a complex of responses to the political future of Israel. But, recognizing the cultural dominance of dispensational themes, Chris Partridge's emphasis is vital. The "technological rapture" of Heaven's Gate is a powerful reminder that millennial ideas never exist in a vacuum, and that ideas of the Christian establishment readily mutate into the expectations of insular new religious movements. The importing and reinterpretation of eschatological symbols, codified in the Christian appropriation of Old Testament apocalyptic, continues to the present day, as dispensationalism provides the basic shape for a series of marginal expectations of the end.

But while the chapters in this volume return to Christian and particu-larly dispensational traditions, they do so addressing a wider context of millennial hope and apocalyptic fear. The social and psychological analysis provided by Richard Landes is illustrated by examples that demonstrate his mastery of the field of millennial studies as well as the potential range of this increasingly consolidated scholarly interest. The instability generated by expectations of the end can have quite distinctive results. Darryl Jones documents the anxieties encoded in *Left Behind* and considers the series' articulation of a potentially dangerous cultural frustration. Chris Partridge examines the means by which a millennial movement can move beyond this kind of frustration to find itself consumed—sometimes literally—by the application of its own ideas, while John Walliss charts the uneasy progress towards the unleashing of millennial violence upon an unsuspecting world. Catherine Wessinger considers the matter of responsibility for millennial violence and concludes that the media and other external actors can play an important role in the escalation of apocalyptic fear and violent anxiety.

But millennial expectations can also be culturally benign. Gordon Allan recounts the trajectories of a number of initially significant millennial movements and hints at the cyclical nature of the cultures he describes. Kenneth Newport charts the differences among Davidian sects and describes a movement that has turned so far in upon itself that its entire missionary activity is restricted to members of a sister denomination. The political passivity of these sects is paralleled in Stephen Hunt's analysis of contemporary charismatic manifestations. For all the media hype they generate, these ecstatic movements have failed to witness or generate the cultural transformation around which their theology often seems constructed. As these chapters demonstrate, contemporary eschatological movements should not be regarded as uniformly threatening to the stability of the outside world.

Nevertheless, this volume's most important contribution may be its clear signal that, in the world of scholarship, millennial studies is moving out of the quietist behavior that is characteristic of "normal time" into the "semiotic arousal" that typifies a movement that begins to believe it has something urgent to say. Perhaps it is perverse to consider the community of millennial scholars as consisting of a millennial movement in itself—but there may be some value in the analogy. There can be little doubt that the academy is more inclined to show interest in millennial studies than it has been at almost any time in the past. Millennial scholars are no longer the intellectual quacks who keep their heads down and elaborate their analyses only among the remnant of the faithful. Our moment has come. The "semiotic arousal" of "apocalyptic time" is extending the field of our millennial inquiry, while geopolitical crises are priming our peers to see the significance of eschatological thinking in contexts that might formerly have been considered mundane. Specialists in millennial studies have never had as much to contribute to the scholarly discussion of the academy—and, perhaps, to the safe continuance of the many and varied societies in which they live and work.

The chapters in this collection illustrate something of the range of subject matter and lively opinion that characterizes the burgeoning project of millennial studies. Its end, it seems, is not yet.

Notes

Chapter One

1 R. Tucker, "The Theory of Charismatic Leadership," *Daedalus* (1967): 731–56.

2 S. D. O'Leary, *Arguing the Apocalypse: A Theory of Millennial Rhetoric* (Oxford: Oxford University Press, 1994).

3 R. J. Lifton, *Destroying the World to Save It: Aum Shinrikyo, Apocalyptic Violence, and the New Global Terrorism* (New York: Henry Holt, 1999).

4 As if to illustrate my point about the ability of the dominant discourse to marginalize and ignore millennialism, although it is one of the great passions of any culture, and certainly of the West, it did not make it into R. Tarnas, *The Passion of the Western Mind: Understanding the Ideas that Have Shaped Our Worldview* (New York: Random House, 1991).

5 The joke tells of a zookeeper who had a fabulous "messianic" exhibit where a lion and a lamb shared the same cage. "How do you do it?" asked an amazed observer. "Easy," he replied, "Lots of lambs." Or, as Woody Allen put it, "The lion lies down with the lamb, but the lamb doesn't get much sleep."

6 The *just* live free in this world. The just *live free* in this world. The just live free *in this world*.

7 A. Lynch, *Thought Contagion: How Belief Spreads Through Society* (New York: Basic Books, 1999).

8 K. Mannheim, *Ideology and Utopia* (London: Essential Books, 1936); N. Cohn, *The Pursuit of the Millennium: Revolutionary Millenarians and Mystical Anarchists of the Middle Ages* (Fairlawn, NJ: Essential Books, 1957); J. Talmon, *The Origins of Totalitarian Democracy* (New York: Praeger, 1961).

241

9   Let us hope this description of the Crusaders entering Jerusalem in 1099 was
        a rhetorical exaggeration—it was only splashing that high—rather than an
        actual event; or else that the language was dependent upon the imagery found
        in Revelation 14:20. The rejoicing in blood is a characteristic element of many
        millennial movements. See the verse of the Marseillaise: "Let the blood of our
        enemies flow in our ploughed furrows."

10   Jung called this synchronicity. Whether, how, or why it happens is not clear;
        that people think it does unquestionably happens often.

11   See below, chapters 12 and 6, respectively.

12   On Tertullian and *ressentiment*, see Nietzsche, *Genealogy of Morals*. This is the
        opposite of Origen's heretical (!) notion that even Satan himself, *a fortiori* all
        people, will eventually be saved.

13   See D. Redles, *Hitler and the Apocalypse Complex: Salvation and the Spiritual
        Power of Nazism* (New York: New York University Press, 2001). See also chap-
        ter 12 of my forthcoming book, *Heaven on Earth: The Varieties of the Millennial
        Experience* (Oxford University Press).

14   Historians, especially historians of theology, often use a more restrictive term
        for millennialism, as, for a recent example, does C. Hill, *Regnum Caelorum: Pat-
        terns of Future Hope in Early Christianity* (Oxford: Clarendon Press, 1992), 1–8.
        Hill rejects the broader term, as I use it here, in favor of a more restrictive one:
        "full blown chiliasm" (the Greek term for millennialism), he insists, includes
        all three elements of: a temporary period (not necessarily 1000 years), an
        earthly location, and messianic agency (individual deliverers playing a key
        role), 5f. If one does not adhere to this specific scenario, he argues, if one
        denies the interim, temporary millennial period, one "remove[s] oneself from
        the millennialist camp," 1n1. Aside from the fact that he is tracing this partic-
        ular configuration in early Christianity, Hill gives no reason so to restrict the
        definition. It does, certainly, permit him to argue that not only is millennial-
        ism not the dominant ideology of the early church (contra many, primarily
        Protestant German historians, 2–4), but that not even the book of Revelation
        (!) is millennial. His analysis would be far more useful if he had a term for the
        larger phenomenon, as well as for this subset which he convincingly correlates
        to other beliefs. If he wishes to define his particular brand of thinking "chil-
        iasm," then fine; but to define it so rigidly in order to marginalize it does not
        help us understand. Hereafter, I refer to the larger phenomenon of expecta-
        tion of the Kingdom of God on earth (Hill's second and third points) as mil-
        lennial.

15   Here I use the term in Augustine's sense of the time-space continuum, the
        embodied, the historical. For Augustine, the *saeculum* could not be redeemed.
        There was no earthly millennium of peace, never would be.

16   For a sense of the full range of millennial beliefs and the various disciplines
        that contribute to this field of study, see T. Daniels, *Millennialism: An Interna-
        tional Bibliography* (New York: Taylor & Francis, 1992). For a recent discussion
        of the anthropological dimensions, see P. Stewart and A. Strathern, eds., *Mil-
        lennial Countdown in New Guinea, Ethnohistory* 47 (2000).

17   For Hill, the socially disruptive dimension is key; see *Regnum Caelorum*, 1n1.
        This seems to be a widespread tendency among historians, drawn largely from
        a (possibly superficial reading) of Cohn's *The Pursuit of the Millennium*.

18 E. Middlefort, "Madness and the Millennium at Münster, 1534–35," in C. Kleinhenz and F. J. LeMoine, eds, *Fearful Hope: Approaching the New Millennium* (Madison: University of Wisconsin Press, 1999), 115–34.

19 Josephus, *Antiquities of the Jews*, book 18, chapter 1.6: "These men agree in all other things with the Pharisaic notions; but they have an invisible attachment to liberty; and they say that God is to be their only Ruler and Lord." Josephus, *Josephus: The Complete Works*, trans. W. Whiston (Grand Rapids: Kregel Publications, 1978), 377.

20 See C. Hill, *Antichrist in Seventeenth-Century England* (London: Oxford University Press, 1971). See also D. V. Erdman, *William Blake: Prophet against Empire* (Princeton: Princeton University Press, 1970); and E. P Thompson, *"Witness Against the Beast": William Blake and the Moral Law* (Cambridge: Cambridge University Press, 1993).

21 Obviously, for most anarchic millennialists, certain forms of religiosity, like human sacrifice, do not qualify as "just." Such people show a strong tendency towards iconoclastic thinking.

22 F. Nietzsche, *On the Genealogy of Morals*, trans. W. Kaufmann (New York: Vintage, 1967). The Nazi use of Nietzsche represents one of the great ironies of history, since they represent precisely the kind of self-pitying *ressentiment* at loss of power that Nietzsche denounced.

23 Thucydides, "Athenians to the Melians," *Peloponnesian War*, book V, 89.

24 See Landes, *Heaven on Earth*, chaps. 7 (Taiping) and 10 (Communists).

25 On coercive purity, see L. Quinby, *Anti-Apocalypse: Exercises in Genealogical Criticism* (Minneapolis: University of Minnesota Press, 1994); on the prediction of reversal with power, see "Athenians to the Melians" in Thucydides (above, n23) or, more acidly, by Nietzsche (n22).

26 E. Peterson, *Der Monotheismus als politisches Problem* (Leipzig: Hegner, 1935).

27 N. Cohn, *Cosmos, Chaos and the World to Come: The Ancient Roots of Apocalyptic Faith* (New Haven: Yale University Press, 1993).

28 P. Alexander, *The Byzantine Apocalyptic Tradition*, ed. D. de F. Abrahamse (Berkeley: University of California Press, 1985).

29 For Buddhism see T. J. Kodera, "Nichiren and his Nationalistic Eschatology," *Religious Studies* 15 (1979): 41–53; Ho Tai Hue-Tam, *Millenarianism and Peasant Politics in Vietnam* (Cambridge, Mass.: Harvard University Press, 1993). On Hinduism, see R. F. Maher, "Tommy Kabu Movement of the Purari Delta," *Oceania* 29 (1958): 75–90.

30 O'Leary, *Arguing the Apocalypse*, 195–206.

31 See also the discussion in B. Witherington, *Jesus, Paul and the End of the World* (Downers Grove, Ill.: InterVarsity, 1992), 15–22.

32 Cohn, *The Pursuit of the Millennium*; Talmon, *The Origins of Totalitarian Democracy*; B. Wilson, *The Social Dimensions of Sectarianism: Sects and New Religious Movements in Contemporary Society* (Oxford: Clarendon, 1990).

33 Josephus describes how the followers of a failed messiah—an Egyptian false prophet—dispersed after his defeat, "every one to his own home and there concealed themselves." *Jewish Wars* II.13.5, in *Josephus: The Complete Works*, 482.

34 The locus classicus of this is the *Protocols of the Elders of Zion* (1920). See its more recent avatars, UFOs, in K. Thompson, *Angels and Aliens: UFOs and the Mythic Imagination* (New York: Fawcett Columbine, 1991); Christian fundamentalist P. Robertson, *The New World Order* (Dallas: Word Publishing, 1991); F. A. Leib, *Behold a Pale Horse* (New York: Tom Doherty, 2000).

35 See below, chapter 7.
36 For example, the postmillennial Reconstructionists, whose cataclysmic scenario made Y2K so attractive to some (Gary North). Chip Berlet has described these groups as "Calvinism on crack."
37 Note the "rooster" rhetoric.
38 Isaiah 2:2-4; Micah 1–4.
39 See C. Hill, "John Mason and the End of the World," in *Puritanism and Revolution* (London: Secker & Warburg, 1992); Lifton, *Destroying the World to Save It.*
40 Middlefort, "Madness and the Millennium at Münster, 1534–35."
41 A. Mendel, *Vision and Violence* (Ann Arbor: University of Michigan Press, 1999).
42 S. Naquin, *Millenarian Rebellion in China: The Eight Trigrams Rebellion* (New Haven: Yale University Press, 1976).
43 Augustine, *Epistolae*, 198 (418 C.E.), trans. W. Parsons, *Letters* (Washington, D.C.: Catholic University of America Press, 1955), iv, 353.
44 Quoted in M. Livermore, *My Story of the War* (Hartford, 1889, as cited in J. C. Scott, *Domination and the Arts of Resistance* [New Haven: Yale University Press, 1989], 5).
45 Scott, *Domination and the Arts of Resistance*, chap. 1. He points out how Aggy had said this not in front of her master (who had just whipped her daughter for a theft she had not committed) but after he had left, in the presence of the governess from New England whom she apparently trusted not to tell the master.
46 T. E. Fulop and A. J. Raboteau, eds., *African-American Religion: Interpretive Essays in History and Culture* (New York: Routledge, 1997).
47 *Byrhtferth's Manual*, ed. S. J. Crawford, Early English Text Society, Original Series 177 (London: Oxford University Press, 1972), 242, lines 3-9.
48 The term "hegemonic discourse" refers to the prevailing public transcript; Scott, *Domination and the Arts of Resistance*, 70–107.
49 Scott astutely notes that the public transcript not only constrains those below, but also those in the elite whose behavior must conform to expectations in order for them to maintain their position of authority (he analyzes Orwell's "The Elephant Hunter" in this connection); Scott, *Domination and the Arts of Resistance*, 10–11.
50 See Brenda Brasher, "Semiotically Aroused: Through the Looking Glass of Millennial Studies." paper presented to the Social Science History Association in a special panel entitled "Presidential Session: Social Science History views the Millennium" Pittsburgh, Pa., October 26, 2000. Most deeply religious monotheists believe that nothing is coincidental, that God wills everything that happens, and that every event has meaning. The apocalyptic believer, however, takes these signs to indicate imminent transformation, as a call to dramatic change—initially for him- or herself, soon for everyone.
51 Even as hyperbole, the passage clearly articulates the break; cf. a milder variant in Matthew 10:37. Other passages have Jesus renouncing his birth family: "What have I to do with thee?" and claiming that those who follow the Lord are his true family. The break with family that the hyperbole suggests seems of a pair with the hostility to Judaism in the same sources.

52   On the cattle slaying that dispatched half a million cattle and caused fifty
     thousand to starve to death, see Landes, *Heaven on Earth*, chapter 1; J. B.
     Peires, *The Dead will Arise* (Johannesburg: Ravan Press, 1989).

53   L. Festinger et al., *When Prophecy Fails: A Social and Psychological Study* (Min-
     neapolis: University of Minnesota Press, 1956). See also the application of
     this to the earliest extensive documentation on prophecy, that of Israelite
     prophets, by R. P. Carroll, *When Prophecy Failed: Reactions and Responses to Fail-
     ure in the Old Testament Prophetic Traditions* (New York: Seabury Press, 1979).

54   See the controversy around "cult mind control": S. Hassan, *Combating Cult
     Mind Control* (Rochester, Vt.: Park Street Press, 1990).

55   Following Lord Acton's principle, this is especially true of millennial move-
     ments that take power, whether briefly (Münster, 1533-1535; Taiping China
     1840-1854; Nazi Germany, 1933-1945), or more lastingly (Ming and Maoist
     China, Soviet Russia).

56   "When a man knows he is to be hanged in a fortnight, it concentrates his
     mind wonderfully . . .," Samuel Johnson, quoted by J. Boswell, *Life of Johnson*,
     ed. G. B. Hill, revised by L. F. Powell, iii, 167 (September 19, 1777).

57   Blake; on the millennial aspects of his thought and the time, see Thompson,
     "Witness Against the Beast."

58   *America*, 6, *The Complete Poetry and Prose of William Blake*, ed. D. Erdman
     (Berkeley: University of California Press, 1982), 52.

59   R. H. Brodhead, "Millennium Prophecy and the Energies of Social Transfor-
     mation: The Case of Nat Turner," in A. Amanat and M. Bernhardsson, eds.,
     *Imagining the End: Visions of Apocalypse from the Ancient Middle East to Modern
     America* (London: I.B. Tauris, 2002); R. Bloch, *Visionary Republic* (New York:
     Cambridge University Press, 1985).

60   Among the many examples, consider Shaker unpatented contributions to
     American technology; Seventh-day Adventists and Kellogg's cereal and Gra-
     ham crackers (to bring Americans over to a vegetarian diet); Protestants and
     the printing press; Nazis and television; see E. Benz, *Evolution and Christian
     Hope: Man's Concept of the Future from the Early Church Fathers to Teilhard de
     Chardin* (New York: Doubleday, 1966), 121-42; D. Noble, *The Religion of Tech-
     nology: The Divinity of Man and the Spirit of Invention* (New York: Alfred A.
     Knopf, 1998).

61   For a frightening example of the power of ADD type II, see the study at an
     Atlanta hospital of Munchausen Syndrome by proxy, in which parents make
     their children sick in order to attract attention and sympathy to themselves,
     Boston Globe, June 6, 2000, A2.

62   Chant of the demonstrators at Chicago in 1968. Cf. the American revolution-
     ary slogan about the onset of the hostilities in Lexington and Concord: "The
     shot heard round the world."

63   Al Baumgarten: "I suggest that there are moments when millennial move-
     ments need to 'up the ante,' by forcing their members to accept risks which
     will increase solidarity and loyalty. At the simplest level, movements 'up the
     ante' in order to take advantage of the bonds established between those who
     share dangers. . . . The risk binds those who will share in the imminent bless-
     ings, unlike the apostates [who refuse to take the risk and are] doomed to
     perdition. Designating and expelling these apostates also contributes to the

sense of solidarity among those who endure." "Introduction" from A. I. Baumgarten, ed., *Apocalyptic Time* (Leiden: Brill, 2000), x–xi.

64   The most recent and extraordinary example of this is the NRM, the Movement for the Restoration of the Ten Commandments in Uganda (March 2000).

65   L. Tiger, *Optimism: The Biology of Hope* (New York: Simon & Schuster, 1979).

66   "Handsome Lake." A.C. Parker, "The Code of Handsome Lake, the Seneca Prophet," in W. N. Fenton, ed., *Parker on the Iroquois* (Syracuse: Syracuse University Press, 1968).

67   "The Temptations of Jesus: Dostoyevsky's 'The Parable of the Grand Inquisitor,'" in *The Brothers Karamazov*, trans. R. Pevear and L. Volokhonsky (New York: Knopf, 1992).

68   A good example of this kind of behavior on the part of "normal" scientists is their readiness to ignore the anomalies in their paradigm, as has been outlined in T. Kuhn, *The Structure of Scientific Revolutions* (Chicago: University of Chicago Press, 1962).

69   I took the imagery of the rooster from Talmudic discussion; but rather than use the bat as its antithesis, I preferred the imagery of the "wise" owl as my nocturnal animal because "bat" seems so invidious; and whether the proud roosters like Reb Simlai like it or not, the historian has to admit that the owls have consistently got it right.

70   Kuhn, *The Structure of Scientific Revolutions*, chap. 3.

71   Northrop Frye points out that "pedantry means . . . that kind of contact with culture which consists in belittling the size and scope of the conceptions of genius, the 'nothing but' principle of reading everything on the minimum imaginative level. . . . Imaginative intensity applied to a wrong or inadequate object can be corrected; a deficiency in intensity never can be"; N. Frye, *Fearful Symmetry* (Princeton: Princeton University Press, 1965), 422.

72   For a good example of the dynamics here, see the interesting, if at points anachronistically post-testosteronic, interaction between Joan of Arc and the French aristocratic military command in the movie *The Messenger* (1999).

73   This dysfunctional relationship was delineated by Blake in the *Marriage of Heaven and Hell* (1796), where the roosters are called energy (desire) and the owls, reason. Substituting the terms works perfectly: "Indeed it appeared to Reason (the owls) as if Desire (the roosters) was cast out, but the Devil's (rooster's) account is that the Messiah (the owl's savior) fell & formed a heaven (ecclesiastical notions of paradise/the Church) of what he stole from the Abyss (the unfettered mind)," plate 5f; *The Complete Poetry and Prose of William Blake*.

74   The classic case here is the Canudos community in the backlands of Brazil at the end of the nineteenth century: around fourteen thousand men, women, and children were wiped out for having the temerity to drop out of a society where they occupied the bottom rungs. See Robert Levine, *Vale of Tears* (Berkeley: University of California Press, 1992).

Chapter Two

1   See, for example, N. Cohn, *The Pursuit of the Millennium: Revolutionary Millenarians and Mystical Anarchists of the Middle Ages* (London: Pimlico, 1993).

2   For an alternative account of how the fire(s) started, see K. G. C. Newport, *The Branch Davidians of Waco: The History and Beliefs of an Apocalyptic Sect* (Oxford: Oxford University Press, 2006).

3   J. Walliss, "Making Sense of the Movement for the Restoration of the Ten Commandments of God," *Nova Religio* (forthcoming).

4   Federal Bureau of Investigation (FBI), *Project Megiddo*, http://permanent. access.gpo.gov/lps3578/www.fbi.gov/library/Megiddo/megiddo.pdf., 1999, 3; Canadian Security Intelligence Service (CSIS), *Doomsday Religious Movements*, http://www.csis-scrs.gc.ca/eng/miscdocs/200003_e.html, 1999.

5   Y. Talmon, "Millenarian Movements," *Archives Européennes de Sociologie* 7 (1966): 159–200.

6   J. Kaplan, *Radical Religion in America: Millenarian Movements from the Far Right to the Children of Noah* (Syracuse, New York: Syracuse University Press, 1997).

7   For a detailed discussion of the incidents, see J. Walliss, *Apocalyptic Trajectories: Millenarianism and Violence in the Contemporary World* (Bern: Peter Lang, 2004).

8   T. Robbins and D. Anthony, "Sects and Violence: Factors Enhancing the Volatility of Marginal Religious Movements," in S. A. Wright, ed., *Armageddon in Waco: Critical Perspectives on the Branch Davidian Conflict* (Chicago and London: University of Chicago Press, 1995), 236–59; T. Robbins and S. J. Palmer, "Patterns of Contemporary Apocalypticism in North America," in T. Robbins and S. J. Palmer, eds., *Millennium, Messiahs and Mayhem: Contemporary Apocalyptic Movements* (New York and London: Routledge, 1997), 1–27; T. Robbins, "Sources of Volatility in Religious Movements," in D. G. Bromley and J. G. Melton, eds., *Cults, Religion and Violence* (Cambridge: Cambridge University Press, 2002), 57–79.

9   Cohn, *The Pursuit of the Millennium*.

10 Talmon, "Millenarian Movements," 168–69.

11 Talmon, "Millenarian Movements," 167–68.

12 C. Wessinger, "Millennialism with and without the Mayhem," in Robbins and Palmer, *Millennium, Messiahs and Mayhem*, 47–59; C. Wessinger, *How the Millennium Comes Violently: From Jonestown to Heaven's Gate* (New York and London: Seven Bridges Press, 2000); C. Wessinger, "Introduction: The Interacting Dynamics of Millennial Beliefs, Persecution and Violence," in C. Wessinger, ed., *Millennialism, Persecution, and Violence: Historical Cases* (New York: Syracuse University Press, 2000), 3–39.

13 Robbins and Anthony, "Sects and Violence," 242.

14 Robbins and Anthony, "Sects and Violence," 243.

15 See, for example, M. Singer, *Cults in Our Midst: The Hidden Menace in our Everyday Lives* (San Francisco: Jossey-Bass, 1995).

16 M. Weber, "The Sociology of Charismatic Authority," in H. H. Gerth and C. W. Mills, eds., *From Max Weber: Essays in Sociology* (London: Routledge, 1991), 245–64; 63.

17 Weber, "Sociology," 63.

18 R. Wallis, "Charisma, Commitment and Control in a New Religious Movement," in R. Wallis, ed., *Millennialism and Charisma* (Belfast: Queen's University, 1982), 73-140, 117.

19 R. Wallis, "Sex, Violence, and Religion," *Update: A Quarterly Journal of Religious Movements* 7, no. 4 (1983): 3-11, 8.

20 Robbins and Anthony, "Sects and Violence," 247.

21 R. Wallis and S. Bruce, "Sex, Violence, and Religion," in R. Wallis and S. Bruce (eds.), *Sociological Theory, Religion and Collective Action* (Belfast: Queen's University, 1986), 115-27, 117.

22 M. Weber, *The Theory of Social and Economic Organization* (London: Collier-Macmillan, 1947), 364; 248.

23 Weber, *Theory*, 248.

24 L. L. Dawson, "Crises of Charismatic Legitimacy and Violent Behavior in New Religious Movements," in Bromley and Melton, *Cults, Religion and Violence*, 80-101.

25 Robbins and Anthony, "Sects and Violence," 246.

26 T. S. Lebra, "Millenarian Movements and Resocialization," *American Behavioral Scientist* 16, no. 2 (1972): 195-217.

27 Robbins, "Sources of Volatility in Religious Movements."

28 M. Galanter, *Cults: Faith, Healing, and Coercion*, 2d ed. (Oxford: Oxford University Press, 1989).

29 Lebra, "Millenarian Movements," 195, 196.

30 Lebra, "Millenarian Movements," 198.

31 Lebra, "Millenarian Movements," 198.

32 R. M. Kanter, "Commitment and Social Organization: A Study of Commitment Mechanisms in Utopian Communities," *American Sociological Review* 33, no. 4 (1968): 499-517.

33 E. W. Mills, "Cult Extremism: The Reduction of Normative Dissonance," in L. L. Dawson, ed., *Cults in Context: Readings in the Study of New Religious Movements* (London: Transaction Publishers, 1998 [1982]), 385-96; L. L. Dawson, *Comprehending Cults: The Sociology of New Religious Movements* (Oxford: Oxford University Press, 1998), 153.

34 Mills, "Cult Extremism," 388.

35 Mills, "Cult Extremism," 388.

36 Mills, "Cult Extremism," 393.

37 Mills, "Cult Extremism," 395.

38 Mills, "Cult Extremism," 395.

39 Kanter, "Commitment and Social Organization."

40 J. R. Hall, P. D. Schuyler, and S. Trinh, *Apocalypse Observed: Religious Movements and Violence in North America, Europe, and Japan* (London: Routledge, 2000).

41 J. T. Richardson, "Minority Religions and the Context of Violence: A Conflict/Interactionist Perspective," *Terrorism and Political Violence* 13, no. 1 (2001): 103-33.

42 D. Anthony, T. Robbins, and S. Barrie-Anthony, "Cult and Anticult Totalism: Reciprocal Escalation and Violence," *Terrorism and Political Violence* 14, no. 1 (2002): 211-39.

43 Hall et al., *Apocalypse Observed*, 38, 147.

44 Hall et al., *Apocalypse Observed*, 38, 147.

45 Hall et al., *Apocalypse Observed*, 12.

46 J. G. Melton and D. G. Bromley, "Challenging Misconceptions about the New Religions-Violence Connection," in Bromley and Melton, *Cults, Religion and Violence*, 42–56, 2; Bromley, "Dramatic Denouements," in Bromley and Melton, *Cults, Religion and Violence*, 11–41.
47 Bromley, "Dramatic Denouements," 11.
48 Bromley, "Dramatic Denouements," 12.
49 Bromley, "Dramatic Denouements," 12.
50 Bromley, "Dramatic Denouements," 12.
51 Bromley, "Dramatic Denouements," 12, 13.
52 M. Barkun, "Introduction: Understanding Millennialism," *Terrorism and Political Violence* 7, no. 3 (1995): 1–9, 6.
53 Barkun, "Introduction," 1–9, 6.
54 Wessinger, *How the Millennium Comes Violently*, 15.
55 Wessinger, *How the Millennium Comes Violently*, 20.
56 Wessinger, *How the Millennium Comes Violently*, 20.
57 Wessinger, *How the Millennium Comes Violently*, 20.
58 Walliss, *Apocalyptic Trajectories*.
59 While all of the factors are analytically distinct and will be discussed independently of each other, in reality they are of course invariably interlinked and, indeed, may impact each other. Although, for example, it is possible to discuss the emergence of dissent and the group's failure to fulfill its "millennial goal" as analytically separate phenomena, in reality the appearance of one may very well be related to the existence of the other. Similarly, while it is again possible to discuss the role of exogenous and endogenous factors separately, in reality it is often the case that one may influence or intersect with the other in complex ways. So, for example, while dissent and defections may be analyzed separately from the campaigns of apostates, in reality it is possible that a group's response to dissent may be influenced by the fear that defectors could become vocal apostates. Equally, it is also possible that the campaigns of apostates and other "cultural opponents" may play a crucial role in the emergence and growth of dissent within a millenarian group.
60 R. Moore, *A Sympathetic History of Jonestown: The Moore Family Involvement in Peoples Temple* (New York: Edwin Mellen, 1985); J. R. Hall, *Gone from the Promised Land: Jonestown in American Cultural History* (London: Transaction Publishers, 1989).
61 M. Introvigne, "The Magic of Death: the Suicides of the Solar Temple," in Wessinger, *Millennialism, Persecution and Violence*, 138–57.
62 Hall et al., *Apocalypse Observed*.
63 I. Reader, *Religious Violence in Contemporary Japan: The Case of Aum Shinrikyo* (Surrey: Curzon, 2000); B. Atuhaire, *The Uganda Cult Tragedy: A Private Investigation* (London: Janus Publishing, 2003).
64 J.-F. Mayer, "Apocalyptic Millennialism in the West: The Case of the Solar Temple," a presentation held on Friday, November 13, 1998, at the University of Virginia, http://www.healthsystem.virginia.edu/internet/ciag/reports/report_apoc_index.cfm.
65 Reader, *Religious Violence in Contemporary Japan*.
66 Atuhaire, *The Uganda Cult Tragedy*.
67 See, for example, Bromley, "Dramatic Denouements," 38–40; Wessinger, *How the Millennium Comes Violently*, 241–43.
68 Hall et al., *Apocalypse Observed*, 180.

69   R. W. Balch and D. Taylor, "Making Sense of the Heaven's Gate Suicides," in
     Bromley and Melton, *Cults, Religion and Violence*, 209–28, 227. See also chap.
     3 of the present volume.

70   "Glnody," "Earth Exit Statement," www.heavensgate.com/misc/exitgln.htm.,
     1997.

71   Quoted in Hall et al., *Apocalypse Observed*, 135.

72   S. J. Palmer, "Purity and Danger in the Solar Temple," *Journal of Contemporary
     Religion* 11, no. 3 (1996): 303–18.

73   R. F. Young, "Lethal Achievements: Fragments of a Response to the Aum
     Shinrikyo Affair," *Japanese Religions* 20, no. 2 (1995): 230–45, 232.

74   Reader, *Religious Violence in Contemporary Japan*.

75   Quoted in "'Our Terrestrial Journey is Coming to an End': The Last Voyage
     of the Solar Temple," in L. L. Dawson, ed., *Cults and New Religious Movements:
     A Reader* (Oxford: Blackwell Publishing, 2003 [1999]), 208–25, 212–13.

76   S. Shimazono, "In the Wake of Aum: The Formation and Transformation of
     a Universe of Belief," *Japanese Journal of Religious Studies* 22, nos. 3-4 (1995):
     314–15; Palmer, "Purity and Danger in the Solar Temple."

77   The sole exception to this state of affairs is Joseph Kibwetere, one of the lead-
     ers of the MRTCG, although there is some speculation that he may have been
     dying of AIDS. This was certainly the view expressed in several reports follow-
     ing the March 2000 conflagration (Uganda Human Rights Commission
     [UHRC], *The Kanungu Massacre: The Movement for the Restoration of the Ten
     Commandments of God Indicted* [Uganda: Uganda Human Rights Commission,
     2002], 3.3).

78   M. M. Maaga, *Hearing the Voices of Jonestown: Putting a Human Face on an Amer-
     ican Tragedy* (New York: Syracuse University Press, 1998).

79   Quoted in Maaga, *Hearing the Voices of Jonestown*, 92.

80   Balch and Taylor, "Making Sense of the Heaven's Gate Suicides." The co-
     founder of the Heaven's Gate group, Bonnie Nettles, or "Ti," had herself died
     of cancer in 1985. (See again Partridge in this volume.)

81   "Glnody," "Earth Exit Statement."

82   Reader, *Religious Violence in Contemporary Japan*.

83   Reader, *Religious Violence in Contemporary Japan*, 170–71.

84   Wessinger, *How the Millennium Comes Violently*.

85   D. Thibodeau and L. Whiteson, *A Place Called Waco: A Survivor's Story* (U.S.:
     Public Affairs, 1999), 174.

86   Wessinger, *How the Millennium Comes Violently*.

87   J.-F Mayer, "Cults, Violence and Religious Terrorism: An International Per-
     spective," *Studies in Conflict and Terrorism* 24 (2001): 361–76, 366.

88   J.-F. Mayer, "The Dangers of Enlightenment: Apocalyptic Hopes and Anxieties
     in the Order of the Solar Temple," in R. Caron, J. Godwin, W. J. Hanegraaf,
     and J.-L. Vieillard-Baron, eds., *Esotérisme, gnoses et imaginaire symbolique Mélanges
     offerts à Antoine Faivre* (Leuven: Peeters, 2001), 437–51.

89   Mayer, "Apocalyptic Millennialism in the West."

90   Mayer, "The Dangers of Enlightenment," 447–48.

91   D. Chidester, *Salvation and Suicide: An Interpretation of Jim Jones, the Peoples Tem-
     ple, and Jonestown* (Bloomington: Indiana University Press, 1988).

92   Maaga, *Hearing the Voices of Jonestown*, 126.

93   Maaga, *Hearing the Voices of Jonestown*, 129.
94   Shimazono, "In the Wake of Aum," 314–15.
95   Reader, *Religious Violence in Contemporary Japan*.
96   See Walliss, *Apocalyptic Trajectories*, chap. 6.
97   Atuhaire, *The Uganda Cult Tragedy*.
98   UHRC, *The Kanungu Massacre*, 6.1.
99   Atuhaire, *The Uganda Cult Tragedy*, 85; G. Banura, C. Tuhirirwe, and J. Begumanya, "Kanungu Research Team's Report," in S. Kabazzi-Kisirinya, D. R. K. Nkurunziza, and G. Banura, eds., *The Kanungu Cult-Saga: Suicide, Murder, or Salvation?* (Uganda: The Department of Religious Studies, Makerere University), 12–46.
100 Reader, *Religious Violence in Contemporary Japan*.
101 Moore, "Demographics and the Black Religious Culture of Peoples Temple," in R. Moore, A. B. Pinn, and M. R. Sawyer, eds., *Peoples Temple and Black Religion in America* (Bloomington: Indiana University Press, 2004).
102 Moore, *A Sympathetic History of Jonestown*, 200.
103 Maaga, *Hearing the Voices of Jonestown*, 90.
104 J. R. Hall, *Gone from the Promised Land*, 275.
105 Wessinger, "Introduction."

Chapter Three

1   For example, all of them were, apparently, devoted fans of *The X-Files* and *Star Trek*. Although many programs were prohibited, these were not. See D. Wojcik, *The End of the World As We Know It: Faith, Fatalism, and Apocalypse in America* (New York: New York University Press, 1997), 181.
2   For discussions of UFO religions, see C. Partridge, ed., *UFO Religions* (London: Routledge, 2003); J. R. Lewis, ed., *The Gods Have Landed: New Religions from Other Worlds* (Albany: State University of New York Press, 1995); J. R. Lewis, ed., *Encyclopedic Sourcebook of UFO Religions* (Amherst, NY: Prometheus, 2003).
3   In his perceptive study of American apocalypticism, published the same year as the suicide, Daniel Wojcik makes this connection: "Although depicted as a bizarre, occult UFO group, the basic theology of Heaven's Gate largely consists of vernacular and personal interpretations of Christian doctrine. Belief in UFOs was a key element in the group's constellation of beliefs, yet its rigid dualism, emphasis on demonic influences and conspiracies, rejection of the world as evil, and yearning for planetary escape clearly resemble various Christian premillennialist worldviews" (Wojcik, *The End of the World As We Know It*, 183). To a large extent, this chapter simply provides flesh for this skeletal comment. Also worthy of note is Mark Muesse's argument that, while we might find some comfort in thinking of Heaven's Gate as a bizarre cult, in fact many of their beliefs are variations on familiar themes. See M. Muesse, "Religious Studies and 'Heaven's Gate': Making the Strange Familiar and the Familiar Strange," in R. T. McCutcheon, ed., *The Insider/Outsider Problem in the Study of Religion* (London: Cassell, 1999), 390–94.
4   R. W. Balch and D. Taylor, "Heaven's Gate: Implications for the Study of Commitment to New Religions," in Lewis, *Encyclopedic Sourcebook of UFO Religions*, 214–15.
5   Balch and Taylor, "Heaven's Gate," 215.

6   See, for example, J. R. Lewis, "Legitimating Suicide: Heaven's Gate and New Age Ideology," in Partridge, *UFO Religions*, 103–28.
7   See C. Hill, "John Reeve and the Origins of Muggletonianism," in C. Hill, B. Reay, and W. Lamont, *The World of the Muggletonians* (London: Maurice Temple Smith, 1983), 64–110.
8   B. Steiger and H. Hughes, *Inside Heaven's Gate* (New York: Penguin, Signet, 1997), xi. I am indebted to Ted Peters's article for drawing this to my attention (T. Peters, "UFOs, Heaven's Gate, and the Theology of Suicide," in Lewis, *Encyclopedic Sourcebook of UFO Religions*, 239–60, 259).
9   An introduction to the thought and influence of Clarence Klug is provided in R. W. Balch, "The Evolution of a New Age Cult: From Total Overcomers to Death at Heaven's Gate," in W. W. Zellner and M. Petrowsky, eds., *Sects, Cults & Spiritual Communities: A Sociological Analysis* (Westport: Praeger, 1998), 6–16.
10 Balch, "The Evolution of a New Age Cult," 2.
11 All committed "students"/members were likewise given special names, such as Brnody, Chkody, Glnody, Snnody, Jwnody, Lvvody, and Yrsody. Balch and Taylor explain that they "gave their followers '-ody' names, such as Jimody or Janody, although the first syllable was spelled with three consonants, so Jimody became Jmmody and Janody became Jnnody. Ti and Do explained that '-ody' is a diminutive for the '-od' in God, just as Jimmy is a child's name for Jim." Balch and Taylor, "Heaven's Gate," 224.
12 Heaven's Gate, "Bible Quotes Primarily from Previous Representatives to Earth from the Evolutionary Level Above Human," http://www.heavensgatetoo.com (accessed August 26, 1999).
13 On creationism in UFO religions, see, for example, G. D. Chryssides, "Scientific Creationism: a Study of the Raëlian Church," in Partridge, *UFO Religions*, 45–61; C. Partridge, "Understanding UFO Religions and Abduction Spiritualities," in Partridge, *UFO Religions*, 23ff.
14 Snnody, "Deposits," http://www.heavensgatetoo.com/exitchk.htm (accessed August 26, 1999).
15 See R. Bauckham and T. Hart, *Hope Against Hope: Christian Eschatology in Contemporary Context* (London: Darton, Longman & Todd, 1999), 147ff.
16 As is often noted by UFO groups, Genesis 1:26 appears to refer to a plurality of creators: "Then God said, 'Let *us* make man in *our* image . . . .'"
17 Snnody, "Deposits."
18 Hinduism, of course, also teaches that we are living in the final *yuga* ("age"), the *Kali-yuga*, and are witnessing an unrelenting deterioration of spirituality, morality, and the quality of life. For a good, concise discussion of *yugas* in Hindu thought, see G. Flood, *An Introduction to Hinduism* (Cambridge: Cambridge University Press, 1996), 111–13. See also J. Brockington, *The Sacred Thread: Hinduism in its Continuity and Diversity* (Edinburgh: Edinburgh University Press, 1981):

> Each period of Manu is divided into the great ages, each of which is divided in turn into four periods of decreasing duration, marked by progressive moral and physical deterioration; within this system the world is now in the middle of the last and worst of these ages, the Kali yuga, popularly held to have begun with the *Mahābhārata* war. . . . This idea that the current age is one of degeneracy seems

to have evolved concurrently with the whole cyclical theory of time-reckoning. There is a progressive decay of all that gives value to life and a continuing decline in moral standard. . . . (194-95)

19 Much of their terminology is drawn from education. They are students with their teachers in this earthly classroom looking forward to an eschatological graduation.

20 Jnnody, "Incarnating and Discarnating," http://www.heavensgatetoo.com/exitchk.htm (accessed August 26, 1999).

21 W. J. Hanegraaff, *New Age Religion and Western Culture: Esotericism in the Mirror of Secular Thought* (Leiden-New York-Köln: Brill, 1996), 471-72. Indeed, as Hanegraaff argues, an evolutionary teleology is a central feature of New Age spirituality (158).

22 Applewhite, quoted in Balch and Taylor, "Heaven's Gate," 233.

23 Chkody, "The Hidden Facts of Ti and Do," http://www.heavensgatetoo.com/exitchk.htm (accessed August 26, 1999).

24 See C. G. Jung, *Flying Saucers: A Modern Myth of Things Seen in the Skies* (New York: Signet Books, 1969).

25 All the knowledge humans have, we are told, "comes from two sources . . . a) the Next Level—the Kingdom of God, or b) the opposition—the Lower Forces—Lucifer, Satan, or the Luciferians and their naïve servants." Jnnody, "Incarnating and Discarnating."

26 For more on the demonologies of UFO religions, see C. Partridge, "Alien Demonology: the Christian Roots of the Malevolent Extraterrestrial in UFO Religions and Abduction Spiritualities," *Religion* 34 (2004): 163-89.

27 Glnody, "Earth Exit Statement," http://www.heavensgate.com/misc/exit-gln.htm (accessed August 26, 1999).

28 Chkody, "Earth Exit Statement," http://www.heavensgate.com/misc/exitchk.htm

29 Heaven's Gate, "'95 Statement by an E.T. Present Incarnate," http://www.wave.net/upg/gate/95upd96.htm (accessed April 12, 2004).

30 Snnody, "Deposits."

31 There are similarities here with both John Calvin's discussion about "seeds of religion" and also with Justin Martyr's *logos spermatikos* thesis.

32 Snnody, "Deposits."

33 There are numerous discussions of theologies of religions. For analyses and critiques of Christian exclusivism, see, for example, G. D'Costa, "Theology of Religions," in D. F. Ford, ed., *The Modern Theologians* (Oxford: Blackwell, second edition, 1997), 626-44; A. Race, *Christians and Religious Pluralism* (London: SCM, second edition, 1994); H. Netland, *Dissonant Voices: Religious Pluralism and the Question of Truth* (Leicester: Apollos, 1991).

34 Heaven's Gate, "'95 Statement by an E.T. Present Incarnate"—italics mine. To some extent, this reminds one of Karl Barth's rejection of the notion that Christianity is a *religion* along with other religions. Religion, he argued, is *Unglaube* (unbelief), an unwillingness to respond to true revelation. "It is the attempted replacement of the divine work by a human manufacture. The divine reality offered and manifested to us in revelation is replaced by a concept of God arbitrarily and willfully evolved by man." Barth, *Church Dogmatics* I/2, trans. G. T. Thomson and H. Knight (Edinburgh: T&T Clark, 1936), 302. For a discussion of this thesis, see C. Partridge, *H. H. Farmer's Theologi-*

cal Interpretation of Religion: Towards a Personalist Theology of Religions (Lewiston, NY: Edwin Mellen, 1998), 58ff.

35 See H. Harris, "Protestant Fundamentalism," in C. Partridge, ed., *Fundamentalisms* (Carlisle: Paternoster Press, 2001), 36–38.

36 J. Hick, *Evil and the Love of God* (London: Macmillan, 1966), 217–21. On Irenaeus, see J. N. D. Kelly, *Early Christian Doctrines*, 5th ed. (London: Adam & Charles Black, 1977), 170–74.

37 Hick, *Evil and the Love of God*, 290.

38 Smmody, "T.E.L.A.H.—The Evolutionary Level Above Human," http://www.heavensgatetoo.com/exitchk.htm (accessed August 26, 1999).

39 See R. Wallis, *Elementary Forms of the New Religious Life* (London: Routledge, 1984).

40 This is a long-standing dictum of the Roman Catholic church: "Outside the church no salvation."

41 Balch and Taylor, "Heaven's Gate," 219.

42 See Kelly, *Early Christian Doctrines*, 167. See also Justin, in J. Stevenson, ed., *A New Eusebius: Documents Illustrating the History of the Church to AD 337* (London: SPCK, 1987), 60.

43 Chkody, "The Hidden Facts of Ti and Do."

44 Jwnody, "Religions are Humans' #1 Killers of Souls," http://www.heavensgatetoo.com/exitchk.htm (accessed August 26, 1999).

45 There is some debate as to the cause of her death. Balch and Taylor record death by spotted fever as a result of a tick bite, whereas Ted Peters, John Hall, and, earlier, Balch himself, claim she died of liver cancer in Parkland Hospital, Dallas. See Balch and Taylor, "Heaven's Gate," 233; Peters, "UFOs, Heaven's Gate, and the Theology of Suicide," 250; Hall et al., *Apocalypse Observed*, 167; Balch, "The Evolution of a New Age Cult," 23.

46 For a helpful discussion of their understanding of suicide, see Peters, "UFOs, Heaven's Gate, and the Theology of Suicide," 239–60.

47 H. H. Farmer, "The Bible: Its Significance and Authority," in G. A. Buttrick et al., eds., *The Interpreter's Bible*, vol. 1 (New York: Abingdon, 1952), 12.

48 R. Montgomery, *Aliens Among Us* (New York, Fawcett Crest, 1985), 8.

49 The following purports to be a statement from "'95 Statement by an E.T. Present Incarnate": "In the early 1970s, two individuals (my task partner and myself) from the Evolutionary Level Above Human (the Kingdom of Heaven) incarnated into (moved into and took over) two human bodies that were in their forties. I moved into a male body, and my partner, who is an Older Member in the Level Above Human, took a female body. (We called these bodies "vehicles," for they simply served as physical vehicular tools for us to wear while on a task among humans. They had been tagged and set aside for our use since their birth.)"

50 On the relationship between the two, see Slvody, "Older Member, Younger Member: Their relationship," http://www.heavensgatetoo.com/exitchk.htm (accessed August 26, 1999).

51 For a short discussion of the ufological theories about Hale-Bopp, see P. Devereaux and P. Brookesmith, *UFOs and Ufology: The First Fifty Years* (London: Blandford, 1998), 114–15.

52 "For whoever wants to save his life will lose it, but whoever loses his life for me will find it" (Matt. 16:25).

53 Heaven's Gate, "'95 Statement by an E.T. Present Incarnate."

54 "There is no life here in the human world. This planet has become the planet of the walking dead. The human plants walk, talk, take careers, procreate and so forth, but there is no life in them." Glnody, "Earth Exit Statement."

55 Heaven's Gate, "Our Position Against Suicide," http://www.wave.net/upg/gate/letter.htm (accessed April 12, 2004).

56 Glnody, "Earth Exit Statement."

57 Heaven's Gate, "'95 Statement by an E.T. Present Incarnate."

58 Heaven's Gate, "'95 Statement by an E.T. Present Incarnate."

59 Heaven's Gate, "'95 Statement by an E.T. Present Incarnate."

60 This, of course, means that, of the countless humans that have stood upon the earth, only a couple of hundred have responded to Next Level teaching, and only forty, including Nettles, have actually entered the Kingdom of Heaven.

61 Lvvody, "Ingredients of a Deposit—Becoming a New Creature," http://www.heavensgatetoo.com/exitchk.htm (accessed August 26, 1999).

62 Wknody, "A Matter of Life or Death? YOU Decide," http://www.heavensgatetoo.com/exitchk.htm (accessed August 26, 1999).

63 M. Applewhite, "Do's Intro: Purpose—Belief," in Lewis, *Encyclopedic Sourcebook of UFO Religions*, 464.

64 It should be noted that, whereas Applewhite seems later, following Nettles's death, to have understood their relationship in terms of that between Jesus and the Father, earlier they were both identified with Jesus. For example, one Heaven's Gate document (which appears to have been written prior to Nettles's death) states the following: "Approximately 2000 years ago an individual of [the] next kingdom forfeited his body of that kingdom and entered a human female's womb, thereby incarnating as the one history refers to as Jesus of Nazareth. . . . There are two individuals here now who have also come from that next kingdom, incarnate as humans, awakened, and will soon demonstrate the same proof of overcoming death. They are 'sent' from that kingdom by the 'Father' to bear the same truth that was Jesus." This is like a repeat performance, except this time by two (a man and a woman) to restate the truth Jesus bore, restore its accurate meaning, and again show that any individual who seeks the kingdom will find it through the same process." Heaven's Gate, "The UFO Two and their Crew," in Lewis, *Encyclopedic Sourcebook of UFO Religions*, 474–75.

65 Glnody, "WARNING: For Those Prone to Hasty Judgments," http://www.heavensgatetoo.com/exitchk.htm (accessed 26 August 1999).

66 Lvvody, "Ingredients of a Deposit—Becoming a New Creature."

67 Peters, "UFOs, Heaven's Gate, and the Theology of Suicide," 245.

68 Brnody, "Up the Chain," http://www.heavensgatetoo.com/exitchk.htm (accessed August 26, 1999).

69 Wknody, "A Matter of Life or Death? YOU Decide."

70 Chkody, "Earth Exit Statement."

71 Heaven's Gate, "Crew from the Evolutionary Level Above Human Offers Last Chance to Advance Beyond Human," http://www.wave.net/upg/gate/index.htm (accessed April 12, 2004).

72 Smmody, "T.E.L.A.H.—The Evolutionary Level Above Human."

73 Illustrations of the genderless, heavenly beings appear on their Web site and look very much like the typical alien—slender, smooth, pale skin, large head, and almond-shaped eyes.

74 Glnody, "WARNING: For Those Prone to Hasty Judgments."
75 Jnnody, "Incarnating and Discarnating."
76 Yrsody, "The Way Things Are," http://www.heavensgatetoo.com/exitchk. htm (accessed August 26, 1999). Indeed, because the spirit world surrounds us, spirits (many of which are malevolent) will continually seek unauthorized access to bodily "vehicles" and will certainly seek to influence humans—hence Heaven's Gate's rationale for withdrawal from the world.
77 Jwnody, "Religions are Humans' #1 Killers of Souls." Cf. Jnnody, "Incarnating and Discarnating": ". . . the only proper application of the term 'death' is the termination of the soul, and only the Kingdom of God can kill the soul."
78 Balch, "The Evolution of a New Age Cult," 18.
79 See, for example, R. L. Román, "Christian Themes: Mainstream Traditions and Millenarian Violence," in M. Barkun, ed., Millennialism and Violence (London: Frank Cass, 1996), 51–82.
80 M. Barkun, "Understanding Millennialism," in Barkun, Millennialism and Violence, 8.
81 R. E. Bartholomew and G. S. Howard, UFOs and Alien Contact (Amherst, N.Y.: Prometheus Books, 1998), 13.
82 Bartholomew and Howard, UFOs and Alien Contact, 248–81.
83 For an excellent discussion of the issues, see J. Cooper, Body, Soul and Life Everlasting: Biblical Anthropology and the Monism-Dualism Debate (Grand Rapids: Eerdmans, 2000).
84 Indeed, arguably, the anthropological dualism of "walk-in" theory has its roots in Christian culture.
85 J. R. Lewis, Legitimating New Religions (New Brunswick, N.J.: Rutgers University Press, 2003), 130–31; Lewis, "Legitimating Suicide," 115.
86 Chkody, "Earth Exit Statement."
87 Glnody, "Earth Exit Statement."
88 For example, there is a section entitled "Soul vs. Flesh Body" in a key document consisting primarily of biblical quotations ("Bible Quotes Primarily from Previous Representatives to Earth from the Evolutionary Level Above Human"). Another key document on the subject, which never refers to "walk-ins," is entitled "Incarnating and Discarnating," by Jnnody. It begins with a discussion of Luke 10:25-37.
     Moreover, James Lewis, who makes a persuasive case for the significance of New Age ideology in Heaven's Gate's thinking, notes that an underlying notion for much theosophical thought is that "Christ was such a highly evolved soul that it would have been difficult, if not impossible, for him to have incarnated as a baby—and, even if he could have done so, it would have been a waste of precious time for such a highly developed soul to have to go through childhood" ("Legitimating Suicide," 115). For Heaven's Gate, however, this is not the case. The Representative from the Next Level did not walk into Christ, but rather the womb of a virgin. For example, one document makes the following point: "Approximately 2000 years ago an individual of that next kingdom forfeited his body of that kingdom and entered a human female's womb, thereby incarnating as the one history refers to as Jesus of Nazareth. He awakened to this fact gradually . . . by his resurrection he proved that death can be literally overcome and that a permanent body for the next kingdom is acquired from the human kingdom" (Heaven's Gate, "The UFO

Two and their Crew," 474). As far as the mechanics of incarnation are concerned, this is closer to traditional kenotic Christology than it is to theosophical adoptionism. That is to say, it is closer to the type of Christology that focuses on a divine Christ who "lays aside" certain attributes pertaining to deity (for example, omniscience, omnipotence) at the incarnation. The British theologian P. T. Forsyth, who developed a form of kenoticism, argued also for a corresponding *plerosis*, which allowed for Jesus' personal and spiritual growth. Jesus genuinely did grow from ignorance of his mission to full awareness. While Applewhite is no Forsyth, the same Christian themes are developed. Forsyth's thesis is developed in *The Person and Place of Jesus Christ* (London: Independent Press, 1909).

Chapter Four

1   H. Kippenberg, "The Restoration of Israel as Messianic Birth Pangs," in A. Baumgarten, ed., *Apocalyptic Time* (Leiden: Brill, 2000), 328.
2   T. Herzl, *The Jewish State: An Attempt at a Modern Solution of the Jewish Question* (London: Zionist Organization, 1936).
3   This overview is limited to Jewish or Christian millennial visions of Israel. It does not address Palestinian or Israeli Arab Muslim millennialism, or the millennial views of radical groups (such as Hamas) that advocate a Middle East absent Israel. Each of these is influential and warrants further study in its own right.
4   A. Ravitzky, *Messianism, Zionism, and Jewish Religious Radicalism*, trans. M. Swirsky and J. Chipman (Chicago: University of Chicago Press, 1996), 236.
5   J. Auerbach, *Are We One? Jewish Identity in the United States and Israel* (New Brunswick, N.J.: Rutgers University Press, 2001), 40.
6   Ravitzky, *Messianism, Zionism, and Jewish Religious Radicalism*, 13.
7   Shimon Peres, 1994 Nobel Prize lecture.
8   Y. Yadgar, "From 'True Peace' to 'The Vision of the New Middle East': Rival Images of Peace in Israel," *Journal of Peace Research* 40, no. 2 (London, Thousand Oaks, Calif., and New Delhi: Sage Publications, 2003): 178.
9   Yadgar, "From 'True Peace,'" 186.
10 Ravitzky, *Messianism, Zionism, and Jewish Religious Radicalism*, 87.
11 Ravitzky, *Messianism, Zionism, and Jewish Religious Radicalism*, 82.
12 Rabbi Tzvi Yehuda Kook, *Le-Netivot Yisraeli* (Jerusalem, 1967), 1:56, 188.
13 Ravitzky, *Messianism, Zionism, and Jewish Religious Radicalism*, 83.
14 Ravitzky, *Messianism, Zionism, and Jewish Religious Radicalism*, 80.
15 Ravitzky, *Messianism, Zionism, and Jewish Religious Radicalism*, 145.
16 Ravitzky, *Messianism, Zionism, and Jewish Religious Radicalism*, 149.
17 Y. Ariel, *Evangelizing the Chosen People: Mission to the Jews in America 1800–2000* (Chapel Hill: University of North Carolina Press, 2000), 31.
18 R. B. Fowler, A. D. Hertzke, and L. R. Olson, *Religion and Politics in America: Faith, Culture and Strategic Choices*, 2d ed. (Boulder: Westview Press, 1999), 76.
19 C. Goldberg and M. Connelly, "For Better or Worse, Israel is 'Special' in U.S. Eyes," *The New York Times*, April 26, 1998, 6.
20 D. S. Katz and R. H. Popkin, *Messianic Revolution: Radical Religious Politics to the End of the Second Millennium* (New York: Hill & Wang, 1999), 222.

21   Peace Now, http://www.peacenow.org.il/site/en/peace.asp?pi=58 (accessed February 20, 2005).

Chapter Five

1   On integralism as a fundamentalism, see J. A. Coleman, "Catholic integralism as fundamentalism," in L. Kaplan, ed., *Fundamentalism in Comparative Perspective* (Amherst: University of Massachusetts Press, 1992), 74-95; on post-Conciliar traditionalism, see M. W. Cuneo, *The Smoke of Satan: Conservative and Traditionalist Dissent in American Catholicism* (New York: Oxford University Press, 1997).

2   *World Missionary Conference, 1910: To Consider Missionary Problems in Relation to the Non-Christian World*, 9 vols. (Edinburgh and London: Oliphant, Anderson, & Ferrier; New York, Chicago, and Toronto: Fleming H. Revell, 1910).

3   This was the "watchword" of the Missionary Volunteers; it had been taken up by the Student Volunteer Movement in 1896 and was publicized at great length by John R. Mott in the years surrounding the emergence of the ecumenical movement.

4   J. Barr, *Fundamentalism* (Philadelphia: Westminster Press, 1978); Barr, *Beyond Fundamentalism* (Philadelphia: Westminster Press, 1984).

5   J. Fitzer, ed., *Romance and the Rock: Nineteenth-Century Catholics on Faith and Reason*, Fortress Texts in Modern Theology (Minneapolis: Fortress, 1989), 5.

6   G. Steiner, *Grammars of Creation: Originating in the Gifford Lectures for 1990* (London: Faber & Faber, 2001), 2.

7   F. Schleiermacher, *On Religion: Speeches to its Cultured Despisers*, Introduction, translation, and notes by R. Crouter, *Texts in German Philosophy* (Cambridge: Cambridge University Press, 1988). Crouter provides the first English translation of the first edition of 1799: subsequent German editions of the *Speeches* toned down considerably the romantic flourishes of the first.

8   Schleiermacher, *On Religion*, 103.

9   Schleiermacher, *On Religion*, 104.

10 Schleiermacher, *On Religion*, 130-31.

11 Schleiermacher, *On Religion*, 134.

12 Famously so in the introductory account of dogmatics and piety in F. Schleiermacher, *The Christian Faith*, H. R. Mackintosh and J. S. Stewart, eds., English translation of the second German edition (Edinburgh: T&T Clark, 1928), 1-128.

13 Schleiermacher, *The Christian Faith*, 12-18. I follow Claude Welch's insistence that the translation should be rendered as "utter" and not "absolute" dependence (C. Welch, *Protestant Theology in the Nineteenth Century: Volume 1, 1799-1870* [New Haven: Yale University Press, 1972], 65n16).

14 H. R. Niebuhr, *Christ and Culture* (London: Faber & Faber, 1952).

15 Niebuhr, *Christ and Culture*, 93-122.

16 There is a helpful assessment of Harnack's theology and social involvement— the "two faces" of the one Harnack—in K.-J. Kuschel, *Born Before All Time? The Dispute over Christ's Origin* (English translation, 1990; London: SCM, 1992), 51-56.

17 K. Barth, *The Word of God and the Word of Man*, trans. D. Horton (New York: Harper & Brothers, 1957). (It is curious that Schleiermacher and Barth both entered English translation in the same year: 1928.)

18 Cited by G. Rupp, *Culture-Protestantism: German Liberal Theology at the Turn of the Twentieth Century*, AAR Studies in Religion 15 (Missoula, Mont.: Scholars Press, 1977), 11. Rupp notes a certain hyperbole in Barth's claim: of the ninety-three signatories, twelve were theologians, and they did not constitute "pretty much all" his former teachers. It is interesting, however, that the twelve theologians included four major figures, two liberal (Harnack and Wilhelm Herrmann) and two conservative (Adolf von Schlatter and Reinhold Seeberg), indicating that for Barth the liberal/conservative tensions of the nineteenth century had been surpassed by the need for a far more radical overhaul.

19 Troeltsch's hermeneutical reflections on the historiographical roots of the quest for the "essence of Christianity" is found in his important essay, "What Does 'Essence of Christianity' Mean?" in R. Morgan and M. Pye, eds., *Ernst Troeltsch: Writings on Theology and Religion* (Atlanta: John Knox Press, 1977), 124–79. This essay was first published in 1903 and reissued in 1913.

20 See D. Charlton, *Secular Religions in France 1815–1870* (London: Oxford University Press for University of Hull Publications, 1963).

21 There is an illuminating presentation of resurgent theosophical religious groupings in this period by J. W. Burrow, *The Crisis of Reason: European Thought, 1848–1914* (New Haven: Yale University Press, 2000), esp. 197–233, 233.

22 See the stimulating account of twentieth-century traditionalism by M. Sedgwick, *Against the Modern World: Traditionalism and the Secret Intellectual History of the Twentieth Century* (Oxford: Oxford University Press, 2004).

23 S. Sykes, *The Identity of Christianity: Theologians and the Essence of Christianity from Schleiermacher to Barth* (London: SPCK, 1984), esp. 239–61. Gallie's book was published in London in 1964.

24 M. E. Marty and R. S. Appleby, *The Glory and the Power: The Fundamentalist Challenge to the Modern World* (Boston: Beacon Press, 1992), 48–56.

25 See G. A. McCool, *Catholic Theology in the Nineteenth Century: The Quest for a Unitary Method* (New York: Seabury, 1977). The work of McCool, and others, makes evident the role of neoscholasticism in defining its discontents as "modernists" after 1907 and of providing a coherent identity to integralist Roman Catholicism in the period before the Second Vatican Council. On the clash between historicist and essentialist interpretations of historical truth, see C. J. T. Talar, *Metaphor and Modernist: The Polarization of Alfred Loisy and his Neo-Thomist Critics* (Lanham, Md.: University Press of America, 1987), esp. 17–44.

26 See G. W. F. Hegel, *The Philosophy of History*, trans. J. Sibree (New York: Dover, 1956), esp. 341–46. On Hegel's philosophy of history, see C. Taylor, *Hegel* (Cambridge: Cambridge University Press, 1975), 389–427.

27 Troeltsch, "What Does 'Essence of Christianity' Mean?" 129.

28 A. von Harnack, *What Is Christianity?* (English translation, 1901; Rudolf, New York: Harper & Brothers, 1957).

29 The *Lehrbuch der Dogmengeschichte* was first published in three volumes between 1886 and 1889, and the English translation, *History of Dogma*, appeared between 1894 and 1899 in seven volumes, in which Harnack

studied the history of Christian dogma between the patristic period and the Reformation.

30 A. Loisy, *L'Évangile et l'Église* (Paris: Nourry, 1902). Loisy's real target lay elsewhere, in contemporary Roman Catholic neoscholasticism, hence the ambiguity of the concept of essence with which he works: he rebukes Harnack for advocating an improbably neoscholastic notion of essence.

31 On Mott's wide-ranging career and interest see B. Mathews, *John R. Mott: World Citizen* (London: SCM, 1934); C. H. Hopkins, *John R. Mott: 1865–1955: A Biography* (Geneva: WCC; Grand Rapids: Eerdmans, 1979).

32 P. Jenkins, *The Next Christendom: The Coming of Global Christianity* (Oxford: Oxford University Press, 2002), 16.

33 See the important biography by K. Clements, *Faith on the Frontier: A Life of J. H. Oldham* (Edinburgh: T&T Clark; Geneva: WCC, 1999). This is an essential resource for understanding the emergence of the ecumenical movement.

34 These eight commissions were: 1. Carrying the Gospel to all the Non-Christian World; 2. The Church in the Mission-Field; 3. Education in Relation to the Christianization of National Life; 4. The Missionary Message in Relation to Non-Christian Religions; 5. The Preparation of Missionaries; 6. The Home Base of Missions; 7. Relation of Missions to Governments; and 8. Cooperation and the Promotion of Unity. For a brief account of the conference and its proceedings see W. H. T. Gairdner, *Edinburgh 1910: An Account and Interpretation of the World Missionary Conference* (Edinburgh and London: Oliphant, Anderson & Ferrier, 1910).

35 *World Missionary Conference, 1910*, vol. 9, *The History and Records of the Conference Together with Addresses Delivered at the Evening Meetings*, 108–10, 110.

36 *World Missionary Conference, 1910*, 9:108.

37 *World Missionary Conference, 1910*, vol. 1, *Report of Commission I: Carrying the Gospel to all the Non-Christian World*, 70.

38 *World Missionary Conference, 1910*, 1:80.

39 Gairdner, *Edinburgh 1910*, 71–72.

40 Cited by J. Pelikan, *Credo: Historical and Theological Guide to Creeds and Confessions of Faith in the Christian Tradition* (New Haven: Yale University Press, 2003), 488.

41 Z. Bauman, *The Individualized Society* (Cambridge: Polity, 2001).

Chapter Six

1 M. Davis, *Ecology of Fear: Los Angeles and the Imagination of Disaster* (New York: Metropolitan Books, 1998), 277.

2 D. Brooks, "One Nation, Slightly Divisible," *Atlantic Monthly*, December 2001. For a penetrating critique of Brooks's argument, see T. Frank, *What's the Matter with America: The Resistible Rise of the American Right* (London: Secker & Warburg, 2004), 18–19.

3 D. Gates, with D. J. Jefferson and A. Underwood, "The Pop Prophets," *Newsweek*, May 24, 2004, 44.

4 J. Meacham, "The Editor's Desk," *Newsweek*, U.S. ed., May 24, 2004, 4.

5 J. Micklethwait and A. Wooldridge, *The Right Nation: Why America is Different* (London: Allen Lane, 2004), 388.

6   It is, however, important to note here the findings of Amy Johnson Frykholm, whose interviews with *Left Behind* readers suggest that their reading experience is not always one of passive acceptance, but that some readers use the series as a means of confronting their own faiths, and vice versa. See A. J. Frykholm, *Rapture Culture: Left Behind in Evangelical America* (New York: Oxford University Press, 2004).

7   T. LaHaye and J. B. Jenkins, *Left Behind: A Novel of Earth's Last Days* (Wheaton: Tyndale, 1995), 60.

8   A. Cowell and D. L. Halbfinger, "A Plot Seen Behind Every Door: Conspiracy Theorists Take Global Viewpoint," *The New York Times*, July 13, 2004, News, 3. For an account of the Bilderberg group and its appeal for conspiracy theorists, see J. Ronson, *Them: Adventures with Extremists* (London: Picador, 2001).

9   T. LaHaye and J. B. Jenkins, *Tribulation Force: The Continuing Drama of Those Left Behind* (Wheaton: Tyndale, 1996), 357, 127.

10   LaHaye and Jenkins, *Tribulation Force*, 298.

11   T. LaHaye and J. B. Jenkins, *Nicolae: The Rise of Antichrist* (Wheaton: Tyndale, 1997), 125.

12   LaHaye and Jenkins, *Nicolae*, 300.

13   LaHaye and Jenkins, *Tribulation Force*, 258.

14   G. Orwell, "Wells, Hitler, and the World State," in J. Carey, ed., *Essays* (London: Everyman, 2002), 369.

15   H. G. Wells, *Experiment in Autobiography* (New York: Macmillan, 1934), 596.

16   H. G. Wells, *The Shape of Things to Come* (London: Everyman, 1999), 312.

17   Micklethwait and Wooldridge, *The Right Nation*, 187.

18   Micklethwait and Wooldridge, *The Right Nation*, 150.

19   J. Steinberg, "One Man and his God," *Financial Times*, Weekend Magazine, June 12, 2004, 26.

20   A. Franken, *Lies and the Lying Liars Who Tell Them: A Fair and Balanced Look at the Right* (London: Allen Lane, 2003), 280.

21   Micklethwait and Wooldridge, *The Right Nation*, 144.

22   Franken, *Lies and the Lying Liars Who Tell Them*, 281.

23   P. Stothard, "The Town of the Rising Son," *The Times*, Features Magazine, July 17, 2004, 22.

24   Stothard, "The Town of the Rising Son," 22.

25   M. Bright, "Powell Caught up in Row over Neo-con 'Crazies,'" *The Observer*, September 12, 2004, 2.

26   Micklethwait and Wooldridge, *The Right Nation*, 146.

27   *Profile: John Ashcroft.* http://news.bbc.co.uk/1/hi/world/americas/1120440.stm.

28   S. Hegarty, "God's Running Mate?," *Irish Times*, Weekend Review, September 4, 2004, 4.

29   Franken, *Lies and the Lying Liars Who Tell Them*, 277.

30   H. Fineman, "Apocalyptic Politics," *Newsweek*, U.S. ed., May 24, 2004, 55.

31   Micklethwait and Wooldridge, *The Right Nation*, 83.

32   N. Shepherdson, "Writing for Godot," *Los Angeles Times*, Magazine, April 25, 2004, 1:16.

33   T. LaHaye, "The Colossal Battle," *Esquire*, U.S. ed., September 2004.

34 T. LaHaye and J. B. Jenkins, *Soul Harvest: The World Takes Sides* (Wheaton: Tyndale), 327.
35 T. LaHaye and J. B. Jenkins, *Are We Living in the End Times?* (Wheaton: Tyndale, 1999), 338.
36 LaHaye and Jenkins, *Soul Harvest*, 305.
37 LaHaye and Jenkins, *Soul Harvest*, 307.
38 J. A. Morone, *Hellfire Nation: The Politics of Sin in American History* (New Haven: Yale University Press, 2003), 484.
39 Morone, *Hellfire Nation*, 454.
40 LaHaye and Jenkins, *Are We Living in the End Times?* 332.
41 LaHaye and Jenkins, *Are We Living in the End Times?* 332.
42 LaHaye and Jenkins, *Are We Living in the End Times?* 34–47.
43 R. Davenport-Hines, *Sex, Death, and Punishment: Attitudes to Sex and Sexuality in Britain since the Renaissance* (Glasgow: Fontana Collins, 1991), 330–83.
44 LaHaye and Jenkins, *Are We Living in the End Times?* 345, 183.
45 Micklethwait and Wooldridge, *The Right Nation*, 149.
46 For the Columbia survey, see "How Effective are Abstinence Pledges?," http://news.bbc.co.uk/1/hi/magazine/3846687.stm; for the North Kentucky University survey, see Franken, *Lies and the Lying Liars Who Tell Them*, 284.
47 LaHaye and Jenkins, *Tribulation Force*, 418.
48 L. Marlowe, "'Regime Change Starts at Home,' say Kansas moderates," *Irish Times*, September 11, 2003, 11.
49 Morone, *Hellfire Nation*, 478–79.
50 Micklethwait and Wooldridge, *The Right Nation*, 149, 285.
51 LaHaye and Jenkins, *Left Behind*, 33.
52 LaHaye and Jenkins, *Nicolae*, 296.
53 M. T. Dalhouse, *An Island in the Lake of Fire: Bob Jones University, Separatism and the Fundamentalist Movement* (Athens: University of Georgia Press, 1996), 3.
54 M. McAlister, "Prophecy, Politics and the Popular: The *Left Behind* Series and Christian Fundamentalism's New World Order," *South Atlantic Quarterly* 102, no. 4 (Fall 2003): 790.
55 LaHaye and Jenkins, *Soul Harvest*, 116–17.
56 McAlister, "Prophecy, Politics and the Popular," 782.
57 McAlister, "Prophecy, Politics and the Popular," 791–92.
58 LaHaye and Jenkins, *Left Behind*, 7, 10.
59 LaHaye and Jenkins, *Are We Living in the End Times?* 61.
60 Micklethwait and Wooldridge, *The Right Nation*, 215; McAlister, "Prophecy, Politics and the Popular," 781.
61 Micklethwait and Wooldridge, *The Right Nation*, 203–204.
62 LaHaye and Jenkins, *Tribulation Force*, 424.
63 LaHaye and Jenkins, *Nicolae*, 20.
64 M. Barkun, *Religion and the Racist Right: The Origin of the Christian Identity Movement* (Chapel Hill: University of North Carolina Press, 1997), 226.
65 A. MacDonald, *Hunter* (Hillsboro, W. Va.: National Vanguard Books, 1989), 259.
66 Barkun, *Religion and the Racist Right*, 275.
67 LaHaye and Jenkins, *Tribulation Force*, 317.
68 Morone, *Hellfire Nation*, 7.

69 LaHaye and Jenkins, *Left Behind*, 22, 31.
70 Micklethwait and Wooldridge, *The Right Nation*, 192.
71 Dalhouse, *An Island in the Lake of Fire*, 3.
72 LaHaye and Jenkins, *Are We Living in the End Times?* 8.
73 S. J. Gould, *Rocks of Ages: Science and Religion in the Fullness of Life* (London: Vintage, 2002), 129.
74 R. Hofstadter, *Anti-Intellectualism in American Life* (New York: Knopf, 1963), 56.
75 S. Sontag, "The Imagination of Disaster," in *Against Interpretation* (New York: Octagon, 1978), 215.

Chapter Seven

1   T. LaHaye and J. B. Jenkins, *The Remnant* (Wheaton: Tyndale, 2002), 402.
2   C. Hill, *Antichrist in Seventeenth-Century England* (London: Verso, 1990), 159. The mainstreaming of millennial beliefs at the end of the twentieth century is indicated by the massive sales of the *Left Behind* series of novels, documented in this and the previous chapter.
3   Something of the range of recent evangelical eschatological thought can be seen in K. E. Brower and M. W. Elliot, eds., *"The Reader Must Understand": Eschatology in Bible and Theology* (Leicester: Apollos, 1997).
4   P. Boyer, *When Time Shall Be No More: Prophecy Belief in Modern American Culture* (Cambridge, Mass.: The Belknap Press of Harvard University Press, 1992), 5.
5   *88 Reasons* was also published as *The Rosh Hash Ana 1988 and 88 Reasons Why*. See Boyer, *When Time Shall Be No More*, 130; and G. North, "Publisher's Preface," in D. Wilson, *Armageddon Now! The Premillenarian Response to Russia and Israel since 1917*, 2d ed. (1977; Tyler, Tex.: Institute for Christian Economics, 1991), xi–xii. Further titles are listed on www.amazon.com, accessed June 25, 2004.
6   H. Lindsey, *Blood Moon* (Palos Verdes, Calif.: Western Front, 1996). On rapture novels and the rewriting of millennial hope, see C. Gribben, "Rapture Fictions and the Changing Evangelical Condition," *Literature and Theology* 18, no. 1 (2004): 77–94.
7   Up-to-date sales statistics are available at www.leftbehind.com.
8   M. McAlister, "Prophecy, Politics and the Popular: The *Left Behind* Series and Christian Fundamentalism's New World Order," *South Atlantic Quarterly* 102, no. 4 (2003): 773.
9   A. J. Frykholm, *Rapture Culture: Left Behind in Evangelical America* (New York: Oxford University Press, 2004), 3.
10 The original series comprised (all by LaHaye and Jenkins and published by Tyndale): *Left Behind* (1995); *Tribulation Force* (1996); *Nicolae* (1997); *Soul Harvest* (1998); *Apollyon* (1999); *Assassins* (1999); *The Indwelling* (2000); *The Mark* (2000); *Desecration* (2001); *The Remnant* (2002); *Armageddon* (2003); *The Glorious Appearing* (2004). Subsequent volumes are also now appearing.
11 Frykholm, *Rapture Culture*, 3.
12 McAlister, "Prophecy, Politics and the Popular," 778.

13   McAlister, "Prophecy, Politics and the Popular," 792–93.
14   LaHaye and Jenkins, *Tribulation Force*, 150, 360, 388.
15   J. B. Jenkins, *Soon: The Beginning of the End* (London: Hodder & Stoughton, 2003), 305.
16   Jenkins, *Soon*, 259.
17   Boyer, *When Time Shall Be No More*, ix. Articles on the subject include T. M. Doyle, "Competing Fictions: the Uses of Christian Apocalyptic Imagery in Contemporary Popular Fictional Works," *Journal of Millennial Studies* 1, no. 1 (2001): available online at www.mille.org; and D. Hertzler, "Assessing the 'Left Behind' Phenomenon," in L. L. Johns, ed., *Apocalypticism and Millennialism: Shaping a Believers' Church Eschatology for the Twenty-first Century* (Kitchener, Ont.: Pandora Press, 2000).
18   C. Tayler, "Rapt Attention," *Times Literary Supplement*, May 7, 2004, 36. The original twelve volumes are to be followed by several prequels and sequels.
19   Frykholm, *Rapture Culture*, 89.
20   McAlister, "Prophecy, Politics and the Popular," 782.
21   Tayler, "Rapt Attention," 36.
22   Frykholm, *Rapture Culture*, 178.
23   Frykholm, *Rapture Culture*, 89.
24   A. Lamott, "Knocking on Heaven's Door," *Traveling Mercies: Some Thoughts on Faith* (New York: Pantheon, 1999), 60, quoted in Frykholm, *Rapture Culture*, 177.
25   McAlister, "Prophecy, Politics and the Popular," 774.
26   McAlister, "Prophecy, Politics and the Popular," 774.
27   J. L. Sheler and M. Tharp, "Dark Prophecies," *U.S. News and World Report*, December 15, 1997, cited in M. Hitchcock, *Is the Antichrist Alive Today?* (Sisters, Ore.: Multnomah Publishers, 2002), 6.
28   Hitchcock, *Is the Antichrist Alive Today?* 11.
29   Jenkins, *Soon*, 55.
30   Frykholm, *Rapture Culture*, 179.
31   Jenkins, *Soon*, 276.
32   Frykholm, *Rapture Culture*, 109.
33   B. Graham, "My Answer," *The Daily Oklahoman*, April 12, 2002, cited in Hitchcock, *Is the Antichrist Alive Today?* 8.
34   Hitchcock, *Is the Antichrist Alive Today?* 67.
35   According to www.amazon.com, accessed June 25, 2004, the novels were republished by Future Events Publications in 1998.
36   "Suddenly from nowhere, it seemed, Helen was by his side. 'But darling, where did you come from and how could you? The doors are closed and we're 50 feet high.' 'Honey, you must remember I have been resurrected by Christ. Resurrected believers are not constrained by physical barriers. Besides, you'll need help in this telecast,'" S. Kirban, *1000* (Chattanooga, Tenn.: Future Events Publications, 1973), 52.
37   Kirban, *1000*, 12.
38   Jenkins, *Soon*, 4.
39   Jenkins, *Soon*, 10.
40   Jenkins, *Soon*, 17.
41   Jenkins, *Soon*, 9.
42   Jenkins, *Soon*, 9.

43 Jenkins, *Soon*, 10.
44 Jenkins, *Soon*, 203.
45 Jenkins, *Soon*, 124.
46 Jenkins, *Soon*, 26.
47 Jenkins, *Soon*, 17; Rev. 1:16.
48 Jenkins, *Soon*, 45.
49 Jenkins, *Soon*, xi. To readers schooled in dispensationalism, the new administration bears the hallmark of antichrist asd it has changed "times and seasons."
50 Jenkins, *Soon*, 157.
51 Jenkins, *Soon*, 199.
52 Jenkins, *Soon*, 231.
53 Jenkins, *Soon*, 317.
54 Jenkins, *Soon*, 318.
55 Jenkins, *Soon*, 19.
56 A summary of their conclusions is provided in Boyer, *When Time Shall Be No More*, 225-53.
57 G. M. Marsden, *Jonathan Edwards: A Life* (New Haven: Yale University Press, 2003), 264-65.
58 Boyer, *When Time Shall Be No More*, 225-53.
59 LaHaye and Jenkins, *Tribulation Force*, 29.
60 McAlister, "Prophecy, Politics and the Popular."
61 Boyer, *When Time Shall Be No More*, 177.
62 Jenkins, *Soon*, 34-35.
63 Jenkins, *Soon*, 94. The expression is drawn from *The Economist*.
64 A survey of readers is available at www.leftbehind.com.
65 Boyer, *When Time Shall Be No More*, 258.
66 Kirban, *1000*, 67.
67 Jenkins, *Soon*, xv.
68 Jenkins, *Soon*, 203.
69 Jenkins, *Soon*, 37-38.
70 Jenkins, *Soon*, 262.
71 Jenkins, *Soon*, 277.
72 Jenkins, *Soon*, 68.
73 Jenkins, *Soon*, 38.
74 Jenkins, *Soon*, 295.
75 Jenkins, *Soon*, 204.
76 R. Landes, "Millennialism," in J. R. Lewis, ed., *The Oxford Handbook of New Religious Movements* (Oxford: Oxford University Press, 2004), 340.
77 Jenkins, *Soon*, 105.
78 Gribben, "Rapture Fictions and the Changing Evangelical Condition," 88.
79 LaHaye and Jenkins, *Nicolae*, 335.
80 LaHaye and Jenkins, *Tribulation Force*, 279.
81 Jenkins, *Soon*, 35.
82 Jenkins, *Soon*, 272.
83 LaHaye and Jenkins, *Soul Harvest*, 318; *Desecration*, 2.
84 LaHaye and Jenkins, *Assassins*, 70.
85 See Gribben, "Rapture Fictions and the Changing Evangelical Condition," 88.
86 *Catechism of the Catholic Church* (Dublin: Veritas, 1994), §677, 155-56.
87 Jenkins, *Soon*, §675, 155.

88   Jenkins, *Soon*, §673, 154.
89   Gribben, "Rapture Fictions and the Changing Evangelical Condition," 86.
90   This process is described in Gribben, "Rapture Fictions and the Changing
     Evangelical Condition."
91   This restructuring is highly ironic, in that *Assassins* (1999) was dedicated to a
     former president of Dallas Theological Seminary, John F. Walvoord, who "has
     helped keep the torch of prophecy burning."
92   LaHaye and Jenkins, *Soul Harvest*, 364.
93   LaHaye and Jenkins, *Soul Harvest*, 64, 84.
94   LaHaye and Jenkins, *The Indwelling*, 90.
95   LaHaye and Jenkins, *Soul Harvest*, 166.
96   LaHaye and Jenkins, *Assassins*, 239.
97   The exodus/battle typology is explained in D. G. Bromley, "Violence and
     New Religious Movements," in Lewis, *The Oxford Handbook of New Religious
     Movements*, 153.
98   Wilson, *Armageddon Now!* 186.
99   Bromley, "Violence and New Religious Movements," 148.
100 Jenkins, *Soon*, 35.
101 Jenkins, *Soon*, 199.
102 Jenkins, *Soon*, 199.
103 Jenkins, *Soon*, 302.
104 Jenkins, *Soon*, 313, 317.
105 Jenkins, *Soon*, 296.
106 Jenkins, *Soon*, 347.
107 Bromley, "Violence and New Religious Movements," 151.
108 Bromley, "Violence and New Religious Movements," 156, 159.
109 Bromley, "Violence and New Religious Movements," 145.
110 Landes, "Millennialism," 334.
111 Jenkins, *Soon*, 304.
112 Jenkins, *Soon*, 28, 201.
113 McAlister, "Prophecy, Politics and the Popular," 775.
114 Frykholm, *Rapture Culture*, 52.
115 For the relationship between *Left Behind* and earlier rapture fiction, see
     Gribben, "Rapture Fictions and the Changing Evangelical Condition,"
     77–94; and Gribben, "Before *Left Behind*," *Books & Culture*, July/August 2003,
     11. For general comment on the series' theology, see Gribben, *Rapture Fiction
     and the Evangelical Crisis* (Auburn, Mass.: Evangelical Press, 2006). See also the
     extensive bibliography of rapture fictions in Frykholm, *Rapture Culture*, but
     note that Frykholm has misdated the works of Sydney Watson.
116 Jenkins, *Soon*, 302.

Chapter Eight

1   The story of post-Waco Branch Davidianism is told in some detail in K. G. C.
    Newport, *The Branch Davidians of Waco: The History and Beliefs of an Apocalyp-
    tic Sect* (Oxford: Oxford University Press, 2006), chap. 16.
2   See J. D. Tabor and E. V. Gallagher, *Why Waco? Cults and the Battle for Religious
    Freedom in America* (Berkeley: University of California Press, 1995).
3   Houteff appears not always to have been of the view that the Kingdom would
    be literal and based in Jerusalem. There is no mention of it, for example, in

his principal early publication *The Shepherd's Rod* (1930–1932). The first clear signs of the doctrine appear in Houteff's 1937 tract *Mount Zion at the Eleventh Hour*. Houteff's theology in general is discussed in Newport, *The Branch Davidians of Waco*, chap. 4.

4   See Newport, *The Branch Davidians of Waco*, chap. 3, for a summary of the historical development of the movement up to 1955. Very useful in this context are the extensive oral memoirs of longtime Davidian George Saether, the transcription of which is held in the Texas Collection at Baylor University in Waco, Texas (hereinafter "TXC").

5   A number of such letters and other documents are now held in the TXC at Baylor.

6   The "old" Mount Carmel was a substantial property located in what was later to become a prime location in Waco, close to the lake. During the period 1955–1959 this property was sold off, initially in an attempt to finance an ambitious plan of seeking to visit in person as many Seventh-day Adventists as possible (the so-called hunting campaign) rather than simply sending out vast amounts of literature (the so-called fishing campaign). A cheaper property near Elk was purchased, and eventually a large percentage of that was similarly sold off. It was on what remained of this latter property that Koresh's Branch Davidians lived, and this was the location of the siege and fire in 1993. See, further, Newport, *The Branch Davidians of Waco*, chap. 5.

7   As is noted below, in 1959 there was an attempt on the part of Houteff's wife, Florence, to get the Davidians to abandon this view. She did not succeed.

8   The precise details of how this date was arrived at need not be spelled out here, and in any case are subject to some dispute. What is clear, however, is that Florence arrived at the date of April 22 by adding 1,260 days (a period she believed to be spoken of in Revelation 12:6 and perhaps elsewhere too) to the date of her announcing to the community that they had entered a "waiting time" (the announcement was made in November 1955). See, further, Newport, *The Branch Davidians of Waco*, chap. 5, and especially Saether, "Oral Memoirs" (transcript held at the Institute of Oral History, Baylor University), 353–54.

9   The view that Houteff would be raised was not new. According to longtime Davidian Don Adair (though he was not present himself), there were people at Houteff's funeral who "cried and weeped [sic] and wailed . . . and said that he was going to be resurrected in three days." This quotation is taken from the transcription of three interviews that Adair gave to the interviewers from the Institute of Oral History at Baylor University. These transcriptions are not as yet in their final form and hence pagination may change; however, in the version used here the remark is found on p. 36.

10   "Shepherd's Rod press release on prophecy of April 22, 1959," unpublished MS, a copy of which is in my possession. It may have been this press release that Saether was given to take into a local newspaper office (see Saether, "Oral Memoirs," 405).

11   A number of these have been preserved in the TXC.

12   See L. Festinger, H. W. Riecken, and S. Schachter, *When Prophecy Fails: A Social and Psychological Study* (Minneapolis: University of Minnesota Press, 1956).

13   D. Adair, *A Davidian Testimony* (privately published, 1997), 223.

14 Another feature of Davidian eschatology, which is not dwelt upon here, is that once the 144,000 have been called out, the rest of the Seventh-day Adventists die in a literal and bloody slaughter (thought to be predicted in Ezek. 9). Only after this do non-Adventists come into the frame as targets for evangelism. See, further, Newport, *The Branch Davidians of Waco*, chap. 4.

15 Adair, *A Davidian Testimony*, 227; see also "Interviews" (transcriptions held at the Institute of Oral History), 57-58.

16 Dates from *Bashan Tidings* 18 (2002): 6. On the publication *Bashan Tidings* generally, see further below, n27.

17 Adair, *A Davidian Testimony*, 227.

18 Adair, "Interviews," 58-59.

19 Bingham had apparently put forth this doctrine during the initial meeting of the group, for according to *Bashan Tidings* on Sunday, July 30 [1961]:

> A study from the Bible and the ROD was presented to us by Brother Bingham, proving conclusively that there are three places of spiritual pasture where God's people are to feed (see 2SR 243:2). The study went on to show that since the Carmel of the ROD (old Mt Carmel) is no more, and since Gilead is the Kingdom (see Jer. 51:8 and 46:11, 12), we are therefore now in the Bashan period and must, accordingly, get our meat in due season *from* the ROD *in* Bashan. (*Bashan Tidings* 18 [2002]: 10)

20 Details are from Adair, "Interviews," 60.

21 Adair, "Interviews," 62.

22 Adair, "Interviews," 62. Adair gives the names of three others (in addition to himself, that is) who had gone with Bingham but who now returned to the group in Riverside. These are "Sister Newsome, Sister Bishop and Brother Beck." They were all accepted back, though Adair was put on probation.

23 Houteff's absence lasted about four months, and at this time the rivalry between Bingham and another would-be leader, E. T. Wilson, came to a head. Houteff resolved the situation upon his return. See, further, Newport, *The Branch Davidians of Waco*, chap. 3.

24 W. Pitts, "Davidians and Branch Davidians: 1929-1987," in S. A. Wright, ed. *Armageddon in Waco: Critical Perspectives on the Branch Davidian Conflict* (Chicago: University of Chicago Press, 1995), 20-42, 38.

25 According to Adair, "Interviews," 68-69, Jemmy Rohoman was from Trinidad, but of mixed descent.

26 See, further, D. Cattau, "Davidians in Missouri Disavow Waco-area Cult," *Dallas Morning News*, March 14, 1993.

27 These include issues of *Bashan Tidings to the Little Flock* and *The Timely Truth Educator*. Other publications put out by this group include a series of tracts with titles such as *God's Battle and the Weapons of War*, *The Mystery Stone*, *The Sanctuary Truth*, and *The Latter Rain*. None of these tracts are dated, but all are published by The Universal Publishing Association, Bashan Hill, Exeter, Mo. Copies of these publications are in my personal possession.

28 April 17, 1994; a transcript of the relevant section of the broadcast is in my personal possession.

29 The address given for this group by Adair is P.O. Box 8, Sprucedale, Ontario, POA 1YO; "Interviews," 81.

30 Adair, "Interviews," 81-181.

31 A little of what the group teaches is reconstructible from the publications designed to counter their arguments put out by the Bashan Davidians. See, for example, *The Timely Truth Educator* (the Bashan Bull Edition, 1982). Proper allowance must, of course, be made for the genre and origin of this source.

32 In 1967 La Sierra University and Loma Linda University formally joined together to create a two-campus institution. The union lasted until 1990.

33 Adair, *A Davidian Testimony*, 237-44.

34 Adair, *A Davidian Testimony*, 245; "Interviews," 63.

35 C. T. Smith is listed as a Bible worker in the 1943 Davidian directory of ministers and other workers (V. Houteff, *Fundamental Beliefs and Directory of the Davidian Seventh-day Adventists* [1943]); her address is given as "Mt. Carmel Center."

36 L. W. Nations is listed as a "worker" in the 1943 *Directory*; his address is given as "Salem, South Carolina."

37 Adair, *A Davidian Testimony*, 251.

38 See the transcript of a series of four interviews conducted at Baylor University on February 1, 1989, with Glenn Green, Sidney Smith, and Bonnie Smith, draft copies of which are available at the Institute of Oral History at Baylor University. The reference here is to the transcript of the fourth interview, page 50; the Salem Seventh-day Adventist church had apparently been financed and was owned by the members. When, therefore, the pastor (and, it seems, his flock) accepted the Davidian message, the Conference was not able to take the building away from them. Green indicates that at the time of the interview (1989), the membership of the Salem Davidian church (they are avoiding using "Seventh-day Adventist" in any part of their name in fear of prosecution) is about twenty.

39 Adair, "Interviews," 171.

40 Adair indicates that this group grew fairly well until at some point in the early 1980s it became bankrupt. Those in Yucaipa joined together with the group that was by this time settled in New York (though not all moved physically to New York). Adair, "Interviews," 192-93. On the New York group, see below.

41 The only two items that have come to me to date are *Has the Judgment for the Living Commenced* (Yucaipa, Calif.: The Universal Publishing Association, undated); and an open letter to "Fellow Believers in the Advent Message," undated.

42 In private correspondence, Adair wrote: "In 1974 our leadership (Executive Council) sent me to the West Indies islands from Trinidad all the way up to Jamaica, and I gave them Bible studies and showed them that M. J. Bingham was wrong. And nearly all of these Davidians joined with the Salem Association, including all of the Jamaicans."

43 The precise issue concerned the 144,000, or more particularly the view that in addition to the 144,000 who had been called out of the Adventist church (and were all Jews), there were to be an unspecified number of additional Adventists who would "go with" the saints to the New Kingdom. This seems to be a doctrine that was developed by Adair on the basis of a passing comment he claims was made by Houteff about some people who "go with" the 144,000. The ones that "go with" are Adventists, but not Jews. Adair, "Interviews," 180; *A Davidian Testimony*, 298.

44 The address of this group is given as General Association of Davidian Seventh-day Adventists, 32 Crescent Street, Mountain Dale, New York 12763.
45 http://www.shepherds-rod-message.org.
46 T. Hibbert, *Before the Flames: Story of David Koresh and the Davidian Seventh-day Adventists* (New York: Seaburn Publishing, 1996). In TXC 2D216 there is a folder marked "Miscellaneous" that has some material that stems from the New York group. This includes a pamphlet "Only 144,000 Translated?" and a number of study sheets on such topics as "The Shepherd's Rod in Prophecy" and "Elijah."
47 Adair also reports that "Winston Rose," a New York Davidian, staked a claim to the prophetic office and claimed that he was Elijah. However, as far as one can tell, Rose's claims fell upon deaf ears ("Interviews," 80). It may be to this person that Adair is again referring when he later talks of someone in New York who claims to be "Solomon David" ("Interviews," 199).
48 Sidney Smith indicates that one of those looking to return has already bought a house in Waco (Green, Smith, and Smith 1, p. 11).
49 The video is located in the Institute of Oral History at Baylor, not in the TXC.
50 Green, Smith, and Smith 1, p.11.
51 Adair, "Interviews," 36–37.
52 Adair, "Interviews," 36–37.
53 Adair, "Interviews," 77, 80. Adair indicates that Norman Archer was a Davidian in Jamaica before leaving for the United States.
54 There is good evidence, for example, though it has not been possible as yet to follow it up, that there is a small group based in Jerusalem.

Chapter Nine

1   J. R. Hall, "Public Narratives and the Apocalyptic Sect: from Jonestown to Mt. Carmel," in S. A. Wright, ed., *Armageddon in Waco: Critical Perspectives on the Branch Davidian Conflict* (Chicago: University of Chicago Press, 1995), 205–35; C. Wessinger, *How the Millennium Comes Violently: From Jonestown to Heaven's Gate* (New York: Seven Bridges Press, 2000); J. T. Richardson, "Minority Religions and the Context of Violence: A Conflict/Interactionist Perspective," *Terrorism and Political Violence* 13, no. 1 (2001): 103–33; D. G. Bromley and J. G. Melton, eds., *Cults, Religion and Violence* (Cambridge: Cambridge University Press, 2002).
2   Uncited factual information summarized in this chapter is drawn from my chapter on the Branch Davidians in Wessinger, *How the Millennium Comes Violently*, which contains full citations. I am deeply indebted to Lee Hancock for providing me with invaluable materials relating to this case. I am equally indebted to surviving Branch Davidians for granting me interviews: Catherine Matteson, Clive Doyle, Bonnie Haldeman, Sheila Martin, and Kimberly Martin. I also thank Brad Borst, Gustav Niebuhr, Kimberly Winston, and Lee Hancock for permitting me to interview them. I am grateful to Kyle Cole and Steve Herrick of the American Academy of Religion, Stuart Wright and Scott Thumma of the Society for the Scientific Study of Religion, Debra Mason of the Religion Newswriters Association, and Robert Mong of the *Dallas Morning News* for their assistance. I greatly appreciate the comments I received from Lee Hancock, Stuart Wright, Rebecca Moore, Eugene Gallagher, and James

T. Richardson on earlier drafts of this chapter. I thank Lonnie Davis and Claire Borowik for sending materials. I wish to thank Crawford Gribben and Gary L. Nebeker for reading and commenting on the text of this chapter.

3 In 1993 the media framing of the Branch Davidians as "cultists" was based on several decades of depictions of new religions as "cults," a stereotype applied to diverse groups (J. T. Richardson and B. van Driel, "Journalists' Attitudes toward New Religious Movements," *Review of Religious Research* 39, no. 2 [1997], 116–36). The mass suicide-murders at Jonestown, Guyana, in 1978 solidified this stereotype that was used to characterize the Branch Davidians in 1993 (Hall, "Public Narratives and the Apocalyptic Sect"). The consequence was that in 1993 most of the news coverage about the tragedy at Mount Carmel depicted the Branch Davidians as members of a "cult" that was solely responsible for the deaths. A poll by CNN/Gallup reported that 73 percent of Americans believed that the FBI decision to use CS gas on the residence was "responsible," and 93 percent of Americans blamed the Branch Davidians' leader, David Koresh, for the deaths (S. A. Wright, "Another View of the Mt. Carmel Standoff," in Wright, *Armageddon in Waco*, xiii–xxvi, xv).

4 D. Maxwell and C. Smith, Report of Investigation, Texas Department of Public Safety, Criminal Law Enforcement Division, May 11, 1993. A dispatcher for an ambulance company on standby for the ATF revealed that she tipped off Mulloney. Witherspoon did not reveal his source.

5 Maxwell and Smith, Report of Investigation.

6 Maxwell and Smith, Report of Investigation, §§54, 68.

7 Maxwell and Smith, Report of Investigation.

8 Maxwell and Smith, Report of Investigation.

9 L. Hancock, personal communications, January 2004.

10 V. Lowe, "FBI Uses Briefings as a Tactical Weapon," *Dallas Morning News*, March 25, 1993.

11 J. D. Tabor and P. Arnold, audiotape of discussion of biblical prophecies on the Ron Engleman radio talk show, April 1, 1993.

12 House of Representatives, *Investigation into the Activities of Federal Law Enforcement Agencies toward the Branch Davidians: Thirteenth Report by the Committee on Government Reform and Oversight Prepared in Conjunction with the Committee on the Judiciary together with Additional and Dissenting Views* (Washington, D.C.: U.S. Government Printing Office, 1996), 165.

13 L. Hancock, "Agents Reach Settlement in Waco Court," *Dallas Morning News*, October 18, 1996.

14 E. S. Herman and N. Chomsky, *Manufacturing Consent: The Political Economy of the Mass Media* (New York: Pantheon Books, 1988).

15 J. T. Richardson, "Manufacturing Consent about Koresh: A Structural Analysis of the Role of the Media in the Waco Tragedy," in Wright, *Armageddon in Waco*, 153–76, 155.

16 Richardson and van Driel, "Journalists' Attitudes toward New Religious Movements."

17 S. A. Wright, "Media Coverage of Unconventional Religions: Any 'Good News' for Minority Faiths?" *Review of Religious Research* 39, no. 2 (1997, 101–15).

18 See, for instance, B. Edelman and J. T. Richardson, "Falun Gong and the Law: Development of Legal Social Control in China," *Nova Religio: The Journal of Alternative and Emergent Religions* 6, no. 2 (2003): 312–31.

19 J. T. Richardson, email dated August 25, 2003.
20 Wessinger, *How the Millennium Comes Violently*, 73–74, 89, 106–12.
21 D. McCormick, "Howell's Mom Flees Home," *Waco Tribune-Herald*, March 2, 1993, 1-A.
22 B. Minutaglio and J. Weiss, "Divided Davidian," *Dallas Morning News*, March 2, 1993, 1, 11-A.
23 Branch Davidians, compilation of three unpublished videotapes of interviews made during the fifty-one-day siege (1993), a copy of which is in the author's possession.
24 In my analysis, Jonestown was a "fragile millennial movement" that initiated violence. The Branch Davidians were an "assaulted millennial movement" (Wessinger, *How the Millennium Comes Violently*).
25 N. T. Ammerman, "Waco, Federal Law Enforcement, and Scholars of Religion," in Wright, *Armageddon in Waco*, 282–96, 285.
26 Ammerman, "Waco, Federal Law Enforcement," 286–89.
27 CNN News, March 2, 1993; NBC News *Today* Show, April 20, 1993.
28 *State of Arizona v. Rick Alan Ross*; *Jason Scott v. Rick Ross* et al.
29 S. A. Wright, "Explaining Militarization at Waco: The Construction and Convergence of the Warfare Narrative," in J. R. Lewis and J. A. Petersen, eds., *Controversial New Religions* (New York: Oxford University Press, 2005), 79–99; Ammerman, "Waco, Federal Law Enforcement, and Scholars of Religion," 286.
30 J. D. Tabor and E. V. Gallagher, *Why Waco? Cults and the Battle for Religious Freedom in America* (Berkeley: University of California Press, 1995), 105, 118–19.
31 Tabor and Gallagher, *Why Waco?* 57.
32 C. Matteson, interviewed August 15–17, 2003.
33 Tabor and Gallagher, *Why Waco?* 117.
34 Tabor and Gallagher, *Why Waco?* 118.
35 Maxwell and Smith, Report of Investigation, §§121–22, 153, 186.
36 W. Rawls, "Debacle at Waco: Print and Broadcast, National and Local, Journalism Displayed its Unseemly Side," *Nieman Reports*, Summer 1993, 12–15.
37 Rawls, "Debacle at Waco," 14.
38 M. England and D. McCormick, "Sinful Messiah" series, *Waco Tribune-Herald*, February 27–March 1, 1993, http://www.wacotrib.com/news/content/coxnet/branchdavidian/1993/, part 1, part 4.
39 England and D. McCormick, "Sinful Messiah," part 1.
40 England and D. McCormick, "Sinful Messiah," part 6.
41 Maxwell and Smith, Report of Investigation, §§182, 191.
42 England and McCormick, "Sinful Messiah," part 7.
43 Maxwell and Smith, Report of Investigation, §187.
44 Tabor and Gallagher, *Why Waco?* 118.
45 Tabor and Gallagher, *Why Waco?* 118.
46 See also the following, all of which appeared in *Nova Religio: The Journal of Alternative and Emergent Religions* 5, no. 1 (2001): S. A. Wright, "Justice Denied: The Waco Civil Trial," 143–51; J. T. Richardson, "'Showtime' in Texas: Social Productions of the Branch Davidian Trials," 152–70; J. E. Rosenfeld, "The Use of the Military at Waco: The Danforth Report in Context," 171–85.

47 L. Hancock, "2 Pyrotechnic Devices Fired at Davidians, Ex-official Says," *Dallas Morning News*, August 24, 1999.

48 See Rosenfeld, "The Use of the Military at Waco," on the Danforth report's limitations.

49 L. Hancock, interviewed September 26, 2003.

50 L. Hancock, "FBI Missteps Doomed Siege Talks, Memos Say," *Dallas Morning News*, December 30, 1999.

51 Hancock, "FBI Missteps."

52 Hancock, "FBI Missteps."

53 Hancock, "FBI Missteps."

54 Hancock, "FBI Missteps"; see also S. A. Wright, "A Decade after Waco: Reassessing Crisis Negotiations at Mt. Carmel in light of New Government Disclosures," *Nova Religio: The Journal of Alternative and Emergent Religions* 7, no. 2 (2003): 101–10.

55 Cable News Network, television broadcast, April 20, 1993.

56 L. Hancock, interviewed September 26, 2003.

57 *Waco Tribune-Herald*, "Flashpoint in History" series, parts 2 ("Church History," March 2, 2003), 4 ("Law Enforcement," March 16, 2003), 9 ("Prophesying," April 19, 2003), and bio on Mike McNulty.

58 Perry's 2003 remarks differed in tone from his assertions in 1993 and 1995. Perry's 1995 congressional testimony stated that in addition to the girls being socialized for eventual sexual relationships with Koresh, the children were disciplined in abusive ways. His written report submitted to Congress said that the children lived in "an abusive and psychologically-destructive" environment. He also reported that he had protested the blaring of high-decibel sounds at Mount Carmel as harmful to the children. During the siege Dr. Perry advised FBI agents that the Branch Davidians had a belief system that made them capable of "'abstract' suicide" and that the aggressive tactical actions made the Branch Davidians feel "under threat under siege, thereby making rational decision-making on the part of Koresh or the Davidians increasingly difficult." Dr. Perry's report stated that he did not know how the analysis he gave the FBI "was used (or misused)." Committee of the Judiciary, *Activities of Federal Law Enforcement Agencies toward the Branch Davidians (Part I)*. Serial No. 72 (Washington, D.C.: U.S. Government Printing Office, 1995), 214–16, 234–41, quotes on 241.

59 Part 8.

60 M. Hall, "The Ghosts of Mount Carmel," *Texas Monthly*, April 2003, 122–27, 132–38; photographs by Misty Keasler.

61 B. Haldeman, interviewed August 17, 2003.

62 J. Dart, *Deities and Deadlines: A Primer on Religion News Coverage*, 2d ed. (Nashville: First Amendment Center, 1998).

63 Religion Newswriters Foundation, *A Guide to Religion Reporting in the Secular Media: Frequently Asked Questions* (Westerville, Ohio: Religion Newswriters Foundation, 2002).

64 S. A. Wright, email message dated November 10, 2003.

65 "Journalists Honored for In-Depth Reporting on Religion," *Religious Studies News* 18, no. 4 (AAR ed., 2003): 12; American Academy of Religion, Awards for Best In-Depth Reporting on Religion, 2003, http://www.aarweb.org/awards/journalism/default.asp, accessed November 7, 2003.

66 Religionsource, http://religionsource.org, accessed November 12, 2003.

67 K. Cole remarks during a panel session, "Are We Public Educators: A Discussion with Journalists of Religion," Society for the Scientific Study of Religion, Norfolk, Va., October 25, 2003.

68 ReligionLink, http://www.religionwriters.com/public/tips/main.shtml, accessed November 14, 2003.

69 K. Winston, interviewed August 7, 2003.

70 D. Mason, email dated November 14, 2003.

71 Maxwell and Smith, Report of Investigation, §75.

72 G. Niebuhr, interviewed September 4, 2003.

73 Television depictions still relied heavily on the "cult" stereotype. The thesis of the ABC *Primetime Witness* show *The Children of Waco*, produced by J. Dratt and J. L. Goldstone (New York: ABC News) that was broadcast on April 17, 2003 was that the children who came out of Mount Carmel during the siege knew that their parents were going to choose to die with David Koresh, and that therefore there was nothing FBI agents could have done to prevent the tragedy. Surviving Branch Davidians (Sheila Martin, interviewed August 16, 2003; Kimberly Martin, also interviewed August 16, 2003) noted that the young people remaining in Waco were not included on the show because their statements did not fit the agenda of the producers. The young people who were depicted on the show refused to accept retired FBI agent Byron Sage's characterization of their parents as being completely to blame, and asked about the responsibility of the federal agents. Brad Borst (age twenty-nine), who lived at Mount Carmel for five years with his mother and subsequently became a police officer, was particularly critical of the producer, Jude Dratt, who he said attempted to get the young people to make certain statements for the camera (B. Borst, press release, April 17, 2003, http://www.anyc-ities.com/mtcarmel/ BradPress.htm; Borst, Website, "The Facts about Waco," http://www.wacofacts.com/, accessed October 3, 2003; Borst, interviewed October 27, 2003).

74 Hall, "Public Narratives and the Apocalyptic Sect"; Wright, "Media Coverage of Unconventional Religions," 101–15; Richardson and van Driel, "Journalists' Attitudes toward New Religious Movements"; Wessinger, *How the Millennium Comes Violently.*

Chapter Ten

1   P. Boyer, *When Time Shall Be No More: Prophecy Belief in Modern American Culture* (Cambridge, Mass.: The Belknap Press of Harvard University Press, 1992), ix.

2   C. Gribben, "*Left Behind* and the Paradox of Evangelical Pessimism," p. 115 of this volume.

3   F. R. Coad, *Prophetic Developments with Particular Reference to the Early Brethren Movement* (Pinner, Middlesex: Christian Brethren Research Fellowship, 1966), 8.

4   Dispensationalism awaits a definitive history. See, however, C. Ryrie, *Dispensationalism* (Chicago: Moody, 1995); A. D. Ehlert, *A Bibliographic History of Dispensationalism* (Grand Rapids: Baker Book, 1965); and, for an overview of the essential elements, J. S. Feinberg, "Systems of Discontinuity," in *Continuity and Discontinuity: Perspectives on the Relationship between Old and New Testaments.*

(*Essays Presented in Honor of S. Lewis Johnson Jr.*) (Westchester, Ill.: Crossway Books, 1988), 67–85.

5   It should be noted that dispensationalists have argued that, while dispensationalism per se was a product of the nineteenth century, its roots could be discerned in the early church. See Ehlert, *A Bibliographic History of Dispensationalism*; F. A. Tatford, *God's Programme of the Ages* (Grand Rapids: Kregel, 1967), 21–22; L. V. Crutchfield, "Rudiments of Dispensationalism in the Ante-Nicene Period, Part 1: Israel and the Church in the Ante-Nicene Fathers," *Bibliotheca Sacra* 144, no. 576 (1987): 254–77; and "Rudiments of Dispensationalism in the Ante-Nicene Period, Part 2: Ages and Dispensations in the Ante-Nicene Fathers," *Bibliotheca Sacra* 144, no. 576 (1987): 377–402. A similar thesis is replicated in Crutchfield, "Early Church Fathers and the Foundations of Dispensationalism," available online at www.tyndale.edu/dirn/source/theology.htm. Also helpful, although more general, is E. Frank, "A Survey of Early Pre-Millennialism," *WRS Journal* 2, no. 1 (1995): 8, 15–19. For a discussion of the rapture in later Christianity see T. J. Demy and T. D. Ice, "The Rapture, an Early Medieval Citation," *Bibliotheca Sacra* 152, no. 607 (1995): 306–17.

6   This tendency can be seen, for example, in A. Miller, *"The Brethren" (Commonly so-called), A Brief Sketch* (Dillenburg: Gute Botschaft Verlag, 1992).

7   F. R. Coad, *A History of the Brethren Movement*, 2d ed. (Exeter: Paternoster Press, 1976).

8   T. C. F. Stunt, *From Awakening to Secession* (Edinburgh: T&T Clark, 2000).

9   Coad, *Prophetic Developments*, 19.

10   Coad, *Prophetic Developments*, 18.

11   On Irving, see Mrs. M. O. W. Oliphant, *The Life of Edward Irving*, 2 vols., 2d ed. (London, 1862); H. C. Whitley, *Blinded Eagle: An Introduction to the Life and Teaching of Edward Irving* (London: SCM Press, 1955); and Stunt, *From Awakening to Secession*, 98–102, 221–71, passim. For the Irvingites (the Catholic Apostolic Church) see R. A. Davenport, *Albury Apostles, the Story of the Body Known as the Catholic Apostolic Church* ([Birdup]: United Writers, 1970); and C. G. Flegg, *"Gathered under Apostles": A Study of the Catholic Apostolic Church* (Oxford: Oxford University Press, 1992).

12   On the birth of the charismatic movement with relation to the Brethren, see T. C. F. Stunt, "Irvingite Pentecostalism and the Early Brethren," *Christian Brethren Research Fellowship Journal* 10 (1965): 40–48. For the wider response to the charismatic movement, see T. C. F. Stunt, "'Trying the Spirits': The Case of the Gloucester Clergyman (1831)," *Journal of Ecclesiastical History* 39, no. 1 (January 1988): 95–105; and, for a contemporary critique, W. Goode, *Charismatic Confusion: A Reprint of the Modern Claims to the Possession of the Extraordinary Gifts of the Spirit*, 3rd ed. (Trelawnyd: K&M Books, 2000).

13   Coad, *Prophetic Developments*, 20.

14   Coad, *Prophetic Developments*, 21.

15   For a helpful historical overview of Irving's prophetic teaching, see I. H. Murray, *The Puritan Hope* (Edinburgh: Banner of Truth Trust, 1971), 187–206. Murray's conclusions require cautious consideration. For a discussion of Irving's importance to later dispensationalism, see M. Patterson and A. Walker, "'Our Unspeakable Comfort'": Irving, Albury, and the Origins of the Pretribulation Rapture," *Fides et Historia* XXXI, no. 1 (1999): 66–81. This article

is especially useful in its discussion of the role of Brethren politics in linking the pretribulation rapture with Irving. However, G. L. Nebeker, "John Nelson Darby and Trinity College, Dublin: A Study in Eschatological Contrasts," *Fides et Historia* XXXIV, no. 2 (2002): 87–108, helpfully nuances some of Patterson and Walker's claims.

16   Patterson and Walker, "Our Unspeakable Comfort," 68.

17   For some rather splenetic examples of the debate about the origins of dispensationalism and the pretribulation rapture, see D. MacPherson, *The Rapture Plot* (Simpsonville, S.C.: Millennium III Publishers, 1994); *The Unbelievable Pre-Trib Origin* (Kansas City, Mo.: Heart of America Bible Society, 1973); *The Three R's: Rapture, Revisionism, Robbery* (Monticello, Utah: P.O.S.T., 1998); *The Great Rapture Hoax* (Fletcher, N.C.: New Puritan Library, 1983); *Rapture?* (Fletcher, N.C.: New Puritan Library, 1987); *The Incredible Cover-Up* (Plainfield, N.J.: Logos International, 1975); and *The Late Great Pre-Trib Rapture* (Kansas City, Mo.: Heart of America Bible Society, 1974). For some responses, see R. A. Huebner, *The Truth of the Pre-Tribulation Rapture Recovered* (Millington, N..J: Present Truth Publishers, 1976); Huebner, *Precious Truths Revived and Defended Through J. N. Darby*, vol. 1 (Morganville, N.J.: Present Truth Publishers, 1991); T. Ice, "Why the Doctrine of the Pre-tribulational Rapture Did Not Begin with Margaret Macdonald," *Bibliotheca Sacra* 147 (1990): 155–68; G. Stanton, *Kept from the Hour*, 4th ed. (Miami Springs, Fla.: Schoettle Publishing, 1991); and, most recently, T. C. F. Stunt, "The Tribulation of Controversy, a Review Article," *Brethren Archivists and Historians Network Review* 2, no. 2 (2003): 91–98.

18   Coad, *A History of the Brethren Movement*, 109.

19   For Darby's biography, see W. G. Turner, *John Nelson Darby* (London: C.A. Hammond, 1944); and Max S. Weremchek, *John Nelson Darby* (Neptune, N.J.: Loizeaux Brothers, 1992). Perhaps the best analysis of Darby is offered in Coad, *A History of the Brethren Movement*. For the influence of Trinity College on Darby's eschatology see Nebeker, "Darby and Trinity College."

20   J. D. Pentecost, *Things to Come: A Study in Biblical Eschatology* (1958) (Grand Rapids: Zondervan, 1964), 203.

21   On Newton, see Stunt, *From Awakening to Secession*, 194–219; and H. H. Rowdon, *The Origins of the Brethren 1825–1850* (London: Pickering & Inglis, 1967), 58–69.

22   Coad, *Prophetic Developments*, 27. See also L. Dixon, "The Importance of J. N. Darby and the Brethren Movement in the History of Conservative Theology," *Christian Brethren Review* 41 (1990): 42–55.

23   Stunt, "The Tribulation of Controversy," 91–92.

24   See Dunlap, "The Origins of the Scofield Bible," *Uplook*, July–August 1999, 17–19; and A. C. Gaebelein, *The History of the Scofield Reference Bible* (Spokane, Wash.: Living Words Foundation, 1991). It should be emphasized that dispensationalism, like any theology, is not static. Thus, Scofield's system differed from Darby's as, later, did Pentecost's from Scofield's. For the relationship between Darby's and Scofield's views, see L. V. Crutchfield, *The Origins of Dispensationalism: The Darby Factor* (Lenden, Md.: University Press of America, 1992). See also D. J. Macleod, "Walter Scott, a Link in Dispensationalism between Darby and Scofield," *Bibliotheca Sacra* 153, no. 610 (1996): 155–76.

25 E. R. Sandeen, *The Roots of Fundamentalism: British and American Millenarianism 1800-1930* (Chicago: University of Chicago Press, 1970), 222.

26 C. Gribben, "Rapture Fictions and the Changing Evangelical Condition," *Literature and Theology* 18, no. 1 (March 2004): 77-94.

27 My use of the term "classical dispensationalism" as a term covering a wide section of the movement is susceptible to considerable nuance. In particular, it disregards the emergence of revised dispensationalism and progressive dispensationalism, both of which have challenged the orthodoxy of classical dispensationalism. See W. R. Willis and J. R. Master, eds., *Issues in Dispensationalism* (Chicago: Moody, 1994); C. A. Blaising and D. L. Bock, *Progressive Dispensationalism: An Up-to-date Handbook of Contemporary Dispensational Thought* (Wheaton: Bridgepoint, 1993), for more details of these developments within dispensationalism.

28 C. I. Scofield, *The Scofield Reference Bible* (New York: Oxford University Press, 1917), 5n5.

29 See Scofield's notes for the following passages: Gen. 1:28, Gen. 3:23, Gen. 8:20, Gen. 12:1, Exod. 19:8, John 1:17, and Eph. 1:10.

30 Sandeen, *The Roots of Fundamentalism*, 62-64.

31 *Scofield Bible*, 941, note on Daniel 9:24. The seventieth week referred to is the seven-year period of tribulation.

32 Pentecost, *Things to Come*, 155.

33 H. F. Rail, "Where Premillennialism Leads," *The Biblical World* LIII (1919): 623.

34 Lindsey is nothing if not prolific. His bibliography includes: *The Late Great Planet Earth* (London: Lakeland, 1970); *Satan Is Alive and Well on Planet Earth* (London: Lakeland, 1973); *There's a New World Coming: A Prophetic Odyssey* (Santa Ana, Calif.: Vision House, 1973); *The Liberation of Planet Earth* (London: Lakeland, 1974); *The World's Final Hour: Evacuation or Extinction?* (Grand Rapids: Zondervan, 1976); *The 1980s Countdown to Armageddon* (New York: Bantam, 1981); *The Promise* (Eugene, Ore.: Harvest House, 1982); *The Rapture: Truth or Consequences* (New York: Bantam, 1983); *The Terminal Generation* (New York: Bantam, 1983); *A Prophetical Walk through the Holy Land* (Eugene, Ore.: Harvest House, 1983); *Israel and the Last Days* (Eugene, Ore.: Harvest House, 1983); *Combat Faith* (New York: Bantam Dell, 1986); *The Road to Holocaust* (New York: Bantam, 1989); *Planet Earth 2000 A.D.* (Palos Verdes, Calif.: Western Front, 1994 [rev. 1996]); *The Final Battle* (Palos Verdes, Calif.: Western Front, 1995); *Amazing Grace* (Palos Verdes, Calif.: Western Front, 1996); *Blood Moon* (Palos Verdes, Calif.: Western Front, 1996); *The Apocalypse Code* (Palos Verdes, Calif.: Western Front, 1997); *Planet Earth: The Final Chapter* (Beverley Hills, Calif.: Western Front, 1998). He also publishes a monthly journal, *International Intelligence Briefing*, and broadcasts a monthly radio program "Week in Review." See also www.hallindseyoracle.org.

35 Lindsey, *The Road to Holocaust*, 195. See also G. M. Marsden, *Understanding Fundamentalism and Evangelicalism* (Grand Rapids: Eerdmans, 1991), 77; and M. Lienesch, *Redeeming America: Piety and Politics in the New Christian Right* (Chapel Hill: University of North Carolina Press, 1993), 311. T. P. Weber, *Living in the Shadow of the Second Coming: American Premillenialism, 1875-1925*, rev. ed. (Chicago: University of Chicago Press, 1987), 5, discusses the significance of the book's presence in "drugstores, supermarkets and 'secular' bookstores,

right alongside gothic romances, cheap westerns, and books on the latest fads."

36 For a more detailed analysis of Lindsey's ongoing revision of his writings, see S. R. Sizer, "Hal Lindsey: Father of Apocalyptic Christian Zionism," available online at www.virginiawater.co.uk/christchurch/articles/hallindsey.htm.

37 Lindsey, *The Final Battle*, back cover; Lindsey, *Apocalypse Code*, back cover.

38 Lindsey, *Planet Earth*, 16.

39 G. North, "Publisher's preface," in D. Wilson, *Armageddon Now! The Premillenarian Response to Russia and Israel since 1917*, 2d ed. (1977) (Tyler, Tex.: Institute for Christian Economics, 1991), x.

40 Quoted in T. D. Ice, "Dispensationalism, Date-setting and Distortion," *Biblical Perspectives* I, no. 5 (Sep/Oct 1988): available online at www.prestoncitybible.org/ BP/3D.htm.

41 Coad, *Prophetic Developments*, 10.

42 For a discussion of Puritan eschatology, see Murray, *The Puritan Hope*; and C. Gribben, *The Puritan Millennium* (Dublin: Four Courts Press, 2000).

43 Historicism, which was an extremely popular method of prophetic interpretation from around 1550 onwards (but which has roots going back well before that), sees the biblical prophecies as being fulfilled throughout the course of the history of the church.

44 Ice, "Dispensationalism, Date-setting and Distortion."

45 Wilson, *Armageddon Now!* 36.

46 H. Pickering, "The World at War," *The Witness* 44 (1914): 165-66.

47 A. T. Schofield, "Can Corsica Conquer Galilee?" *The Witness* 45 (1915): 85-86.

48 H. Stone, "God's Voice to His People through the War," *The Witness* 44 (1914): 167.

49 T. Robinson, "Is this War 'Armageddon?'" *The Witness* 44 (1914): 168-69.

50 Special Number II: "The Coming of the Lord," *The Witness* 46 (1916): 73-96.

51 R. M'Murdo, "The Next Great Event: Or the Time of His Coming," *The Witness* 46 (1916): 82-83.

52 F. Ferguson, "The War and the Coming," *The Witness* 46 (1916): 82.

53 For Anderson's biography see A. P. Moore-Anderson, *Sir Robert Anderson, K.C.B., LL.D.: A Tribute and Memoir* (London: Morgan & Scott, 1919).

54 Sir R. Anderson, "The Christian and the Crisis," *The Witness* 44 (1914): 134-35.

55 Robinson, "Is this War 'Armageddon?'" 169.

56 J. R. Caldwell, "The Times of the Gentiles," *The Witness* 44 (1914): 151-52.

57 W. E. Vine, "The Roman Empire in Prophecy," *The Witness* 45 (1915): 18, 27-30, 45-48, 61-62, 93-95, 109-11, 141-43, 157-59, 173-76, 189-91. See also W. E. Vine, "The Roman Empire in the Light of Prophecy," in *The Collected Writings of W. E. Vine*, vol. 5 (Nashville: Thomas Nelson, 1996), 255-90.

58 W. E. Vine, "The Future 'European Federation.' The Revival of the Roman Empire," *The Witness* 44 (1915): 157-58.

59 F. A. Tatford, *Going into Europe: The Common Market and Prophecy* (Eastbourne: Prophetic Witness Publishers, 1971), back cover.

60 Tatford, *Going into Europe*, 15.

61 Tatford, *Going into Europe*, 22.

62 Tatford, *Going into Europe*, 27.
63 F. A. Tatford, *10 Nations–Now What?* (Eastbourne: Upperton House, 1980).
64 Coad, *Prophetic Developments*, 26.
65 W. MacDonald, "Y2K–Is This the Time?" *Uplook*, December 1999, 16.

Chapter Eleven

1   T. Smail, "The Cross and the Spirit: Towards a Theology of Renewal," in T. Smail, A. Walker, and N. Wright, eds., *Charismatic Renewal: The Search for a Theology* (London: SPCK, 1995), 49–70.
2   Smail, "The Cross and the Spirit," 50.
3   M. Hamilton, "Sociological Dimensions of Christian Millenarianism," in S. Hunt, ed., *Christian Millenarianism: From the Early Church to Waco* (London: Hurst Publishers, 2001), 12–25.
4   Y. Talmon, "Millennial Movements," *Archives Européennes de Sociologie* 7 (1966): 159–200, 166.
5   M. Weber, "The Social Psychology of the World Religion," in H. Gerth and C. W. Mills, eds., *From Max Weber: Essays in Sociology* (London: Routledge, 1991).
6   H. Cox, *Fire from Heaven* (Reading, Mass.: Addison-Wesley, 1994); D. Martin, *Tongues of Fire: The Explosion of Pentecostalism in Latin America* (Oxford: Blackwell, 1990).
7   P. Wagner, *Warfare Prayer* (Ventura, Calif.: Regal Books, 1992).
8   R. Anderson, *Vision of the Disinherited: The Making of American Pentecostals* (Oxford: Oxford University Press, 1980).
9   A. Walker, "Thoroughly Modern: Sociological Reflections on the Charismatic Movement from the End of the Twentieth Century," in S. Hunt, M. Hamilton, and T. Walter, eds., *Charismatic Christianity: Sociological Perspectives* (Basingstoke: Macmillan, 1997), 17–42, 23.
10 P. Hocken, *Streams of Renewal: Origins and Early Development of the Charismatic Movement in Great Britain* (Exeter: Paternoster, 1986).
11 D. McBain and S. Hunt, "Mainstream Charismatics: Some Observations of Baptist Renewal," in Hunt et al., *Charismatic Christianity*, 43–59, 49.
12 W. Thompson, "Charismatic Politics: The Social and Political Impact of Renewal," in Hunt et al., *Charismatic Christianity*, 160–83.
13 D. Martin, *The Dilemma of Contemporary Religion* (Oxford: Blackwell, 1978), 41–43.
14 M. Patterson and A. Walker, "'Our Unspeakable Comfort': Irving, Albury, and the Origins of Pretribulation Rapture," in Hunt, *Christian Millenarianism*, 98, 115.
15 P. Elbert, "Renewal Movement 'Losing the War,'" *Eternity* 33, November 1981, 5–6.
16 S. Hunt, "The Radical Kingdom of the Jesus Fellowship," *Pneuma* 20, no. 1 (1998): 21–41.
17 S. Hunt, M. Hamilton, and T. Walter, "Introduction" to Hunt et al., *Charismatic Christianity*, 2.
18 A. Walker, "Pentecostal Power: The 'Charismatic Renewal Movement' and the Politics of Pentecostal Experience," in E. Barker, ed., *Of Gods and Men: New Religious Movements in the West* (Macon, Ga.: Mercer University Press, 1983).

19 R. Wallis, *Elementary Forms of New Religious Life* (London: Routledge, 1984); Martin, *The Dilemma of Contemporary Religion*, 41–43.

20 A. Walker, *Restoring the Kingdom: The Radical Christianity of the House Church Movement* (London: Hodder & Stoughton, 1985), 28.

21 S. Bruce, *Religion in Modern Britain* (Oxford: Oxford University Press, 1995), 111.

22 G. Davie, *Religion in Britain since 1945: Believing without Belonging* (Oxford: Blackwell, 1994), 34.

23 E. Barker, "New Religious Movements. Yet Another Great Awakening?" in P. Hammond, ed., *The Sacred in a Secular Age* (Berkeley: University of California Press, 1985).

24 C. Patrides, "Renaissance and Modern Thought on the Last Things: A Study in Changing Conceptions," *Harvard Theological Review* L, no. 93 (1958): 169–86.

25 W. Hood, *The Plan of the Apocalypse* (York, Pa.: Anstadt, 1990), 164–77.

26 A. Shupe, "Christian Reconstructionism and the Angry Rhetoric of Neo-Post-millenarianism," in T. Robbins and S. Palmer, eds., *Millennium, Messiahs, and Mayhem: Contemporary Apocalyptic Movements* (New York: Routledge, 1997), 195–206.

27 N. Wright, "The Nature and Variety of Restorationism and the 'House Church Movement,'" in Hunt et al., *Charismatic Christianity*, 60–76, 74–75.

28 M. Percy, *Words, Wonders, and Power* (London: SPCK, 1997).

29 J. Beckford, "The Restoration of 'Power' to the Sociology of Religion," *Sociological Analysis* 44, no. 1 (1983): 11–32.

30 N. Kokosalakis, "Legitimation, Power, and Religion in Modern Society," *Sociological Analysis* 46, no. 4 (1985): 367–76.

31 H. Chalfont, R. Beckley, and C. Palmer, *Religion in Contemporary Society* (Palo Alto, Calif.: Maxfield Publishing, 1987).

32 S. Hunt, "'Doing the Stuff': The Vineyard Connection," in Hunt et al., *Charismatic Christianity*, 77–96.

33 P. Lawrence, *The Hotline* (Eastbourne: Kingsway, 1990), 35.

34 M. Noll, *The Scandal of the Evangelical Mind* (Leicester: InterVarsity, 1994).

35 Walker, "Pentecostal Power."

36 S. Hunt, "Letting the Devil Get More than his Due. Some Problems with the Deliverance Ministry," in A. Walker, ed., *Harmful Religion* (London: SPCK, 1997), 43–65.

37 N. Wright, "The Rise of the Prophetic," in Smail et al., *Charismatic Renewal*, 117–30, 117.

38 Report of a Leadership Consultation on the Current Situation in the Charismatic Churches (Sheffield: 1995), 12.

39 S. Hunt, "The 'Toronto Blessing': A Rumor of Angels," *The Journal of Contemporary Religion* 10, no. 3 (1995): 257–72.

40 P. Richter, "God is not a Gentleman," in S. Porter and P. Richter, eds., *The Toronto Blessing, Or is It?* (London: Darton, Longman & Todd, 1995); Richter, "The Toronto Blessing: The Charismatic Evangelical Global Warming," in Hunt et al., *Charismatic Christianity*, 97–119.

41 E. Durkheim, *The Elementary Forms of the Religious Life* (London: Allen & Unwin, 1915).

42 M. Poloma, *Main Street Mystics: The Toronto Blessing and Reviving Pentecostalism* (New York: Altamira, 2003).

43 S. Hunt, *Anyone for Alpha: Evangelism in a Post-Christian Society* (London: Darton, Longman & Todd, 2001), 26–30.
44 S. Hunt, *The Alpha Enterprise: Evangelism in the Post-Christian Era* (London: Ashgate, 2004).
45 Walker, "Thoroughly Modern," 36.

Chapter Twelve

1   This chapter is based in substantial part on personal correspondence of the author and on materials held in a private archive in the United Kingdom. Much of that archive is yet to be catalogued properly, and hence some of the references given here are necessarily rather imprecise. Readers who would like further information on sources mentioned in the chapter are invited to contact the author by email: gordon.allan@theology.oxford.ac.uk.
2   In the last fifty years, two books have been specifically written about the "New and Latter House of Israel" (or "Jezreelites," as they are known to the general public). These are: R. A. Baldwin, *The Jezreelites: The Rise and Fall of a Remarkable Prophetic Movement* (Orpington: Lambarde Press, 1961); and P. G. Rogers, *The Sixth Trumpeter: The Story of Jezreel and his Tower* (London: Oxford University Press, 1963). Baldwin states that almost all the information in his book is from records in various libraries, or national and local newspapers, although he has included interviews with local residents. Rogers's bibliography states that the chief sources of information are two local newspapers supplemented with other published sources. G. R. Balleine (*Past Finding Out: The Tragic Story of Joanna Southcott and her Successors* [London: SPCK, 1956]) attempts to record the history of all the Southcottian sects, beginning with Richard Brothers, down to the middle of the twentieth century. It lacks any references or bibliography, and it is therefore impossible to determine whether his sources are reliable. While there are definitely some errors of fact, this book has been the best (and really the only) introduction to the whole subject until the present.
3   A good example is the cover of the Jezreelite magazine, the *Guide to Life*, which in every issue lists their beliefs, with extracts from Scripture alone, making no reference to *The Flying Roll*.
4   The Oxford University Prophecy Project is directed by Prof. Christopher Rowland and Dr. Jane Shaw.
5   *Extracts from the Flying Roll*, Sarah Bone edition (undated), vol. 1, no. iii.
6   Believers in Benjamin and Mary Purnell, however, believe that Joanna Southcott was the first, and that Richard Brothers was number two. This is based on the message to the second church (Smyrna) at Revelation 2:10—"Beware, the devil is about to throw some of you into prison so that you may be tested, and for ten days you will have affliction. Be faithful until death, and I will give you the crown of life." The argument is that as Richard Brothers was thrown into prison, he must be number two; Southcott was never thrown into prison.
7   For example, Ponsonby and the Countess of Buckinghamshire. See Brothers, *Revealed Knowledge of the Prophecies and Times*, vol. 1 (1794), 42.
8   A detailed study of Richard Brothers and his theology, by Dr. Deborah Madden (a member of the Prophecy Project), is currently being written.

9 The Joanna Southcott website, www.joannasouthcott.com, contains the text of all sixty-five published books and some unpublished manuscripts, as well as a short biography.
10 See F. Brown, *Joanna Southcott: The Woman Clothed with the Sun* (Cambridge: Lutterworth Press, 2002).
11 See, for example, J. Klausner, *The Messianic Idea in Israel* (London: George Allen & Unwin, 1956), 400–401, 492–97.
12 A detailed study of Joanna Southcott and her theology, by Dr. Frances Kennett (a member of the Prophecy Project), is nearing completion.
13 See Diagram 1 in the Appendix.
14 For example, George Turner and others were expelled from the Methodists for believing in Southcott.
15 The Panacea Society Web site is www.panacea.fsbusiness.co.uk.
16 Letter of A. Baylis of Bath to Samuel Gompertz, July 8, 1822.
17 The website of the Christian Israelite Church, www.cichurch.asn.au, contains statement of beliefs, details of online broadcasts, and other information.
18 See Diagram 2 in the Appendix.
19 Letter of Jeanette Lambert to Miss Green, October 29, 1924.
20 The website is www.nlhouseofisrael.com.
21 For developments into the twentieth century, see Diagram 3 in the Appendix.
22 The Panacea Society, now based in Bedford, is another group that is important here. Jane Shaw has conducted extensive research into this group as another part of the Oxford Prophecy Project, so they are not examined here. Her forthcoming book will be published in England by Jonathan Cape and in the United States by Knopf.
23 J. Southcott, Book 17: *A Word to the Wise or A Call to the Nation, That They May Know the Days of their Visitation, etc.* (Stourbridge: J. Heming, 1803), 1.
24 Based on Galatians 4:26 "But the other woman corresponds to the Jerusalem above; she is free, and she is our mother."
25 For typical discussion of this, see *The Flying Roll*, Sermon 1, 129, or Sermon 2, iii–iv.
26 The chronology is summarized in a table, which is inserted in some copies of "Commandment of the Law and Testimony" (Christian Israelite Press, Ashton-under-Lyne, undated).
27 Republished as *The United States and Britain in Prophecy* by the Philadelphia Church of God, following successful legal action against the Worldwide Church of God.
28 The Mary's City of David website, www.maryscityofdavid.org, contains interesting history, publications, doctrine, and pictures.
29 This comment is based on interviews with members of various groups.

Chapter Thirteen

1 J. Berger, "Twentieth-century Apocalypse: Forecasts and Aftermaths," *Twentieth Century Literature* 46 (2000): 388.

Bibliography

Adair, Don. *A Davidian Testimony*. Privately published, 1997.
———. "Interviews." Transcriptions held at the Institute of Oral History, Baylor University, Waco, Tex.
Aho, James. *The Politics of Righteousness: Idaho Christian Patriotism*. Seattle: University of Washington Press, 1995.
Alexander, Paul. *The Byzantine Apocalyptic Tradition*. Edited by Dorothy de F. Abrahamse. Berkeley: University of California Press, 1985.
Amanat, Abbas and Magnus Bernhardsson, eds. *Imagining the End: Visions of Apocalypse From the Ancient Middle East to Modern America*. London: I. B. Tauris, 2002.
American Academy of Religion. Awards for Best In-Depth Reporting on Religion, 2003. Available at http://www.aarweb.org/awards/journalism/default.asp.
Ammerman, Nancy T. "Waco, Federal Law Enforcement, and Scholars of Religion." In S. Wright, *Armageddon in Waco*.
Ammi, Ben. *The Messiah and the End of This World*. Washington, D.C.: Communicators Press, 1991.

Anderson, R. *Vision of the Disinherited: The Making of American Pente-costals.* Oxford: Oxford University Press, 1980.

Anderson, Sir Robert. "The Christian and the Crisis." *The Witness* 44 (1914).

Anthony, D., T. Robbins, and S. Barrie-Anthony. "Cult and Anticult Totalism: Reciprocal Escalation and Violence." *Terrorism and Political Violence* 14, no. 1 (2002).

Applewhite, M. "Do's Intro: Purpose—Belief." In *Encyclopedic Source-book of UFO Religions*, edited by James R. Lewis. Amherst, N.Y.: Prometheus, 2003.

Ariel, Yaakov. *Evangelizing the Chosen People: Mission to the Jews in America 1800–2000.* Chapel Hill: University of North Carolina Press, 2000.

Armstrong, H. W. *The United States and Britain in Prophecy.* Edmund, OH: Philadelphia Church of God, 2005.

Atuhaire, B. *The Uganda Cult Tragedy: A Private Investigation.* London: Janus Publishing, 2003.

Auerbach, Jerald. *Are We One? Jewish Identity in the United States and Israel.* New Brunswick, N.J.: Rutgers University Press, 2001.

Augustine. *Epistolae*, 198 [418 CE]. Translated by Wilfrid Parsons [*Letters*]. Washington, D.C.: Catholic University of America Press, 1955.

Balch, R. W. "The Evolution of a New Age Cult: From Total Overcomers to Death at Heaven's Gate." In *Sects, Cults & Spiritual Communities*, edited by William W. Zellner and Marc Petrowsky.

———. "Waiting for the Ships: Disillusionment and the Revitalization of Faith in Bo and Peep's UFO cult." In *The Gods Have Landed*, edited by James R. Lewis.

Black, R. W., and David Taylor. "Heaven's Gate: Implications for the Study of Commitment to New Religions." In *Encyclopedic Sourcebook of UFO Religions*, edited by James R. Lewis.

———. "Making Sense of the Heaven's Gate Suicides." In *Cults, Religion and Violence*, edited by David G. Bromley and J. Gordon Melton.

Baldwin, R. A. *The Jezreelites: The Rise and Fall of a Remarkable Prophetic Movement.* Orpington: Lambarde Press, 1961.

Balleine, G. R. *Past Finding Out: The Tragic Story of Joanna Southcott and her Successors.* London: SPCK, 1956.

Banura, G., C. Tuhirirwe, and J. Begumanya. "Kanungu Research Team's Report." In *The Kanungu Cult-Saga: Suicide, Murder, or Salvation?* edited by S. Kabazzi-Kisirinya, D. R. K. Nkurunziza, and G. Banura. Uganda: Department of Religious Studies, Makere University, 2000.

Barker, Eileen. "New Religious Movements. Yet Another Great Awakening?" In *The Sacred in a Secular Age*, edited by Phillip B. Hammond.

——, ed. *Of Gods and Men: New Religious Movements in the West.* Macon, Ga.: Mercer University Press, 1983.

Barkun, M. "Introduction: Understanding Millennialism," *Terrorism and Political Violence* 7, no. 3 (1995).

——, ed. *Millennialism and Violence.* London: Frank Cass, 1996.

——. *Religion and the Racist Right: The Origin of the Christian Identity Movement.* Chapel Hill: University of North Carolina Press, 1997.

Barr, James. *Beyond Fundamentalism.* Philadelphia: Westminster, 1984.

——. *Fundamentalism.* Philadelphia: Westminster, 1978.

Barth, Karl. *Church Dogmatics* I/2. Translated by G. T. Thomson and H. Knight. Edinburgh: T&T Clark, 1936.

——. *The Word of God and the Word of Man*, 1928. Translated by Douglas Horton. New York: Harper & Brothers, 1957.

Bartholomew, R. E., and G. S. Howard. *UFOs and Alien Contact.* Amherst, N.Y.: Prometheus Books, 1998.

Bashan Tidings to the Little Flock. Bashan Hill, Exeter, Mo.: The Universal Publishing Association, undated.

Bauckham, R., and T. Hart. *Hope Against Hope: Christian Eschatology in Contemporary Context.* London: Darton, Longman & Todd, 1999.

Bauman, Zygmunt. *The Individualized Society.* Cambridge: Polity, 2001.

Baumgarten, Albert I., ed. *Apocalyptic Time.* Leiden: Brill, 2000.

Beckford, J. "The Restoration of 'Power' to the Sociology of Religion." *Sociological Analysis* 44, no. 1 (1983).

Benz, Ernst. *Evolution and Christian Hope: Man's Concept of the Future from the Early Church Fathers to Teilhard de Chardin.* New York: Doubleday, 1966.

Berger, James. "Twentieth-century Apocalypse: Forecasts and Aftermaths." *Twentieth Century Literature* 46 (2000).

Blaising, Craig A., and D. L. Bock. *Progressive Dispensationalism: An Up-to-date Handbook of Contemporary Dispensational Thought.* Wheaton: Bridgepoint, 1993.

Blake, William. *The Complete Poetry and Prose of William Blake.* Edited by David Erdman. Berkeley: University of California Press, 1982.

Bloch, Ruth. *Visionary Republic.* New York: Cambridge University Press, 1985.

Borst, Brad. Press release, April 17, 2003. http://www.anycities.com/mtcarmel/BradPress.htm

——. "The Facts about Waco." http://www.wacofacts.com. Accessed October 3, 2003.

——. Interview, October 27, 2003.

Boswell, James. *Life of Johnson*. Edited by G. B. Hill, revised by L. F. Powell. 6 vols. Oxford: Clarendon, 1934–1950.

Boyer, Paul. *When Time Shall Be No More: Prophecy Belief in Modern American Culture*. Cambridge, Mass.: The Belknap Press of Harvard University Press, 1992.

Brasher, Brenda. *Godly Women: Fundamentalism and Female Power*. New Brunswick, N.J.: Rutgers University Press, 1998.

——. "Semiotically Aroused: Through the Looking Glass of Millennial Studies." Paper presented to the Social Science History Association in a special panel entitled "Presidential Session: Social Science History Views the Millennium," Pittsburgh, Pa., October 26, 2000.

Bright, Martin. "Powell Caught up in Row over Neo-con 'Crazies.'" *The Observer*, September 12, 2004.

Brnody. "Up the Chain." http://heavensgatetoo.com/exitchk.htm. Accessed August 26, 1999.

Brockington, J. *The Sacred Thread: Hinduism in its Continuity and Diversity*. Edinburgh: Edinburgh University Press, 1981.

Brodhead, Richard H. "Millennium Prophecy and the Energies of Social Transformation: The Case of Nat Turner." In Amanat and Bernhardsson, *Imagining the End*.

Bromley, David G. "Dramatic Denouements." In *Cults, Religion, and Violence*, edited by D. G. Bromley and J. Gordon Melton. Cambridge: Cambridge University Press, 2002.

——. "Violence and New Religious Movements." In Lewis, *The Oxford Handbook of New Religious Movements*.

Bromley, David G., and J. Gordon Melton, eds. *Cults, Religion and Violence*. Cambridge: Cambridge University Press, 2002.

Brooks, David. "One Nation, Slightly Divisible." *Atlantic Monthly*, December 2001.

Brothers, Richard. *Revealed Knowledge of the Prophecies and Times*. London, 1794.

Brower, K. E., and M. W. Elliot, eds. *"The Reader Must Understand": Eschatology in Bible and Theology*. Leicester: Apollos, 1997.

Brown, Frances. *Joanna Southcott: The Woman Clothed with the Sun*. Cambridge: Lutterworth Press, 2002.

Bruce, S. *Religion in Modern Britain*. Oxford: Oxford University Press, 1995.

Burrow, J. W. *The Crisis of Reason: European Thought, 1848–1914*. London and New Haven: Yale University Press, 2000.

Buttrick, G. A. et al., eds. *The Interpreter's Bible*. New York: Abingdon, 1952.

Byrhtferth's Manual. Edited by S. J. Crawford, Early English Text Society, Original Series 177. London: Oxford University Press, 1972.

Caldwell, J. R. "The Times of the Gentiles." *The Witness* 44 (1914).

Carey, John, ed. *Essays.* London: Everyman, 2002.

Caron, R., J. Godwin, W. J. Hanegraaf, and J.-L. Vieillard-Baron, eds. *Esotérisme, gnoses et imaginaire symbolique Mélanges offerts à Antoine Faivre.* Leuven: Peeters, 2001.

Carpenter, Joel A. *Revive Us Again: The Reawakening of American Fundamentalism.* New York: Oxford University Press, 1997.

Carroll, Robert P. *When Prophecy Failed: Reactions and Responses to Failure in the Old Testament Prophetic Traditions.* New York: Seabury Press, 1979.

Casanova, Jose. *Public Religions in the Modern World.* Chicago: University of Chicago Press, 1994.

Catechism of the Catholic Church. Dublin: Veritas, 1994.

Cattau, Daniel. "Davidians in Missouri Disavow Waco-area Cult." *Dallas Morning News,* March 14, 1993.

Chalfont, H., R. Beckley, and C. Palmer. *Religion in Contemporary Society.* Palo Alto, Calif.: Maxfield Publishing, 1987.

Charlton, Donald. *Secular Religions in France 1815–1870.* London: Oxford University Press for University of Hull Publications, 1963.

Chidester, D. *Salvation and Suicide: An Interpretation of Jim Jones, the Peoples Temple, and Jonestown.* Bloomington: Indiana University Press, 1988.

The Children of Waco. Jude Dratt and Jennifer Lew Goldstone, producers. *Primetime: Witness: The Children of Waco.* Television broadcast. New York: ABC News, April 17, 2003.

Chkody. "Earth Exit Statement." http://www.heavensgate.com/misc/exitchk. htm.

———. "The Hidden Facts of Ti and Do." http://heavensgatetoo.com/ exitchk.htm. Accessed August 26, 1999.

Christian Israelite Church. *Doctrinal Articles of the Christian Israelite Church.* Privately published in Australia, 1983.

———. *The Hope of Life of the Body.* Privately published in Australia, 1983.

Chryssides, G. D. "Scientific Creationism: A Study of the Raëlian Church." In Partridge, *UFO Religions.*

Clements, Keith. *Faith on the Frontier: A Life of J. H. Oldham.* Edinburgh: T&T Clark; Geneva: WCC, 1999.

Coad, F. R. *A History of the Brethren Movement.* Second edition, Exeter: Paternoster Press, 1976.

———. *Prophetic Developments with Particular Reference to the Early Brethren Movement*. Pinner, Middlesex: Christian Brethren Research Fellowship, 1966.

Cohn, Norman. *Cosmos, Chaos and the World to Come: The Ancient Roots of Apocalyptic Faith*. New Haven: Yale University Press, 1993.

———. *The Pursuit of the Millennium: Revolutionary Millenarians and Mystical Anarchists of the Middle Ages*. Fairlawn, N.J.: Secker & Warburg, 1957. Second edition, London: Pimlico, 1993.

Cole, Kyle. "Are We Public Educators: A Discussion with Journalists of Religion." Remarks during a panel session by the Society for the Scientific Study of Religion. Norfolk, Va., October 25, 2003.

Coleman, John A., SJ. "Catholic Integralism as Fundamentalism." In Kaplan, *Fundamentalism in Comparative Perspective*.

Colson, Charles and R. J. Neuhaus. "Evangelicals and Catholics Together: The Christian Mission in the Third Millennium." *First Things* 43 (May 1994): 15–22.

"The Coming of the Lord." *The Witness* 46 (1916).

"Commandment of the Law and Testimony." Ashton-under-Lyne: Christian Israelite Press, undated.

Committee of the Judiciary. *Activities of Federal Law Enforcement Agencies toward the Branch Davidians (Part I)*. Serial No. 72. Washington, D.C.: U.S. Government Printing Office, 1995.

Continuity and Discontinuity: Perspectives on the Relationship between Old and New Testaments. (*Essays Presented in Honor of S. Lewis Johnson Jr.*). Westchester, Ill.: Crossway Books, 1988.

Cooper, J. *Body, Soul and Life Everlasting: Biblical Anthropology and the Monism-Dualism Debate*. Grand Rapids: Eerdmans, 2000.

Cowell, Alan, and David L. Halbfinger. "A Plot Seen Behind Every Door: Conspiracy Theorists Take Global Viewpoint." *The New York Times*, July 13, 2004.

Cox, H. *Fire from Heaven*. Reading, Mass.: Addison-Wesley, 1994.

Crutchfield, Larry V. "Early Church Fathers and the Foundations of Dispensationalism." www.tyndale.edu/dirn/source/theology.htm.

———. *The Origins of Dispensationalism: The Darby Factor*. Lenden, Md.: University Press of America, 1992.

———. "Rudiments of Dispensationalism in the Ante-Nicene Period." *Bibliotheca Sacra* 144, no. 576 (1987).

Cuneo, Michael W. *The Smoke of Satan: Conservative and Traditionalist Dissent in American Catholicism*. New York: Oxford University Press, 1997.

Dalhouse, Mark Taylor. *An Island in the Lake of Fire: Bob Jones University, Separatism and the Fundamentalist Movement.* Athens: University of Georgia Press, 1996.

Daniels, Ted. *Millennialism: An International Bibliography.* New York: Taylor & Francis, 1992.

Dart, John. *Deities and Deadlines: A Primer on Religion News Coverage.* Second edition, Nashville: First Amendment Center, 1998.

Davenport, Rowland A. *Albury Apostles, the Story of the Body Known as the Catholic Apostolic Church.* [Birdup]: United Writers, 1970.

Davenport-Hines, Richard. *Sex, Death, and Punishment: Attitudes to Sex and Sexuality in Britain since the Renaissance.* Glasgow: Fontana Collins, 1991.

Davidson, Lawrence. "Christian Zionism as a Representation of American Manifest Destiny." *Critique: Critical Middle Eastern Studies* 14, no. 2 (2005).

Davie, Grace. *Religion in Britain Since 1945: Believing without Belonging.* Oxford: Blackwell, 1994.

Davis, Mike. *Ecology of Fear: Los Angeles and the Imagination of Disaster.* New York: Metropolitan Books, 1998.

Dawson, L. L. *Comprehending Cults: The Sociology of New Religious Movements.* Oxford: Oxford University Press, 1998.

——. "Crises of Charismatic Legitimacy and Violent Behavior in New Religious Movements." In Bromley and Melton, *Cults, Religion, and Violence.*

——, ed. *Cults and New Religious Movements: A Reader.* Oxford: Blackwell, 2003 [1999].

——, ed. *Cults in Context: Readings in the Study of New Religious Movements.* London: Transaction Publishers, 1998 [1982].

D'Costa, G. "Theology of Religions." In Ford, *The Modern Theologians.*

Demy, Timothy J., and Thomas D. Ice. "The Rapture, an Early Medieval Citation." *Bibliotheca Sacra* 152, no. 607 (1995).

Devereaux, P., and P. Brookesmith. *UFOs and Ufology: The First Fifty Years.* London: Blandford, 1998.

Dixon, Larry. "The Importance of J. N. Darby and the Brethren Movement in the History of Conservative Theology." *Christian Brethren Review* 41 (1990).

Docherty, Jayne Seminare. *Learning Lessons from Waco: When the Parties Bring their Gods to the Negotiation Table.* Religion and Politics Series, Syracuse, N.Y.: Syracuse University Press, 2001.

Dostoyevsky, Fyodor. *The Brothers Karamazov.* Translated by Richard Pevear and Larissa Volokhonsky. New York: Knopf, 1992.

Doyle, Thomas M. "Competing Fictions: The Uses of Christian Apocalyptic Imagery in Contemporary Popular Fictional Works." *Journal of Millennial Studies* 1, no. 1 (2001).

Dunlap, Dave. "The Origins of the Scofield Bible." *Uplook*, July–August 1999.

Durkheim, E. *The Elementary Forms of the Religious Life*. London: Allen & Unwin, 1915.

Edelman, Bryan, and James T. Richardson. "Falun Gong and the Law: Development of Legal Social Control in China." *Nova Religio: The Journal of Alternative and Emergent Religions* 6, no. 2 (2003).

Ehlert, Arnold D. *A Bibliographic History of Dispensationalism*. Grand Rapids: Baker Book, 1965.

Elbert, P. "Renewal Movement 'Losing the War.'" *Eternity* 33, November 1981.

England, Mark, and Darlene McCormick. "Sinful Messiah" series, *Waco Tribune-Herald*, February 27–March 1, 1993.

Erdman, David V. *William Blake: Prophet against Empire*. Princeton: Princeton University Press, 1970.

Extracts from the Flying Roll. Sarah Bone edition, undated.

Farmer, H. H. "The Bible: Its Significance and Authority." In Buttrick et al., *The Interpreter's Bible*, vol. 1.

Federal Bureau of Investigation (FBI). Project Megiddo. http://permanent.access.gpo.gov/lps3578/www.fbi.gov/library/Megiddo/megiddo.pdf. 1999.

Feinberg, C., ed. *Millenarianism*. Chicago: Malstrom, 1936.

Feinberg, John S. "Systems of Discontinuity." In *Continuity and Discontinuity: Perspectives on the Relationship between Old and New Testaments. (Essays Presented in Honor of S. Lewis Johnson Jr.)*. Westchester, Ill.: Crossway Books, 1988.

Fenton, William N., ed. *Parker on the Iroquois*. Syracuse, N.Y.: Syracuse University Press, 1968.

Ferguson, Franklin. "The War and the Coming." *The Witness* 46 (1916).

Festinger, Leon, H. W. Riecken, and S. Schachter. *When Prophecy Fails: A Social and Psychological Study*. Minneapolis: University of Minnesota Press, 1956.

Fineman, Howard. "Apocalyptic Politics." *Newsweek*, U.S. ed., May 24, 2004.

Fitzer, Joseph, ed. *Romance and the Rock: Nineteenth-century Catholics on Faith and Reason*, Fortress Texts in Modern Theology. Minneapolis: Fortress Press, 1989.

Fitzgerald, Frances. *Cities on a Hill: A Journey through Contemporary American Cultures*. New York: Simon & Schuster, 1981.

Flegg, C. G. *"Gathered under Apostles": A Study of the Catholic Apostolic Church*. Oxford: Oxford University Press, 1992.

Flood, G. *An Introduction to Hinduism*. Cambridge: Cambridge University Press, 1996.

Ford, D. F., ed. *The Modern Theologians*. Second edition, Oxford: Blackwell, 1997.

Forsyth, P. T. *The Person and Place of Jesus Christ*. London: Independent Press, 1909.

Fowler, Robert Booth, Allen D. Hertzke, and Laura R. Olson. *Religion and Politics in America: Faith, Culture and Strategic Choices*. Second edition, Boulder: Westview Press, 1999.

Frank, Eric. "A Survey of Early Pre-millennialism." *WRS Journal* 2, no. 1 (1995).

Frank, Thomas. *What's the Matter with America: The Resistible Rise of the American Right*. London: Secker & Warburg, 2004.

Franken, Al. *Lies and the Lying Liars Who Tell Them: A Fair and Balanced Look at the Right*. London: Allen Lane, 2003.

Frye, Northrop. *Fearful Symmetry*. Princeton: Princeton University Press, 1965.

Frykholm, Amy Johnson. *Rapture Culture: Left Behind in Evangelical America*. New York: Oxford University Press, 2004.

Fulop, Timothy E., and Albert J. Raboteau, eds. *African-American Religion: Interpretive Essays in History and Culture*. New York: Routledge, 1997.

Gaebelein, Arno C. *The History of the Scofield Reference Bible*. Spokane, Wash: Living Words Foundation, 1991.

Gairdner, W. H. T. *Edinburgh 1910: An Account and Interpretation of the World Missionary Conference*. Edinburgh and London: Oliphant, Anderson & Ferrier, 1910.

Galanter, M. *Cults: Faith, Healing, and Coercion*. Second edition, Oxford: Oxford University Press, 1989.

Gallagher, Eugene V. "'Theology Is Life and Death': David Koresh on Violence, Persecution, and the Millennium." In Wessinger, *Millennialism, Persecution, and Violence*.

Gallie, W. B. *Philosophy and the Historical Understanding*. London: Chatto & Windus, 1964.

Gates, David, with David J. Jefferson, and Anne Underwood. "The Pop Prophets." *Newsweek*, U.S. edn., May 24, 2004.

Gerth, H. H., and C. W. Mills, eds. *From Max Weber: Essays in Sociology*. London: Routledge, 1991.

Glnody. "Earth Exit Statement." www.heavensgate.com/misc/exitgln.htm. 1997.

——. "WARNING: For Those Prone to Hasty Judgments." http://www. heavensgatetoo.com/exitchk.htm. Accessed August 26, 1999.

God's Battle and the Weapons of War. Bashan Hill, Exeter, Mo.: The Universal Publishing Association, undated.

Goldberg, Carey, and Marjorie Connelly. "For Better or Worse, Israel is 'Special' in U.S. Eyes." *New York Times*, April 26, 1998.

Goode, William. *Charismatic Confusion: A Reprint of the Modern Claims to the Possession of the Extraordinary Gifts of the Spirit*. Third edition, 1934. Trelawnyd: K & M Books, 2000.

Gould, Stephen Jay. *Rocks of Ages: Science and Religion in the Fullness of Life*. London: Vintage, 2002.

Graham, Billy. "My Answer." *The Daily Oklahoman*, April 12, 2002.

Green, Glenn, Sidney Smith, and Bonnie Smith. Interview, February 1, 1989. Draft copies at the Institute for Oral History, Baylor University, Waco, Tex..

Gribben, Crawford. "Before *Left Behind*." *Books & Culture*, July/August 2003.

——. *Rapture Fiction and the Evangelical Crisis*. Auburn, Mass.: Evangelical Press, 2006.

——. *The Puritan Millennium*. Dublin: Four Courts Press, 2000.

——. "Rapture Fictions and the Changing Evangelical Condition." *Literature and Theology* 18, no. 1 (March 2004).

Hall, John R. *Gone from the Promised Land: Jonestown in American Cultural History*. London: Transaction Publishers, 1989.

——. "Public Narratives and the Apocalyptic Sect: From Jonestown to Mt. Carmel." In Wright, *Armageddon in Waco*.

Hall, John R., P. D. Schuyler, and S. Trinh. *Apocalypse Observed: Religious Movements and Violence in North America, Europe, and Japan*. London: Routledge, 2000.

Hall, Michael. "The Ghosts of Mount Carmel." *Texas Monthly*, April 2003.

Hamilton, M. "Sociological Dimensions of Christian Millenarianism." Hunt, *Christian Millenarianism*.

Hammond, P., ed. *The Sacred in a Secular Age*. Berkeley: University of California Press, 1985.

Hancock, Lee. "2 Pyrotechnic Devices Fired at Davidians, Ex-official Says." *Dallas Morning News*, August 24, 1999.

——."Agents Reach Settlement in Waco Court." *Dallas Morning News*, October 18, 1996.

——. "FBI Missteps Doomed Siege Talks, Memos Say." *Dallas Morning News*, December 30, 1999.

Hanegraaff, Wouter J. *New Age Religion and Western Culture: Esotericism in the Mirror of Secular Thought*. Leiden/New York/Köln: Brill, 1996.

Harnack, Adolf von. *What Is Christianity?* English translation, 1901, with an introduction by Rudolf Bultmann. New York: Harper & Brothers, 1957.

——. *History of Dogma*. London: Williams & Norgat, 1894.

Harris, H. "Protestant Fundamentalism." In Partridge, *Fundamentalisms*.

Harrison, J. F. C. *The Second Coming: Popular Millenarianism 1780–1850*. London: Routledge and Kegan Paul, 1979.

Has the Judgment for the Living Commenced. Yucaipa, Calif.: The Universal Publishing Association, undated.

Hassan, Steve. *Combating Cult Mind Control*. Rochester, Vt.: Park Street Press, 1990.

Heaven's Gate. "'95 Statement by an E. T. Present Incarnate." http://www.wave.net/upg/gate/index.htm. Accessed April 12, 2004.

——. "Bible Quotes Primarily from Previous Representatives to Earth from the Evolutionary Level above Human." http://www.heavensgatetoo.com/. Accessed August 26, 1999.

——. "Crew from the Evolutionary Level above Human Offers Last Chance to Advance Beyond Human." http://www.wave.net/upg/gate/index.htm. Accessed April 12, 2004.

——. "Our Position against Suicide." http://www.wave.net/upg/gate/index.htm. Accessed April 12, 2004.

——. "The UFO Two and their Crew." In Lewis, *Encyclopedic Sourcebook of UFO Religions*.

Hegarty, Shane. "God's Running Mate?" *Irish Times*, Weekend Review, September 4, 2004.

Hegel, Georg Wilhelm Friedrich. *The Philosophy of History*. Translated by J. Sibree. New York: Dover, 1956.

Herman, Edward S., and Noam Chomsky. *Manufacturing Consent: The Political Economy of the Mass Media*. New York: Pantheon Books, 1988.

Hertzler, Daniel. "Assessing the 'Left Behind' Phenomenon." In Johns, *Apocalypticism and Millennialism*.

Herzl, Theodor. *The Jewish State: An Attempt at a Modern Solution of the Jewish Question*. London: Zionist Organization, 1936.

Hibbert, Tony. *Before the Flames: Story of David Koresh and the Davidian Seventh-day Adventists*. New York: Seaburn Publishing, 1996.

Hick, J. *Evil and the Love of God.* London: Macmillan, 1966.

Hill, Charles. *Regnum Caelorum: Patterns of Future Hope in Early Christianity.* Oxford: Oxford University Press, 1992.

Hill, Christopher. *Antichrist in Seventeenth-Century England.* London: Oxford University Press 1971; London: Verso, 1990.

——. "John Mason and the End of the World." In *Puritanism and Revolution.* London: Secker & Warburg, 1958.

——. "John Reeve and the Origins of Muggletonianism." In Hill, Reay, and Lamont, *The World of the Muggletonians.*

Hill, Christopher, Barry Reay, and William Lamont. *The World of the Muggletonians.* London: Maurice Temple Smith, 1983.

Hitchcock, Mark. *Is the Antichrist Alive Today?* Sisters, Ore.: Multnomah Publishers, 2002.

Hocken, P. *Streams of Renewal: Origins and Early Development of the Charismatic Movement in Great Britain.* Exeter: Paternoster, 1986.

Hofstadter, Richard. *Anti-Intellectualism in American Life.* New York: Knopf, 1963.

Hood, W. *The Plan of the Apocalypse.* York, Pa.: Anstadt, 1990.

Hopkins, C. Howard. *John R. Mott: 1865–1955: A Biography.* Geneva: WCC; Grand Rapids: Eerdmans, 1979.

Hopkins, J. K. *A Woman to Deliver Her People: Joanna Southcott and English Millenarianism in an Era of Revolution.* Austin: University of Texas Press, 1982.

House of Representatives. *Investigation into the Activities of Federal Law Enforcement Agencies toward the Branch Davidians: Thirteenth Report by the Committee on Government Reform and Oversight Prepared in Conjunction with the Committee on the Judiciary together with Additional and Dissenting Views.* Washington, D.C.: U.S. Government Printing Office, 1996.

Houteff, Victor. *Fundamental Beliefs and Directory of the Davidian Seventh-day Adventists,* 1943.

——. *Mount Zion at the Eleventh Hour,* 1937.

——. *The Shepherd's Rod,* 1930–32.

"How Effective Are Abstinence Pledges?" http://news.bbc.co.uk/1/hi/magazine/3846687.stm.

Huebner, R. A. *Precious Truths Revived and Defended Through J. N. Darby,* vol. 1. Morganville, N.J.: Present Truth Publishers, 1991.

——. *The Truth of the Pre-Tribulation Rapture Recovered.* Millington, N.J.: Present Truth Publishers, 1976.

Hue-Tam Ho Tai. *The Alpha Enterprise: Evangelism in the Post-Christian Era.* London: Ashgate, 2004.

———. *Millenarianism and Peasant Politics in Vietnam*. Cambridge, Mass., 1993.

Hunt, S. *Anyone for Alpha: Evangelism in a Post-Christian Society*. London: Darton, Longman & Todd, 2001.

———, ed. *Christian Millenarianism: From the Early Church to Waco*. London: Hurst Publishers, 2001.

———. "'Doing the Stuff': The Vineyard Connection." In Hunt, Hamilton, and Walter, *Charismatic Christianity*.

———. "Letting the Devil Get More than his Due. Some Problems with the Deliverance Ministry." In Walker, *Harmful Religion*.

———. "The Radical Kingdom of the Jesus Fellowship." *Pneuma* 20, no. 1 (1998).

———. "The Rise, Fall and Return of Post-millenarianism," in Hunt, *Christian Millenarianism*.

———. "The 'Toronto Blessing': A Rumor of Angels." *The Journal of Contemporary Religion* 10, no. 3 (1995).

Hunt, S., M. Hamilton, and T. Walter, eds. *Charismatic Christianity: Sociological Perspectives*. Basingstoke: Macmillan, 1997.

Ice, Thomas. "Dispensationalism, Date-setting, and Distortion." *Biblical Perspectives* I, no. 5 (1988). http://www.prestoncitybible.org/BP/3D.htm.

———. "Why the Doctrine of the Pretribulational Rapture Did Not Begin with Margaret Macdonald." *Bibliotheca Sacra* 147 (1990).

Introvigne, M. "The Magic of Death: The Suicides of the Solar Temple." In Wessinger, *Millennialism, Persecution and Violence*.

Jelen, Ted G. "Dimension of Religious Free Exercise: Abstract Beliefs and Concrete Applications." *Review of Religious Research* 40, no. 4 (1999).

Jenkins, Jerry B. *Soon: The Beginning of the End*. London: Hodder & Stoughton, 2003.

Jenkins, Philip. *The Next Christendom: The Coming of Global Christianity*. Oxford: Oxford University Press, 2002.

Jezreel, James Jershom. *The Flying Roll*. London, 1879.

Johns, Loren L., ed. *Apocalypticism and Millennialism: Shaping a Believers' Church Eschatology for the Twenty-first Century*. Kitchener, Ont.: Pandora Press, 2000.

Josephus: The Complete Works. Translated by William Whiston. Grand Rapids: Kregel Publications, 1978.

"Journalists Honored for In-Depth Reporting on Religion." *Religious Studies News* 18, no. 4, AAR ed. (2003).

Jung, C. G. *Flying Saucers: A Modern Myth of Things Seen in the Skies.* New York: Signet Books, 1969.

Jwnody. "Religions Are Humans #1 Killers of Souls." http://www.heavens gatetoo.com/exitchk.htm. Accessed August 26, 1999.

Kanter, R. M. "Commitment and Social Organization: A Study of Commitment Mechanisms in Utopian Communities." *American Sociological Review* 33, no. 4 (1968).

Kaplan, J. *Radical Religion in America: Millenarian Movements from the Far Right to the Children of Noah.* Syracuse, N.Y.: Syracuse University Press, 1997.

Kaplan, Lawrence, ed. *Fundamentalism in Comparative Perspective.* Amherst: University of Massachusetts Press, 1992.

Katz, David S., and Richard H. Popkin. *Messianic Revolution: Radical Religious Politics to the End of the Second Millennium.* New York: Hill & Wang, 1999.

Kelly, J. N. D. *Early Christian Doctrines.* Fifth edition, London: Adam & Charles Black, 1977.

Kippenberg, Hans. "The Restoration of Israel as Messianic Birth Pangs." In Baumgarten, *Apocalyptic Time.*

Kirban, Salem. *1000.* Chattanooga, Tenn.: Future Events Publications, 1973.

Klausner, J. *The Messianic Idea in Israel.* London: George Allen & Unwin, 1956.

Kleinhenz, C. and F. J. LeMoine, eds. *Fearful Hope: Approaching the New Millennium.* Madison: University of Wisconsin Press, 1999.

Kodera, Takashi James. "Nichiren and his Nationalistic Eschatology." *Religious Studies* 15 (1979).

Kokosalakis, N. "Legitimation, Power, and Religion in Modern Society." *Sociological Analysis* 46, no. 4 (1985).

Kook, Rabbi Tzvi Yehuda. *Le-Netivot Yisraeli.* Jerusalem, 1967, 1:56.

Kosmin, Barry A., and Seymour P. Lachman. *One Nation Under God: Religion in Contemporary American Society.* New York: Harmony Books, 1993.

Kuhn, Thomas. *The Structure of Scientific Revolutions.* Chicago: University of Chicago Press, 1962.

Kuschel, Karl-Josef. *Born Before All Time? The Dispute over Christ's Origin.* English translation, 1990. London: SCM, 1992.

Jnnody. "Incarnating and Discarnating." http://www.heavensgatetoo.com /exitchk.htm. Accessed August 26, 1999.

LaHaye, Tim. "The Colossal Battle." *Esquire*, U.S. ed., September 2004.

LaHaye, Tim, and Jerry B. Jenkins. *Apollyon*. Wheaton: Tyndale, 1999.

———. *Are We Living in the End Times?* Wheaton: Tyndale, 1999.

———. *Armageddon*. Wheaton: Tyndale, 2003.

———. *Assassins*. Wheaton: Tyndale, 1999.

———. *Desecration*. Wheaton: Tyndale, 2001.

———. *The Glorious Appearing*. Wheaton: Tyndale, 2004.

———. *The Indwelling*. Wheaton: Tyndale, 2000.

———. *Left Behind: A Novel of Earth's Last Days*. Wheaton: Tyndale, 1995.

———. *The Mark*. Wheaton: Tyndale, 2000.

———. *Nicolae*: The Rise of Antichrist. Wheaton: Tyndale, 1997.

———. *The Remnant*. Wheaton: Tyndale, 2002.

———. *Soul Harvest: The World Takes Sides*. Wheaton: Tyndale, 1998.

———. *Tribulation Force: The Continuing Drama of those Left Behind*. Wheaton: Tyndale, 1996.

Lamott, Anne. "Knocking on Heaven's Door." In *Traveling Mercies: Some Thoughts on Faith*. New York: Pantheon, 1999.

Landes, Richard. *Heaven on Earth: The Varieties of the Millennial Experience*. Oxford University Press, forthcoming.

———. "Millennialism." In Lewis, *The Oxford Handbook of New Religious Movements*.

The Latter Rain. Bashan Hill, Exeter, Mo.: The Universal Publishing Association, undated.

Lawrence, P. *The Hotline*. Eastbourne: Kingsway, 1990.

Lebra, T. S. "Millenarian Movements and Resocialization." *American Behavioral Scientist* 16, no. 2 (1972).

Leib, Franklin Allen. *Behold a Pale Horse*. New York: Tom Doherty, 2000.

Levine, Robert. *Vale of Tears: Revisiting the Canudos Massacre in Northeastern Brazil*. Berkeley: University of California Press, 1992.

Lewis, James R., *Legitimating New Religions*. New Brunswick, N.J.: Rutgers University Press, 2003.

———. "Legitimating Suicide: Heaven's Gate and New Age Ideology." In Partridge, *UFO Religions*.

———. ed. *Encyclopedic Sourcebook of UFO Religions*. Amherst, N.Y.: Prometheus, 2003.

———, ed. *The Gods Have Landed: New Religions from other Worlds*. Albany: State University of New York Press, 1995.

———, ed. *The Oxford Handbook of New Religious Movements*. Oxford: Oxford University Press, 2004.

Lewis, James R., and Jesper Aagaard Petersen, eds. *Controversial New Religions*. New York: Oxford University Press, 2005.

Lienesch, Michael. *Redeeming America: Piety and Politics in the New Christian Right*. Chapel Hill: University of North Carolina Press, 1993.

Lifton, Robert J. *Destroying the World to Save it: Aum Shinrikyo, Apocalyptic Violence, and the New Global Terrorism*. New York: Henry Holt, 1999.

Lindsey, Hal. *The 1980s Countdown to Armageddon*. New York: Bantam, 1981.

——. *Amazing Grace*. Palos Verdes, Calif.: Western Front, 1996.

——. *The Apocalypse Code*. Palos Verdes, Calif.: Western Front, 1997.

——. *Blood Moon*. Palos Verdes, Calif.: Western Front, 1996.

——. *Combat Faith*. New York: Bantam Dell, 1986.

——. *The Final Battle*. Palos Verdes, Calif.: Western Front, 1995.

——. *Israel and the Last Days*. Eugene, Ore.: Harvest House, 1983.

——. *The Late Great Planet Earth*. London: Lakeland, 1970.

——. *The Liberation of Planet Earth*. London: Lakeland, 1974.

——. *Planet Earth 2000 A.D.* Palos Verdes, Calif.: Western Front, 1994 (revised 1996).

——. *Planet Earth: The Final Chapter*. Beverly Hills, Calif.: Western Front, 1998.

——. *The Promise*. Eugene, Ore.: Harvest House, 1982.

——. *A Prophetical Walk through the Holy Land*. Eugene, Ore.: Harvest House, 1983.

——. *The Rapture: Truth or Consequences*. New York: Bantam, 1983.

——. *The Road to Holocaust*. New York: Bantam, 1989.

——. *Satan Is Alive and Well on Planet Earth*. London: Lakeland, 1973.

——. *The Terminal Generation*. New York: Bantam, 1983.

——. *There's a New World Coming: A Prophetic Odyssey*. Santa Ana, Calif.: Vision House, 1973.

——. *The World's Final Hour: Evacuation or Extinction?* Grand Rapids: Zondervan, 1976.

Livermore, Mary. *My Story of the War*. Hartford, 1889. Reprint, New York: DaCapo Press, 1995.

Loisy, Alfred. *L'Évangile et l'Église*. Paris: Nourry, 1902.

Lowe, Victoria. "FBI Uses Briefings as a Tactical Weapon," *Dallas Morning News*, March 25, 1993.

Lvvody. "Ingredients of a Deposit—Becoming a New Creature." http://www.heavensgatetoo.com/exitchk.htm. Accessed August 26, 1999.

Lynch, Aaron. *Thought Contagion: How Belief Spreads through Society*. New York: Basic Books, 1999.

Maaga, M. M. *Hearing the Voices of Jonestown: Putting a Human Face on an American Tragedy*. New York: Syracuse University Press, 1998.

MacDonald, Andrew. *Hunter*. Hillsboro, W. Va.: National Vanguard Books, 1989.

MacDonald, William. "Y2K–Is This the Time?" *Uplook*, December 1999.

Macleod, David J. "Walter Scott, a Link in Dispensationalism between Darby and Scofield." *Bibliotheca Sacra* 153, no. 610 (1996).

MacPherson, Dave. *The Great Rapture Hoax*. Fletcher, N.C.: New Puritan Library, 1983.

——. *The Incredible Cover-Up*. Plainfield, N.J.: Logos International, 1975.

——. *The Late Great Pre-Trib Rapture*. Kansas City, Mo.: Heart of America Bible Society, 1974.

——. *Rapture?* Fletcher, N.C.: New Puritan Library, 1987.

——. *The Rapture Plot*. Simpsonville, S.C.: Millennium III Publishers, 1994.

——. *The Three R's: Rapture, Revisionism, Robbery*. Monticello, Utah: P.O.S.T., 1998.

——. *The Unbelievable Pre-Trib Origin*. Kansas City, Mo.: Heart of America Bible Society, 1973.

Maher, Robert F. "Tommy Kabu Movement of the Purari Delta." *Oceania* 29 (1958).

Mannheim, Karl. *Ideology and Utopia*. London: Routledge, 1936.

Markowitz, Fran. "(Still) Sacrificing for Salvation: Millenarian Motherhood Reconsidered." *Social Compass* 50, no. 1 (2003).

Marlowe, Lara. "'Regime Change Starts at Home,' Say Kansas Moderates," *Irish Times*, September 11, 2003.

Marsden, George M. *Jonathan Edwards: A Life*. New Haven: Yale University Press, 2003.

——. *Understanding Fundamentalism and Evangelicalism*. Grand Rapids: Eerdmans, 1991.

Martin, David. *The Dilemma of Contemporary Religion*. Oxford: Black-well, 1978.

——. *Tongues of Fire: The Explosion of Pentecostalism in Latin America*. Oxford: Blackwell, 1990.

Marty, Martin E., and R. Scott Appleby. *The Glory and the Power: The Fundamentalist Challenge to the Modern World*. Boston: Beacon Press, 1992.

Mathews, Basil. *John R. Mott: World Citizen*. London: SCM, 1934.

Maxwell, David, and Coy Smith. Report of Investigation, Texas Department of Public Safety, Criminal Law Enforcement Division, May 11, 1993.

Mayer, J.-F. "Apocalyptic Millennialism in the West: The Case of the Solar Temple." A presentation held on Friday, November 13, 1998, at the University of Virginia. http://www.healthsystem.virginia.edu/internet /ciag/reports/report_apoc_index.cfm.

——. "Cults, Violence and Religious Terrorism: An International Perspective." In *Studies in Conflict and Terrorism* 24 (2001).

——. "The Dangers of Enlightenment: Apocalyptic Hopes and Anxieties in the Order of the Solar Temple," in Caron, Godwin, Hanegraaf, and Vieillard-Baron, *Esotérisme, gnoses et imaginaire symbolique Mélanges offerts à Antoine Faivre.*

McAlister, Melani. "Prophecy, Politics and the Popular: The *Left Behind* Series and Christian Fundamentalism's New World Order." *South Atlantic Quarterly* 102, no. 4 (2003).

McBain, D., and S. Hunt. "Mainstream Charismatics: Some Observations of Baptist Renewal." In Hunt, Hamilton, and Walter, *Charismatic Christianity.*

McCool, Gerald A. *Catholic Theology in the Nineteenth Century: The Quest for a Unitary Method.* New York: Seabury, 1977.

McCormick, Darlene. "Howell's Mom Flees Home." *Waco Tribune-Herald,* March 2, 1993.

McCutcheon, R. T., ed. *The Insider/Outsider Problem in the Study of Religion.* London: Cassell, 1999.

Meacham, Jon. "The Editor's Desk." *Newsweek,* U.S. ed., May 24, 2004.

Melton, J. G., and D. G. Bromley. "Challenging Misconceptions about the New Religions-Violence Connection." In Bromley and Melton, *Cults, Religion, and Violence.*

Mendel, Arthur. *Vision and Violence.* Ann Arbor: University of Michigan Press, 1999.

Mercer, Joye. "For Fund Raisers at Religious Colleges, the Millennium Means Business as Usual." *The Chronicle of Higher Education,* January 15, 1999.

Micklethwait, John, and Adrian Wooldridge. *The Right Nation: Why America is Different.* London: Allen Lane, 2004.

Middlefort, Erik. "Madness and the Millennium at Münster, 1534–35." In Kleinhenz and LeMoine, *Fearful Hope.*

Miller, Andrew. *"The Brethren" (Commonly So-called), A Brief Sketch.* Dillenburg: Gute Botschaft Verlag, 1992.

Miller, Donald E. *Reinventing American Protestantism: Christianity in the New Millennium.* Berkeley: University of California Press, 1997.

Mills, E. W. "Cult Extremism: the Reduction of Normative Dissonance." In Dawson, *Cults in Context.*

Minutaglio, Bill, and Jeffrey Weiss. "Divided Davidian." *Dallas Morning News,* March 2, 1993.

Misztal, Bronislaw, and Anson Shupe, eds. *Religion, Mobilization, and Social Action.* Westport, Conn.: Praeger, 1998.

M'Murdo, Robert. "The Next Great Event: Or the Time of His Coming." *The Witness* 46 (1916).

Montgomery, R. *Aliens Among Us.* New York, Fawcett Crest, 1985.

Moore, Carol. *The Davidian Massacre: Disturbing Questions about Waco Which Must be Answered.* Franklin, Tenn., and Springfield, Va.: Legacy Communications and Gun Owners Foundation, 1995.

Moore, R. *A Sympathetic History of Jonestown: The Moore Family Involvement in Peoples Temple.* New York: Edwin Mellen, 1985.

Moore, R, A. B. Pinn, and M. R. Sawyer, eds. *Peoples Temple and Black Religion in America.* Bloomington: Indiana University Press, 2004.

Moore-Anderson, A. P. *Sir Robert Anderson, K.C.B., LL.D.: A Tribute and Memoir.* London: Morgan & Scott, 1919.

Morgan, Robert, and Michael Pye, eds. *Ernst Troeltsch: Writings on Theology and Religion.* Atlanta: John Knox Press, 1977.

Morone, James A. *Hellfire Nation: The Politics of Sin in American History.* New Haven: Yale University Press, 2003.

Muesse, Mark. "Religious Studies and 'Heaven's Gate': Making the Strange Familiar and the Familiar Strange." In McCutcheon, *The Insider/Outsider Problem in the Study of Religion.*

Murray, Iain H. *The Puritan Hope.* Edinburgh: Banner of Truth Trust, 1971.

The Mystery Stone. Bashan Hill, Exeter, Mo.: The Universal Publishing Association, undated.

Naquin, Susan. *Millenarian Rebellion in China: The Eight Trigrams Rebellion.* New Haven: Yale University Press, 1976.

Nebeker, Gary L. "John Nelson Darby and Trinity College, Dublin: A Study in Eschatological Contrasts." *Fides et Historia* 34, no. 2 (2002).

Netland, H. *Dissonant Voices: Religious Pluralism and the Question of Truth.* Leicester: Apollos, 1991.

Newport, Kenneth G. C. *Apocalypse and Millennium: Studies in Biblical Eisegesis.* Cambridge: Cambridge University Press, 2000.

———. *The Branch Davidians of Waco: The History and Beliefs of an Apocalyptic Sect.* Oxford: Oxford University Press, 2006.

Niebuhr, H. Richard. *Christ and Culture.* London: Faber & Faber, 1952.

Nietzsche, Friedrich. *Genealogy of Morals.* Oxford: Oxford University Press, 1996.

Noble, David. *The Religion of Technology: The Divinity of Man and the Spirit of Invention.* New York: Knopf, 1998.

Noll, Mark. *The Scandal of the Evangelical Mind.* Leicester: InterVarsity, 1994.

North, Gary. "Publisher's Preface." In D. Wilson, *Armageddon Now!*

O'Leary, Stephen D. *Arguing the Apocalypse: A Theory of Millennial Rhetoric.* Oxford: Oxford University Press, 1994.

Oliphant, Mrs. M. O. W. *The Life of Edward Irving.* 2 vols. Second edition, London, 1862.

Orwell, George. "Wells, Hitler and the World State." In Carey, *Essays.*

Palmer, S. J. "Purity and Danger in the Solar Temple." *Journal of Contemporary Religion* 11, no. 3 (1996).

Parker, Arthur C. "The Code of Handsome Lake, the Seneca Prophet." In Fenton, *Parker on the Iroquois.*

Partridge, C. "Alien Demonology: The Christian Roots of the Malevolent Extraterrestrial in UFO Religions and Abduction Spiritualities." *Religion* 34 (2004).

——. *H. H. Farmer's Theological Interpretation of Religion: Towards a Personalist Theology of Religions.* Lewiston, N.Y.: Edwin Mellen, 1998.

——. "Understanding UFO Religions and Abduction Spiritualities." In Partridge, *UFO Religions.*

——, ed. *Fundamentalisms.* Carlisle: Paternoster, 2001.

——, ed. *UFO Religions.* London: Routledge, 2003.

Patrides, C. "Renaissance and Modern Thought on the Last Things: A Study in Changing Conceptions." *Harvard Theological Review* L, no. 93 (1958).

Patterson, Mark, and Andrew Walker, "'Our Unspeakable Comfort': Irving, Albury, and the Origins of the Pretribulation Rapture." *Fides et Historia* 31, no. 1 (1999).

Peace Now. http://www.peacenow.org.il/site/en/peace.asp?pi=58. Accessed February 20, 2005.

Peires, J. B. *The Dead Will Arise.* Johannesburg: Ravan Press, 1989.

Pelikan, Jaroslav. *Credo: Historical and Theological Guide to Creeds and Confessions of Faith in the Christian Tradition.* New Haven: Yale University Press, 2003.

Pentecost, J. Dwight. *Things to Come: A Study in Biblical Eschatology.* 1958. Grand Rapids: Zondervan, 1964.

Percy, M. *Words, Wonders, and Power.* London: SPCK, 1997.

Peters, T. "UFOs, Heaven's Gate, and the Theology of Suicide." In Lewis, *Encyclopedic Sourcebook of UFO Religions.*

Peterson, Eric. *Der Monotheismus als politisches Problem; ein Beitrag zur Geschichte der politischenTheologie im Imperium Romanum.* Leipzig: Hegner, 1935.

Pickering, Hy. "The World at War." *The Witness* 44 (1914).

Pipes, Daniel. "The New Anti-Semitism." Philadelphia Jewish Exponent, January 1998.

Pitts, William. "Davidians and Branch Davidians: 1929–1987." In S. Wright, *Armageddon in Waco*.

Poloma, M. *Main Street Mystics: The Toronto Blessing and Reviving Pentecostalism*. New York: Altamira, 2003.

Porter, S., and P. Richter, eds. *The Toronto Blessing, Or Is It?* London: Darton, Longman & Todd, 1995.

Price, Randall. *Jerusalem in Prophecy: God's Stage for the Final Drama*. Eugene, Ore.: Harvest House Publishers, 1998.

Profile: John Ashcroft. http://news.bbc.co.uk/1/hi/world/americas/1120440.stm.

Protocols of the Meetings of the Learned Elders of Zion. Translated by Victor E. Mars. London: Briton Publishing Society, 1920.

Quinby, Lee. *Anti-Apocalypse: Exercises in Genealogical Criticism*. Minneapolis: University of Minnesota Press, 1994.

Race, A. *Christians and Religious Pluralism*. Second edition, London: SCM, 1994.

Rail, Harrison Franklin. "Where Premillennialism Leads." *The Biblical World* 53 (1919).

Ravitzky, Aviezer. *Messianism, Zionism, and Jewish Religious Radicalism*. Translated by Michael Swirsky and Jonathan Chipman. Chicago: University of Chicago Press, 1996.

Rawls, Wendell. "Debacle at Waco: Print and Broadcast, National and Local, Journalism Displayed its Unseemly Side." *Nieman Reports*, Summer 1993.

Reader, I. *Religious Violence in Contemporary Japan: The Case of Aum Shinrikyo*. Surrey: Curzon, 2000.

ReligionLink. http://www.religionwriters.com/public/tips/main.shtml. Accessed November 14, 2003.

Religion Newswriters Foundation, *A Guide to Religion Reporting in the Secular Media: Frequently Asked Questions*. Westerville, Ohio: Religion Newswriters Foundation, 2002.

Religionsource. http://www.religionsource.org. Accessed November 12, 2003.

Rendles, David. *Hitler and the Apocalypse Complex: Salvation and the Spiritual Power of Nazism*. New York: New York University Press, 2001.

Report of a Leadership Consultation on the Current Situation in the Charismatic Churches. Sheffield, 1995.

Richardson, James T. "Manufacturing Consent about Koresh: A Structural Analysis of the Role of the Media in the Waco Tragedy." In S. Wright, *Armageddon in Waco*.

——. "Minority Religions and the Context of Violence: A Conflict/ Interactionist Perspective." *Terrorism and Political Violence* 13, no. 1 (2001).

——. "'Showtime' in Texas: Social Productions of the Branch Davidian Trials." *Nova Religio: The Journal of Alternative and Emergent Religions* 5, no. 1 (2001).

Richardson, James T., and Barend van Driel. "Journalists' Attitudes toward New Religious Movements." *Review of Religious Research* 39, no. 2 (1997).

Richter, P. "God Is Not a Gentleman." In Porter and Richter, *The Toronto Blessing, Or Is It?*

——. "The Toronto Blessing: the Charismatic Evangelical Global Warming." In Hunt, Hamilton, and Walter, *Charismatic Christianity*.

Robbins, T. "Sources of Volatility in Religious Movements." In Bromley and Melton, *Cults, Religion, and Violence*.

Robbins, T., and D. Anthony. "Sects and Violence: Factors Enhancing the Volatility of Marginal Religious Movements." In S. Wright, *Armageddon in Waco*.

Robbins, T., and S. J. Palmer, eds. *Millennium, Messiahs, and Mayhem: Contemporary Apocalyptic Movements*. New York: Routledge, 1997.

Robertson, Pat. *The New World Order*. Dallas: Word Publishing, 1991.

Robinson, Thomas. "Is this War 'Armageddon?'" *The Witness* 44 (1914).

Rogers, P. G. *The Sixth Trumpeter: The Story of Jezreel and his Tower*. London: Oxford University Press, 1963.

Román, R. L. "Christian Themes: Mainstream Traditions and Millenarian Violence." In Barkun, *Millennialism and Violence*.

Ronson, Jon. *Them: Adventures with Extremists*. London: Picador, 2001.

Rosenfeld, Jean E. "The Use of the Military at Waco: The Danforth Report in Context." *Nova Religio: The Journal of Alternative and Emergent Religions* 5, no. 1 (2001).

Ross, Robert. *So It Was True: The American Protestant Press and the Nazi Persecution of the Jews*. Minneapolis: University of Minnesota Press, 1980.

Rowdon, H. H. *The Origins of the Brethren 1825–1850*. London: Pickering & Inglis, 1967.

Rupp, George. *Culture-Protestantism: German Liberal Theology at the Turn of the Twentieth Century*. AAR Studies in Religion 15. Missoula, Mont.: Scholars Press, 1977.

Ryrie, Charles. *Dispensationalism*. Chicago: Moody, 1995.

Saether, George. "Oral Memoirs." Transcription held in the Texas Collection, Baylor University, Waco, Texas.

The Sanctuary Truth. Bashan Hill, Exeter, Mo.: The Universal Publishing Association, undated.

Sandeen, Ernest R. *The Roots of Fundamentalism: British and American Millenarianism 1800–1930*. Chicago: University of Chicago Press, 1970.

Schleiermacher, Friedrich. *The Christian Faith*. Second German edition translated into English and edited by H. R. Mackintosh and J. S. Stewart. Edinburgh: T&T Clark, 1928.

———. *On Religion: Speeches to its Cultured Despisers*. Texts in German Philosophy. Cambridge: Cambridge University Press, 1988.

Schofield, A. T. "Can Corsica Conquer Galilee?" *The Witness* 45 (1915).

Scofield, C. I. *The Scofield Reference Bible*. New York: Oxford University Press, 1917.

Scott, James C. *Domination and the Arts of Resistance*. New Haven: Yale University Press, 1989.

Sedgwick, Mark. *Against the Modern World: Traditionalism and the Secret Intellectual History of the Twentieth Century*. Oxford: Oxford University Press, 2004.

Sheler, Jeffery L., and Mike Tharp. "Dark Prophecies." *U.S. News and World Report*, December 15, 1997. Cited in Hitchcock, *Is the Antichrist Alive Today?*

Shepherdson, Nancy. "Writing for Godot." *Los Angeles Times*, Magazine, April 25, 2004.

Shimazono, S. "In the Wake of Aum: The Formation and Transformation of a Universe of Belief." *Japanese Journal of Religious Studies* 22, nos. 3–4 (1995).

Shupe, A. "Christian Reconstructionism and the Angry Rhetoric of Neo-postmillenarianism." In Robbins and Palmer, *Millennium, Messiahs, and Mayhem*.

Singer, M. *Cults in Our Midst: The Hidden Menace in our Everyday Lives*. San Francisco: Jossey-Bass, 1995.

Sizer, Stephen R. "Hal Lindsey: Father of Apocalyptic Christian Zionism." www.virginiawater.co.uk/christchurch/articles/hallindsey.htm.

Slvody. "Older Member, Younger Member: Their Relationship." http://www. heavensgatetoo.com/exitchk.htm. Accessed August 26, 1999.

Smail, Tom. "The Cross and the Spirit: Towards a Theology of Renewal." In Smail, Walker, and Wright, *Charismatic Renewal*.

Smail, Tom, Andrew Walker, and Nigel Wright, eds. *Charismatic Renewal: The Search for a Theology.* London: SPCK, 1995.

Smith, Tom W. "The Religious Right and Anti-Semitism." *Review of Religious Research* 40, no. 3 (1999).

Smmody. "T.E.L.A.H.–The Evolutionary Level above Human." http://www.heavensgatetoo.com/exitchk.htm. Accessed August 26, 1999.

Snnody. "Deposits." http://www.heavensgatetoo.com/exitchk.htm. Accessed August 26, 1999.

Sontag, Susan. "The Imagination of Disaster." In *Against Interpretation*, New York: Octagon, 1978.

Southcott, Joanna. Book 17: *A Word to the Wise or A Call to the Nation, That They May Know the Days of their Visitation, etc.* Stourbridge: J. Heming, 1803.

——. *The Strange Effects of Faith*, 1801.

Stanton, Gerald. *Kept from the Hour.* Fourth edition, Miami Springs, Fla.: Schoettle Publishing, 1991.

Steiger, B., and H. Hughes. *Inside Heaven's Gate.* New York: Penguin, Signet, 1997.

Steinberg, Jonathan. "One Man and his God." *Financial Times*, Weekend Magazine, June 12, 2004.

Steiner, George. *Grammars of Creation: Originating in the Gifford Lectures for 1990.* London: Faber & Faber, 2001.

Stevenson, J., ed. *A New Eusebius:Documents Illustrating the History of the Church to AD 337.* London: SPCK, 1987.

Stewart, Pamela and Andrew Strathern, eds. *Millennial Countdown in New Guinea. Ethnohistory* 47 (2000).

Stone, Huntington. "God's Voice to His People through the War." *The Witness* 44 (1914).

Stothard, Peter. "The Town of the Rising Son." *The Times*, Features Magazine, July 17, 2004.

Stunt, Timothy C. F. *From Awakening to Secession.* Edinburgh: T&T Clark, 2000.

——. "Irvingite Pentecostalism and the Early Brethren." *Christian Brethren Research Fellowship Journal* 10 (1965).

——. "The Tribulation of Controversy, a Review Article." *Brethren Archivists and Historians Network Review* 2, no. 2 (2003).

——. "'Trying the spirits': The Case of the Gloucester Clergyman (1831)." *Journal of Ecclesiastical History* 39, no.1 (1988).

Sykes, Stephen. *The Identity of Christianity: Theologians and the Essence of Christianity from Schleiermacher to Barth.* London: SPCK, 1984.

Tabor, James D., and Phillip Arnold. Audiotape of discussion of biblical prophecies on the Ron Engleman radio talk show, April 1, 1993.

Tabor, James D., and Eugene V. Gallagher. *Why Waco? Cults and the Battle for Religious Freedom in America*. Berkeley: University of California Press, 1995.

Talar, C. J. T. *Metaphor and Modernist: The Polarization of Alfred Loisy and his Neo-Thomist Critics*. Lanham, Md.: University Press of America, 1987.

Talmon, Jacob. *The Origins of Totalitarian Democracy*. New York: Praeger, 1960.

Talmon, Y. "Millenarian Movements." *Archives Européennes de Sociologie* 7 (1966).

Tarnas, Richard. *The Passion of the Western Mind: Understanding the Ideas that have Shaped our World View*. New York: Random House, 1991.

Tatford, Frederick A. *10 Nations–Now What?* Eastbourne: Upperton House, 1980.

———. *God's Programme of the Ages*. Grand Rapids: Kregel, 1967.

———. *Going into Europe: The Common Market and Prophecy*. Eastbourne: Prophetic Witness Publishers, 1971.

Tayler, Christopher. "Rapt Attention." *Times Literary Supplement*, May 7, 2004.

Taylor, Charles. *Hegel*. Cambridge: Cambridge University Press, 1975.

Thibodeau, D., and L. Whiteson. *A Place Called Waco: A Survivor's Story*. U.S.: Public Affairs, 1999.

Thompson, E. P. *"Witness Against the Beast": William Blake and the Moral Law*. Cambridge: Cambridge University Press, 1993.

Thompson, Keith. *Angels and Aliens: UFOs and the Mythic Imagination*. New York: Fawcett Columbine, 1991.

Thompson, William. "Charismatic Politics: The Social and Political Impact of Renewal." In Hunt, Hamilton, and Walter, *Charismatic Christianity*.

Tiger, Lionel. *Optimism: The Biology of Hope*. New York: Simon & Schuster, 1979.

The Timely Truth Educator. Bashan Hill, Exeter, Mo.: The Universal Publishing Association, undated.

Troeltsch, Ernst. "What Does 'Essence of Christianity' Mean?" In Morgan and Pye, *Ernst Troeltsch*.

Tucker, Robert. "The Theory of Charismatic Leadership." *Daedalus*, 1967.

Turner, George. *A Testimony to the Prophetical Mission of Richard Brothers*. London, 1795.

Turner, W. G. *John Nelson Darby*. London: C. A. Hammond, 1944.

Uganda Human Rights Commission, *The Kanungu Massacre: The Movement for the Restoration of the Ten Commandments of God Indicted*. Uganda: Uganda Human Rights Commission, 2002.

Vine, W. E. "The Future 'European Federation.' The Revival of the Roman Empire." *The Witness* 44 (1915).

——. "The Roman Empire in Prophecy." *The Witness* 45 (1915).

——. "The Roman Empire in the Light of Prophecy." In *The Collected Writings of W. E. Vine*. Vol. 5. Nashville: Thomas Nelson Publishers, 1996.

Wagner, Peter. *Warfare Prayer*. Ventura, Calif.: Regal Books, 1992.

Walker, A. "Pentecostal Power: The 'Charismatic Renewal Movement' and the Politics of Pentecostal Experience," in Barker, *Of Gods and Men*.

——. *Restoring the Kingdom: The Radical Christianity of the House Church Movement*. London: Hodder & Stoughton, 1985.

——. "Thoroughly Modern: Sociological Reflections on the Charismatic Movement from the End of the Twentieth Century." In Hunt, Hamilton, and Walter, *Charismatic Christianity*.

——, ed. *Harmful Religion*. London: SPCK, 1997.

Wallis, R. *Elementary Forms of the New Religious Life*. London: Routledge, 1984.

——. "Sex, Violence, and Religion." *Update: A Quarterly Journal of Religious Movements* 7, no. 4 (1983).

——, ed. *Millennialism and Charisma*. Belfast: Queen's University, 1982.

Wallis, R., and S. Bruce. *Sociological Theory, Religion and Collective Action*. Belfast: Queen's University, 1986.

Walliss, John. *Apocalyptic Trajectories: Millenarianism and Violence in the Contemporary World*. Bern: Peter Lang, 2004.

——. "Making Sense of the Movement for the Restoration of the Ten Commandments of God." Forthcoming in *Nova Religio*.

Weber, Max. "The Social Psychology of the World Religion." In Gerth and Mills *From Max Weber*.

——. "The Sociology of Charismatic Authority." In Gerth and Mills, *From Max Weber*.

——. *The Theory of Social and Economic Organization*. London: Collier-Macmillan, 1947.

Weber, Timothy P. "How Evangelicals Became Israel's Best Friend." *Christianity Today* 42, no. 11, October 5, 1998.

——. *Living in the Shadow of the Second Coming: American Pre-millennialism, 1875–1925*. Chicago: University of Chicago Press, 1987.

Welch, Claude. *Protestant Theology in the Nineteenth Century: Volume 1, 1799–1870.* New Haven: Yale University Press, 1972.

Wells, H. G. *Experiment in Autobiography.* New York: Macmillan, 1934.

——. *The Shape of Things to Come.* Edited by John Hammond, 1933. London: Everyman, 1993.

Weremchek, Max S. *John Nelson Darby.* Neptune, N.J:. Loizeaux Brothers, 1992.

Wessinger, Catherine. *How the Millennium Comes Violently: From Jonestown to Heaven's Gate.* New York: Seven Bridges Press, 2000.

——. "Millennialism with and without the Mayhem." In Robbins and Palmer, *Millennium, Messiahs, and Mayhem.*

——, ed. *Millennialism, Persecution, and Violence: Historical Cases.* Syracuse, N.Y.: Syracuse University Press, 2000.

Whisenant, Edgar. *88 Reasons Why the Rapture Will Be in 1988.* Nashville: World Bible Society, 1988. *88 Reasons* was also published as *The Rosh Hash Ana 1988 and 88 Reasons Why.*

Whitley, H. C. *Blinded Eagle: An Introduction to the Life and Teaching of Edward Irving.* London: SCM Press, 1955.

Willis, Wesley R., and John R. Master, eds. *Issues in Dispensationalism.* Chicago: Moody, 1994.

Wilson, Brian. *The Social Dimensions of Sectarianism: Sects and New Religious Movements in Contemporary Society.* Oxford: Oxford University Press, 1990.

Wilson, D. *Armageddon Now! The Premillenarian Response to Russia and Israel since 1917, 1977.* Second edition, Tyler, Tex.: Institute for Christian Economics, 1991.

Witherington, Ben. *Jesus, Paul and the End of the World.* Downers Grove.: InterVarsity, 1992.

Wknody. "A Matter of Life or Death? YOU Decide." http://www.heavens gatetoo.com/exitchk.htm. Accessed August 26, 1999.

Wojcik, Daniel. *The End of the World As We Know It: Faith, Fatalism, and Apocalypse in America.* New York: New York University Press, 1997.

World Missionary Conference, 1910: To Consider Missionary Problems in Relation to the Non-Christian World. 9 volumes, Edinburgh and London: Oliphant, Anderson, & Ferrier; New York, Chicago, and Toronto: Fleming H. Revell, 1910.

Wright, N. "The Nature and Variety of Restorationism and the 'House Church Movement.'" In Hunt, Hamilton, and Walter, *Charismatic Christianity.*

——. "The Rise of the Prophetic." In Smail, Walker, and Wright, *Charismatic Renewal*.

Wright, Stuart A. "Another View of the Mt. Carmel Standoff." In S. Wright, *Armageddon in Waco*.

——. "A Decade after Waco: Reassessing Crisis Negotiations at Mt. Carmel in light of New Government Disclosures." In *Nova Religio: The Journal of Alternative and Emergent Religions* 7, no. 2 (2003).

——. "Explaining Militarization at Waco: The Construction and Convergence of the Warfare Narrative." In Lewis and Petersen, *Controversial New Religions*.

——. "Justice Denied: The Waco Civil Trial." *Nova Religio: The Journal of Alternative and Emergent Religions* 5, no. 1 (2001).

——. "Media Coverage of Unconventional Religions: Any 'Good News' for Minority Faiths?" *Review of Religious Research* 39, no. 2 (1997).

——, ed. *Armageddon in Waco: Critical Perspectives on the Branch Davidian Conflict*. Chicago and London: University of Chicago Press, 1995.

Yadgar, Yaakov. "From 'True Peace' to 'the Vision of the New Middle East': Rival Images of Peace in Israel." *Journal of Peace Research* 40, no. 2 (2003). London, Thousand Oaks, Calif., and New Delhi: Sage Publications.

Young, R. F. "Lethal Achievements: Fragments of a Response to the Aum Shinrikyo Affair." *Japanese Religions* 20, no. 2 (1995).

Yrsody. "The Way Things Are." http://www.heavensgatetoo.com/exitchk. htm. Accessed August 26, 1999.

Zellner, W. W. and M. Petrowsky, eds. *Sects, Cults & Spiritual Communities: A Sociological Analysis*. Westport, Conn.: Praeger, 1998.

Notes on Contributors

GORDON ALLAN has spent over thirty years studying the theology and history of a number of religious groups that have been influenced by English prophetess Joanna Southcott. He is personally acquainted with many members of these groups and has studied their literature in depth. While studying theology at the University of Chichester, he was invited to join the Oxford University Prophecy Project, which focuses on millennialist religions, particularly those influenced by Joanna Southcott. He is now developing a database of all of Southcott's prophecies and communications held in various collections, public and private, throughout the world.

BRENDA E. BRASHER is the author of *Give Me That Online Religion* (2001) and *Godly Women: Fundamentalism and Female Power* (1998). She is editor-in-chief of the *Encyclopedia of Fundamentalism* with Routledge and editor-in-chief of the *Millennialism and Society* series with Equinox Publishing. She took her PhD at the University of Southern California in social ethics. A former Fulbright scholar, Dr. Brasher is currently a lecturer in the School of Social Science at the University of Aberdeen, Scotland.

CRAWFORD GRIBBEN is lecturer in Renaissance literature and culture at the University of Manchester, UK. He is the author and editor of a number of publications on millennial studies, including *The Puritan Millennium: Literature and Theology, 1550–1682* (2000).

STEPHEN J. HUNT is a reader in the sociology of religion. Based at the University of the West of England, Bristol, he is director of the Unit for the Study of Religion and Spirituality. His published volumes include: *Religion in Everyday Life* (2005), *The Alpha Enterprise* (2004), *Alternative Religion* (2003), and *Religion in Western Society* (2002). He is editor of *Christian Millenarianism* (2001).

DARRYL JONES is director of the MPhil program in popular literature in the School of English at Trinity College, Dublin. He is the author of *Jane Austen* (2004), *Horror: A Thematic History in Fiction and Film* (2002), and, with Stephen Matterson, *Studying Poetry* (2000). His current project is entitled "Apocalypse: Mass Death and Catastrophe Fiction since the Enlightenment."

RICHARD LANDES is professor of medieval history at Boston University. His publications include: *The Apocalyptic Year 1000: Studies in the Mutation of European Culture*, ed. R. Landes, A. Gow, and D. Van Meter (2003); *Encyclopedia of Millennialism and Millennial Movements* (2000); *Relics, Apocalypse, and the Deceits of History: Ademar of Chabannes 989–1034* (1995); and *The Peace of God: Social Violence and Religious Response in France around the Year 1000*, ed. T. Head and R. Landes (1992). For the past ten years he has directed the Center for Millennial Studies at Boston University. He has written and lectured widely on millennialism, especially in the medieval period.

KENNETH G. C. NEWPORT is assistant vice-chancellor and professor of Christian thought at Liverpool Hope University. He is the author of a number of books, including *The Branch Davidians of Waco: The History and Beliefs of an Apocalyptic Sect* (Oxford, 2006) and *Apocalypse and Millennium: Studies in Biblical Eisegesis* (2000).

CHRISTOPHER PARTRIDGE is professor of contemporary religion at the University of Chester and codirector of the Research Centre for Religion, Film, and Contemporary Culture. He has a particular interest in popular music and religion. He is coeditor of the journal *Fieldwork in Religion* and author of *The Re-Enchantment of the West*, 2 volumes (2004–2005) and *H. H. Farmer's Theological Interpretation of Religion* (1998). He is the editor of several volumes, including *The World's Religions* (2005), *Encyclopedia of New Religions* (2004), *UFO Religions* (2003), *Fundamentalisms* (2001), *Finding and Losing Faith* (with Helen Reid, 2005), and *Mysticisms East and West* (with Theodore Gabriel, 2003).

ANDREW PIERCE is a lecturer in the Irish School of Ecumenics at Trinity College, Dublin. He is editor of *The Critical Spirit: Theology at the Crossroads of Faith and Culture* (2003) and the author of a number of publications on religious fundamentalism and religions in modernity.

MARK S. SWEETNAM read English literature and mathematics at Trinity College, Dublin. In 2005, he was awarded a scholarship under the sponsorship of the Irish Research Council for the Humanities and Social Sciences. He is currently a Government of Ireland Scholar in the English Department at Trinity College, reading for a PhD on the theology and thought of John Donne. Besides Renaissance literature, his main research interests are dispensational millennialism and evangelical missionary writing. A revised version of his BA dissertation, on the nineteenth-century Plymouth Brethren missionary Dan Crawford, is forthcoming in the *Journal of Ecclesiastical History*.

JOHN WALLISS is a lecturer in sociology in the Deanery of Sciences and Social Sciences at Liverpool Hope University. His research interests are within the study of apocalyptic violence, a topic he has explored in his recent book *Apocalyptic Trajectories: Millenarianism and Violence in the Contemporary World* (2004). He has published works on several topics, including: millenarianism within the Hindu new religious movement, the Brahma Kumaris; "fringe archaeology," relationships between the living and dead within contemporary spiritualism; and the secularization of weddings in the United Kingdom. He is also coeditor, with James Beckford, of *Theorising Religion: Classical and Contemporary Debates* (Ashgate, forthcoming).

CATHERINE WESSINGER is professor of history of religions at Loyola University, New Orleans. She is co-general editor of *Nova Religio: The Journal of Alternative and Emergent Religions*. Her books include *How the Millennium Comes Violently: From Jonestown to Heaven's Gate* (2000) and an edited work, *Millennialism, Persecution, and Violence: Historical Cases* (2000). She is currently working on an oral history project with some surviving Branch Davidians and is editing *The Oxford Handbook on Millennialism*.

Index